D1163417

THE GRIM REAPERS

Foreword

Over thirty years ago I began to probe the Mafia and its component parts, beginning in New York City where I grew up and, as a young reporter, first watched the wretched men of the underworld peddle their illicit services to an unsuspecting and often willing segment of the public. And for the whole period, the close comfort lent by dedicated "watchers" of the syndicate across our country has been a source of inspiration.

The watchers have done as much again for this project. Without the information compiled and furnished by such bodies as the Kefauver, McClellan, and other governmental investigative committees, metropolitan and state crime commissions, federal, state, and city police intelligence departments, crime reporters, and my writing colleagues in all the media, a study of this scope would be impossible. Most of these sources are named within the text, and I hereby gratefully acknowledge one and all for the help they have given.

I should like also to acknowledge the valuable assistance of all who feel as I do: that as long as Americans are free to choose the kind of society in which they and their children wish to live, they should at least be fully informed as to what their decisions may mean. And this is an endless task, for reader as well as for writer; for, remember, while most of us like to get a good night's sleep now and then, the mob boys keep busy *all* the time.

ED REID
Chicago

As this volume went to press, news arrived of the death in federal penitentiary of Vito Genovese, "boss of bosses" in the Mafia organization that controls the crime syndicate in the United States. Genovese's influence and importance are clearly detailed in *The Grim Reapers,* and his death will undoubtedly lead to the accession to supreme power in the Mafia of one of the persons appearing in the book. Who that person will be is open to conjecture. What means will be used to grasp the Mafia scepter is not yet clear. But that someone will assume the mantle is certain.

Ed Reid, the author of *The Mafia* and co-author of *The Green Felt Jungle,* has spent most of his working life tracking down and exposing small- and big-time hoods and their operations. While on the Pulitzer Prize-winning *Brooklyn Eagle,* he broke the story that led to the exposing of the Brooklyn "don," Joseph Profaci, and as associate editor of the *Las Vegas Sun,* he enjoyed a unique opportunity to investigate mob operations in the "green felt jungle."

Henry Regnery Company

CHICAGO

PROLOGUE

The Mafia is a mailed fist on the scabrous arm of organized crime girdling the earth.

The fist has its fingers in the very bowels of the human economy, on whatever level people are found: digging into the swank parlors of the White House; grubbing in the opium fields of Red China; pulling lanyards on graceful yachts for the pleasure-loving nabobs of the Mafia hierarchy; running the lives of the peoples of the world, the coinages, the factories, the shipyards, the docks, the mills, the farms, the pleasure palaces such as Kublai Khan never dreamed of; killing or maiming people who stand in its way. No one is immune from its attacks. The innocent bystander, the honest cop, the crusading journalist, a thousand men in one dissolute city, Chicago, in two decades—a thousand murders never solved—all fall victim to the Mafia.

In the minds of the men of the Mafia, evil is perpetuated in the womb; the princelings are predestined to marriage according to an ancient code of *Sangre Nostru* (Our Blood). This dissolute concept, patterned after that of the worst of the Egyptian dynasties, seeks to preserve the "good" blood of the Sicilian latifondi on the basis of a biologic theory that genes transmit criminal tendencies. The Mafia is way off, genetically, but when you have the power of life and death over people, lead is the prime catalyst. And who can question those who hold such power in conscienceless hands? When you play Sicilian roulette, all the chambers of the revolver are loaded.

Some years ago a leading Mafioso had two fingers on his right hand shot off while still in the womb of his mother, who was tied to a tree in Jericho, Long Island. She had given information to the police. There is no record that he ever resented the circumstances of her death or of his disfigurement. Why not? Because there is an outstanding difference between a syndicate man and a "free-lance" criminal. The "ordinary" criminal knows when he is breaking a law, and he knows, too, that if he is caught, he will suffer the consequences. But a Mafia-trained syndicate man is devoid of any moral concepts. He believes he has the right to steal, corrupt, even murder. His world of crime and punishment is different. In the place of shame and degradation he expects rewards: power, money, honor, glorification by a fraternity that has spread its influence around the world. And in the United States many have become quite willing to accept a poverty of spirit, born of crime, corruption, and national dishonor, in which more or less everyone participates, from the housewife who bets pennies with the local bookmaker or numbers racketeer to the big-time influence men who stalk the halls of Congress.

We have been attacked right here in our own country, not in strange, exotic lands, and we are losing the war.

We must recognize the enemy. Look for him in our businesses, our legislative bodies, our media of communication and entertainment. Find him in the cities and villages, next door to our homes. He may be the president of a corporation, a jukebox operator, a mill hand, or even the quiet, mannerly fellow hanging out his wife's washing. Or he may merely be the man who—innocently or otherwise—works hand-in-hand with the syndicate because it makes for "good business" or, as in the case of legalized gambling, because the nature of his own business requires the know-how of the "boys" if it is to be a success.

It is, therefore, to this constant war that this book is directed. If vigilance is the watchword, information is one of the keys to eventual success. Consequently, this book intends to chart for its readers a large part of the membership of the crime syndicate in the United States and to outline the influence of those members and their nonmember associates throughout North America and other pertinent places. Then it is up to the public. At present too few are fighting the battle. There can never be too many.

1

EVEN APES HAVE FAMILY TREES

Getting into a speaking or a writing involvement with the Mafia is much like making love to someone who doesn't love you. It is perhaps best, therefore, to approach the criminal organization on a "belly-button" basis, for an "umbilical cord" attaches the men of the Mafia to an innocent public that unknowingly nurtures the secret society by means of a gold-plated attachment centuries old.

Compromise on the part of a public basking in the steady and secure sun of the "establishment" is a hook on which the man of the Mafia hangs his hat. To understand the murders, the letting of blood, the easy way the Mafia has achieved its purpose is next to impossible for most human beings. How can one understand a virus that can't be seen, even if the cause is as certain as the prognosis?

The Mafia has a way of screening things out, hiding them, and our modern society is an example of the complacent ease with which rather desperate things can be hidden and then forgotten—which brings us to the point: What is the Mafia? Who are the apes on the branches of its family tree? How did they evolve?

To begin to understand the secret society, you have to go back to the year in which it is said to have begun, 1282, and to the city of its birth, Palermo, Sicily, a gem-like cluster of buildings on a gulf of the same name, exporting sulphur, citrus fruits, wines, olive oil, and, eventually, a crime syndicate. A well-supported legend—and legends sometimes do have factual backgrounds—holds that the Mafia gained its first breath of life on March 30th of that long-ago year.

Certainly, it is a fact that on that day the Sicilian revolt known as the Sicilian Vespers broke out against the French Angevin rulers of Sicily. And it may well also be true that the actual cause of the outbreak was the assault on a Sicilian bride-to-be by a drunken French sergeant, Pierre Druet. In any case, the story goes that the terrified girl tore away from her tormentor, fell, cracking her skull against a sharp projection of the church wall, and died just minutes before the wedding ceremony was to have taken place. The grief-stricken bridegroom fell upon Sergeant Druet and beat him, screaming: "*Morte alla Francia!*" "Death to all the French!"

As the news spread, thousands of maddened Sicilians took up the refrain and added to it, so that their slogan became: "*Morte alla Francia Italia anela!*" "Death to the French is Italy's cry!"

The uprising led to the massacre of most of the French in Palermo and all of Sicily. And for a hundred years Sicily was free of foreign domination.

Here the story clouds again, but it is believed that in a short time a secret organization was formed to protect the welfare of poor or ill-treated Sicilians. Its name, "Mafia," was made up of the initial letters in the death slogan, and for years it was the benefactor and defender of the poor and downtrodden who made up a large part of the population of Sicily.

Italy's ultimate political unification, in the nineteenth century, isolated the nearby island of Sicily, and, having played out its role as savior to the people, the Mafia turned about-face. Discarding its ideal of fighting oppression, it began to mount an unceasing reign of terror that, over the years, has been exported to many places around the world. Extortion, arson, and murder perpetrated on all classes became the trinity of terror that ruled Sicily.

Over the foundations of walls laid by Phoenicians and Carthaginians, the ruined temples, theaters, and fortresses of the Greeks, the bridges, aqueducts, and amphitheaters of the Romans, shimmered the black flag of the Mafia.

The hooves of horses owned by marauding Mafiosi clattered over the cobbles of edifices haunted by Byzantine architects, rang through mosques and towers of Saracenic and Norman origin. In the channeled grooves of the Mafia brain were woven the threads of generations of intrigue. In their shining knives were reflected the tortures and mutilations employed by Muslim caliphs who at one time held domination over Sicily. In the blood of the Mafia are the tears of six hundred years.

During its rise to power in Sicily the Mafia absorbed the Camorra, a secret society formed at Seville in 1417 and transported to Sicily and adjacent states by the Bourbons, last of the foreign dynasties to control Sicily. The Camorra started, unlike the Mafia, as an organization of criminals who divided amicably the products of their robberies with the police and the clergy. The Bourbons tolerated the Camorra as the source of their assassins, much as the crime syndicate in the United States tolerated the trouble-making Murder, Inc., gang of Brooklyn hoodlums.

This group was extremely powerful in Naples, and there was a time when nothing was more honorable for a young Neapolitan than to belong to the Camorra. For him to go to jail for robbery or murder was not considered degrading. To girls of his association he was a hero. The Camorra was entrenched strongly among municipal employees of Naples as well as in the army. To realize a political ambition in Naples, one had to be a Camorrista.

King Victor Emmanuel II made a desperate effort to eradicate the Camorra, and some arrests were made. Some unimportant people were sent to jail for various types of crimes, but this only resulted in the Camorra's becoming active in the penitentiary system.

In 1907, after the murder of many influential people in Naples, public sentiment rebelled, and huge numbers of arrests of Camorristi were made. Many others fled to America and began to prey upon the Italian population here. In many cities the Camorristi ran across the Mafia, and bloody feuds resulted. One of the most disastrous gang wars was in New York City. After dozens of persons had died, the public became aroused, and the two societies joined hands shortly after 1920. Finally, at a meeting in Atlantic City the bond was cemented, and the foundation laid for the present syndicate, or combine.

Also in the physical makeup of the modern Mafia are strains of other secret societies, one of which was formed in Italy to combat foreign despotism. This was the sect of the Carbonari, which gave invaluable aid to the Mafia when Giuseppe Garibaldi landed in Sicily with a thousand men and drove the Bourbons out of the island.

In the salad days of the Mafia in Sicily, when its main object was to harass the Bourbon tyranny, the secret society operated in sections. Monreale and the province of Palermo had the *Stoppaglieri* (not translatable) and the *Fratuzzi* (Little Brothers). The province of Messina had *Beati Paoli* (Blessed Pauls); the province of Caltanisetta had the *Fratellanza* (Brotherhood). For the original noble purpose of mutual assistance among the members, the duties of all comrades were: reciprocal aid in case of any need whatsoever; absolute obedience to the chief; an offense received by one of the members to be considered an offense against all and avenged at any cost; no appeal to the state's authorities for justice; no revelation of the names of members or any secrets of the association.

These are exactly the rules of the present American crime syndicate ruled by the hard core of Sicilian and other Italian immigrants.

The Mafia reached the apex of its power in Sicily in 1912 after universal suffrage was adopted. The poorer classes, with the power to vote, yielded to "suggestions" made by the Mafiosi and supported their candidates. The nobility and wealthier classes joined the Mafia in self-protection—better steady payments of tribute than sudden robbery.

It was around the turn of the century that mass migration of Mafiosi took place, with the destination in most cases being America. Many Mafiosi changed their ways upon entering a new life. But, unfortunately, not all changed their outlook. Instead, they brought with them the terror and lawbreaking associated with their secret society, which had evolved into a sort of religion.

This religion, difficult to explain but easy to understand if one considers that a sharp knife at a soft throat really needs no explanation, revolves around a little-known Sicilian word, *omerta*. *Omerta* has bound together the men of the Mafia—and their victims—in a sinister drama that is now being played in all the back alleys of the globe and has assumed such an importance that it has become the keystone of the whole immoral concept of the Mafia.

A word of somewhat obscure genesis, *omerta* apparently derives from the Latin word *homo*. In Sicily it was a purely local expression, correctly spelled *umirta*, meaning "humility"—the quality members of the Mafia were supposed to display. It connoted quality and manliness, but its primitive and most lasting meaning was, and is, "golden silence." And because "silence" has become the watchword for modern Mafia lawbreakers, an understanding of its full meaning may make possible a more complete appraisal of the Mafia and its success in eluding the forces of justice.

Basically, "Keep your lip buttoned," is just another way of saying, "Talk and you die." Humility seems to play only a small part in the activities of today's Mafiosi, but it is worth noting that those few Mafiosi who have retained some of the original concepts of humility and the simple family life have outlasted the streamlined youngsters who attempted completely to shake off the old ways.

Omerta is itself rarely mentioned now by the old-timers, for it is much easier simply to explain to the younger generation of the Mafia and to their non-Mafia underlings that whether a man lives or dies depends on how much he talks. For the modern Mafia, terror, not the concept denoted by a time-honored word, has achieved a simplicity of operation that continues to create something even more time-honored than a word: profit.

Suppose a man had a modest business, or was even a prince of industry. Suppose the Mafia wanted the business and told the man so. Suppose the man was made to understand a certain fact of life—a small matter, such as, for instance, the certainty that his children would go through the very cruel but, from the Mafia viewpoint, sane process of having their limbs broken across a handy curb, or that his wife would be violated, in conformance with a *quid pro quo* ideology that offers the businessman no way out. Suppose all that and you have *profit*—for the Mafia at least.

It is difficult to tell a story that people who have never been touched by the terror can scarcely believe, so let us delve into a few facts about the men who make up the skeleton of the Mafia—men whose activities are as elusive as the Mafia mystery through which law-enforcement agencies are trying to chart a course.

The first hard thrust of the Mafia into the peace of mind of the American public came on January 24, 1889, when a man named Vincenzo Ottumvo was knifed during a card party in New Orleans and thrust at dawn into the Sixteenth Street canal. The second murder was that of Giuseppe Mataino, a month later in the same city. Giuseppe was found in a fire grate in his home, where he was roasting merrily. But the reason for his death, which occurred in the course of an obscure vendetta that attracted the attention of New Orleans Police Chief Peter Hennessey, was never made clear.

Both Ottumvo and Mataino had been associated with the first wave of Italian immigrants brought to the United States from various provinces of Italy and Sicily, and they represented the first pricklings of terror that was to assault the minds of a bewildered public. It could well be that these two murders came about because of keen competition over contracts for the handling of cargoes on the New Orleans docks, as well as because of the existence of factions within the Mafia divided in allegiance by the geography and diverse patois of northern and southern Italy and Sicily.

Whatever the motivation, late in 1890 Chief Hennessey was the target of a rumor indicating that he was taking sides in the dock controversy. On October 15, 1890, he was shot down in front of his home and died ten hours later. The terror expanded and engulfed an indignant group of citizens.

The first reports indicating official recognition of the existence of the secret society in this country came, therefore, from two New Orleans grand juries, sixty years before the Kefauver revelations and seventy-five years before Joseph Valachi testified at the Senate hearings about the organization and its related "families" throughout the United States.

One grand jury report stated:

> The range of our researches has developed the existence of the secret organization styled "Mafia." The evidence comes from several sources fully competent in themselves to attest its truth, while the fact is supported by the long record of blood-curdling crimes, it being almost impossible to discover the perpetrators or to secure witnesses.

This same 1890 report concluded: "Today there is recorded in the office of the Italian consul the names of some 1100 Italians and Sicilians landed here during several years past, showing the official record of their criminality in Italy and Sicily."

A further influx of the secret society occurred in New York City in 1908, when a festive occasion took place in the borough of Brooklyn. The Sicilian population turned out in force to welcome Raffaele Palizzola of Palermo at the Bush docks. Palizzola was a refugee from his own country, where rumors (also spread in Brooklyn) claimed he was king of the Mafia and that he had been behind the murder in 1893 of Baron Emanuele Notarbartolo, head of the Sicilian bar association. The baron had advocated a cleanup of local graft and named Palizzola as one of those responsible for the situation. The baron's body was later found, with sixteen dagger wounds, in a forest near Palermo.

After three trials separated by many delays, Palizzola was finally convicted in Sicily and went into glorious exile in Brooklyn. Five men who had testified against him had preceded Palizzola to New York City, and, in the ensuing years, each was found murdered—along with dozens of relatives and friends, including one Salvatore Marchinne, whose body was found in two pieces in a vacant lot in Flatbush.

Marchinne's murder was "clean," unlike the executions of most of Palizzola's other victims. Their bodies were cut into several pieces, wrapped in tarpaper to prevent blood spillage, and shipped in barrels to doting relatives outside New York—who had no trouble understanding the message of terror. During the Palizzola exile in this country, which saw forty homes bombed as a counterpoint to the revenge murders, the transportation of chopped-up bodies in barrels became popular. And the use of tarpaper-lined sarcophagi may well have been responsible for the name "Black Handers" that was tagged onto the Mafia killers, for their hands often were stained by the telltale black tar.

In the years between the beginnings of the terror in this country and the advent to power of Brooklyn-bred gangster Alphonse Capone—who started his take-over of Chicago, its illicit liquor industry, and most of its public officials in the early 1920's —a gang known as "The Green Ones" went to St. Louis and bathed the city in blood. Partners in the invading gang were Vito Giannola, his brother John, and Alphonse Palizzola, farm boys from the plains of Sicily "blessed" with the approval of the Mafia.

The Green Ones set up shop in 1915, and murder followed murder in St. Louis until a bootlegger named Dinty Colbeck, who had controlled activities in St. Louis County, tossed in the towel for the "Irish Mafia" and ran for his life. The Green Ones took over not only the "alky" production and distribution but also the produce markets, including those of the vegetable and meat vendors, who paid them for the privilege of staying in business.

Gradually spreading out from St. Louis itself, the gang helped spread terror, thinly at first, over a great triangle of the country, which at its peak had its corners set in New Orleans, New York, and their own bailiwick near the center of the country.

Then, at the height of the gang's power, on September 14, 1925, a resort owned by John Gray and his wife was divested of its proprietors a few days after the gang found out that the Grays had purchased part of their liquor stock from non-Mafia sources. The young mobsters ambushed the Grays near their resort in Madison County, and Palizzola shot them to death in their touring car and burned their bodies in a nearby pine grove.

It was from St. Louis that well-indoctrinated and seasoned Mafiosi later migrated to Detroit. However, it took an Al Capone in Chicago to gather in the first bits and pieces of real power and to achieve a kind of gangland supremacy—a sophistication that gained a further measure of polish when Frank Costello, known as "The Prime Minister," got the eastern boys together and worked out a division of assets and a method of operation. The division occurred in May, 1929, and the assets were those of Arnold Rothstein, the famed gambler and "big bankroll" of the Italian boys on the way up in New York, who had been shot during a card game in the Park Central Hotel in Manhattan some six months earlier.

Costello, whose real name was Francesco Seriglia, had worked his way up through Mafia echelons and wormed his way into the inner councils of Tammany Hall, which ran the politics in New York City for almost half a century. He had a monopoly on the good-quality bootleg liquor brought in from Canada and England, unloaded at Montauk Point at the eastern tip of Long Island, and dribbled into every speakeasy and nightclub on the East Coast.

Indeed, it was Prohibition, the Eighteenth Amendment to the Constitution of the United States, that set the seal of success on the activities of Costello and his mobsters, and he therefore doled out the territories and at the same time split the Rothstein assets in a divvy that was to become typical—moneys held by syndicate members went back into the pot, to be used again and again, gathering greenbacks like moss as they rolled around. Once the division was made, Costello wanted to be sure, the Mafia would be firmly in the driver's seat—for good.

A few of the deals handed out, as Leo Katcher points out in

The Big Bankroll (Harper & Bros., 1958), were: (1) bookmaking to Frank Erickson, whose later nemesis was Fiorello LaGuardia, the "Little Flower" of New York politics who was to destroy Tammany Hall; (2) narcotics to Charles (Lucky) Luciano and Louis (Lepke) Buchalter, the industrial racketeer; (3) the garment center also to Buchalter, aided by Thomas (Three Finger Brown) Lucchese, up-and-coming darling of Tammany Hall; and (4) the political empire to Costello himself.

An even more comprehensive and far-reaching framework for this "syndicate" of crime—which has evolved into the current "family" groups across the country, as was made clear by the 1963–1964 Senate hearings—was apparently laid two years later, when another meeting is said to have been held at which additional "parcels" of territory were handed out to gang bosses across the country and a ruling council was organized.

At this meeting New Orleans was given to Phil (Dandy Phil) Kastel and Meyer Lansky, who was to become a power in Florida and, more recently, mastermind behind the gaming industry in the Bahamas. Las Vegas and southern California were earmarked for Benjamin (Bugsy) Siegel, onetime enforcer with Meyer Lansky of Buchalter's dictates in the garment district of New York City. New Jersey went to Abner (Longy) Zwillman, king of the New Jersey rackets until Joseph (Joe Adonis) Doto took over. Longy, incidentally, did not have too much luck in life. A few years ago he died at the end of a rope fastened to a waterpipe in the cellar of his home. Florida was given to Willie (Willie Moore) Moretti, who paved the way for such worthies as Brooklyn gangster Anthony (Little Augie Pisano) Carfano and Detroit Mafiosi Joe Massei, habitué in his late years of the famous though now defunct Wofford Hotel in Miami.

Many other princelings were created, and they all took their orders at one time or another from Capone, Luciano, and Costello.

It is not easy to say how the Mafia will be conquered, or even if it will. Scores of dedicated people have been appalled, then frustrated, at the invisible forces aligned against them once it became known they were hacking at the tap roots of the gigantic Mafia family tree.

One such opponent of the Mafia is Senator John L. McClellan of Arkansas. Senator McClellan, as chairman of both the Senate Permanent Subcommittee on Investigations and the Senate Select

Committee on Improper Activities in the Labor or Management Field, went to work on the Mafia more than ten years ago with the comment: "No man need apologize for devotion to duty."

A curious divergence of logic, McClellan noted, became evident when he began his probes into the criminal element. As his committees began hearing evidence pointing to Mafia influence in labor circles, they were quickly labeled "anti-labor." This prompted the senator to ask, with some justification: "Does this mean that the criminals are 'pro-labor'?"

Undaunted, committee investigators began to accumulate evidence, and in 1963 and 1964, during the Senate hearings into organized crime and illicit traffic in narcotics, they released impressive amounts of material.

Information for the hearings had been secured from countless sources, including the Department of Justice, the Federal Bureau of Narcotics, and experienced police and crime-commission officials from numerous metropolitan areas across the country. Federal, state, and municipal records and other data accumulated over a period of years, colorfully but meaningfully reinforced in part by the extensive testimony of Joseph Valachi, a New York hoodlum for thirty years, brought to light a revealing picture of the workings and organization of the criminal conspiracy.

The purpose and methods of the Mafia were outlined in the framework established by eight overall characteristics (still remarkably similar to the original list of duties set up by Mafiosi in their early days in Sicily), which were summed up in the permanent subcommittee's final report as follows:

> 1. A substantial number of members.
> 2. The group aggressively engaged in attempts to subvert the process of government by well-organized endeavors to capture or otherwise make ineffectual the three branches of our local and Federal Government by various forms of bribery and corruption.
> 3. The primary purpose of this group is to dominate those categories of crime which we refer to as "organized crime." By "organized crime" is meant the following: gambling, illegal distribution of narcotics, commercialized prostitution, labor and management racketeering, loansharking, and the infiltration of the crime syndicate into legitimate enterprises.
> 4. The group anticipates a continuous, indefinite lifespan of operations.

5. Members habitually engage in similar criminal activity as a primary source of income.

6. Top leadership and management people primarily engage in crimes of conspiracy, and are usually divorced from operations by two or more levels.

7. The group is dedicated to commit murder and other acts of violence upon any member who informs on the group, and to commit similar violence on any outsider who seriously threatens the security of the group.

8. . . . the group does not recognize any geographical boundaries of operations and is often associated in crime with similar groups in other cities, states, and, in some instances, in other countries.

The report (published by the Government Printing Office at a price of $1.25 to the public) summarizes the testimony given over two years of hearings (also published in five similar handbooks) and would have made the best-seller list because it details an amazing series of facts—if only we, as a nation of readers, were as interested in what is happening to our country as we seemingly are in what purportedly happens in other people's bedrooms.

For example, the report offers noteworthy clues as to how the organization is so successful in eluding those who would pursue and examine it and lists ten self-protective measures used by syndicate leaders:

1. *Insulation.*—Top-ranking members avoid involvement in actual crimes. They limit social contacts and eliminate all obvious links to criminal operations. The strongest insulation is Cosa Nostra's inherent philosophy that bosses must be protected. A combination of fear and traditional distaste for informing has helped preserve 30 years of silence, broken publicly only by Joseph Valachi . . .

2. *Respect.*—Deference is given to position, authority, and seniority, and is unmistakable when observed. Status is often revealed by the tone of voice, the held door, the proffered seat. "Sleepers" (high-ranking members whose importance was relatively unknown) have been revealed to police by displays of respect . . .

3. *The buffer.*—Leaders do not mix or deal with underlings, but use a trusted aide to stand between the boss and trouble. This buffer has many functions and knows all the boss' operations . . .

4. *The appointment.*—Infrequently, with utmost security a

leader may meet an underling upon an urgent matter. Ordinarily, even the most important matters go through regular channels . . .

5. *The sitdown.*—Meetings known as "sitdowns" are peace conferences within families or among allied families. Usually these are held at lower levels, although sometimes the heads of Cosa Nostra families must meet on vital questions. Decisions at the upper level are final . . .

6. *Discipline.*—Whenever necessary, as it frequently is, discipline is kept within a family and is carried out by associates. Punishment ranges from warnings to sanctions on criminal enterprises to murder . . .

7. *The disappearance.*—When murder is decreed, trusted fellow members carry out the sentence, and the man vanishes without a trace—no violence, no gunplay, no blood, no body, no public outcry. The case is carried by police as a disappearance; the victim is a missing person . . .

8. *Permission.*—All illicit activities within a family require the approval of the boss. The family that gives permission will help if anything goes wrong. Family policy is the criterion; crimes which arouse the public are forbidden . . .

9. *The money mover.*—One or more trusted members handle much of the cash pouring into a family from its illegal sources. The money mover has commercial connections; he puts the profits to work while hiding their sources. He invests in importing, real estate, trust funds, stocks and bonds, and certain other favored enterprises. The bulk of the profits clandestinely go to the bosses . . .

10. *Public relations.*—The organization is always concerned with public opinion, and all strong actions which might influence the public must be cleared with the Cosa Nostra leaders. Failures in this area reflect upon the boss. The front of respectability and propriety must be maintained.

When he was Attorney General, the late Senator Robert Kennedy, who had served as the subcommittee's chief counsel in the years prior to his appointment to President John F. Kennedy's cabinet, testified at the Senate hearings that organized crime had clearly become a national problem, and that "illegal gambling alone" had a gross volume of $7 billion annually in the United States.

This sum includes the take from the numbers racket, horse and card parlors, floating crap games, and the like, and the take from this kind of gambling helps finance operations involving narcotics smuggling and distribution and loan sharking in every big city in the country. Financed in turn by these and other shady operations are many "legit" enterprises ranging from legal gambling (with its obvious opportunities for "skimming"—the practice of tapping gambling profits before casino income is declared) to more mundane endeavors such as laundries, trucking firms, travel agencies, wholesale meat markets, vending-machine firms, insurance underwriting, fat-rendering plants, paving-contract firms, taxicab fleets, bus lines, restaurants, and countless other operations. And the legitimate businesses are used not only in an orthodox manner—to make money—but also increasingly for illicit practices. For example, two favorite means of "earning" money are burning down a building to collect the insurance and going into bankruptcy after high credit accounts have been run up. In fact, often furnishings and equipment are purchased on credit and passed on to associates who know where to dispose of the inventories.

Consequently, Kennedy's estimate of syndicate income is on the low side. An educated guess often made by Mafia experts, but of course never substantiated, for the current overall annual income of the syndicate is $20 billion, derived from such basic criminal activities as gambling, loan sharking, narcotics, infiltration into legitimate businesses, labor racketeering, and, in a smaller way, prostitution and bootlegging.

As in all inquiries into Mafia operations, it is hard to get at the truth. Mafia wheels are well greased; they make little noise. But at least some of the fat was scraped off publicly by McClellan's prize canary, Valachi, who put on record for the first time the facts of the existence of "families" of Mafia lawbreakers. Valachi told of his belonging to the New York family controlled by Vito Genovese, successor to Luciano and Costello in the chain of syndicate royalty, overall ruler of five New York families (the Mafia's most powerful), and perhaps the last of the secret society's supreme commanders.

Valachi placed other families in Buffalo, Chicago, Detroit, Tampa, Boston, and Providence, Rhode Island—picturing them as a kind of "in" group called "Cosa Nostra," a loose Sicilian phrase meaning "Our Thing." (The 1951 Kefauver investigations had made "Mafia" something of a dirty word.)

Valachi, a gray-haired, husky-voiced, squat man, outlined a river of criminality which has never known a dry spell in over six hundred years of bloodbaths. He said the Cosa Nostra families in New York City contained two thousand active members and perhaps up to three thousand inactive members. Five charts, submitted by local lawmen and supplemented by McClellan investigators, listed the apparent family membership, and Valachi identified 289 hoodlums of the 338 men whose pictures and names appeared on the charts. Other data upped the number of men in one criminal cartel controlled by mobster Genovese to close to five hundred.

Vito Genovese, at present a federal prisoner on a narcotics conviction serving a fifteen-year sentence received in 1959, is considered by experts to be the guiding genius who pulls the wires of criminal enterprises throughout the United States. He has a long history of activity in the unsavory society that has pushed its way into the sociological maw of an apparently uncaring public, which keeps the deadly merry-go-round going by supplying it with financial support—such as two-dollar bets on horses it has never seen, running on tracks in towns thousands of miles away.

Valachi's testimony to the McClellan committee was supplemented by that of federal and local intelligence-bureau police officers and other Mafia buffs. When it was all put together, it brought into the open for the first time some of the details of the secret society's chain of command.

The top-ranking Mafia men are "dons." The term "don" is one of respect and is more an indication of top authority than of a consistently specific position in the organizational structure. The "ruling council" is made up of "commissioners" (many of whom are dons), and each commissioner is boss of one or more "families." Families have pretty much of a free rein over the rackets in their jurisdiction, but territorial disputes generally are settled by the ruling council.

The family "boss," who has a respected *consiglieri* for consultation, passes down his decisions to an "underboss," who is responsible for keeping the family running smoothly with the help of *capiregime,* each of whom is put in charge of a particular branch of the family's illegal activities.

The *capiregime* are in closer contact with the operational level—the chiefs, lieutenants, and section leaders within each regime, the "button men" or "soldiers" who do the dirty work such as contacting bookmakers and loan sharks, who may or may not themselves be members of the Mafia—than their superiors.

The chain of command extending down from Genovese indicates there are over a hundred button men in his family, and twenty-seven of these are classified as millionaires by investigators who almost certainly know but cannot prove their facts. The lower echelons of workers provide the all-important buffers for the top men who make up the ruling council.

The top men across the country are, of course, all known to one another, but they rarely get together. The famous Apalachin meeting in 1957 had its closest parallel in Cleveland in 1928, when twenty-three suspected Mafia leaders were seized and local Sicilians rushed to raise bail for them. Police found thirteen guns in the leaders' baggage at the hotel in which the meet was held. Five of those arrested were from Brooklyn; some are still alive today. A less formal but equally star-studded gathering of thirteen Mafia chieftains was rousted by the police from a New York restaurant during a luncheon in 1966, and a so-called, but misnamed, Little Apalachin meet was supposedly held in Palm Springs in 1965. But generally the big boys try not to congregate any more than necessary.

Along with Vito Genovese, other family bosses and underbosses listed by the McClellan committee, some of whom were also identified by Valachi, included: Santo Trafficante, Jr., of Florida; Salvatore (Momo) Giancana, Tony Accardo, Rosario (Ross Prio) Fabricini, and Giuseppe (Joey Glimco) Glielmi, all of Chicago; Raymond Patriarca, Henry Tamello, and Frank Cucchiara of Providence, Rhode Island, and Boston, Massachusetts; Joseph Zerilli, John (Papa John) Priziola, Peter Licavoli, Angelo Meli, and William (Black Bill) Tocco, all of Detroit; Stefano Magaddino, Frederick Randaccio, Salvatore Pieri, and John Montana of Buffalo, New York.

The bosses of the four other New York families were identified as Carlo Gambino, Giuseppe Magliocco, Thomas Lucchese, and Joseph Bonanno—called "Joe Bananas," but not by his friends.

Genovese's close association with such top Mafia men as Three Finger Brown Lucchese, now deceased but once the power behind the garment-district truckers in New York, is well documented by local police. Other close associates include the late Charles Luciano and former owner of swank gaming joints in New York State and Florida, Joe Adonis. Adonis accepted deportation in 1956 after being unable to prove to authorities that he was born in Jersey

City, and it is believed he may have taken Luciano's place in Italy.

More recent information, as ensuing chapters indicate, has tended to shuffle around some of the names and their order of importance—listing, for example, the powerful Carlos Marcello as boss of the Louisiana family and showing Meyer Lansky's influence in Florida and the Bahamas and some West-Coast faces as well—but Valachi was the first "insider" to put the pieces in place officially. He tied together in considerable detail the hitherto sketchy information gathered by law-enforcement agencies and others—"outsiders" who had always hoped for a closer look. And it must have been invigorating for the lawmen to know that some of their theories had finally been given credence.

Valachi's indictment of the crime syndicate was underscored by the McClellan committee, which stated in its summary report that "the source of the appalling power of Cosa Nostra in the underworld is the well-known inevitability of the death penalty for offenders and informers."

This source of power was further confirmed by Captain William Duffy, then director of intelligence for the Chicago police department, who told the committee:

> From countless investigations and after long analysis, we have concluded that the one single characteristic which is most responsible for the success and continuity of this crime syndicate is the ability of the group to commit murder and other acts of violence without compunction.

This protective veil of secrecy and terror was what, in breaking the code of *omerta*, Valachi cut to ribbons. The golden silence was shattered. But is not the fact that Valachi did break the code the explicit reason for the very close protection he now enjoys? In other words, Valachi proved that the code exists by breaking it and living the rest of his life in fear. The mob has no doubt noted his heroics and laid out his future, should he ever leave the protective prison walls now provided him by the law.

Perhaps, then, the most persuasive and lasting contribution Valachi has given the world is something that hinders rather than helps the fight against the syndicate: the very clear realization the "good" people now have that to become directly involved to the point of testifying against any of the boys or their activities is to invite certain death. As Captain Duffy said: "People have just refused to cooperate, stating that they were afraid for their lives."

The monolith of force and terror hinted at by Valachi's testimony and followed up in the Senate committee report must always lie heavily on a public that may want to help but will not make too many sacrifices in the doing. And the sacrifices to be made *are* real, as can be seen by examining some of the pressures the mob uses on its victims.

For example, in its inquiries into loan sharking the Senate small business committee found that loan sharking and legitimate business (other people's) go hand-in-hand. For instance, the committee heard the case of a former New York businessman who testified on May 15, 1968, that loan sharks—the "juice men" of the underworld—forced him to pay more than $14,000 interest on loans totaling a mere $1,900. The man, who wore a black hood to retain his anonymity and was known only as John Doe, came to the hearing accompanied by Assistant New York County District Attorney Michael Metzger, who urged congressional action to legalize wiretapping and electronic surveillance as "invaluable law enforcement tools."

Doe told the committee, headed by Senator George A. Smathers of Florida, that the original loan was given him in October, 1963, and that when he finally went to authorities in 1967, he still owed $5,800. At one point, he testified, he was "sold" to another loan shark for $5,000. This "new" shark said he wanted $100 a week, "and I don't care how you get it."

Frank Costello, who originally "refined" the syndicate methods, could hardly have imagined in his fondest dreams that one of his juice men would ever achieve enough sophistication to secure a loan for one of his victims from the Small Business Administration. But John Doe said this is exactly what was worked out for him in just two weeks by his shark; $900 was secured from the government, and the loan was used to keep up his payments.

Once the loan shark sent a floral wreath to Mr. Doe on the occasion of the funeral of his son, who had died in an industrial accident. Then the shark told Doe to sue the company and to reassign any settlement to him, his "patron."

Metzger tied into the John Doe incident the names of Ralph Lombardo, Nathan Sackin, and Sebastian (Buster) Aloi, who were subpoenaed and took the Fifth Amendment. Aloi has a record of twelve arrests and three convictions for various crimes.

Both he and Lombardo belong to the New York Mafia family of the late Thomas Lucchese.

The senators heard other testimony from a heavily veiled woman. She told how a loan shark suggested she become a prostitute in order to make payments owed by her husband to Chicago juice men. Her spouse had committed suicide when the pressure for repayment became too great. He was identified by Senator Smathers as Tony Franchina, a truck driver for the *Chicago Sun-Times*, which had editorially blasted the loan sharks, whose activities had been brought to light by crime reporters Ray Brennan and Sandy Smith.

The Chicago boys may have thought that the prostitution request of Mrs. Franchina was a "refinement." If so, they were surely wrong. But, then, mobsters always make the claim that they restrict physical punishment to members of the syndicate who have betrayed the outfit. The claim is, of course, spurious, but it is based on a certain amount of truth: regardless of all the refinements, *omerta* is still the law of the criminal jungle. The fear instilled in their victims is the Mafia's trump card when all the other cards are down, and the Mafia reserves its worst punishments for derelict members of the family.

In this connection, perhaps the cruelest bit of bloodletting and torture was inflicted on an enforcer for the juice racket in Chicago, William (Action) Jackson, and another hoodlum, Al Ageuci, who dared speak out against a member of the Mafia hierarchy. Jackson was hanged from a meat hook in a Chicago cellar until he was dead, and Ageuci was flayed alive in a field near Rochester, New York. It is obvious that the very men who seek to make life easier for the syndicate, because it stuffs their pockets with dollars, are often themselves victims of the terror; best men at a shotgun wedding who suddenly find themselves bridegrooms.

Such cruelty typifies all the men who live by the gun and are banded together for the purpose of doing peaceful citizens out of what assets and comforts they have. In the case of ruthless syndicate gangs actively seeking a wedge into the heart of a community, an act of cruelty and fear becomes one of the strongest arguments with which to confront civilized people. Thus, while probably there was no one to weep for Jackson or Ageuci, who is to say their deaths did not serve as deterrents to individuals honestly dedicated to destroying organized crime?

Today the Mafia has "class." There is still "muscle," but perhaps not so much. There are still assassinations, but instead of the machine-gun variety, the guns are muffled by silencers—and by the clinking of gold being stashed away in foreign bank accounts protected by wealthy and quiet officials in the lofty world of "high finance." The overt violence has mostly gone; it is no longer necessary. For example, as U.S. Attorney Robert M. Morgenthau has said, the new Mafiosi no longer have to rob banks since, "passing between the criminal and legitimate worlds of financial enterprise with greater and greater ease every day," they can merely "drain" them. Yet for all the syndicate's class, its blatant disruption of peaceful activities, little is known of the top men or even of the men who finance, and are financed in turn by, the mob's activities, men who do business not only in this country but with such other nations as Red China, where the production of heroin is carried out on a wholesale scale and distributed through syndicate pipelines in a sort of "balance of payments" program.

One of the more recent outlets for huge Mafia cash reserves is real estate, "by its nature a clandestine operation," according to Nicholas Pileggi, who wrote in the January, 1966, *Esquire:*

> Easily disposed to secret ownership, second mortgages, false fronts, absentee landlords, and labyrinthian holding companies, real estate has become the Mafia's new source of legitimate income. It is suspected that hundreds of millions of Mafia dollars lie just beneath the libelous surface of firms controlling well-known skyscrapers and hotels.
>
> The pertinent question of the day is whether the Mafia has taken over big business or big business has taken over the Mafia . . . There is so much complicity and general hanky-panky between the two that it is apparent America's business community and her racketeers, playing the strongest suits in profits rather than ethics, are sending an almost equal number of soldiers from their ranks to jail annually. Arm in arm, they have recently been linked to so many dubious bankruptcies, suspicious fires, defunct corporations, fraudulent stock issues, tainted unions, anemic insurance firms and rigged prices that the Mafia, through this strange marriage of connivance, is finding itself chronicled in the *Wall Street Journal* as often as in the racing tabloids.

The machinations, financial and otherwise, of organized crime are of such gargantuan proportions that to untangle and lay them out for all to see clearly is an impossible task. But we must assume, from what is already known, that there is a "second government" in this country—a government of crime—and even an inscrutable second religion. Mafiosi seem to have their own God, their own Christ, their own devil. And Frank Costello is his prophet.

The syndicate is a great nail in the heel of the public. The Mafia is the hammer that drives the nail home, the real grim reapers, and it is a hammer held by men who deal out death without scruple. Syndicate members, the shrubs around a tomb doing the bidding of a caretaker who clips them and transplants them at will, can be of any race—and they are—but the actual Mafiosi are of Sicilian or Italian birth or extraction. Thus, although Mafia families are made up exclusively of such men, they also work with criminals of other ethnic backgrounds within the syndicate. Consequently, one can well refer to the syndicate, the mob, and the Mafia (Cosa Nostra) as one and the same thing. For practical purposes they are, inasmuch as they all work hand-in-hand. But if you are not of the right blood, you will always be an outsider in the eyes of the Mafiosi, as Meyer Lansky and a host of others have learned. Blood does make a difference.

As we tour the criminal hot spots across the country, the qualities of the component parts of the syndicate will become more and more apparent. The pattern indicates that this second government has a constitution that recognizes the rights of wrongdoers and the principle that not all men—unless they are Mafiosi—are created equal. But the syndicate is not concerned only with "big" matters. There also exists, for the use of the brotherhood, a free lunch counter at which members may feed and a theatrical boarding house deal in which everything smells not of cabbage but of blood.

And whatever else happens, the money keeps pouring in, though no one seems to know its ultimate destination. The money deposited abroad constantly circulates, often finding its way back to the United States through a myriad of banks in such places as Switzerland, Lichtenstein, Panama, and more recently Nassau in the Bahamas. Meanwhile, in this country, men of the syndicate and their nonmember cohorts not only have been depositors but also have bought their way into banks and savings and loan associations across America and in many foreign countries—which helps immeasurably to cover their trail and confuse their trackers.

Such is the complexity of syndicate operations, moreover, that it is almost impossible ever to know of the wealth of an individual syndicate member. In this connection, the death of Jake (Greasy Thumb) Guzik of Chicago may be one lead into the secret of Mafia purse strings and how they are pulled. Guzik handed out, used, and controlled for the mob hundreds of millions of dollars in his lifetime. Yet when he died a few years ago, the probate of his estate revealed the existence of a paltry $10,000 in cash, which accrued to his widow. The rest of it? One can only surmise that Mafia money is all one big pot, with refinements that permit feeding from both sides of the trough—a golden side for the big shots and their bought-and-paid-for flunkies, and a silver side for the gunmen and button men trying to work their way up in the world.

This common ownership, however, also makes more difficult the task of cracking the Mafia. So what can be done? What can ordinary citizens accomplish if they are concerned about the thieves who are to change their lives and the lives of their children who will have to exist under laws dictated by the mob?

It is difficult to say, precisely. But the more knowledge we can gain about the workings of this criminal cartel, the better we can understand how to fight it. And it will take the cooperation of all of us—the legislative and law-enforcement agencies cannot defeat the Mafia on their own—to rid ourselves and our nation of the cancer that is crippling us.

So get involved. Don't turn your face the other way when the disturbing subject of organized crime comes up. Listen and learn. Be aware of what is happening and how it can and does affect the lives of every one of us. And perhaps someday, with your help, there will be enough courageous witnesses to terror to turn the Mafia code of *omerta*, which is their best weapon, into a lead balloon.

2

NEW YORK:

Momma, Momma, Momma!

New York City's first crisis was solved when the Indians sold Manhattan Island to some Dutchmen, who thought, rightly enough, that they had a bargain for their forty bucks. Many years have since passed and consolidated the Dutchmen's initial idea, not only in the minds of historians, but also in those of real estate men, who kick themselves because they weren't on the scene with a few blue beads when Fifth Avenue was up for grabs.

Few Dutchmen really made big money out of the deal, but one who did, a couple of hundred years later, was Arthur Flegenheimer, known to local police as "Dutch Schultz," scourge for a long time of the Irish and Italian mobsters who inherited a criminal legacy in the town during Frank Costello's regime. The trouble with the Dutch was that they didn't quite know what to do with the island, but that was before Flegenheimer and the others discovered that politicians were not much different from Indians.

Tammany Hall, for instance, was just another tepee open for trading with various kinds of wampum, even including blue beads when the price was right. During Boss Tweed's control of Tammany, in fact, before the turn of the century, gang riots were common and many gangs grew up and flourished—only to disappear, victims of the changing times and the fluctuating power and influence of the politicians they followed. No real union of criminals evolved in New York City until gangs of Mafiosi from Sicily disembarked almost simultaneously there and in New Orleans as the new century was ushered in.

The Mafiosi liked what they saw and launched themselves headfirst into the honey pots of the new land. Unfortunately for America, however, they brought with them a new concept of death, terror, and criminal efficiency—one that united them in their lawless pursuits.

At first, however, the new immigrants remained only loosely united politically, for often they were divided according to regions of origin and prior loyalties. Factions were numerous; the common front was directed only against the outsider.

Most powerful of the factions were the Camorra and the Mafia. Bloody feuds marked meetings of the two groups through the years, but something of a climax was reached on September 7, 1917, when the two factions—police generally lumped them together as Mafiosi—fought it out on Navy Street, in Brooklyn, with the result that many members of both sides were wiped out.

One of the first to die was Nicholas Morello, a hoodlum generally described as a member of the Mafia, who hailed from Harlem. His brother Ciro was later to become famous as Ciro Terranova, "The Artichoke King" who shook down Italian vegetable distributors in New York for every "choke" brought into the city.

Convicted a few months later as a result of the killings were Pelligrino Morano and Allessandro Vollero, early bosses of the Italian gang in the borough of Brooklyn. Both men eventually received life terms, and the trial of Morano provided the first testimony in any American courtroom regarding the secret initiation rites of the Mafia, which were apparently the same as those of the Camorra and no different from the rites undergone by Joe Valachi twelve years later.

Valachi testified that early in 1930 he was made a member of the Mafia in ceremonies at a private house ninety miles upstate from New York City. He said that about thirty-five men were there and that the man who handled the details was Salvatore Maranzano. Maranzano told Valachi that when the Mafia oath was taken, members inducted were "expected to die by the gun and by the knife," in accordance with the rules of the society. There was a ritual of burning paper and the adoption of a godfather—in Valachi's case it was Joseph Bonanno, boss of one of the other New York families. A little of Valachi's blood was let, and he became a button man in the organization.

The McClellan committee did not bring out the ritualistic meaning of all that happened in relation to Valachi's taking the brotherhood oath, but the Morano trial in 1918 makes Valachi's testimony clearer and perhaps even more terrifying.

In that trial, the district attorney elicited testimony from a witness, Tony Notaro, a hired killer from Springfield, Massachusetts. Notaro, in describing his own initiation into the secret society, said:

> . . . a man named Tony the Shoemaker [Anthony Paretti] gave me a penknife. He gave me a little penknife, so big. There was so much blade outside (witness illustrating). There was a piece of string attached to that penknife. He had one. Tony the Shoemaker extended his arm in this fashion (witness illustrates). He said to me, "Strike here." I did with the penknife, and just a little blood came out. Pelligrino went near the Shoemaker's arm and sucked the blood, and a little more blood came out. He said to me, "You have gained."

The initiation rites of the old Mafia had religious overtones. The burning of paper represented the immolation of a saint. The oath taken read: "I pledge my honor to be faithful to the Mafia like [sic] the Mafia is faithful to me. As this saint and a few drops of my blood were burned, so will I give all my blood for the Mafia when the ashes and my blood will return to their original status." And whatever its meaning, once the oath is taken, the new member is tied to the association—and is usually the first to be used when a murder is desired.

The Camorra languished with the jailing of Vollero and Morano, and subsequent feuds eventually resulted in the fusing of northern and southern Italian gangsters into a component organ of destruction in the United States, the Mafia, though there were still some antagonistic sections.

At the heart of the Mafia take-over in Manhattan after Vollero's departure in 1918 was Ignatzio Saietta, "Lupo the Wolf," who founded a human abattoir, the Murder Stable, near One Hundred and Seventh Street in Harlem. The Wolf, whose bodyguard was Ciro Terranova, thought nothing of hanging his enemies from meat hooks in the Murder Stable or of tossing them alive into the big furnace that was fired up the day before Ignatzio had his "discussion" with the boys who got out of line.

The story is told that when the recalcitrant Mafiosi were tossed into the coals, they would cry, "Momma, Momma, Momma!" before the gases and flames snuffed out their lives. The rough, brutal Mafiosi, stripped of the veneer provided by their wanton use of terror, could only cry out for their mothers when confronted with painful death.

"Normal" murders were also, of course, carried out at the Murder Stable. One, perhaps apocryphal, story repeated over the years has it that thirty-nine men were shot by the organization, not only as punishment, but also to further the ambitions of the leaders. Supposedly, the "old ladies" of the neighborhood would wail, whenever they heard shots coming from the stable: "They had to shoot another poor horse, God bless him."

The specific number of deaths—thirty-nine—recorded in neither police records nor the annals of the Mafia, points to the zeal of the person who originally published the details in his attempt to get the facts from a human welter of superstitions and terror. This is not always easy, for the Mafia is exceedingly inventive. For example, murder graves have included plain ditches dug on the property of Mafia chiefs, lime pits in which the bodies of victims were chemically destroyed after gangster lead had done its lethal work, furnaces, and the concrete foundations of housing developments. Watery graves are no exception, either.

In New York City, a favorite "drop off" place, nearly as popular as the East River, was a snaky stretch of water in Brooklyn known as the Gowanus Canal. The canal is an oily turgid arm of the East River lined by processing plants handling coffee, sugar, spices, and other products. For many years funds were voted either by the New York State or by the federal government to widen and deepen the canal. Somehow the effort was always circumvented. Skeletons with their bony feet encased in concrete would be hard to explain and might open up new murder inquiries.

The final fusion of the secret society's warring factions came about in the early 1930's and was, in part, the result of a bloody conflict since labeled the "Masseria-Maranzano War." Begun in New York in 1930 by Giuseppe Masseria, a gang leader of Neopolitan birth who passed death sentences on some of the top Sicilian Mafiosi in America, it ended some fourteen months later following the murder of Masseria himself and of his strongest opponent, Salvatore Maranzano, Joe Valachi's family boss.

Valachi testified that after gangland slayings had almost annihilated his forces and power, Masseria was murdered (in April, 1931) by three of his most trusted lieutenants: Charles Luciano, Vito Genovese, and Ciro Terranova. Then, according to Valachi, the opposing families were brought together under the rule of Maranzano, whose first assassination order was directed against

Luciano and Genovese because of their obvious dissatisfaction with subordinate roles. But Luciano and Genovese made their move first, hired some assassins of their own, and had Maranzano murdered in his New York City office on September 11, 1931.

This left Luciano and Genovese in a position to seize power over the New York-New Jersey combine, which they quickly did. Within a few years, however, Luciano was convicted of compulsory prostitution and imprisoned and Genovese became the subject of investigation by New York law authorities and fled to Italy. In 1937, therefore, Frank Costello stepped in officially as "boss of all bosses" in New York, a position he held until his attempted assassination outside his Manhattan apartment house in May, 1957.

Prime "powder man" suspect in the Costello assassination attempt was Vincent (The Chin) Gigante, but he was tried and acquitted. Later, however, in 1959, he was convicted on narcotics charges and sent to jail. Notes found by police when frisking Costello after the shooting, on May 2, 1957, revealed the mobster's connections with the Tropicana Hotel in Las Vegas, an establishment built by Dandy Phil Kastel, Frank's partner in gaming joints in Louisiana. Kastel, whose body was found a few years later with several bullet holes in it, "committed suicide," according to police reports. If so, he had to shoot himself about six times!

In the meantime, Genovese returned to New York in 1945 after his long exile in Italy. It took some time and considerable ruthlessness to consolidate his former strength and prestige, for in putting together the pieces of his regime and regaining his power he found that several men stood in his way. The first to go was Willie Moretti, New Jersey family boss. He was shot in 1951, and the others followed. When the attempt on Costello's life in May, 1957, and the subsequent publicity about his Las Vegas interests caused his removal from the position of supremacy in the Mafia hierarchy and Albert Anastasia was murdered in a barber shop in October, 1957, the way was clear for Genovese to assume the throne once more.

Genovese, moreover, is a different man from Anastasia, who typified the high-water mark of crude Mafia power in New York City. Anastasia, who succeeded Vincent Mangano as head of what is now the Carlo Gambino family upon Mangano's disappearance in 1951, was "Mr. Terror" of the mob, Lord High Executioner for the syndicate, and original boss of Murder, Inc. For years he determined when a murder would happen and when it wouldn't.

However, all good things come to an end, even for Mafiosi, and finally someone—probably Don Joseph Profaci, the Brooklyn boss later succeeded by Giuseppe Magliocco—decided Albert was getting too powerful. Anastasia had been stepping on the toes of Profaci's pal, Santo Trafficante, Jr., and annoying Vito Genovese's cohort, Meyer Lansky, probably because both Trafficante and Lansky had interests in Cuban gambling casinos coveted by Anastasia.

It is also thought by some that Anastasia was guilty of selling Cosa Nostra memberships for $40,000 apiece, a not unlikely occurrence since the membership rolls had supposedly been closed by Luciano between 1931 and 1954 and a growing number of hoodlums were therefore waiting to get into the select secret society—a situation paralleled since 1958, when the books were again reportedly closed.

Whatever the reasons, Anastasia was killed on the orders of his associates, and at the Apalachin conference, just three weeks after Anastasia's murder, Genovese aparently was scheduled to justify this and other killings within the organization, settle the internal disputes, and pull together his ranks. The conference, however, was broken up almost before it began, because its fifty-some participants became aware that they were under police surveillance and decided to run, thereby getting themselves picked up and identified.

Genovese's subsequent arrest in 1958 and later conviction for narcotics conspiracy earned him a fifteen-year prison sentence and at least outwardly put an end to his tremendous power over the New York families and to his overriding voice in the ruling council.

Vito Genovese's career is especially interesting because it demonstrates both the ruthlessness and the efficiency of the successful don. Born in Italy in 1897, Genovese came to America in 1913. He was arrested on a variety of charges while an apprentice gangster and then naturalized in 1936, a mistake the government didn't correct until 1953, when he was denaturalized and considered for deportation.

Meanwhile, in 1937, Vito deported himself when he fled to the old country to avoid arrest for the 1934 murder in a Brooklyn back alley of a Mafia colleague, Ferdinand (The Shadow) Boccia. Brooklyn police cracked the case when an informant named Ernie (The Hawk) Rupolo told of being hired to kill Boccia. Rupolo's gun failed to go off, and another gunman had to be brought in to do the job. The Hawk, thoroughly flustered, told authorities about meeting Vito and planning the murder, thereby prompting Genovese to hightail it out of the country for Italy.

Prior to the Allied invasion of Italy, Vito was close to Mussolini and was decorated by the dictator. In turn Vito got the boys back home to chip in handsomely for a fascist public building in Nola. Genovese may also have taken time out to arrange the murder of anti-fascist editor Carlo Tresca in New York City in January, 1943. Testimony heard at the McClellan committee hearings indicated that Vito "pressed a button" in Italy and a pal, Carmine (Lillo, Little Cigar) Galante, fired the bullet that slew Tresca, editor of *The Hammer*, a publication devoted to the destruction of Mussolini and his Fascists. Two hours before Tresca was shot, Galante, current underboss of the Joe Bonanno family, was seen getting into a car identified later as the vehicle used by the killer.

Sidney Gross, a parole officer stationed in downtown Manhattan, had just been told by Galante, who reported to him regularly after having served a sentence for robbery, that he was reformed and going straight. Gross was skeptical and detailed two investigators, Fred Berson and George Talianoff, to follow Galante. A few months previously, however, state officials had banned the use of autos by parole officers because of the wartime shortage of gasoline and tires, so all Berson and his colleague could do was note the license number of the car Galante sped away in: LC-9272. It was a car with this number that was identified by witnesses as being that from which the murderer had emerged to fire his pistol at Tresca.

Berson found himself in hot water with the parole board when he persisted in his investigation, which definitely tied Galante and his friends into the murder. Hidden wheels seemed to be working, and Berson was shortly notified by the division of parole that he was being dismissed for the "good of the service." A letter written by a fellow parole officer charging Berson with insulting a superior officer was read to him, and Berson left the service to become a businessman. But if Berson was silenced, his case still had repercussions. A week after his departure from the parole service, the man who wrote the note shot himself, leaving a statement that he was killing himself because of what he had been forced to do to Berson.

Needless to say, Genovese was little exercised by these complications; he continued to prosper in Italy. But given these circumstances, lawmen were flabbergasted when Genovese turned up as "adviser" and interpreter for the brass who staffed the offices of the Allied Military Government in the district of Nola. During the war, in fact, with the help of the Allied Military Government, Vito cornered the black market in important Italian cities, splitting the take with certain top officers in Nola. He also rounded up whores and other entertainment for them, becoming something of a glorified pimp.

The wheel nearly came full circle, however, when the Swiss government reportedly threatened to make public the deposit records of the numbered bank accounts of these and other American officers involved in European postwar black-market activities. The threat was made when the Internal Revenue Service, during the Eisenhower administration, secured from a disgruntled Zurich bank clerk a file recording cash stashed away by a prominent American businessman then under investigation. The IRS had enough information from the bank records to put the tax-dodger behind bars, but the Swiss, in an effort to protect their reputation for complete secrecy in banking, had their embassy in Washington demand that the IRS take no legal action. When the IRS flatly refused, according to a news story written by Edwin Hartrich for the *Boston Globe* on November 22, 1965, the Swiss told them: "Drop this case or the Swiss government will make public the names of these American officers, together with the amounts of their hidden deposits. That would create a real international scandal and damage U.S. prestige in Europe."

The IRS, which thinks nothing of putting the investigative bite on banks, backed off without reminding the Swiss that their government was helping perpetuate the power of the greatest criminal syndicate in history. It is estimated that Swiss banks hold some $80 billion in securities and funds for depositors located in every part of the world. Vito Genovese and the men below him, in and out of the Mafia, must certainly be responsible for a substantial portion of the funds in the more than four thousand commercial and private banking houses in Switzerland—to say nothing of the growing number of other banks around the world holding "secret" deposits. But this seems to affect the Swiss not at all.

Genovese maintained a chauffeured limousine in Nola, and his apartment was filled with short-wave radio equipment. One coup brought off by the cunning Mafioso, on June 2, 1944, involved the use of U.S. Army trucks for the theft of flour and sugar from the quartermaster supply depot in Nola. The stolen loads were sold in nearby towns, and the trucks later were found destroyed by fire in a vineyard in the commune of San Gennaro, seven miles away. Ultimately, however, Genovese was arrested by agent O. C. Dickey, of the criminal investigation division of the U.S. Army, who had been sent to Italy to apprehend Genovese and return him to the United States to face trial for the 1934 murder of Boccia.

Dickey later gave sworn testimony before the Brooklyn district attorney as to his many findings regarding Genovese's activities in Nola. On the day of Vito's arrest, a vault he owned in Nola's Bank of Labor was cleaned out by a henchman, Salvatore Profeta. Piles of PX supplies were found among his possessions, and Dickey found evidence later that indicated Vito was a ham radio operator with a set strong enough to send signals three thousand miles or more and should have been suspected of spying—a possibility never checked out.

Genovese was returned to Brooklyn on June 1, 1945, but there appeared to be no case against him in the murder of Boccia. It seems that Vito had again pushed a button before leaving Italy. Six months earlier the principle witness against him, Peter La-Tempa, a hoodlum who could have put Vito in the electric chair by providing corroboration for Ernie Rupolo's testimony as to Genovese's part in planning Boccia's demise, conveniently died in the Raymond Street Jail in Brooklyn.

While in jail, on January 15, 1945, LaTempa, who had gall-stones and was seemingly in great distress, was handed a glass of water supposedly laced with pain-killing tablets. He downed the "medicine" and died the same day. Enough tablets "to kill eight horses," according to the city toxicologist, had been mixed in La-Tempa's glass.

On June 11, 1946, County Judge Leibowitz was forced to release Genovese, who was dressed for the happy occasion in a blue suit, white shirt, maroon tie, and a faint sneer.

In our research into the early days of the secret society in New York and the jailing of Vollero and Morano, we came upon an interesting document, which revealed that Vito's roots in the Mafia may go even deeper than the law has been able to determine. A henchman of both Vollero and Morano known as "Tony the Shoemaker" to the boys and as Anthony Paretti to the law was sent to the electric chair for one of the murders that caused the Vollero-Morano façade to fall apart. The murder was only one of a long series of assassinations committed in the name of progress in the march of the Mafia toward local control of the Brooklyn rackets, but its connotations are significant.

The fact is that on July 20, 1926, Supreme Court Justice Mitchell May signed an order in Brooklyn permitting Genovese to visit Paretti in the death house. The implications are clear. Paretti, supposedly a Neopolitan Camorrista and on no good terms with such Mafiosi as Genovese, may well have been planted in the Vollero-Morano gang by the very man who was soon to become top dog in American syndicate activities. A curious fact is that early immigration records show Vito's birthplace as Resigliano—not Naples, as Joe Valachi later told investigating senators. The explanation could easily lie in the theory that Vito was playing both sides of the ethnic fence; if so, he managed to come out smelling like a rose to his gang buddies, despite the odds against this feat.

Vito really "arrived," though unofficially, in 1949, when Frank Costello threw a dinner for a charitable organization at the Copacabana in Manhattan. The seating arrangements at the dinner and the deference with which Genovese was treated made it pretty obvious to those in the know that he would soon emerge as top man throughout the country.

Genovese had somehow survived when dozens of gang bosses, such as Joe Masseria, Salvatore Maranzano, Gaetano Reina, and Joseph Pinzola, were murdered during the mob's "transition" from bootlegging to other rackets in the thirties. And his progress has been continuous. Today, even from prison, Genovese has kept his boys "honest"—and dishonest. Only one member of the mob has tried to move in on his personal command, which includes most of New England and New York City. The rackets, including the profitable numbers game, are seemingly still operating full blast, and the money is being stashed away for Don Vitone during his incarceration.

The Mafioso who got out of line was Anthony (Tony Bender) Strollo, long one of Genovese's lieutenants. Bender began to import pure heroin in kilo lots and, for some unexplained reason, employed the Gallo gang to plague Brooklyn's reigning don, Joseph Profaci. The Gallos, led by brothers Larry and Joe, kidnapped and then released Profaci's chief lieutenants in February, 1961, in a coup that staggered and puzzled the underworld and was fully detailed at the McClellan hearings by Sergeant Ralph Salerno, then one of the New York City police department's top investigators into organized crime.

After experiencing numerous other, less serious, annoyances by the Gallo gang, the inner circle of the Mafia finally went to work. At 10:00 P.M. on April 8, 1962, Bender walked out of his house at 1015 Palisades Avenue, Fort Lee, New Jersey. He told his wife he was going to buy cigarettes—and hasn't been seen since. The hint was enough. The Gallos folded up shop, and Larry Gallo died of cancer in May, 1968.

Joseph Profaci, Brooklyn's don, had a career equally significant to that of Genovese. Profaci came to the United States in 1922 with a friend, the soon-to-become-notorious Vincent Mangano, and Vincent's father, Gaetano. At first he was overshadowed by Mangano, who became boss of what is now the Carlo Gambino family and is believed to have served a term as boss of bosses in the ruling council for several years before his disappearance in 1951. But Profaci enjoyed a career that was not much less dramatic. He became an associate of Lucky Luciano in 1928, and over the years, using mob money garnered from numbers, prostitution, and narcotics, he bought into no fewer than twenty businesses operating within the law. At one time he was the largest single importer of olive oil and tomato paste in the United States and owned a hunting lodge with private airport on a 328-acre estate at Hightstown, New Jersey. Pretty good for a man born into poverty in 1897 in Villabati, a village in the province of Palermo, Sicily!

In 1953 Profaci was prosecuted—later one of the leading government attorneys in the case against him became president of one of Profaci's business enterprises—for income-tax evasion, and it was determined that he owed the government $1,484,807. However, this sum was found to be uncollectable when authorities discovered that Profaci's properties had been taken over by relatives through second mortgages.

Profaci was a man of many interests. In 1949, for example, he was almost made a Knight of St. Gregory by Pope Pius XII. Supreme Court Justice Miles McDonald, a noted Catholic layman who was then district attorney of Brooklyn, found out about the impending honor for Profaci and scotched the whole thing. Profaci had weaseled his way into the good graces of the local church community via some Italian prelates and judges he knew as well as by means of huge cash gifts, and the churchmen were unaware of Profaci's connection with the Mafia until McDonald pointed it out. Even then, however, they expressed shock and indignation at such accusations. But Profaci's honor was withheld.

The day before his knighthood was canceled, Profaci got some really bad news. The *Brooklyn Eagle* ran a story that eventually exposed the Brooklyn don by alluding to a mysterious "Mister X" who ran the rackets. Profaci, who was eating lunch in the Brooklyn Navy Yard restaurant owned by Ralph (Peaches) Conti when the paper was laid on his table, promptly emptied his stomach of steaming spaghetti. He was never the same man again, and a later conviction for dosing olive oil imports with a substance known as squalene sent him even further down the ladder.

The end came in 1962, a bad year for Mafia bosses. Lucky Luciano, who had been deported to Italy in 1946, died unexpectedly at Naples airport on the afternoon of January 26th, and Joe Profaci died of cancer in the South Side Hospital on Long Island, New York, on June 7th.

It has been estimated that during the twenty-five years of Profaci's reign as Brooklyn boss his total illegal receipts from rackets under his control were between $100 and $200 million. It can be assumed that no taxes were paid on the money; Profaci would have had to gross something like $200 billion to amass legally $200 million after taxes. He left no will providing for relatives and no estate. His holdings had been parceled out, and they simply vanished. It was the story of Greasy Thumb Guzik all over again.

Luciano? He had an empty paper cup in his hand when he died, and owned the clothes on his back.

Genovese? Despite the fact that he is in jail, Vito now commands possibly ten times as much money as Profaci did in his lifetime. As titular boss of the Mafia in the United States, with direct control of the rackets in the most important cities of the East, Genovese is probably the richest man in the world. But it is money he cannot leave to anyone or anything except the syndicate, money that is piling up around the world for him and the mob.

Since, however, Genovese does control the New York Mafia, and by extension is the leading Mafia figure in the country, the boss of bosses, an understanding of his organization is vital if one is to appreciate the complexity and extent of current Mafia activities. Fortunately, the McClellan investigation unearthed a New York City police department organization chart showing the membership of the Vito Genovese family, and the ensuing testimony of Joe Valachi and others reinforced and substantiated information gathered over the years by various law agencies and gave precise details as to Vito's subordinates. Also made clear were their order of importance and many of their activities. Consequently, we have a pretty clear idea of current Mafia operations.

Now that he is incarcerated, Vito's orders are carried out by three men within his own family: Thomas Eboli, alias "Tommy Ryan"; Gerardo (Jerry) Catena; and Michele (Mike) Miranda.

Tommy Eboli has on his record six arrests and two convictions, one for an assault on a fight promoter in Madison Square Garden. At the time of the report, he owned vending machines and restaurants in Greenwich Village, including a piece of the Burger Village, and had taken time out to visit Lucky Luciano in Italy before Luciano's death, spending a few days at the crime boss's hotel. John F. Shanley of the New York City police department has testified that Eboli may have been the "wheel man" who drove the car used in the shooting of Frank Costello. Eboli's bookmaking operator in New York is Tony (The Priest) Mousto, who reportedly does a $20,000-a-day business for the boss.

Second-in-command during Genovese's absence is Jerry Catena, who tells everyone he is a truckman. At the time of the testimony, Catena, who attended the Apalachin meeting in 1957, resided at 21 Overhill Road, South Orange, New Jersey, and had interests in People's Express Company, Advance Vending Company, Runyon Vending Sales Company, and Kool Vent Awning Company, all in Newark—and he was not averse to using strong-arm methods to get his way. Arrests of Catena, who is swarthy and pudgy with blue eyes and graying brown hair, include pickups since 1923 for robbery, hijacking, bribing a federal juror, and suspicion of murder.

If Eboli and Catena let Genovese down while he is in prison, control of Vito's empire may fall to Mike Miranda. This much-feared Mafioso is considered an elder in the organization and is sought after for counseling by syndicate bigwigs. Born in Naples in 1896, Miranda lives at 167 Greenway North, Forest Hills, Long Island, when he is not doing time in jail. His summer home is at 629 East Olive Street, Long Beach, Long Island. (Addresses given for all hoodlums are, of course, subject to change at a moment's notice, depending on whether or not the heat is on.)

Miranda, known as "Mr. Big" and "Frank Russi," listed his occupation as Cadillac salesman for Huntoon and Raffo in New York City. He has engaged in narcotics smuggling, murder, and extortion and is one of the controlling racketeers in the garment section of Manhattan, having shared jurisdiction with Thomas Lucchese before Lucchese died.

Law officials are haunted by the thought of what will happen when Vito dies, in jail or out. Since Don Vitone seems to have indicated his favorite heirs—subject, of course, to a change of heart—the feeling is that one of the most vicious gang wars in history may take place if those not chosen by the don decide to take issue with his decision and to fight it out for the throne.

Actually, Catena has not built up a personal following in the organization and would probably not figure too strongly. He was placed in his somewhat exalted position by Joseph Valachi's testimony, and it could be an embarrassing situation for him. It seems more likely that the Genovese empire, the most lucrative in the world, will split up among such powerful mobsters as Carlo Gambino, who replaced the murdered Albert Anastasia, and the heirs of Giuseppe (Bad Eyes) Magliocco—when they emerge, which might be soon, for Magliocco, also known as "The Fat Man" and "Joe Malyak," died of natural causes in December, 1963, after a short term as successor to his late brother-in-law, Joe Profaci.

One of the mobsters who has been quietly trying to pick up pieces of the Profaci barony is Carmine Lombardozzi, a *capo* in the Carlo Gambino family and good pal of Profaci, who once saved him from being sentenced to death by the Mafia peerage. Carmine, who tried to patch up the Profaci-Gallo warfare in Brooklyn in 1961, was protected by Profaci when charged by the bosses with mismanagement of the jukebox-industry racket in Brooklyn, according to police officials in that borough. Now in his late fifties, Lombardozzi has a rugged, handsome face and silvery hair. His one vanity is a pair of diamond cuff links set with star sapphires that cost him, at a conservative estimate, $800. He has been arrested for vehicular homicide, burglary, abduction, rape, unlawful entry, and carrying concealed weapons, yet he has served less than five months in jail since his first arrest in 1929—an enviable record by Mafia standards.

Lombardozzi might have to take on Magliocco's confidant and relative by marriage, Salvatore (The Sheik) Mussachio, who has a police record that includes twenty-two arrests but only one conviction. Mussachio was official underboss to Magliocco before the latter's death, but he appears to be less intelligent than Lombardozzi. Mussachio once told police that he was in the fish business and was also a barber, yet he used an automobile registered to a Brooklyn bakery. The police went to the bakery, found the car outside with a gun on the floor, and arrested him.

Another combatant in the scramble, one who not only is looking to the top position in the Magliocco family but also has his eye on the Genovese throne as well, is forty-five-year-old Joe Colombo. Before Magliocco's death, Colombo was a *capo* in the family, working under Mussachio, but he seems quickly to have assumed the top spot—in terms of power if not in name.

According to Sandy Smith, former *Chicago Sun-Times* crime reporter now with *Life*, Colombo has assumed substantial power and status since 1963 and even serves as one of the commissioners on the ruling council. He is named, in *Life*, September 8, 1967, as the brains behind one of the syndicate's newest rackets: traffic in stolen securities. Since 1962, according to *Life*, authorities have attributed to Colombo's men responsibility for six Manhattan thefts involving $8 million in securities. The securities from these and other robberies are said to have been sold to various foreign banks, and it is also thought that these banks are sometimes induced to send the stolen securities back to this country for resale. Another, even riskier, method of disposal is to put up the stolen stocks as collateral for a bank loan in this country. The borrowed money brings in a quick and sizable profit from loan sharking and is then returned to the bank, with little interest due; whereupon the stolen stocks and bonds are retrieved. Bankers "devious enough to accept the stolen collateral . . . are 'hooked' by the Mob in some way, through physical fear or blackmail," the article continued. "Federal officials have identified a dozen such bankers in the New York area."

In *Life*, September 1, 1967, an article relates a series of events that supposedly led to Colombo's present position in the hierarchy. His rise began in 1963 when council commissioner and New York family boss Joe Bonanno attempted to seize control of the combine by issuing contracts for the killing of three fellow commissioners, Carlo Gambino, Thomas Lucchese, and Stephano Magaddino, boss of the Buffalo, New York, family, and of a California mobster, Frank DeSimone. Bonanno is said to have assigned the New York "contracts" to Giuseppe Magliocco, who in turn farmed them out to Joseph Colombo.

Instead of carrying out his orders, however, Colombo told the commission of the planned "coup," and they summoned Magliocco and Bonanno to face the charges. "Magliocco appeared in a panic," the article states, "made a full confession, was banished from Cosa Nostra, fined $50,000 and sent home. Shortly thereafter he died of a heart attack. Meanwhile, his Family and his Commission seat were given to the stool pigeon Colombo."

Bonanno never did show up for trial. He disappeared temporarily, only to reappear in Canada, "poaching once more on Magaddino's grounds." The infuriated Magaddino is said to have called a commission meeting in September, 1964, but this was also ignored by Bonanno. As a result the commissioners issued his death warrant as a penalty for the insult. A month later Bonanno was "kidnapped" from a Manhattan street as he was about to enter an apartment building and apparently held captive until sometime in December. Although there is other speculation about the reasons for Bonanno's disappearance, it is claimed:

> He was held for about six weeks somewhere in the Catskills. There he talked his captors out of killing him by raising the specter of a nationwide gang war if they knocked him off. But if they let him go, he promised to turn over his gang and his rackets in gratitude. Apparently the Commissioners' lust for loot exceeded their lust for vengeance, for they turned him loose in December of 1964.
>
> Bonanno was only fooling. He went to Haiti to bide his time, then returned to New York last year to rally his gang, claim his place on the Commission and continue his invasion of Canada. Magaddino still howls about it, but the other Commissioners, perhaps afraid of the guns in Bonanno's Family, seem intent on trying to ignore him, hoping he'll go away, or something.

When asked at the McClellan hearings if Vito Genovese had full control over the Brooklyn family of Joe Bonanno, Joe Valachi replied: "No, he don't . . . they stay on the ground . . . In other words, the boss of that family, no one tells them what to do."

If Joe Colombo should someday, somehow succeed in assuming

Genovese's power over the New York families, and if he does indeed serve on the ruling council, then it seems he will be faced with the presence in this brotherhood of crime of a sixty-four-year-old, somewhat scrappy, and certainly dangerous adversary: Joe Bonanno.

With Vito in jail and bosses Lucchese and Magliocco dead, the argument within the Mafia for younger men to take over in New York is accentuated by the fact that Carlo Gambino, the one remaining elder boss in addition to Bonanno is sixty-seven and ailing. Long a shylock in Manhattan and also a labor relations consultant with a Madison Avenue firm, Gambino is said to be looking to retirement.

Thomas Lucchese, long-time elder in the Mafia and boss of one of New York's families, died at the age of sixty-seven in July, 1967. There seemingly has been no final determination as to who will take his place as family boss, although several have been in the running at one time or another.

Vincent John Rao, for example, a *consigliere* and potential heir, who attended the Apalachin meeting, was offered the top spot, but recent troubles with federal authorities have forced him to decline the "honor." Another contender is *capo* Anthony Corallo (who will be mentioned in more detail shortly). Apparently he is trying his best to make the grade, but he, too, has run afoul of the law. Current estimates are that *capo* Carmine Tramunti, alias "Mr. Gribs," is moving up fast in the race to the top. Tramunti is relatively unknown to lawmen, and certainly his activities have been little publicized, but he has been arrested at least fifteen times and convicted on six occasions. Also, Tramunti was listed before the McClellan committee as being involved in the gambling, labor racketeering, shylocking, extortion, strong-arm, and murder fields of syndicate activity.

Lucchese, who was in partial retirement prior to his death, owned many dress firms in Manhattan and factories in eastern Pennsylvania, where labor comes cheap and there is little union trouble. He was for many years a patron of a number of public officials in New York City. Indeed, a study of the seating lists of only two of the many charity dinners Lucchese attended shows that no fewer than twenty-two judges, of every level of jurisprudence, were guests at tables purchased by him.

Lucchese was a great one for "personal" favors and often picked up tabs for friendly officials. One switch on this routine occurred, however, when Lucchese's own tab for rooms 300 and 302 at the Hotel Astor in New York City, totaling $25.08 for March 18 and 19, 1948, was transferred to the hotel account of Armand Chankalian, then assistant to U.S. Attorney Myles Lane.

In his last years Miami claimed most of Lucchese's attention, visitors included Vincent (Jimmy Blue Eyes) Alo, Meyer and Jake Lansky, and Rocco Pelligrino, the "Old Man" of White Plains, New York. Alo, who actually has brown eyes, runs things in the Bronx, and it was Pelligrino who brought the Black Hand to Westchester County years ago when he shook down workers on the Pocantico Hills estate the Rockefellers were building.

There are many who would like to reach out and pick up pieces of the Genovese empire when Vito passes away. But they will have to wait for that day, and they know it; Genovese is still in full command. Even then, it will take a number of meetings such as the Apalachin as well as conferences with the shadowy financial bigwigs who are behind the Mafia both in Europe and the Americas before it will be possible for a decision to be made as to Don Vitone's successors. Either that, or a series of the devastating gang wars so feared by all who know the terror and bloodshed such disputes have brought in the past.

If gang war is violent, however, "ordinary" life with a Mafioso is not without moments of terror, as the Coppola story makes clear. Michael (Trigger Mike) Coppola, long-time Genovese lieutenant who had a record of more arrests than any member of Vito's Mafia ménage and was a likely candidate to be the don's successor, died in a Boston hospital on October 1, 1966. His body was rushed to New York and buried the next day. Federal agents did not know of his demise until the funeral was over, and the press didn't hear about it for two days after that—which is a pity, because Coppola had led an interesting and intriguing life.

Coppola spent most of the last years of his life in Miami Beach, moving around occasionally to Europe, while Lucky Luciano was alive, or to Mexico and Central and South America on syndicate business. His private life was secretive, although it was no secret to the police that Mike owned the numbers racket in East Harlem, a territory he shared with his mentor, Genovese. And it remained for Coppola's second wife, Ann, to blow the whistle on her husband's privacy in a way that must have made even his Mafiosi pals wince.

The story came out in the form of a diary Ann kept hidden, until her death by suicide in a hotel room in Rome on September 18, 1962, led to its discovery. Her diary, and a last letter to Attorney General Robert F. Kennedy, confirmed her wish for surcease.

"Death shall be a blessing to me," she had written. "Mike and I shall both pay . . . One must have compassion, love and a conscience to break."

The diary was suppressed for four years until details of its contents were revealed by crime reporter Hank Messick in a story filed in Miami on November 30, 1966, to the *Chicago Daily News.*

Ann began her story in the diary: "I met Mike Coppola—the swine—September 20, 1955. He pursued me like I don't think too many women have been pursued . . ."

Ann, whose first husband was Charles Drahmann, a casino manager for the syndicate-controlled Lookout House near Covington, Kentucky, met Mike's friends before he ever laid eyes on her. She had opened a dress shop in Cincinnati after Drahmann was killed in a plane crash in 1952. Messick's story relates that Louis (Sleep-out Louie) Levinson, brother of Eddie Levinson (of whom more will be said in subsequent chapters), helped get the pair together, and a whirlwind courtship was followed by a wedding on December 28, 1955, at the plush Beverly Hills Club outside Newport, Kentucky.

The couple went to the home in Miami that Coppola had purchased from John (King) Angersola, a member of Cleveland's Mayfield Road mob, for a honeymoon that lasted three weeks. Not much later, Ann wrote, Mike became angry after a dinner party, called her flat-nosed and frog-eyed, fetched a gun, and took a shot at her.

"Unfortunately," she told her diary, "God made me duck!"

Ann was also subjected to abortions. Coppola used a syndicate doctor who, Messick claimed, was house physician at one of the leading Miami Beach hotels. This man performed four abortions for her on the kitchen table at the Coppola home and, according to Ann, received $1,000 for each one.

Life with Coppola was never dull. Once, Ann relates, Mike came home to dinner from his favorite hangout, the Midtown

Social Club. Suddenly he clapped his hand to his head and called the manager of the club. He ordered the man to look in the freezer unit at the club kitchen and send the package he found there over to Coppola's house. This was just before Christmas, and Ann thought it might be a present. But, instead, the package contained $219,000 in cash, and Mike explained to her that it was his share of the Harlem numbers profits. A courier had delivered it to him at the club, and Mike had put it in the freezer and forgotten about it. The money was secreted in one of five hiding places Coppola had in the house, and at one time, according to Ann, the amount on hand totaled $340,000. She wrote that Mike had given her $250,000 in jewelry, furs, and fine clothes: not to please her, but "to prove to people how big and successful he was."

Christmas lists drawn up by Ann included such persons as Vito Genovese, Philip Lombardardo, Frank Livorsi, Joe Rao, Joe (Joe Stretch) Stracci, and Al Rosato. Vincent Alo and a "Mr. Sal Luçania, 464 Via Lasso, Naples, Italy," were also among the names on her lists. Lucania is, of course, Charles Luciano, who at that time was alive and living in Rome.

The Coppolas were divorced in 1960, when Mike sued and claimed that Ann used bad language in front of his children, and soon after the Internal Revenue Service decided to investigate Trigger Mike's sources of income. Ann reluctantly offered to help, noting in her diary: "I learned at an early age it was most admirable not to be a stool pigeon."

Coppola, who used threats, a beating, and bribe offers, was unable to keep Ann from testifying, and, after changing his plea to guilty, he was sent to federal prison in Atlanta, where he met up with Genovese and Valachi, for nine months.

Coppola got out of prison two months after Ann was found dead. Death may have been a blessing for her—as she had hoped in her diary—but Mike never really paid for his cruelty and apparently had no conscience or compassion to make him think about what had happened. He returned to Miami Beach and, until his own death in 1966, further increased his wealth as a banker for shylocks and top layoff bettors, developing a new hobby at the same time: orchid growing—in the very house that had seen his wife's abortions.

Such is the life and death of the average Mafioso, and of such there is no end. Despite the imprisonment of Genovese, the deaths of Luciano, Profaci, Magliocco, and Lucchese, and the westward and southward migrations of many of the clan, the syndicate is obviously on anything but its last legs, in New York or anywhere else. For example, a story by Ronald Kessler in the *Wall Street Journal* of June 3, 1968, gives another example of the varieties of hoodlum enterprise. Taking advantage of disparate tax laws in different states, the Mafia is "siphoning off as much as $50 million a year" from cigarette bootlegging; "39 million in New York City, alone," according to Queens District Attorney Thomas J. Mackell.

All five New York Mafia families are reportedly involved. The method of operation involves trucking cigarettes from a state where there is no cigarette tax to one in which a tax is charged, and the following example was given as to how it works:

> Until Saturday, a smuggler could rent a one-ton panel truck, load it with 40,000 packs, or $12,400 worth of cigarets, in North Carolina, which has no state cigaret tax. Two days later he could sell them in New York for $18,800, based on a general city retail price of 47 cents a pack, at a profit of $6,400 . . . On Saturday, New York raised its per-pack tax to 12 cents from 10 cents, in addition to a 4-cent city tax and a 2-cent sales tax, increasing illicit profits on the same $12,400 investment to $7,200—or a 58% profit.

Some of these truck shipments are said to require cash payments of between $20,000 and $30,000, which small-time operators could hardly afford. The operation is, therefore, strictly a syndicate venture concentrated primarily in New York State, which has the nation's highest cigarette tax.

While this new racket may seem to contain a strange and surprising twist to those who have not done some previous delving into the syndicate mind, it is neither strange nor surprising to those who know the dedication the mob brings to the task of undermining every possible foundation stone in the structure and maintenance of a lawful, moral society. Thus, the Mafia has even reached its scandal-tainted fingers into the administration of New York's young and vigorous mayor, John V. Lindsay, through one of his commissioners, James L. Marcus.

Lindsay admitted to "great anguish and anger" and believed he had been "ill-served" by his friend and trusted aide when Marcus, then commissioner of water supply, gas, and electricity, was indicted by a federal grand jury in December, 1967, on charges of conspiracy in connection with the letting of an $800,000 reservoir-cleaning contract.

The indictment also named Mafia chieftain Anthony Corallo, a union local president, two labor lawyers, and the president of a contracting firm. All were released without bail except Corallo, who had to post $10,000 and was later convicted along with two of the others. Corallo, a fast-rising *capo* in the family of the late Thomas Lucchese, is known as "Tony Ducks" because of his ability to avoid court appearances. He first came into prominence in the trucking rackets in Queens County, where he did exceptional work for the Mafia and still wields considerable power. He is a close friend of the Teamster Union's Jimmy Hoffa and, with Hoffa's apparent approval, has been instrumental in bringing scores of fellow racketeers into the labor movement.

James Marcus, family friend of Mayor Lindsay, who is godfather to Marcus' son, was accused of accepting a $16,000 kickback on the disputed contract and is also believed to have borrowed money from Corallo at loan-shark interest rates.

Even more surprising than the scandal—syndicate-connected scandals are nothing new in New York—is the revelation by the FBI that one of the men under indictment, Herbert Itkin, had been one of its undercover agents. The bureau said he infiltrated the world of organized crime and reported regularly on his findings. One federal official added more mystery to the case by calling Itkin, Marcus' forty-three-year-old Manhattan lawyer and partner in several business ventures, a "strange" man who risked his life to "stand up to the Mafia."

Itkin is a potential witness, officials say, in numerous cases involving labor racketeering, gambling, bribery, income-tax evasion, and other felonies at the city, state, and federal levels together with action on an international scale. He has told close friends that he provided information to the Central Intelligence Agency on activities of persons in the Dominican Republic and in Haiti, where he is known to have had dealings. A probe by the *New York Times* early in March, 1968, indicated that Itkin's dealings in the Caribbean included a relationship with an export concern headed by a Haitian-born Miami businessman, Robert Deschamps, but Deschamps denied Itkin was ever authorized to represent him or his company, a Coral Gables outfit called Westrade, Inc.

In 1963 Itkin filed a form with the Justice Department as a foreign agent of the Dominican Republic, saying he sought to act for Westrade in efforts "to negotiate on behalf of the Dominican Republic and a bank or brokerage company in the United States, a bond issue in the amount of $35,000,000 to extend over a period of 15 years." Deschamps told the *New York Times* that Itkin spoke of getting financing from a union pension fund—"I think he said the teamsters"—but nothing came of the discussion.

Corallo traveled with Itkin to London in 1966 and was kicked out by the British government. Their excuse for giving him the boot, according to the *New York Times*, was that he was trying to gain control of some of England's legal gambling casinos for Mafia families in the United States.

John F. Malone, FBI assistant director in New York City, and U.S. Attorney Henry Morgenthau both remained mum on the case involving Itkin, but one anonymous federal official told the *New York Times:* "[Itkin] is damned near broke, his family life is in a mess, he can't practice law and he can't do anything but wait it all out." The official would not say whether Itkin was a paid or unpaid informant. It was revealed, however, that he was under protective custody. If he traveled with Corallo and gleaned Mafia secrets, he may need that protection. Certainly, however, he knows something about the first big scandal in Mayor Lindsay's official family.

In the case of Marcus, who resigned after his indictment, pleaded guilty to a charge of bribery conspiracy, and is serving a fifteen-month jail term, Lindsay commented: "I've been through some rough ones but I guess this is the roughest yet." He didn't elaborate on the other "rough ones" he's been through, but, given the history of New York, Lindsay's two years as mayor—up to the Marcus-Itkin-Corallo imbroglio—might be just a warm-up. The ghosts do not chuckle; neither do they envy him.

The shadow hanging over New York is no darker than the shadows that have gone before. The hoods who cried for their mothers as they roasted over the hot coals in the Mafia furnace and the sophisticated, high-riding gangsters of today are separated by many long years of violence, but the play seems always to be the same. Only the actors have changed.

3

BUFFALO:

Niagara Powerhouse

In the files of the Buffalo police department there lies the murder story of narcotics smuggler Al Agueci, of how the Mafia took his clothes, his skin, the very flesh from his bones. Agueci was a man practically no one, except the Mafia, knew. His widow found out, though, what it means to cross the barons of the brotherhood, however right you may be. Crossing the top Mafiosi does not necessarily involve going against their wishes; it is enough to go against the grain of their egos, for they believe they can do no wrong—and there is little chance for appeal. Indeed, it is the insecurity that they themselves feel when they wrong one of their own that apparently leads, at times, to violence.

"*Sangu lava sangu*," the Mafiosi say. "Blood washes blood." And a lot of blood, other than Agueci's, has been spilled in trying to wash the slate clean. Because of Al's murder, his brother Vito set his sights on the throat of one of the top gangsters in this country, Stefano Magaddino, Buffalo-based Mafia powerhouse servicing the western New York, Ohio valley, and Toronto, Canada, areas.

The Agueci brothers were born and raised in Sicily, eventually working their way to Canada, where they became heavy traffickers in narcotics for Stefano Magaddino's Mafia family. The brothers then obtained Magaddino's permission to branch out and soon began to engage in the narcotics business in the greater Buffalo area. On July 20, 1961, however, they were arrested in New York City for violation of the federal narcotics law, thereby setting in motion a chain of events that eventually led to Joe Valachi and his remarkable testimony concerning the Mafia.

Magaddino's agreement with the Aguecis called for a percentage of their profits to be paid to Don Stefano. The don, in turn, was bound to provide protection for his boys: freedom from the interference of other gangsters, bail money in the event of arrest, and many other things.

The evidence indicates, however, that Magaddino, perhaps on a whim, reneged on his end of the deal when the arrest was made and did nothing to aid the Mafiosi brothers, who were depending on him for assistance. Al's wife finally managed to provide bail for her husband, and the angry man set out to avenge himself on Magaddino. He was not seen again until November 23rd, when his burned and mutilated body was found in a field near Rochester, New York. The Buffalo police department records the murder thus:

> On November 23, 1961, the body of Albert G. Agueci of 21 Armitage Drive, Scarsborough, Canada, was found in a field near Rochester, N.Y. His hands were bound behind his back, and his ankles were tied with long cord and he was strangled. His jaw was broken, half his teeth had been kicked or knocked out. Substantial portions of meaty tissue were removed from the calves of his legs. His body was doused with gasoline and ignited. His body was mutilated beyond recognition. This was not only to cause his death, of course, but this was to send a message to anyone else who had the temerity or the gall to try to resort to vengeance against one of the dons of the empire.

Al Agueci had learned the horror of a Mafia death-lesson, and in his tortured and ebbing consciousness at the end he must have begun to realize the wisdom behind the old Mafia proverb: *"Tra la legge e la Mafia, la piu temibile non e la legge."* "Between the law and the Mafia, the law is not the most to be feared." The message was clear, but to one the message appeared to have little meaning: brother Vito.

Vito Agueci was convicted on the narcotics charge and sent to Atlanta federal prison. There he met up with Joe Valachi, who, as a member of Vito Genovese's New York family, had been invited to share the Genovese prison cell with five other inmates.

Agueci told Valachi he would like a meeting with Genovese, and since he didn't know the don personally, he asked Valachi to arrange it. Valachi relayed the message, but Genovese refused to meet Agueci. Vito had already made known his declaration that he would do anything to avenge his brother's murder, and Genovese knew what "anything" meant. Consequently, he looked on

Agueci as a personal threat to himself as well as his close Mafia *compare*, Magaddino.

From that moment on Genovese began playing Agueci against Valachi, and vice versa, hoping thereby to do away with Agueci. Genovese told Valachi to walk Agueci around the prison yard so he could identify him. This Valachi did, and within a short time Valachi found himself under surveillance by other ominous members of the Mafia also doing time in Atlanta—Johnny Dioguardi, a convicted extortionist, Trigger Mike Coppolo, and Joe Beck, alias "Joe Palermo," all of them high-ranking Mafiosi from New York.

To add to Valachi's suspicions of a plot, Agueci, at the instigation of Genovese's pals, began calling him "a rat"—an informer—while Genovese in his cell at night began telling him to "get" Agueci for calling him names. Valachi testified later that he became convinced Genovese wanted to "kill two birds with one stone," for Valachi knew that his killing of Agueci in prison would also seal his own destiny, as far as the law was concerned. He realized he was being used as a tool and that, as a button man, he was expendable to the Mafia.

According to Valachi, his reluctance to do the job assigned to him caused Genovese to give him the Mafia kiss of death, which greatly increased his continuing fear for his life. Valachi became almost paranoid in suspecting everyone in the prison of being determined to kill him and even had himself thrown into solitary confinement, which, he said, was the same as walking into the safety of a police station.

Upon his release from the "hole," Valachi's fears rose until he was almost irrational. For days he sat in his cell and wouldn't leave it even to eat. Then, during an outdoor rest period one day, Valachi went for a walk in the yard. Near a construction project he suddenly looked up and saw a man he thought was hoodlum Joe Beck; he was sure that Beck had been sent to murder him for not following Genovese's instructions to eliminate Vito Agueci. Valachi felt that this was it. Grabbing a piece of pipe, he began slamming it down on Beck's head until his adversary lay motionless.

Unfortunately, for Valachi, the man he killed was not Joe Beck, though he looked very much like him. Fortunately, for the American public, Valachi was tried and convicted of murder and sentenced to life imprisonment—fortunately, that is, because

Valachi's sentence decided him to ask for the protection of the law and to "blow the whistle" on the entire structure of the Mafia, for he knew that if he ever returned to prison, no matter which one or where it was, the violent black hand of the Mafia would search him out. In prison it would be kill or be killed. So he talked, and the nation listened.

But while Valachi filled in one side of the picture, the repercussions of Al Agueci's murder were providing some details of the other side. For example, Assistant Chief of Detectives Michael Amico, who was in charge of the criminal intelligence division of the Buffalo police department, reported to the McClellan committee about the "Niagara Powerhouse" himself.

> Stefano Magaddino, alias "The Boss," "The Old Man," and "Don Stefano," lives at 5118 Dana Drive, in an exclusive area of Lewiston, N.Y., with his wife. His luxurious home is located on a plot of land adjacent to a similarly luxurious home occupied by his daughter and son-in-law, James LaDuca, who was in attendance at the Apalachin convention.
>
> Don Stefano (who is 77) is the irrefutable lord paramount and titular head of syndicated organized crime in the Buffalo-Niagara Falls and Toronto areas.
>
> Stefano is known to be the "don" and in absolute control of all illegal operations in the area as pertains to organized criminal activities. No crime by members of the organization is permitted without his permission and guidance.
>
> Don Stefano was arrested on August 16, 1921, as a fugitive from justice relative to a homicide at Avon, N.J., and turned over to the Avon, N.J., Police Department.
>
> Informed police authorities believe Stefano Magaddino was among visitors to the notorious Apalachin meeting, November 14, 1957. His clothes were found on the premises where the meeting was held.
>
> It has been reasonably theorized that a meeting with such magnitude of important notorious Apalachin guests would not proceed without the presence of Don Stefano Magaddino, who has extensive criminal interests and influence in syndicate decisions.
>
> Don Stefano, before the Apalachin disclosures, was known to wield a great deal of influence in Niagara Falls politics. In the late 1930's Magaddino was reported to be associated with John C. Montana in the Empire State Brewery in Olean, N.Y.
>
> It was during this time that Montana was regarded as a trusted

> lieutenant of Magaddino, and second in command. This close association with the Stefano Magaddino dynasty of criminal activity in the western New York area has been more closely cemented by intermarriage of the two families.
>
> Also closely associated with Magaddino is Herman Weinstein, who is alleged to have profited handsomely from his illegitimate transactions with the mob in the way of bootlegging, black market gasoline operations during World War II, and many other illegitimate transactions. Weinstein is now regarded as a successful motel operator, owning the plush Peace Bridge Motel, which is considered a meeting place for prominent syndicate members.
>
> I mention this association because our surveillance, I might add, takes us many, many times into this plush motel, where many of these syndicated individuals from in and outside of the Buffalo area tend to congregate.
>
> Since Apalachin, Stefano Magaddino has relinquished immediate control over legitimate businesses such as Magaddino Memorial Chapel, the Power City Distributing Co. of Niagara Falls and Camellia Linen Supply Co. of Buffalo, N.Y.
>
> Stefano Magaddino is ostensibly considered to be in retirement from legitimate business holdings, passing on his interests directly or indirectly to members of his immediate family.
>
> Magaddino's present chief lieutenant in charge of Buffalo syndicate operations is Fred "Lupo" Randaccio. Randaccio indisputably controls all gambling, labor racketeering, and other illegitimate activities for the old man.
>
> Associates of Stefano Magaddino include John C. Montana, Samuel Freedman, Herman Weinstein, Roy Carlisi, Fred Randaccio, Fred Magavero, James Zerilli (Detroit), Joseph Falcone (Utica), Anthony Perna, James LaDuca, Dominic D'Agostino, Samuel Rangatore, Dominic Mantele, and Benjamin Nicoletti, the last five from Niaraga Falls and Samuel Pieri, of Buffalo.
>
> I have given the names there of those associates.

He truly did. The men Lieutenant Amico named cannot forget Agueci, the lonely field, and the pitiful remnants of a man seared beyond recognition because he stood up for his rights—or for what passes for them within the peculiar government of the underworld. Suffice it to say that Magaddino's funeral parlor did not handle the funeral, though Amico pointed out to the Senate committee that "we see no illegitimacy at this time [in Magaddino's undertaking business] other than, of course, he enjoys a virtual monopoly of servicing those individuals that are deceased from the families of individuals from the criminal underworld."

Not content merely to name names, however, Lieutenant Amico also sketched the full extent of Mafia operations in the Buffalo area—a sketch substantiated by details collected from many sources. For instance, Lieutenant Amico explained to the senators the business perhaps best loved by the dons—supplying snowy linens to restaurants, barber shops, motels, and other places—using the Buffalo area as an example.

The boys attend to the smallest details of the linen business with consummate courtesy, and it is this occupation that enables the soldiers in the Mafia army to work their way up fom bedsheets to the more serious business of winding-sheets—where the money really is.

Camellia Linens typifies the Magaddino operational ploy. According to Lieutenant Amico:

> This is a type of business that catered to restaurants and barber shops, and what came to my attention, not in the form of an official complaint but undertones of perhaps extortion in this respect. Many times they would contact these barbers, perhaps some of the members of the gang would get a haircut and perhaps tip them a substantial amount, and then go in a few weeks later and indicate to them that they would like to leave their business there, their linen supply business.
>
> These individuals would indicate to them a tendency not to change because they certainly were happy with their linen supply at that particular time. Well, the mere presence of these individuals many times, dressed in the way they were, the demeanor that they showed, would tend to sort of discourage some of these individuals to resist them and to, in effect, acquiesce, and it is said it is better to get their linens than to fight them.
>
> Now, you might wonder what is so important, perhaps, with some linen supply. They might, at the outset, even come in and say, "We will supply your linens for maybe a penny or two per linen cheaper," but after the individual has once changed his services or supply, he is then stuck, and this outfit might, and it has been in cases in the past, perhaps not only increase the prices to where they were, but even add to it. This wouldn't be all.
>
> In many instances, if there were, for example, 50 pieces of linen that were counted by the barber-shop proprietor, and this individual would come in and say you had 100 pieces of linen this time, and he would say I only counted 50, and he would say we counted 100, and

because of his presence and because of what he represented, perhaps, the fellow would acquiesce and say, "Well, I guess I had a hundred." This was the means, at that time, whereby I feel they gained monies in an illegal way.

Amico, a staunch individual, held the senators spellbound as he traced, in a simple, sometimes ungrammatical but always sincere way, syndicate workings at the operational, money-making level:

The same will go for cigarette vending machines and jukeboxes. I had an experience in one instance where they had made a movement; [Fred "Lupo"] Randaccio and a fellow named Fred McGove really had gone into business in a cigarette-vending-machine operation. They had attempted to monopolize the entire predominantly [Italian] west side of Buffalo. In many instances they did this in a legitimate manner.

However there were instances where some were recalcitrant individuals who felt that certainly after some other supplier had been loyal to them they didn't want to change individuals in the middle of the stream. They again came in there in their typical fashion and dressed up in this normal Hollywood style, that you might see in the movies or television, and with their persuasive tones or undertones would sell the idea that they should change their cigarette-vending services to their own. In one instance, one fellow had the gall, or at least the ability and the guts to resist them, and he came to me and asked me what he could do. I said, "Well, you are aware perhaps that this does take guts, and there are going to be threats," and he said, "That is fine." He was willing to go along, and it was only because of insistent intervention by our unit that they gave up trying to change him to take their machines.

They indicated very persuasively and strongly that he would not open his particular restaurant, that they would break the place down, and he might find his body out in the alley, but here was an individual with real guts, and with the real temerity, and it wasn't easy. I will explain here it wasn't easy even for me to get out and harass these individuals with the defense I had at my disposal, it wouldn't be enough for an arrest or conviction. The individual indicated to me, "What do I have to do, be found dead before the police can do something?"

In Buffalo, certainly, the Mafia is well entrenched, and Randaccio's personal touch, in an open and flagrant attempt to "muscle" a restaurant owner, indicates the close attention the leading Mafiosi pay to the details of their rackets. Even a November, 1968, arraignment of Magaddino on charges of international racketeering and conspiracy and a huge tax lien filed against him by the IRS would seem unlikely to shake up Buffalo's Mafia family much.

Randaccio is, according to the Buffalo police department, second-in-command of the Magaddino empire and apparently heir presumptive to the legitimate and illegitimate baronies set up by The Old Man. At the time of the investigation Randaccio's address was given as 562 Richmond Avenue, Buffalo, New York. And since he was born July 1, 1907, in Palermo, Sicily, he is one of the few members of the American Mafia who can claim Italian birth.

Randaccio was first arrested in this country in 1922 for juvenile delinquency. Two years later he was collared for gambling and bootlegging. In 1930 he received a ten-year sentence for felonious assault—reduced from robbery, first degree—when he held up a garage proprietor, but this merely hoisted his personal flag a little higher on the Mafia mainmast. In 1956 deportation proceedings were brought against him by the immigration authorities in the Justice Department, but the legal division of this dedicated branch of the government was horrified to learn that Randaccio had somehow gotten into the U.S. Army in 1945 and served six months—which automatically gave him citizenship. The proceedings were dropped.

Randaccio's interests are varied and somewhat in line with the syndicate *modus operandi* that dictates that money be put anywhere, as long as it becomes legitimate and goes to work somehow. Accordingly, Randaccio and others formed the Delaware Vending Company, which handles all kinds of "slots," the Frontier Lathers, Inc., the services of which are not specified in the Senate records, and the Tur-Ran Builders, operating out of Amherst, New York, a Buffalo suburb.

These legitimate companies, according to Amico, are paralleled by Randaccio's operation of Magaddino's criminal empire, backed by a corps of "muscle men," such as John Cammillieri, who handles labor and union racketeering, Pat Natarelli, Joseph Fino, and Daniel Sansanese, who take care of organization bookmaking interests, and Steven Cannarozzo, who handles the policy, or numbers, racket.

Lupo, who effects a Windsor knot in his conservative ties and a touch of gray at the temples, has no formal education, but the slick gangster with the Palermo label is regarded as a great organizer with ample ability to hold the organization together in times of stress.

Randaccio and his buddies commute frequently between the United States and Canada (Toronto and Hamilton), where the Mafia is firmly established and whence citizen-Mafiosi are branching out throughout what is left of the British empire—especially its remnants in the Caribbean.

Randaccio, who is a young man compared to the oldsters in the syndicate, is waiting for his inheritance to drop into his arms, and it is a safe bet that he will succeed Magaddino, keeper of the keys to the gang treasury in his particular territory—unless a federal court conviction, obtained in Buffalo in February, 1968, for conspiracy to commit armed robbery, alters his plans.

Until recently Randaccio's chief rival for Magaddino's mantle was John Charles Montana, a curious individual who was undercover heir apparent to Magaddino until the Apalachin raid. Born on June 30, 1893, in Montedore, Italy, Montana, who died in 1967, lived to regret that he ever went to that notable gathering in upper New York State. Gray-haired and distinguished-looking, with hard lines that ran down his face to the corners of his mouth, Montana was one of the rarities of the Mafia organization: he had no criminal record until, as a result of his Apalachin appearance, he was accused and convicted of conspiracy to obstruct justice in federal court, and even that conviction was later reversed on appeal.

Testimony at the Senate hearings revealed that Montana lived with his wife at 340 Starin Avenue, Buffalo. His rags-to-riches climb began while he was a messenger boy in a candy shop during his grade-school days. Somehow he made enough money to purchase a taxicab, and somehow he got to know the men who run the Mafia. A cloak of mystery surrounded Montana, and even Amico was forced to admit that until the Apalachin raid, no one, not even the police, suspected that Montana was working with the upper echelon of the New England syndicate. Indeed, his arrest confounded business associates and politicians who had counted him as a friend.

At the time of the Apalachin raid, Amico testified, Montana controlled the largest taxi company in western New York State, formed through a merger of the Yellow Cab Company and the Van Dyke Taxi and Transfer Company. His cabs had a monopoly at preferred taxi locations at Buffalo Airport, the then New York Central railroad station, and the better hotels, including the Statler-Hilton. After November, 1957, Montana's former patrons permitted other cab companies and a host of independents to use the taxi stands, but his cabs continued to do much of the business in Buffalo.

John Montana was elected councilman in Buffalo in 1928 and 1930 and was appointed to other important city posts as the years went by. He was named "Man of the Year" by the local chapter of the National Junior Chamber of Commerce in 1956, in recognition of his services to his home town, where he also was a member of the zoning board and constantly expounded the value of good government. The Elks, the Buffalo Athletic Club, and the Erie Downs golf course, to mention but a few organizations, owe him a debt of gratitude.

Nevertheless, Amico tied Montana in with the notorious Joseph (The Wolf) DiCarlo, a Sicilian-born former Buffalo public enemy No. 1 whose police record includes arrests for assault, coercion, intimidating witnesses, and violation of federal narcotics laws, who is supposedly engaged in illegal gambling in the greater Miami area, and has been reported to frequent the Esquire Smoke Shop, the Carib Hotel, the Tahiti Bar, and the Grand Barber Shop—all in Miami Beach.

In evaluating Montana's contribution to the body politic, Amico was terse and to the point. Then, prodded by McClellan committee member Jacob Javits (R., N.Y.), Amico added:

> I believe I would compare this, that I would say is our great American way of life, that it is such a great nation that anyone, regardless of who he may be, is certainly given an opportunity to succeed and become successful in business. Now it is an apathetic, lethargic public that is enhancing Mr. Montana's position, and maybe a public hearing of this type might do much toward awakening the public to show that this type of organized crime does exist and some of these people perhaps, it is best not to patronize them and not to go along and not encourage this particular setup. So it is the public themselves that either contribute or detract from such an endeavor.

Incidentally, when Javits took time to deny Amico's charge that an area of crime overlordship was run by "Jewish ties," he must have been unaware that police throughout the country long ago divided the syndicate into Italian and Jewish elements, simply because these ethnic groups controlled the rackets—though the Jewish mobsters have been mostly eliminated over the years. Louis Buchalter, a Manhattan racketeer, his buddy, Bugsy Siegel, the Las Vegas gambling pioneer, Phil (Pittsburgh Phil) Straus, and the notorious Murder, Inc., mobster, Abe Reles, who ostensibly dove to his death from the Half Moon Hotel in Coney Island, were among the so-called Jewish element in the mob for many years. But they were only following in the footsteps of the murdered Arnold Rothstein, Frank Costello's mentor. There were also plenty of Irish mobsters, such as "Peg-Leg" Lonergan, killed by Al Capone in Brooklyn before Capone went to Chicago, and Owney (Owney the Killer) Madden, who died a natural death recently in Hot Springs, Arkansas. Italian, Jewish, Irish, it is doubtful that any one of these gangsters really believed in any god but one: profit.

Lieutenant Amico sounded a clarion call for ordinary people whose accepted norms have to do with the everyday things that affect them: their children, their pots and pans and household duties, their jobs. Such people have precious little time to be concerned about crime and the people who operate the business. It is difficult to rouse them. But as Nicholas Murray Butler once said, the little people are good for a grand splurge of morality if the message can be gotten across to them, even though they return to their own affairs soon enough. Thus, we are not entirely without hope. But it is only a small hope, for even respite from the Mafia is difficult to obtain, as the story of James Delmont shows.

A former bookkeeper for one of the Montana interests, the Madison Cab Company, Delmont witnessed an attempt on the life of another employee, Steven (Flat Top) Cannarozzo. Delmont was present when a volley of shots was fired through a window of the cab company office in Buffalo in June, 1959. Cannarozzo, who has a long record of crimes dating from 1939 to 1959, survived, despite multiple bullet wounds, but his assistant, Delmont, did not wait around to read the medical reports. He had been a witness to the crime—and he fled to California, where he became another "Brother Orchid" inspired by fear to spend the last days of his life along the California mission trail.

Word spread that Delmont was marked for death because he

could identify the assailants of Cannarozzo and that the Mafia was out to do the job. In a desperate attempt to square himself, Delmont confessed his past to a brother at one of the monasteries, a priest of Italian origin who in turn contacted the Los Angeles branch of the underworld brotherhood in order to intercede for the worried Delmont.

The naïve holy man, after making what he thought was a convincing argument for the life of his brother, gave Delmont a bus ticket to Los Angeles and a name and address where he said the worried witness would find that his problems were being resolved. Delmont made the trip as instructed and was seemingly cheered by the results, for he then telephoned his wife and told her that all was well and that he would be home in two weeks. But amnesty was not forthcoming despite the façade of forgiveness. At the end of those two weeks—in April, 1960—Delmont's body was found in a field on the outskirts of San Bernardino. He had been shot and tossed from a car a scant sixty miles from Los Angeles and some three thousand miles from his unyielding adversaries in Buffalo.

And Steven Cannarozzo? He stayed mute after the attempt on his life, refusing to tell Buffalo police investigators who shot him, and, at the last report, was a Randaccio "muscle man" in the numbers racket.

Perhaps James Delmont loved his fellow men, if a little late. Seeking surcease, he went from an evil brotherhood, the Mafia, to a blessed brotherhood, but he found that there is really no middle ground between good and evil, and for a resting place he had to pay with his life. In Buffalo, as elsewhere in this country, the Mafia is fully entrenched. It takes real courage either to break out of its tangled web or to resist its encroachments. The Mafia cannot deny anyone the choice, but it often exacts a high price for the privilege of exercising that choice.

4

BOSTON:

Home of the Bean and the Rod

And this is good old Boston,
    Plymouth and Providence, too;
Where the hoodlums talk to no one,
    And even God eschew.

—with apologies to John Collins Bossidy

August, 1961: a hot day on the beach at Salisbury on the fringe of greater Boston. Edward J. (Punchy) McLaughlin and his brothers, Bernie and George, were lolling on the soft sand. A voluptuous female strolled by. Punchy got up, walked over to the young lady, grabbed her head, and, apparently in the throes of an oddly directed sexual impulse, tried to bite off her ear.

The girl in question was a special pal of hoodlum James J. (Buddy) McLean, who happened to be close by on the day in question. Not close enough to stop the affront, McLean ran over to McLaughlin and gave him what newspapermen called the "beating of his life."

Thus began one of the strangest gang wars in history. The police are appalled and bemused by it, but in seven years over forty men—including the two gang leaders, McLaughlin and McLean, who were murdered within ten days of each other, Bernie McLaughlin and seven associates, and at least two other members of the McLean faction—have died because of it.

Responsible papers in Boston talk curiously and cautiously about the killings in their town. A headline on the bottom of the first page of the *Boston Sunday Globe*, November 21, 1965, read: "27 Dead—but no one knows why, or how to stop it." Since then, the number of dead has risen; the long arm of the underworld wields a frightening and devastating weapon that may have as its target anyone from a two-bit hood who has stepped out of line to a top law-enforcement official who is dogging the trail of the syndicate.

In its news story, which was cozily wrapped around a blurb about shopping hours, the *Globe* asks: "Why are they killing each other? 'You'll have to give me two or three guesses,' answers a high police official. 'There isn't one basic pattern.' "

The fact that there is "no basic pattern" could well explain the police official's reluctance to talk, but theories are rife. A *Globe* staff writer, for example, expounded two theoretic reasons for the killings thus: "the instinctive reaction of brother to help brother and of gang member to avenge for gang member. The lust for money from two of history's most fantastic robberies, ordinary crimes and the entrapment of loan sharking."

And he added: "There was not a single underlying motive for the deadly series of murders which have generated increasing public demands for not only a solution but firm action by law enforcement officials to end the blood bath."

But to get back to the initial incident, there are divergent opinions as to just who did insult the young lady during the beach picnic. The *Globe* still claims it was Punchy McLaughlin, but in its February 24, 1967, issue, *Life* states that it was brother George who did the biting. It matters little, except that the incident supposedly triggered the greatest destruction of hoodlums over so short a period of time in gangland history. Murder and jail have wiped out the three McLaughlins (George is now on death row in Walpole State Prison); Buddy McLean was gunned down shortly after the beach incident (following an unsuccessful attempt to dynamite his car); and both gangs have been largely decimated in the forty-some killings thus far.

Police and crime reporters have mulled over the possibility that unrecovered funds totaling around $3 million from three robberies—the famous Brink's robbery in 1950, the 1962 Plymouth, Massachusetts, mail holdup, and the 1966 Brink's holdup at Bedford, Massachusetts—have somehow got stuck in the New England gangland financial web. The theory is that this money has been available, in one fashion or another, over the years and that the warfare among the Boston gangs may well concern its final resting place. The tough boys, the scavengers of the underworld, will always try to move in to "arrange" the division of any holdup money, like so many hyenas chivvying a lion seeking to protect its kill.

Theory after theory has been studied, but seemingly little attention has been given to the possibility that these killings might have some connection with the Mafia. Almost all of the men eliminated as the result of what was, and still is, called the McLaughlin-McLean feud were non-Italians. But it is significant that the McLaughlins and McLeans were enforcers for loan sharks. Bernie McLaughlin was said to favor a sash weight wrapped in newspaper for breaking the arms of delinquent debtors; Buddy McLean supposedly did roadwork to keep in shape for the "muscle" needed in his business. And loan sharking *requires* the broad base of syndicate financing.

When all the facts are examined, there seems little doubt that the man behind the scenes, and the murders, is Mafioso Raymond Loreda Patriarca, sixty-one-year-old hatchet-faced don of the moderate-sized Cosa Nostra family that embraces a good share of Massachusetts, Rhode Island, Connecticut, and Maine. Patriarca's position of power was brought to public attention at the Senate committee hearings by Colonel Walter E. Stone, superintendent of the Rhode Island state police, who labeled him:

> the controlling force behind organized crime in Rhode Island and New England . . . Behind the front of his business enterprises, Patriarca, through his lieutenants, is still involved in one of his old specialties, that of strong-arming. Now it's being done for unions in the New England area instead of for his fellow gangsters during prohibition . . . he has the controlling interest in lotteries, bookmaking, dice games, and the provision of wire service in this area. Moreover, he settles any disputes within the organization working this section, sometimes using force or intimidation to accomplish his designs.

According to Stone, Patriarca was born on March 17, 1908, in Worcester, Massachusetts. Sometimes using his alias "John D'Nabile," Patriarca, whose headquarters now are in Providence, Rhode Island, began his criminal career as a bodyguard for bootleggers in the early twenties and gained a wide reputation as an effective strong-arm man. His police record began while he was still a teenager and includes arrests for hijacking, jail escape, violations of gambling laws, violations of the Mann Act, which prohibits transporting women across state lines for immoral purposes—for which he went to jail—safe cracking, armed robbery, adultery, motor vehicle code offenses, the carrying of firearms, conspiracy, assault, auto theft, and accessory before the fact of murder (two counts). Patriarca, indeed, is no stranger to the charge of murder. He was indicted for this crime by a Rhode Island grand jury for his part in the 1930 Easter Saturday attempt to free two vicious criminals from a prison that resulted in the death of four people.

Until he was thirty Patriarca seems to have been a loser, despite the help of the Mafiosi whose orders he had been following, for he had five convictions and had spent a total of ten years in jail. But his loyalty and persistence, not to mention his excessive nerve, paid off, and today these characteristics are perhaps matched by his influence among top politicians in his area. He began traveling with these high-ranking allies in 1938, possibly through the good offices of his boss, Phil Buccola, who headed the New England Mafia family until he was deported to Italy in the forties.

Buccola, attracted by Patriarca's obvious promise, as indicated by his being arrested at the age of eighteen and breaking out of jail after being convicted of hijacking, took Patriarca under his wing. The young button man soon became a *capo*, a cut much above the soldiers with whom he had been trooping. In 1938 he was convicted of burglarizing a Brookline, Massachusetts, jewelry store and sentenced to five years in prison. This sentence was to run concurrently with two others, the three combined sentences covering convictions for breaking and entering, armed robbery, and arson. But this was no real setback for Patriarca. After only eighty-four days behind bars, he received a full pardon from the Massachusetts governor, who acted on the advice of Executive Councilor Daniel H. Coakley.

The reasons for Coakley's action were hinted at some twenty years later when a Massachusetts investigating commission found that he was guilty of, among other things, "deceit and fraud" in pressing the petition to free Patriarca. Finally, in 1959, Coakley was impeached and became the first member of the governor's executive council to be removed from office since 1821.

One of the distinguishing features of Don Raymond's career is the lack of publicity he has been given. Somehow he and his organization have, until recently, managed to keep away from the eye of the press—although the appearance at the Apalachin meeting of one of his Boston lieutenants, Frank Cucchiara, a naturalized American born in Salemi, Sicily, embarrassed the whole New England mob to such a degree that Cucchiara, then co-owner of the Purity Cheese Company in Boston and also known as Frank (The Spoon) Caruso, was relegated to a position of relative unimportance in the Patriarca setup.

The theory that the McLaughlin-McLean chain of murders should be tied to the Mafia is further strengthened by the fact that the top man and financier in the New England juice rackets—for which the non-Mafia Irish feuders were strong-arm men—is Gennaro (Jerry) Angiulo, second-in-command to Patriarca and one of six brothers who, according to Senate testimony, are all involved in gaming and loan-shark operations.

It is not difficult to believe—and Colonel Stone did believe—that Angiulo, who operates through Mafioso Henry Tamello—both men being insulated by Mafia lieutenant Larry Baioni, who controls some two hundred button men—could have given the word to do away with the troublesome non-Italian McLaughlins and McLeans. The juice racket purportedly provides a million dollars a week to the Patriarca combine and is therefore most sensitive to any sort of interference—from police, journalists, or hot-headed younger gangsters. No well-established Mafioso could stomach the furor caused by the Irish gang leaders.

Indeed, the Mafia move to wipe out the non-Italian opposition in New England may have begun as far back as 1951, with the murder of Carlton O'Brien, an ex-convict and strong-arm man who not only opened several bookie joints in Patriarca territory but also set up a wire service in an adjoining state to bootleg racing information into his own parlors and to other bookmakers. The up-and-coming Patriarca, who owned the Mafia-licensed wire service, moved in fast, and O'Brien was slain early one morning outside his home in a Providence suburb.

In 1956 Patriarca made his next move, into the cigarette-vending-machine business. He followed this up with jukeboxes, cleaning-and-dyeing stores, linen services, auto agencies, drugstores, and garbage-collecting firms. He now controls numerous nightclubs and restaurants, ranging from greasy spoons in the Revere area and the equally seamy Federal Hill district in Providence to some of the top gourmet eating places in New England. His mob owns cemeteries, dude ranches, a New Hampshire ski resort, and a country club north of Boston.

Also, according to Bill Davidson, writing in the *Saturday Evening Post* of November 18, 1967, the Patriarca family had a well-placed Boston drugstore making L.S.D.—"one of the newer Mafia industries"—and distributing the stuff to the many ready customers abounding in three nearby college campuses.

Such enterprises have over the years provided financing for Patriarca's Mafia influence elsewhere, including at one time the Dunes Hotel in Las Vegas—an influence maintained by a front man named Joe Sullivan. Joe did the best he could. He knew the restaurant business and really tried, but Vegas newspapermen who knew Sullivan's backer gave him no peace. One pastime they enjoyed was calling the Dunes switchboard from the house phones in the lobby and having the operators page Raymond Patriarca. Then they would watch while Joe Sullivan, who was usually seated comfortably savoring a drink in the lounge just across the lobby, quietly went into a frenzy. He didn't know whether the big man was really in the hotel or not and would run about frantically trying to find out.

Patriarca, and Sullivan, of course, were not the only targets of newsmen's horseplay in Las Vegas. Pete Licavoli of the Detroit mob, which had a signal interest in the Desert Inn before Howard Hughes took it over, also had his problems with trick paging. Even J. Edgar Hoover's name got some of the play, but that invariably produced a frozen silence that seemed to put the chill on everybody.

In New England there is evidence, on the record, that Patriarca has always played both ends against the middle. For example, Colonel Stone told the McClellan committee that Patriarca was without honor "even among his fellow thieves," having at one time set up the hijacking of the very shipments of alcohol he had been hired to guard. And Stone pointed out that the constancy of the lawlessness of the men who operate within the framework of the syndicate was especially exemplified by Patriarca.

> He is a shrewd, scheming individual as well versed in the ways of crime today as he was in yesteryear. He is as ruthless in the sixties as he was in the thirties.

> Another one of the rackets that Patriarca worked was the so-called past posting. This is the placing of a wager on a horserace that has been run and a winner has been determined. These risky but profitable activities were carried on by the goons of Patriarca throughout the East.

Working for Patriarca was John (Jackie) Nazarian, one of the "animals" used by the don several years ago to instill fear in people he wanted to intimidate. Nazarian once killed another triggerman for Patriarca, George (Tiger) Balletto. There were twenty-two witnesses to the murder at the Bella Napoli Cafe in Providence. One man, an ex-boxer by the name of Eddie Hannan, thought he might step up and testify, but he was promptly strangled by Nazarian and left in a local dump. The baling wire Nazarian wound around Hannan's neck added emphasis to the threat to any other potential witnesses.

In this context, the confidence offered to Senator McClellan's committee by Colonel Stone that Patriarca lived in fear, not knowing whether he would also be a victim of Nazarian, was perhaps understandable. If he was, indeed, afraid of the "animal," Patriarca must have been relieved of a great weight in 1962, when Nazarian was murdered while walking the streets of Federal Hill, a short distance from Patriarca's residence.

Nazarian's murder not only freed Patriarca from fear, however, it also demonstrated the attitude of the public to hood killings. Two indictments in the murder were returned, but nothing happened. The public, it seems, feels that mobsters get what they deserve when they are killed, that "due process" is a privilege hoods don't deserve. But by taking the attitude that the killers of killers are not to be bothered with unduly, the public is allowing to go free the very people who not infrequently kill innocent people who stand in their way—a dangerous practice indeed.

The Nazarian type of Mafia terror is exemplified by the words of a loan shark to whom a bankrupt Boston businessman offered some other kind of collateral than money to repay, partially at least, a $2,000 loan that had given rise to an indebtedness of $3,900 in one year. Replied the loan shark as he slammed a .45-caliber pistol on a table in the retail store owned by his victim: "Your body is our collateral!"

On the subject of this kind of collateral, Charles Rogovin, the Massachusetts attorney general's expert on organized crime, has been quoted as saying:

> All other Mafia families have a tradition which they call "stopping the clock." That is, when you're bled dry, they stop the clock on the interest and just let you give back the principal. They stop short of killing, on the theory that a dead man can't pay. But not here. They're totally ruthless about loan-shark debts. Two thirds of the murders and maimings in New England involve people who have surrendered the collateral of their bodies to the loan sharks.

The Patriarca family, then, are even more ruthless—if that is possible—than the ordinary Mafiosi. And yet lacking in the record on Patriarca are many of the sordid little details of his "business." However, we do know that having worked his way to the top of the heap as don of the New England Mafia family, Patriarca not only commands the boys who take care of syndicate crime in his territory but also passes judgment on the "lesser" crimes—bank robberies, kidnappings, jewel thefts, hijackings, arson, and the like—committed by the younger punks who will perhaps join the big-time someday, if they survive. And we also know that he has any number of non-Mafia allies, representing at least a dozen different nationalities, who operate as executive-class silent partners with some of his own boys in various enterprises involving bookmaking, loan sharking, and illegal wire-service operations.

Even when this kind of information is made available to the public—as is finally happening, little by little—it is difficult to determine whether there is any real fight left in the citizenry against such criminals as Raymond Patriarca; whether the slow and easy way of life, replete with the pleasures that go along with this concept of existence—pleasures such as those provided by men of Patriarca's ilk in the gaming palaces of Las Vegas, the Bahamas, and other such meccas—has stultified all resistance. We can only hope that perhaps the cupidity and ego of the Mafia chieftains themselves may somehow lead to the downfall of the syndicate and to the beginning of the end of the secret society.

An example of just such a slip is found in the story of Al Agueci, who got into trouble with the law but was not given the help he had been promised by Don Stefano Magaddino. His subsequent pursuit of vengeance against Magaddino was the first link in a chain of circumstances which led to his death, to his brother's vendetta, and finally to the Valachi testimony exposing the modern Mafia to the world.

In New England Agueci has something of a counterpart in hoodlum Joe Barboza, a young man of Portuguese descent who came under Patriarca's influence in 1959 after he had served a series of jail terms for various offenses.

Barboza, who had met Mafia members at the state prison in Walpole, Massachusetts, was on a Mafia assignment on October 6, 1966, when he and three friends were stopped by traffic police in the heart of Boston. In their car were found a fully loaded Army M-1 rifle and a .45-caliber pistol. The four were arrested for illegal possession of firearms, and Barboza was held in the unusually high bail of $100,000, probably because at the time of his arrest he was already out on bail on a stabbing charge.

After Barboza had waited in vain for the Patriarca group to bail him out once again, two of his friends, Thomas DePrisco and Arthur Bratsos, decided to raise bail for him on their own. DePrisco and Bratsos collected $60,000 and then sought further funds from an important Mafiosi named Ralph (Ralphie Chiong) Lamattina, who owned a café in the north end of Boston. Chiong asked the pair to wait until the café closed and then invited them into a back room. Next day both men were found shot to death in a black Cadillac in south Boston.

Tipped off by an informant, the police arrived at Chiong's café and found Ralphie mopping up bloodstains in the back room and covering up bullet holes in the wall with a mirror. They therefore arrested him and put him on trial for murder. A few weeks later Patriarca and his Rhode Island executive officer, Henry Tamello, decided that in order to avoid publicity Chiong should plead guilty to being an accessory to the murder. He was told he would get only two years in prison and be rewarded with a profitable Mafia enterprise when he emerged, but he apparently got the wrong judge. Instead of a light two-year term, Ralph Lamattina received two concurrent maximum sentences: eight to fourteen years.

The heavy sentences gave newspapers an opportunity to play up the story—which they did. Joe Barboza, who was by then serving a four-to-five-year sentence on the gun charge and faced life imprisonment as a habitual criminal, read about the case and began to realize its significance: that Patriarca not only had abandoned him and killed two of his good friends but also was so determined to keep Barboza in jail that he had lost the trusted services of Mafioso Lamattina in the process.

Barboza was visited in jail by FBI agents who confirmed the newspaper stories and gave him additional evidence about his betrayal. They added insult to injury by stating that the Mafia had tipped off the police to pick him up on the gun charge. They played a tape made from a "bug" planted in Patriarca's office, and Barboza heard the Mafia chief say: "Barboza's a —— bum. He's expendable."

It was then that Barboza decided to tell everything he knew, and another thread of truth was stitched into the net with which lawmen hope to catch, and put out of action, the Mafia leaders.

Barboza apparently never took the oath of silence and fealty to the secret society, as Valachi had done, but it probably would not have made any difference once his fear and anger made him decide to talk.

With the information given to authorities by its newest canary, the government, represented by U.S. Attorney Paul Markham, went to the federal grand jury in Boston on June 20, 1967, and obtained an indictment charging that Patriarca and Henry Tamello conspired with Barboza and another man to commit murder—a charge that arose from the shooting of William Marfeo, a relatively unknown forty-one-year-old gambler who had the nerve to run an unauthorized crap game in Providence.

Patriarca was charged with causing Barboza to travel interstate for Marfeo's "hit." Tamello was charged with an additional count alleging he made the interstate phone call that brought Barboza from Boston to Providence. Another hood, Ronald Cassesso, who is now serving a term for armed robbery, was also tried. The three men were convicted on March 8, 1968, and later sentenced to five years in prison and fined $10,000 each. Defense attorneys immediately filed appeals and continued Patriarca free in $25,000 bond, so any or all of them may be in the clear by the time this book sees print. But at least some progress is being made in getting through the insulation to a few of the bigger Mafiosi.

If the police are making progress, the New England junior Mafia are not. First, there appears to be little effort to supplant Patriarca, despite the rumor that Larry Baioni would like the job.

And, second, Patriarca's second-in-command, Jerry Angiulo, is in trouble with the law—once again as a result of Barboza's testimony —over the 1967 killing of an ex-boxer, Rocco DeSeglio, who planned to hold up a Mafia floating crap game in Boston.

Thus in New England it's three down for the top Mafia command, and no one knows for sure where it will stop. If Larry Baioni, whose real name is Ilario Anthony Zannino but who is carried on most police records as Larry Zannino, manages a take-over when Patriarca's throne is empty, he will bring with him the necessary prerequisites for a Mafia don. He was born in Boston on June 15, 1920, which makes him old enough to have learned the game but young enough to maintain power. In his many pickups by police over the years since 1938, for questioning on traffic, weapon carrying, gambling, assault and battery, mayhem, extortion, armed robbery, and murder charges, Baioni has variously described his occupation to police as that of a clerk, laborer, salesman, farmer, chauffeur, nightclub manager, and truck driver. In 1960 he was given two four-to-seven-year sentences for extortion, to be served concurrently in the state prison at Walpole. During the 1963 McClellan hearings on organized crime in Boston, Baioni, who was still serving time, was described as a "favorite of Raymond Patriarca." Small in stature—5 feet 7½ inches, 170 pounds—the black-haired, dark-complexioned Mafioso, who carries a small scar on the outer rim of his left eye, may yet become a big man among his confreres.

As a result of all these eruptions, it seems certain that the usually serene Patriarca faces an uncertain future because he disobeyed an unwritten Mafia law that requires reciprocal aid for all members in case of any need whatsoever. And in disobeying the law, he sold his New England organization down the river—just as Magaddino did in Buffalo over the Aguecis. The six brothers of William Marfeo are sure to want revenge and will no doubt wait for Patriarca to get to a quiet spot where the job can be done. In June, 1968, two of them supposedly tried to kill him on the day his indictment was announced.

There are many, however, who would not bet against Patriarca, protected as he is by the wall of insulation and insurance he has built over the years. One well-documented strip of tape made during three years of FBI eavesdropping in Patriarca's Providence office indicates that "in the bag" for the Mafia chief are, among others, a high-ranking court administrator, a top state official, a police chief, two licensing officials, and a few powerful state senators and representatives.

In fact, although he is running out of time and appeals, it is likely that Raymond Patriarca will spend many more pleasant hours, replete in white turtleneck sweater, sunning himself on the doorstep of his Nu-Brite Cleansers, on Atwells Avenue in the Federal Hill district of Providence, over which he has built the bug-proof apartment he calls home—pleasant hours, perhaps, but somewhat less carefree than in the past.

5

DETROIT:
Body by Mafia

On February 21, 1962, Frankie Gerlando, owner of a bar in Detroit, heard a noise. It was 2:00 A.M., chilly, damp. The sound came from outside the rear door of the bar. Gerlando tried to push the door open and found it blocked by something piled against it. He pushed harder and the object gave way. Frankie stepped outside and looked down. He saw a dead pig. The porker's legs were bound with rope, and later examination disclosed it had died by asphyxiation.

Frankie walked quietly back into the bar. A dozen patrons swiveled heads toward him. He nodded to the door, and one by one they filed out to take a look at the pig.

The message was obvious: "Squealers Die."

To the bar patrons the real squealer was a man named Ubal (Roy) Calabresse, their former drinking buddy. Calabresse was in the rackets. He had been arrested a couple of times, found guilty at least once, and flashed more money than the top Mafiosi thought proper for a person at the level of operation assigned to him.

Calabresse's mother told police that he had disappeared a week earlier, after receiving a phone call, telling her he had "an appointment with one of Capone's boys."

Several days later, on February 19, Calabresse was found by police in St. Clair Shores, a suburb of Detroit beyond Grosse Point. He had been garroted, and the arms of a coat were still wrapped around his neck. Calabresse died about two hours after he had eaten dinner at his mother's home on St. Valentine's Day, according to testimony by Detroit Police Commissioner George Edwards before the McClellan committee.

The fate that stalked the two men was set in motion years before, partly because of a vast dissatisfaction felt by three youths who sat in a field outside Palermo, Sicily, one day in 1915.

All three belonged to a class known as "The Green Ones," meaning people who live on Sicily's broad latifondi where herding and farming are the main occupations. They were junior members of the Mafia, of the *Stoppaglieri* faction, and as they sat there, they made up their minds to try to get to St. Louis, in America.

The boys were Vito Giannola, his brother John, and a friend, Alphonse Palizzola. They obtained money from a Palermo banker at stiletto-point, and three days later were in the steerage of a ship bound for the New World. Vito became leader and principal don in St. Louis, where he gathered a few Sicilians together into a gang called by the police of that city The Green Ones.

Alphonse was the enforcer who brought "Little Italy" in St. Louis under the thumb of the gang and collected a tax on every item of food sold to the Italians. Bananas, for instance, were taxed five cents a bunch and bread two cents a loaf. The first murders began in 1923, when Vito went into the wholesale-meat business and signed up Italian butchers. Alphonse was the front man in this deal. When one butcher was recalcitrant, complaining that the gang price for meat was much higher than what he was paying his regular wholesaler, Alphonse pointed out quite truthfully that the extra money was insurance for continued good health. The butcher remained adamant and shouted at the Mafioso: "No orders for you!"

Alphonse stalked out. At 3:00 A.M., two days later, an auto pulled up beside a man walking slowly down the street. There was no moon on that cool September night, and the butcher who had refused to buy meat from the Mafia never saw the men who ran toward him. St. Louis police department records show that on the morning of September 16, 1923, the body of Angelo Pastori, of 1914 Hereford Avenue, was found beneath the Kingshighway Viaduct. He had been stabbed once in the heart and twice in the head and beaten with a couple of baseball bats, which were found nearby. Pastori left a widow and two children.

The most vicious killing performed by The Green Ones was that of two men who were buried in the same grave near one of the stills owned by the gang at Horseshoe Lake.

Deputy Constable Homer Hockett and another officer and friend, John Balke, who had been deputized by the older man, were stationed in nearby Edwardsville when the pair decided to go out and shake down the gang on the night of January 29, 1926. Hockett and Balke walked straight into an ambush. Knocked unconscious as they entered the farmhouse where the still was located, they were bound with baling wire and dragged outside at dawn. Then the frightened men were forced to watch while members of the gang dug a large pit in the ground.

Balke panicked. "For God's sake," he screamed, "what are you going to do?"

"That's all right," came the answer. "We're not going to hurt you, we're just going to kill you."

Then a man came over to the trussed officers and smiled. "We were only fooling, fellows," he said. "Stand up. It's all right."

He cut their wire bonds, and they stood up, rubbing their arms and legs to restore circulation. Then both men started to walk away. As they went by the hole in the ground, two men in the gang drew their guns and began firing. Balke and Hockett fell to the ground, one of the gravediggers ran up and kicked both of them into the pit, and four shovels went to work to level the ground. If the earth heaved a little as the two writhed in their death throes, no one noticed.

The killings put the seal to the power of The Green Ones; the Mafia took over St. Louis' rackets. Then they looked toward Detroit.

Early in 1927 a man named Pete Licavoli left St. Louis for Detroit. He had the proper credentials and did all the right things. First, he married the sister of a fairly well-established hoodlum, Joseph (Scarface Joe) Bommarito, and Joe married Pete's sister, Mamie. Over the years intermarriage between various gang factions in Detroit created a monolith of crime that the authorities have not been able to dent. Indeed, sons and daughters of the criminal combine in Detroit have been tossed out, like bait to sharks, for marriage within other crime factions throughout the country. The resulting unions have forged a steel net in which law-enforcement officials swim blindly, like so many anchovies.

The next thing Pete Licavoli did was to get into the business of rum-running, and while his brother, Yonnie Thomas Licavoli, and a brother-in-law, Frank Cammarata, were in prison, he took over a group known as "The River Gang." Licavoli then formed a union with a hoodlum named Joe (Misery) Moceri and ultimately gained control of the smuggling of Canada's liquor into Detroit's East Side.

Licavoli gave the business his personal touch. Armed with a pair of binoculars, he would get out in the "field"—either the blue waters of Lake Erie or those of the smaller Lake St. Clair to the north—and direct rum-running boats to snug harbors.

Pete's modern approach to gang organization soon dissipated the power of "The Purple Gang," which was comprised mostly of Jewish mobsters. Several of these went to Reno, Nevada, and bought into the Riverside Hotel on the Truckee River, which bisects the town. Meanwhile, an East Side gang combined with a West Side gang in Detroit. And the Italian dons who joined with Licavoli soon controlled gang activities in most of the Great Lakes section and branched out as far to the southwest as Las Vegas and Arizona.

The ruling council in the Detroit area, as the police intelligence chart submitted to the McClellan committee shows, consists of Pete Licavoli, Joseph Zerilli, John Priziola, the elder of the group, Angelo Meli, and William Tocco.

Of the ruling council, four were born in Italy: Priziola, Meli, Zerilli, and Tocco—the latter two in the same year and the same town, Terrasina. Licavoli's parents also were born in Terrasina, as were the parents of Joseph Bommarito, Pete's brother-in-law and heir apparent prior to his death.

All five Detroit leaders have been under fire at one time or another, but mostly they try to avoid getting directly involved—except in such high-level meetings as the Apalachin. Usually they send emissaries when minor Mafia business is to be disposed of.

Meli and Tocco learned this technique early in the history of Detroit's gang wars. A few years after Licavoli came to Detroit, the portion of the West Side mob not yet taken over by the Mafia was operated by a man named Chester LeMar. LeMar thought he would pull a fast one and called for a meeting with Meli and Tocco at a fish market at 2739 Vernor Highway, on the near East Side—a place that had previously served as a rendezvous for gang leaders.

Meli and his pal thought things smelled more than a little fishy and sent representatives to the meet. Thus it was Sam Parino and Gaspare Sibilia, known as a peacemaker in the troubled city where gangland murders even today average two a year, who were ambushed and shot to death by LeMar henchmen. The LeMar men were subsequently arrested, tried, and set free by a jury, but shortly thereafter LeMar was killed by his bodyguards, who had made a deal for their own lives with the Licavoli gang.

LeMar was the last really potent underworld figure to oppose the Licavolis. But there were others, not in the underworld, who fared just as badly, and the fate of Gerald Buckley, in particular, seemed totally inconsistent with the rules and regulations of the Mafia.

Buckley, a crusading radio news commentator who had threatened to reveal the identity of the overlords of crime in Detroit, was shot to death in the lobby of his hotel on July 23, 1930. His demise threw the city of Detroit into a turmoil, and four men were indicted for the crime: Joe Bommarito, Theodore Pizzino and Angelo Levecchi, two of Licavoli's pet assassins, and Licavoli himself. Pete didn't wait around. He fled Michigan and did not return until the other three had been tried and acquitted. The prosecution found that none of the witnesses it had counted on were willing to tell the court the same thing they had recounted in the district attorney's office.

The police did not give up, however. In July the home of hoodlum Joe (Cockeyed Joe) Catalanotte was raided. Police found fifty-four firearms, one of which was identified by ballistic tests as the murder weapon in the Buckley case. But the only punishment for Cockeyed Joe was his deportation to Canada, where he settled down in Windsor, Ontario, just across the Detroit River from his pals. There he still sits, apparently as deeply involved in Mafia affairs as ever. The Royal Canadian Mounted Police seem unconcerned, and though he has visited Detroit many times, the local police have yet to collar him.

Perhaps after all the Buckley murder is not so strange. Licavoli's predeliction for murder has always hewed close to the Mafia method and tradition, which is aimed at producing terror as well as results. A man is not just murdered—especially if he is a Mafia hoodlum who has squealed or double-crossed his associates—he is held up as an example. Buckley's murder, like Calabresse's years before, offered a clear warning, but in his case it was: "Stay Away."

The tactic of fear was, and is, very successful. For example, the old Black Handers, the Italians who terrorized their fellow countrymen in America around the turn of the century by chopping up the bodies of people who defied them, produced an atmosphere of terror around their operations that won many battles before they had begun.

Today the dead pig, the lime pit, and mutilation are most commonly used methods. But the mobsters are making continual improvements in their methods, especially when they are dealing with defectors from, or opponents in, the syndicate. Thus, a few years ago several dead Mafiosi were found in New York: shot but with their genitals cut off and jammed down their throats. There is speculation as to whether the mutilation occurred before or after death.

Licavoli's overlordship of gambling in Detroit requires that he inject himself personally into the everyday mob affairs, and he does it with much the same dedication he evinced when in Prohibition days he directed his rum-runners into Michigan harbors. But his job is not too hard, for the fate of the attackers of one of his principal lieutenants, Max Stern, serves as a constant reminder to those who would undermine Licavoli and his circle of dons that something more than a bullet awaits them.

Stern was shot one day after Licavoli had called a conference to clear up some arguments about the handling of gaming operations in Detroit. The malefactors seemed to have been hoodlums Peter Lucido and Sam Scroy. In any case, Licavoli had specifically asked that they be present at the conference, but they did not show up. Then, on June 12, 1948, both Scroy and Lucido disappeared.

Sam Scroy had a brother named Chris, and he got angry, grabbed a gun, and fired a couple of shots at Stern, only wounding him. The attack lead to Chris Scroy's arrest, and he was sent to prison, where he served seven years. Scroy was freed on July 14, 1955, and on April 10, 1959, he disappeared, only to reappear in the suburbs—in a lime pit. Scroy's body had been chopped into seven pieces. The lime had been spread too thinly—probably a habit developed during the mob's "alky" days—and Chris was identified from both fingerprints and a belt buckle. Licavoli, the natural suspect, was in federal prison for income-tax evasion when Scroy disappeared, so he easily avoided the investigative hook, and Scroy's death became another unsolved murder.

When Licavoli got out in the fall of 1960, he decided to celebrate, so he financed an elaborate wedding for one of his daughters. Actually, the wedding served as a sounding board for his ego. The underworld had heard, while Pete was in prison, that he was going to be retired and put out to pasture by the Mafia. The big party indicated not only that Pete had power but that he still had money—access to the honey pot the Mafia makes available to working dons.

Soon after, moreover, Licavoli had a chance to display his talents and, at the same time, to prove that the Mafia believes in the segregation of Negroes but does not object to deriving financial benefit from them.

The Gotham Hotel is a nine-story fleabag with 174 rooms located in the Negro section of Detroit. Just about every citizen in town knew that it was headquarters of the numbers racket. When a reform spree had swept Detroit several years before, the former mayor, prosecuting attorney, sheriff, superintendent of police, and 250 police officers had gone to jail for the acceptance of graft from the gamblers. It seemed that only Licavoli and his boys did not go to jail. They continued to flourish, at the Gotham and elsewhere.

Police raided the Gotham on November 9, 1962, but only eight people knew where the action was going to take place right up until 112 policemen were herded on buses. In fact, the policemen were given their raid instructions only *after* the bus doors had been closed, and Police Commissioner George Edwards used a federal search warrant.

Michigan state police and the intelligence unit of the IRS accompanied the raiders and found a numbers factory in full operation. The raiders seized 160,000 betting slips and $60,000 in cash. Forty-two Negroes were arrested, but as the raiders fanned out through the rooms of the hotel, they found not a single white person.

Commissioner Edwards discovered that Licavoli's outfit supplied all of the "working" apparatus in the hotel, which housed seven major numbers banks representing districts apportioned by the Mafiosi to servile Negro gang chiefs, and controlled the whole operation from the outside: the Mafia supplied the number, based on mutuals payoffs at races on various tracks or on a lottery; the Mafia supplied the numbers pads used by the sellers who took pennies, nickels, and dimes from Negro customers; and the Mafia supplied the dream books so essential to the Negro numbers bettor.

Licavoli was clearly implicated by the raid on the Gotham Hotel. For example, about ten thousand dream books, which are sold for two dollars each, were seized in a raid on his house prior to the Gotham incident, but because of a faulty search warrant—so the court ruled—no prosecution was possible. In addition, the operator of a dice game found going full blast at the Gotham, one Johnny White, had Licavoli's private phone number in his office.

Thirty-five hundred dollars were lying on the crap table when raiders broke into the Gotham, and of the eighteen pairs of monogrammed dice seized, fifteen were crooked. Even the decks of cards on nearby tables were crooked, and they demonstrated that Licavoli was not only a crook but also a student of at least one opthalmological phenomenon: the card decks looked like any others, with the name of a reputable manufacturer on each wrapper, and the police thought nothing of them until an officer in another room found a set of contact lenses with which it was possible to read the backs of the cards. The suckers never had a chance. "Who cares if we are cheating ourselves?" asked Johnny White, rather ambiguously.

Police also found that if there were too many hits on a particular number, the operators at the Gotham merely changed the number.

Commissioner Edwards estimated that the operation at the Gotham yielded about $21 million a year, with the overall illegal Mafia enterprises in the Detroit area probably netting the mob $150 million annually.

Despite what must be some profitable investments in Las Vegas, where gaming is legal in a free and open atmosphere—in swank casinos where the plushest carpets and the finest materials and woods are used in lavish interiors—Licavoli and his Mafia boys hang on to methods in Detroit that are reminiscent of old-time movies about the sin dens of the Volstead era.

For example, one entered the Lesod Club, which now operates outside the jurisdiction of the Detroit city police, through a locked door at the bottom of a flight of stairs leading up to a gambling room. There was also a locked door at the top of the stairs and a peephole. Buzzers and buzzer controls draped the doors. A guard at the bottom of the stairs screened all who wished to enter for a little action. The guard was most gracious to police who came to look around. On one such visit, Commissioner Edwards escorted a justice of the U.S. Supreme Court on an inspection tour. They were wafted airily through the first door. The guard stepped on a hidden button, and the sound of scurrying came from above. When the probers got upstairs, they found a mob of people gathered around tables on which hot checker games were being played. At nearby billiard tables dedicated players were stroking the ivory spheres across the green felt. One of the players was addressing a billiard ball with the butt end of the cue. The judge was rather taken aback by this newest method of playing until Commissioner Edwards explained that the man wasn't being stupid. He was merely showing contempt.

Afterward Edwards ordered his men to interview all who went into the club and to take photographs of the more sensitive types. Operators of the club sought relief by asking for an injunction to halt the police harassment. Edwards went into the same court, filed a petition for abatement of a nuisance, and then subpoenaed every person who had been interviewed. All took the Fifth Amendment, and the judge was convinced that something was amiss. He issued a search warrant, and on the same day the club closed. Licavoli took the operation a few miles away, outside city limits, and carried on business just as before.

Licavoli's success is due in part to his generosity to other hoodlum types who seek to settle down in Detroit. He remembers when he came to Detroit from The Green Ones' wars, found the right people, and married into the right family. He, in turn, extended the hand of friendship to Joseph Barbara, Jr., who had left New York State after the Apalachin raid on his father's home on November 14, 1957. Young Barbara went west and married the daughter of Detroiter Peter (Bozzi) Vitale. He then promptly became secretary, treasurer, and resident agent for an outfit called Tri-County Sanitation Company, subsidiary of a company with the same name in New York City.

In February, 1962, Joe Barbara's father-in-law, Peter Vitale, and Peter's brother, Paul, formed the Tri-County Leasing Company to provide motorized equipment for the sanitation firm. The mob had moved into a new field of endeavor, and the take-over was rapid.

The new corporation purchased the most modern rubbish-collecting equipment available, and Tri-County launched itself into the highly competitive refuse-hauling business. Its Detroit rivals were companies of long standing, but they couldn't match Barbara's outfit in the equipment area. Hydraulic units purchased for Barbara cost upward of $20,000 each, were highly mobile, and could haul twice as much as the average competitor's truck. Advance assurance of success apparently inspired the layout of the necessary money, for almost immediately Tri-County became big business and took over several of the most lucrative contracts held by competitors.

Strangely enough, Barbara's truckdrivers, who earned an average of $40 a week less than drivers hired by the competition, were never organized by the Teamsters Union in Detroit, home of Jimmy Hoffa.

Barbara's rabbit foot must have been worked overtime. Just a year after he went into business, twenty-nine employees of the Detroit public works department and five employees of rubbish-hauling companies were indicted for defrauding the city of legal dumping fees at city incinerators. It developed that the rubbish companies bribed the public works employees to cheat on the weight and volume of rubbish dumped.

Testimony at the McClellan hearings by Inspector Earl Miller of Detroit's criminal intelligence bureau showed that the companies involved—all defendants pleaded guilty on April 4, 1963—were Variety Trucking Company, Michigan Business Hauling, Les's Trucking, A. N. Reitzloff Corporation, and the Roulo Trucking Company.

Tri-County Sanitation employees were also observed by probers in the act of paying bribes, but none of the recipients were willing to testify against the Barbara outfit. Curiously, the city ordered the private rubbish haulers barred from city incinerators pending the outcome of the court case, and Tri-County, for whom a warrant could not be issued, thrived on its competitors' misfortune.

In addition, legitimate businesses in Detroit, fearful of adverse publicity, canceled contracts with the offending rubbish companies. Tri-County had further insurance in the fact that it was able to use the facilities of the municipal incinerator in a nearby suburb controlled by a Licavoli henchman.

From rubbish collecting to the sport of kings is a jump the Mafiosi take with almost aristocratic aplomb. The Hazel Park Racetrack, just outside Detroit, is, Police Chief Edwards testified, a state-licensed monopoly operation "subject to influence by the

Mafia." On August 26, 1963, the officers and directors were listed as Anthony J. Zerilli, the son of Joseph Zerilli, a member of the ruling council of Detroit dons; Jack W. Tocco, son of Black Bill Tocco, also on the ruling council; Anthony J. Tocco, another son of Black Bill; and Dominic P. (Fats) Corrado. Relatives of a strange Mafioso named Santo (Cockeyed Sam) Perrone also held stock.

The Michigan racing commission started to probe the track and came up with an exposé that, in spite of its rather surprising findings, brought about no action. There was quite a fuss at the beginning, especially when a deposition in the Wayne County circuit court established the fact that Anthony J. Zerilli, at age twenty-one, made an investment of $50,000 in the track. Zerilli explained that this was a loan from his father, and the probe failed to provoke continued interest. Perhaps nobody cares. The operation nets a million dollars a year, and the horse-racing devotees seem to like it.

Santo Perrone, one of the old so-called Moustache Petes, is a big man in Detroit Mafia circles and a very rich man, with assets that include auto washes, scrap-metal firms, and real estate developments. He is worth well over $1 million and can afford to insulate himself from the work of the rank-and-file Mafiosi, but he insists on keeping a hand in the "business" as though he were a mere button man in the organization.

District Inspector Vincent W. Piersanti testified at the McClellan hearings that the criminal intelligence bureau of the Detroit police department has developed evidence that Perrone was responsible for a series of five bombings in Detroit in 1960. Santo had put a new twist on an old Mafia technique. According to police, instead of asking for protection money first and, if refused, bombing afterward, Santo bombed victims *before* trying to shake them down.

A case in point, related by Piersanti, is that of the Victor Oil Company in Detroit, where a bomb went off near a rear door at 7:45 P.M. on October 17, 1961.

Perrone's "pilot fish," Richard Lambert, listed by police as a long-time associate of Perrone, "cased" the oil company for several days before the bombing. He reported back to Perrone, who then called a meeting with his two favorite bombardiers, Paul Tendiglia, who has a police record showing twelve arrests with two convictions for burglary dating back to 1932, and Peter Guastello, whose criminal record includes arrests for armed robbery, burglary, and Office of Price Administration violations.

All four men were observed meeting in St. Clair Shores at the Village Supermarket owned by Guastello. After the meeting on September 13, 1961, police observed Perrone, the millionaire mobster, going to a gun shop, where he purchased a one-pound can of gunpowder before returning to an auto-wash establishment he owned.

On September 30, police observed Perrone and Lambert again investigating the oil company at Warren and St. Jean Streets. The bombing followed on October 17. Early the next morning the owner of the oil company, Eugene Epstein, received a phone call. The caller did not identify himself, but he warned: "The next bomb will blow your place out of business and you into your graveyard."

That afternoon a private citizen, John Harness, reported to police that he had observed the perpetrators of the Victor Oil bombing. He said that during the evening of October 17, he had parked his car in the Chrysler employees' parking lot behind the oil company building as another vehicle had driven up. Two men got out of this car and walked to the Victor Oil Company property. A short time later they came back to their car.

"You don't have to move the car," Harness heard one of the men say, "because the fuse is long enough to give us plenty of time to get away." Their car, however, left the parking lot at a high rate of speed, and Harness, also, decided to leave. When he stopped for a traffic signal half a block away, he heard an explosion from the direction of the Victor Oil property.

Harness went to the police, he said, because he felt a sense of outrage. His life had been placed in jeopardy, and he wanted to testify. As a result of the descriptions supplied by him, police arrested Perrone, Lambert, Guastello, and Tendiglia. Specifically, Harness identified Lambert and Tendiglia as the men he saw in the parking lot. Nitrate tests showed a positive reaction on Perrone, Lambert, and Tendiglia. Guastello's test came up negative.

It was at this point that Harness learned whom he had identified. Police, to allay his fears of reprisal, took maximum security measures to ensure the safety of Harness and his wife and children. In October Harness testified at a preliminary examination held in Recorders Court in Detroit and repeated the facts he had previously given the police. Perrone, Lambert, and Tendiglia were bounded over for trial. The case against Guastello was dismissed.

After many delays the trial was set for September 27, 1962. Police were still guarding Harness' family, but the witness' personal guard was discontinued at his request. At about the same time startled police learned that Harness had visited the office of the defendants' attorney, Joseph Louisell, and signed an affidavit stating that he had been at the scene of the bombing in the company of a girl friend. He said he had observed the two men he had previously identified but now could not with assurance make a positive identification.

Police had not been aware there was an additional witness. The girl was questioned but would not describe or identify anyone. It developed that Harness had been ridiculed by friends and acquaintances, including his union steward, for getting involved with the powerful Perrone.

The trial started on schedule, but Harness recanted the testimony he had given at the pretrial examination. The defendants were acquitted, and Perrone went home, all grains of guilt apparently cleansed from his hands.

So goes Detroit, seat of Mafia power and criminal nepotism second to none in the history of the world, where the dons sift gold or gunpowder through their fingers, depending on whom they want to influence.

Detroit Police Inspector Earl Miller testified at the McClellan hearings as to the extensive infiltration of Mafia elements into legitimate businesses in and around the city, and he put into evidence a chart prepared by his department's criminal information bureau listing businesses that, currently or at one time, were "owned, infiltrated or influenced by" the Detroit Mafia. Placing the names of the firms in proper context with regard to the Mafiosi who either own them in their entirety or have a part of them posed a difficult problem for the law-enforcement group, but it is quite clear that the Detroit Mafia leaders exercise an amazingly diverse influence over the people of Detroit and of the United States, as a study of the list below makes clear (the addresses refer to Detroit unless otherwise indicated). The Detroit Mafia controls or has interest in hundreds of other business interests—in the United States, Mexico, and Canada. Indeed, there are many top businessmen in every big city in the country who owe their financial well-being to Licavoli and his associates. How so? Because the mobsters are interested in anything that can make a dollar.

Peter Licavoli

Lakeshore Underwriters, Inc., 16135 Harper
Office building, 16135 Harper
Lakeshore Insurance, Inc., 16135 Harper
Gold Cup Coffee Co., 6353 W. Vernor
Fototronics, Inc., 6230 John R.
Apache Nickel Surplus, 6230 John R.
Grace Ranch, Tucson, Arizona
Casa Catalina Motel, Tucson, Arizona
Riding stable, Tucson, Arizona
Tanque Verde, property, Tucson, Arizona
Tucson Printing Co., Tucson, Arizona
(*with Joseph Bommarito*)
Apache Realty, 15126 Mack
Michigan Mutual Distributing Co.
Hart Center, 1135 Beaufait
Chrysler Office Bldg., 6230 John R.

John Priziola

Harper Metro Park subdivision
Moravian Acres subdivision
Rental property, 16905 to 16915 Harper
Tocco Wholesale Food Co.
City Barber College
Balmoral Gardens
St. Clair Terrace Corp., 830 St. Clair
Motel and Bar, Gratiot and Masonic Blvd., Roseville, Michigan
Starlite Motel, 19021 Florida, Roseville, Michigan
(*with his sons-in-law, Frank and Joseph Matranga*)
Papa Joe's Restaurant, San Diego, California
Tropics Bar, San Diego, California
La Mesa Bowl Corp., San Diego, California
Bar of Music, San Diego, California
Cactus Bar, San Diego, California

Angelo Meli

Flint Cold Storage, 925 S. Dort
Pure Oil Co., gas station, 2970–98 E. Vernor
Income rental property, 13127 Harper; 19565 Mack
Meltone Music, 2971 Grand River
SC & CC Trucking Co., 1640 E. Six Mile Road
Ace Automatic Music Co., Saginaw, Michigan
Bel-Aire Lodge Motel, Saginaw, Michigan
480-acre farm, Marine City, Michigan

William Tocco and Joseph Zerilli

T & M Construction, 11896 E. Outer Drive
Grocery store, 710 Jos. Campau
Hazel Park Racing Association
Pfeiffer Macomb, distributors
Melrose Linen Service, 4630 Crane
Lakeshore Coach Lines
Detroit Italian Bakery
Jarson-Zerilli Co.
Income property, 4120 Woodward
South Branch Ranch, Roscommon, Michigan
Elias Big Boy, Ann Arbor, Michigan
(*with Peter Licavoli*)
Office building, 16135 Harper
Muller Foods, Jersey City, New Jersey
Deer Valley Citrus Association, Glendale, Arizona

Tucson, Arizona, has for years been a favored spa for a number of misplaced and displaced eastern mobsters, including Pete Licavoli and Joe Bonanno, a resident since 1943 when not on the move, and Anthony Tisci, son-in-law of Sam Giancana of Chicago. However, an increasing number of bombing and shooting incidents, beginning in 1968 and involving the homes or properties of these three and others, may tend to cool the welcome Tucson has given such syndicate investors in the past.

While Licavoli, an Italian-American and therefore not subject to deportation, has generally been considered to be the Detroit don for many years, the combined power of Joseph Zerilli and William Tocco would seem at present to hold the ruling votes in the council of five that rules Detroit, and together they probably wield the upper hand.

Intertwined with the top dons are the men who actually look after the various income-producing properties. They, in turn, are given fiefs of their own. Men such as Mike Polizzi and Anthony Giacalone and his brother Vito operate, according to McClellan committee testimony, on a lower level of command in such firms as Michigan Metal, Garomot Corporation, Roseland Club, and the Home Juice Company, which distributes soft drinks and exchanged hands, police claim, via an Italian craps game called Barbudi.

The junior Mafiosi's level of activity is not insignificant, however. For example, Tony and Vito Giacalone were arrested and arraigned in October, 1968, along with five others, on conspiracy charges stemming from a loan-shark racket allegedly resulting in at least two violent murders in the Detroit area. A six-month investigation by the state crime commission led to thirteen grand jury indictments, involving thirty-two defendants including known Mafiosi, and exposed, among other things, an illegal interstate horse-race betting ring.

The Sport of Kings is kept up, at the race-horse level—as against the business-office level—by Mike (The Enforcer) Rubino, one of the big men reported to operate the Double "D" Farm at 8351 McKinley Road, Algonac, Michigan.

Men such as Dominic and Anthony Corrado, pals of Black Bill Tocco and Joseph Zerilli, ran a variety of businesses in Detroit, among them, according to testimony, the Grecian Gardens, Kozani Bar, Selco Management Company, Gunn Dairies, vending-machine outfits, and income property including a one-hundred-acre farm in Price, Ontario.

The bakers of the Detroit Mafia seem to be confined to the Cavataio family. Nine members of this family headed by Julian, Peter, and, until his death, Dominic run a variety of business enterprises in addition to their many bakeries, including, according to testimony, four auto-wash companies, the Chesterfield Lounge at 4721 John R., Eastland Court apartments at 10410 Cadieux, Prince Macaroni at 3261 Belleview, and several dry-cleaning establishments.

Of course, it's no crime to be interested in anything that can make a dollar. In fact, it's a typically American pastime. But the devious methods used by the mob in the making and dispensing of the green stuff, as evidenced by the testimony at the McClellan hearings, should give pause to those who say that when a mobster goes into business and turns "honest," he ought to be left alone by the lawmen. The four speakers in the following testimony from the McClellan hearings are Jerome Adlerman, general counsel to the permanent subcommittee on investigations; Senator John L. McClellan, Chairman; and Commissioner Edwards and Inspector Miller of the Detroit police department:

MR. MILLER. . . . The logical belief that Hart Center, Inc. was in fact a three-way partnership between Licavoli, Scarface Joe Bommarito and Matthew "Mike" Rubino, was confirmed when the property was sold on March 26 of this year to a New York City investor.

Wayne County records indicate a sale price of $620,000; after indebtedness of about $125,000 was satisfied leaving proceeds of $495,000, the president of the corporation purchased a total of 36 cashiers' checks made payable to Licavoli, Bommarito, and Rubino.

MR. ADLERMAN. The last three you mentioned are on your chart?

MR. MILLER. Yes, sir.

MR. EDWARDS. Yes, and these are very high-up figures.

Mr. Chairman, it might be desirable at this point for me to point out that Peter Licavoli, who has run through this whole presentation, is at this point in debt to the people of the United States by official court decree to the tune of $411,000 for income tax not paid and penalties for failing to pay income tax.

THE CHAIRMAN. I wonder why these checks could not be impounded and money collected?

MR. EDWARDS. We have a unit of the Intelligence Division of the Department of Internal Revenue for whom we have a great respect. I am sure if they knew that those checks were going to be issued at a given time, they would have been there.

I am also reasonably sure they feel they have already levied liens which will protect the people in relation to the collection of that $411,000.

It is just interesting to note that here is a fellow who has been operating this way for all these years, he owes $411,000 on income taxes up to 1951, Senator. I don't have any idea what he owes from that point forward.

THE CHAIRMAN. You mean that was prior to 1951 that he owes that much?

MR. EDWARDS. Yes, sir, this indebtedness concerning income tax evasion prior to 1951.

> MR. MILLER. The cashiers' checks rendering each of the principals $165,000 for a total of $495,000.
>
> THE CHAIRMAN. I assume there is no lien placed on that building. Maybe the Revenue Department did not know it. They were able to conceal that ownership.
>
> MR. EDWARDS. The record ownership was indeed concealed until actually after the transaction was over.
>
> THE CHAIRMAN. As I point out, it is not always the fault of the officials.
>
> These folks are cunning. They are very resourceful in evading not only the law but in evading taxes.

It is perhaps time the powers that be among our various law-enforcement and crime-detection and prosecution agencies put their collective heads—and information—together and begin to heed the wisdom of the esteemed Judge Learned Hand, who said, in 1923:

> Our dangers do not lie in too little tenderness to the accused. Our procedure has always been haunted by the ghost of the innocent man convicted. It is an unreal dream. What we need to fear is the archaic formalism and the watery sentiment that obstructs, delays, and defeats the prosecution of crime.

6

FLORIDA:
Fun in the Sun

All Florida has been divided into two parts, insofar as the Mafia is concerned. One part is the west coast of Florida, the center of which, from the standpoint of mob influence, is Tampa. And the west coast was the first to be exploited. The men of the Mafia have been in that area for a long time, sharing the loot with, and the lawless endeavors of, the adjoining, widespread New Orleans Mafiosi. In fact, the two families have been so successful that together they have brought the whole southern tier of the United States under control.

The other part is the lush east coast, which came into its own in 1933 when a jockey-sized tough known as Little Augie Pisano, a henchman of New Jersey gambling boss Joe Adonis, went south to establish a beachhead for Adonis in the form of lush "carpet joints," establishments that were copied from some of the lavish gaming houses operated by Adonis in New Jersey.

A carpet joint is several cuts above a "sawdust joint," where that stratum of society known as the middle class is wont to gamble, and Adonis saw his future in the richer rooms even though the less pretentious places and their customers were the backbone of his gambling empire in the thirties. Today, most of the gaming salons, in Las Vegas and elsewhere, are carpet joints, but the clientele, a far richer middle class than existed in Adonis' salad days in New Jersey, is the same; it is still largely made up of "grinds," one-dollar bettors. When a carpet joint "busts out" a member of the jet set, credit, established by consulting the hieroglyphics imprinted on a card in the cashier's office, is usually forthcoming. The grinds, however, must wire home for money when they go broke in Vegas, as they did in Joey's New Jersey joints once upon a time.

To Adonis it seemed that if the wealthy jet set of the thirties flocked from New York City across the Hudson River to his pleasure palaces—the chief of which was Ben Marden's Riviera at the west end of the George Washington Bridge—it would also flock to new establishments in Florida. Events proved him right.

When Joe's advance man, Pisano, went to Florida, his first move was to make peace with the brotherhood in Tampa. There sat such members of the Mafiosi as Ignazio Antinori, later assassinated, James Lumia, a Mafia chief killed in 1950, and Santo Trafficante, Sr., who had arrived much earlier and laid the foundations of the narcotics trade. Once he had done this, Pisano was free to set up the eastern Florida operation, and the fact that it was to be primarily a carpet-joint operation showed that Adonis was out to take the rich. But Adonis and his henchmen were not so stupid as to try to freeze out the old guard, Trafficante and his friends. There was plenty for everyone.

Trafficante, who had been born in Sicily in 1886, arrived in Tampa in 1904 and became a naturalized citizen in 1925, at a time when the notorious non-Mafioso Charles M. Wall was acknowledged boss of most of the illegal gambling in Tampa and central Florida. Wall called himself "dean of the underworld," but he made the mistake of cutting Trafficante in on the proceeds and of opening the newcomer's eyes to gambling profits that made blackmail and extortion money from Italian businessmen seem small potatoes indeed.

In 1954, after experiencing three unsuccessful attempts on his life, Wall announced that he was retiring, without saying exactly what he was retiring from. But in April, 1955, he really retired: his brutally beaten body was found in his own home; his throat had been slashed.

Wall had provided valuable information to the Kefauver committee in 1951, at which time he was one of the few non-Mafia gamblers who talked about the organization and its operation in Tampa. This action probably sealed his death, but he was able to speak even from the grave: in 1960 Sergeant Jack de la Llana of the Tampa police department's criminal intelligence unit obtained a report made by Wall in 1945 about the Mafia, naming some of the members of the national board including Brooklyn's Vincent Mangano, Detroit's Joe Massei, and Chicago's Frank Nitti. Wall also put the finger on Joe Profaci.

The line of influence from Joseph Profaci of Brooklyn, where Adonis got his early start, to the Trafficantes, Senior and Junior, is laid out on police blotters for all to see. Trafficante, Sr., got a leg up and a lot of ideas from Little Augie Pisano, who was backed by Adonis. Adonis, in turn, gained ascendancy in the New York-New Jersey area with the help of Profaci, lifetime friend of Trafficante. The circle, though plated with murders and hard cash, seems always to be completed on the graph paper used by the Mafia, whether it begins in New York, Florida, or some unpronounceable city in a far corner of the earth.

As Trafficante and his Tampa thugs watched with undisguised interest, Adonis worked with the members of the Detroit mob on many of his financial forays at the Mafia level. For example, Adonis' top gaming place in east Florida was the Colonial Inn, near Hallandale, which he started in the late thirties with Mert Wertheimer, Detroit gang wheel, Meyer Lansky, who gravitated to gambling from New York City's industrial racketeering, and Vincent Alo of the Bronx. The Inn's gross profit for the year ending October 31, 1946, after many years of police-free operation, was $685,538.76, which was split between the partners.

It has been estimated that within a few years, up until the time that gambling was outlawed in the Miami area following a public outcry, Adonis had banked over $13 million in cash, using the Merchants Bank of New York. Trafficante and others really blinked when the total was racked up by accountants for Manhattan District Attorney Frank Hogan, who probed Joe Adonis and all angles of his gaming activities.

Adonis' now-defunct Greenacres Club, in Hollywood, north of Miami, was a forerunner of what was to come in Las Vegas in the early forties, and experience garnered in the gambling tourist traps of east Florida was to prove invaluable when Bugsy Siegel opened up Las Vegas for the syndicate.

So it was that Florida gangdom gained through the know-how of Adonis. Adonis' success, however, did not help his pal, Pisano, whose real name was Anthony Carfano. Little Augie was slain in New York City on September 25, 1959, probably as the result of the Vito Genovese take-over—but, then, not even Mafiosi win them all.

When Adonis left Florida, he centered his activities on his old stamping ground in the north and seemed able to get along with everyone, including public officials, and even with the aspirations of Genovese. Joe's hobby was riding to hounds on Shore Road in the Bay Bridge section of Brooklyn. In the full regalia of a fox-hunting *aficionado* he would pound the bridle path, the pride and joy of his hoodlum pals. Finally, however, he made an error, or perhaps his time for playing and being a big man was over. False testimony before a Bergen, New Jersey, County grand jury to the effect that he had been born in Passaic at an address that turned out to be a vacant lot once occupied by a livery stable led to his deportation in 1956. Adonis then joined his pal, Lucky Luciano, as crown prince of "displaced" Mafiosi in Italy: both had come home again.

Adonis' Florida associate, Santo Trafficante, Sr., died on August 11, 1954, leaving behind six sons, one of whom bears his name and wears his Mafia garments with pride.

During his formative years Santo Trafficante, Jr., had been rewarded by his father with control of the numbers racket in central Florida and ownership of the Sans Souci gaming casino in Havana—a casino formerly owned by Gabriel Mannarino of Pittsburgh, Pennsylvania, a fellow delegate with young Santo Trafficante at the Apalachin crime convention in 1957.

Trafficante, Jr., was a pioneer in Cuban gambling and shared the proceeds of the Sans Souci casino with Cuban dictator Fulgencio Batista y Zaldivar for many years. Indeed, so powerful did Trafficante eventually become in Cuba before the advent to power of Fidel Castro that four gunmen who arrived on the island from America to kill him, probably on the instruction of an envious Albert Anastasia, were told by Cuban police they would have to accomplish their purpose on American soil—if they could.

Young Trafficante publicly ascended his father's throne a year after the latter's death when he was introduced to "polite society" in Brooklyn at the wedding of the daughter of Don Joe Profaci to Anthony Tocco, son of Detroit mobster William Tocco. On June 4, 1955, Santo, Jr., was among the guests at a reception following the ceremony at the Hotel Commodore in Manhattan and was greeted with "royal" deference by such gangsters as Frank Livorsi, Thomas Dioguardi, his brother John—"Johnny Dio"—Albert Anastasia, and Three Finger Brown Lucchese. It is, of course, highly unlikely that Trafficante knew then that Anastasia had an eye on his gambling interests in Cuba.

The slick road Adonis laid out in Florida for a short time helped put Trafficante, Jr., on the way to a kind of wealth very different from that amassed by such earlier Mafiosi as his father and Lumia and Antinori, Mustache Petes who were connecting links between the first wave of Mafia immigrants to this country and Joe Adonis. But Santo Trafficante, Jr., did not inherit the easy life. Another legacy was a quarrel born of an incident created by Cuban narcotics smugglers who had sold Antinori a shipment of tainted drugs. Antinori had carried the drugs to the Midwest and peddled them to distributors for the crime cartel. But when it was found that the drugs were tainted, Antinori was not able to make restitution to the distributors and was eliminated, leaving a lot of bad blood between the distributors and the Florida family.

It was probably Little Augie Pisano, a veteran of New York City gang wars and one of the least publicized of the New York-New Jersey Mafia gang, who ironed out the feud between the Cuban mob element and the syndicate brotherhood. At any rate, Pisano certainly stirred up the Floridan criminal waters. During Little Augie's Florida years there were fourteen murders and six attempted assassinations in and around Tampa; Adonis' strong-arm man was keeping the Tampa crowd on a friendly basis and paving the way for his boss's entrance into Florida.

In testifying before the McClellan hearings as to the domination of Santo Trafficante, Jr., over Tampa's criminal organization, Tampa Police Chief Neil Brown presented a chart showing the interrelationships of the boys under Trafficante's thumb and stated:

> It is our considered conclusion that the Mafia exists in Tampa, that it controls most illegal gambling in Tampa and central Florida, and that its members have interstate and international ties to other Mafia groups.

That Trafficante's power extends over more than merely the Tampa area is clearly indicated by his presence in the hotel suite of Albert Anastasia in New York on the night of October 24, 1957, during what appeared to be a showdown discussion about Albert's attempt—despite the fact that concessions had already been handed out by the syndicate, not only to Trafficante, but also to men such as Meyer Lansky and his brother Jake—to move in on Trafficante's gambling operations in Cuba. Trafficante moved out of the hotel approximately one hour after Anastasia was murdered in a nearby barber shop the next morning. He had been registered under the alias "B. Hill," and neither the local police nor federal officials knew of his presence until much later. Trafficante, in fact, may well be the one who gave Anastasia the traditional Mafia kiss of death.

Trafficante showed up again at the famous Apalachin conference, which was held, partly at least, to discuss the division of Anastasia's rackets "estate." And he has never parted company from the Mafia leaders since. Moreover, Trafficante, who has been busy building his own empire, maintains his ties with the organization throughout the country in entirely typical fashion, depending largely on the movements of various couriers. There are few phone calls made, and no mail is sent. Word of mouth—away from all possible recording devices—is the principal mode of communication.

Trafficante and the syndicate depend upon couriers to carry not only information but also cash around the country in order to balance accounts. The couriers are, therefore, extremely important cogs in the Mafia wheel. And the gang leaders make their selections carefully, sometimes even choosing women—such as Virginia Hill, former sweetheart of both Adonis and Bugsy Siegel, who was established in a penthouse atop the Hotel Flamingo in Las Vegas when Bugsy was kingpin in town.

Certainly, the courier method of communication has its advantages. In spite of the fact that well-known gangsters are always subject to being stopped and questioned by the police, by keeping their mouths shut or using their imagination to say the "right" things, they can often turn the officers' probing into a reverse asset. False information can tie up the police longer than trustworthy facts.

For many years the chief courier for the Mafia was Gaetano Ricci, alias "Tony Goebbels," who twenty years ago made his headquarters at 5 Court Square, Brooklyn, in a restaurant beneath the local Democratic party headquarters. Goebbels, who is six feet four inches tall, has been picked up by police in every large city in the country and in many of the smaller towns, but he has now dropped out of sight and is presumably living in retirement in Florida—although his reported appearance in Chicago with other crime bosses in November, 1968, makes his "retirement" questionable.

One of his replacements appeared to be Louis Coticchia, alias "Lou Brady," who came into prominence in April, 1962, when members of the Tampa police department spotted him in the company of veteran Tampa Mafioso Frank Diecidue and a pal, Augustine Primo Lazzara. It is thought that Coticchia served as a trusted courier until he did "something bad," as Tampa police surmise, because a year later he walked out of his house in Miami bound for a luncheon date with Santo Trafficante, Jr., and was never seen again. His wife told police Coticchia received a phone call just before leaving the house.

Coticchia may well have been the victim of foul play because he had taken a contract to collect money due Tommy Eboli, acting boss of the Genovese family. The funds represented interest due on a juice-loan advance to the operator of a New York tractor company. Police believe that the courier may have collected the money but failed to pass it on to Eboli—thus losing not only his job but also his life.

Coticchia is a good example of how a Mafioso works his way up in the world of crime. Born on February 25, 1920, in Cincinnati, Ohio, Coticchia was first arrested in 1936, for robbery in Ohio. In 1937 he was arrested in Miami for investigation of a "shakedown," but after being held for four days, he was released without having charges filed against him. Arrested again and held for investigation, this time in Hot Springs, Arkansas, a noted center of Mafia activity, he was released with the understanding that he would leave the city. A few weeks later, in Cleveland, Coticchia was picked up and charged with assault to commit rape. He was convicted and received a sentence of from one to fifteen years. He served four years and was released in 1941.

Coticchia's next arrest was in Los Angeles. Police arrested him there in 1942 on a warrant issued in Baltimore for grand theft. Tried in Baltimore for receiving stolen goods, he then served five years in prison. Thereafter, for almost fifteen years, Coticchia virtually dropped out of sight, but apparently he was exceedingly active on behalf of the syndicate, cementing ties and contacts throughout the country, and learning new and important duties. He had graduated from soldier to button man in the organization and was picking up the experience needed by a courier. His last arrest came in Tampa, in January, 1963, when he was picked up and booked in connection with a charge of grand larceny, but the charge was dropped for lack of evidence. At the time of his arrest Coticchia had $1,775 in cash on him; he was a trifle shorter than usual because a few days earlier he had plunked down $3,625 in long green for a new car.

Also found on Coticchia were papers indicating that he had lived for a while at the Aloha Motel in Miami under the alias "Luiz Paulino Bailey," of Rio de Janeiro, Brazil. Another paper listed gambling equipment and the statement: "Empress Lines, Ltd., Nassau—via Wappen Von Hamburg—German boat loading pier No. 3."

An investigation indicated that Coticchia had worked as a pit boss in gaming casinos in Las Vegas and Havana and had contacts that would enable him to buy gambling equipment. The cargo listed on the paper included fifty slot machines valued in excess of $65,000. The equipment had been shipped air freight from Las Vegas to Nassau and placed in the German vessel. The information received indicated that the German ship was to travel between Miami and Nassau as a floating gambling casino, but the chances are the cargo finally wound up in the gaming casino of the Lucayan Beach Hotel in the Bahamas, which opened a few months later.

Phone calls are of course frowned on by the Mafia, for obvious reasons, but a record of at least one of Coticchia's long distance calls does exist. The record, submitted to the McClellan hearings by Sergeant de la Llana of the Tampa police department, indicates that late in 1962 Coticchia phoned from Tampa to Sonny's restaurant in Miami Beach, which was owned by Thomas Altamura, reputed Mafia member and an associate of Santo Trafficante, Jr. Coticchia was no doubt well acquainted with Altamura, "The Enforcer," who was killed five years later, on October 30, 1967, as he entered another restaurant in Miami. One of Altamura's lieutenants, Anthony (Big Tony) Esperti, who had fallen out with his boss, has been charged with the murder, and both men have weighty files in the intelligence division of the Los Angeles police department. One question not answered by the files, however, concerns the presence of a $10,000 cashier's check found on Altamura's bullet-ridden body, drawn on a bank in Sherman Oaks, a Los Angeles suburb.

While couriers are essential to Trafficante's successful operation in Florida, his success can be credited even more to his adherence to the Mafia code of *omerta* and to his ability to maintain himself as the power behind the throne in Florida with none of the accoutrements of power: the creature comforts that usually are associated with powerful and financially successful men the world over.

To the syndicate, Trafficante must seem to be a model. Thus, on October 14, 1968, Trafficante once again found time to illustrate to the syndicate the value of *omerta:* he merely coughed and guffawed politely when questioned by counsel for a Florida legislative committee probing lawlessness. Santo took the Fifth Amendment when asked if he was a member of the Mafia. No one knew precisely why he laughed. But then he is a secretive man. Authorities, for example, know of no legitimate businesses, not even of any real estate, owned or controlled by Santo Trafficante. His house, car, and other possessions are held in the names of others. If the rules of humility and austerity, in the old tradition of the Mafia, are thus observed by Trafficante, he must be one of the few true Mafiosi left in the United States. And whatever the motivation behind Trafficante's simple mode of life, it seems to keep him healthy. The downfall of the more polished members of the secret society in Florida over the years has often come through their violation of the old concepts of the Mafia. When a Mafioso gets away from the traditions, he runs into trouble.

Take, for instance, the case of ex-convict Harry I. Voiler, who founded a newspaper, the *Daily Mail,* in Miami in 1949—years before Trafficante, Jr., emerged as a power. A woman witness close to the Mafia testified at the McClellan hearings that the purposes of the paper "were (1) to provide prompt dissemination of racing results and (2) to create a favorable atmosphere toward out-of-state racketeer elements to be found in Miami." Chief backer of the paper was Martin Accardo, brother of Chicago mobster Tony Accardo, who invested $125,000. Voiler said that no money had come from the mob, but Mrs. Oretta Y. Carroll, who had once been married to Martin Accardo but was obviously not bound to a code of silence, produced documentary proof that Accardo had indeed been the money man behind the journal.

Everything went down the drain for the *Daily Mail,* however, when, no doubt in a burst of loyal feeling, the paper published an editorial welcoming the notorious Frank Costello to Miami when the big boss went south one year to take the sun. It was a momentary visit, to say the least.

The old-time racketeers who had a finger in the pie of Miami have now all gone by the board. One was Samuel (Gameboy) Miller, who had been a partner in the Island Club in Miami, from which he gleaned, he said, $15,000 a year. Another Miami stalwart, now out of business, is John Angersola of Cleveland, a member of the old Mayfield Road gang, which operated the Desert Inn in its early days in Las Vegas. Angersola, an associate of Mike Coppola, used to own the Grand Hotel in Miami and a piece of the Wofford Hotel in that area. At present Angersola is reportedly an organizer for the Cleaners and Dyers International Union in Florida at a salary of $100 a week, but he is somewhat vague as to what his duties are. He is also employed by the "23" room, a Miami Beach establishment, at $100 a week. No work is involved here, either, but, as Angersola puts it, "they may need me."

While Angersola awaits his call to duty, Trafficante awaits his greatest opportunity. A windfall of refugees from Castro's Cuba may be providing the wherewithal to launch Trafficante into a truly golden financial orbit. Besides the usual requirements of food and lodging, the Cuban refugees hanker for daily knowledge of the main gambling activity on the island: Bolita or Cuba.

> Bolita is a numbers lottery where the winning number is drawn daily. Cuba is a numbers lottery where the winning number is drawn weekly. Bettors can place bets on any number from 1 to 100 and receive a 60-to-1 return if they win. The Cuba winning number is the last two digits from the Cuban national lottery number, which is five digits, and is broadcast over a Havana radio station each Saturday shortly after 2:00 P.M.

Thus testified Sergeant William Branch of the Orlando, Florida, police department at the McClellan Senate hearings.

The public—over three hundred thousand Cuban refugees have swelled the fertile fields of the lottery boys to incredible proportions—is contacted by peddlers or sellers who receive a commission of 15 per cent of their sales. Pickup men who take the bets from the sellers to the checkup houses receive 20 per cent of what they collect. Employees such as checkup men, adding-machine operators, and supervisors usually receive salaries for their duties.

Mafia watchdog of the lush Bolita-Cuba dough is Sam Cacciatore, cousin of Santo Trafficante, who with another Trafficante relative, Armando Rios, was picked up in a raid staged before the current influx of Cuban refugees and found even then to be doing a business of $160,000 a week in Orange County, Florida—a mere segment of the Trafficante operation.

Santo Trafficante, however, seldom makes mistakes. One is constantly confronted with evidence of his canniness; for example, his tolerance of non-Mafia men in his organization. One such non-Mafioso is Harlan Blackburn, a convicted felon born in Sand Lake, Florida, in 1919. Blackburn was convicted in 1935 of forging a U.S. government check and served four and one-half years in prison. He was arrested again, in March, 1956, for operating a lottery in Polk County, Florida, and received a five-year prison sentence. Released in 1959, Blackburn has since remained active in Trafficante's operation.

When he testified about Blackburn's operations, Sergeant Branch referred to the chart of the Mafia organization in the Tampa area and pointed out that of the twenty-seven people listed as working on the Florida lottery under Blackburn's supervision only five were without criminal records or arrests for gambling and other crimes.

In view of the records of even comparatively unimportant members of the Mafia organization in Florida, it is interesting to note that while the police have solved all but 4 of the 145 murders of "ordinary" people occurring between 1958 and 1962 in the Tampa area alone—a solution ratio of better than 97 per cent—and all 83 "regular" homicides occurring between 1960 and 1962, only 1 of 23 gangland murders has been solved.

With the departure from the syndicate scene in Florida of such elite members of the Mafia as Joe Adonis, Frank Costello, who had more important gold mines to pursue in New Orleans, Joe Massei, who owned cheese companies, and others—all of whom wanted to escape the limelight after a sudden upsurge of morality on the east coast of Florida—it became easy for Trafficante to impose his special brand and organization on many people. Thus while the carpet-joint Mafiosi have moved on, preferring to deal with some of the pushover public officials in the Caribbean's expanding gaming *boites de nuit* as well as with those in Nevada, the diehard Mafiosi who remain are well established, determined, and well organized.

Trafficante's personal touch is best exemplified by the division of organization between the "dirty dollar" boys, who handle the narcotics trade, and the soft-sell fellows, who ply the gambling trade and are finding the refugee Bolita enterprise a fantastic treasure trove. But, according to the Tampa police department, Trafficante has been ably assisted by Salvatore (Sam) Scaglione, now dead, and Gaetano (Joe) Mistretta, both classified as Mafia elders and as old friends of Trafficante's father, who himself started the wholesale take-over of Florida gambling as the carpet-joint boys moved out.

Directly under this local board of directors are other influential Mafiosi, as linked on a chart submitted to the McClellan committee by the Tampa police department: Frank Diecidue, member of a pioneer Mafia clan whose hand was weakened by the demise of Brooklyn's Vincent Mangano some years ago; Angelo Bedami, whose specialty is receiving stolen goods and bootlegging. Trafficante's underboss, Augustine Primo Lazzara, who liked to bribe public officials and assault people who wouldn't go along with him, died in 1968.

The Diecidue clan was given a rather loosely woven barony in Florida when, in 1929, Frank Costello called a meeting in Atlantic City to try to unite warring Mafia groups throughout the United States and to form a cohesive Mafia, subject to its ancient rules and regulations, to take advantage of the huge treasure pot in America that dwarfed the combined riches of all the countries of the world.

Costello was able to integrate the warring factions, and, through the influence of Vincent Mangano, the Diecidue family was able to maintain its power in Florida for some time. The power of the Trafficantes, Senior and Junior, was locked in, however, in 1952 after Mangano, a member of the Mafia governing board, disappeared from sight and became part of the concrete foundations of a well-known housing project in Nassau County, New York.

A current handhold on the rackets for the Diecidues is James (Jimmy) Costa Longo, a gambler who likes to tell the judge off when he stands before the bench—a real loud mouth.

Working with and for these men are the usual assortment—records indicate that forty Mafia members and affiliated hoodlums operate in south Florida—of button men and soldiers who have helped to make Florida a fruit just ripened for picking by the syndicate of crime, which never seems to run out of harvest. In Dade

County (the greater Miami area) alone crime investigator Richard B. Wallace estimated in 1966 that organized vice—bookmaking, lottery operations, prostitution, and abortions—was grossing $50 million a year.

Wallace also strongly urged the creation of a state crime commission, and the war on organized crime in Florida was in fact stepped up recently because of developments stemming as much from crusading zeal as from a desire to make the state appear politically and ethically acceptable, both to its own citizens and to the tourists who wonder whether Florida is a better place than Las Vegas to take the kiddies during vacation.

In a report to Governor Claude Kirk climaxing a six-month probe into syndicate activities in Florida, Director Ed Yarborough of the Florida sheriff's bureau claimed that information developed by his staff indicated that hoodlums, with the aid of eighty-seven corporate structures, control forty-five hotels and twenty-five cocktail lounges and restaurants in the Miami area. Also in his report, delivered to the governor's office in March, 1967, Yarborough asked for more money to continue the investigation, which came to a close after six months of gumshoeing by three full-time agents.

In the meantime, in December, 1966, a new Dade County sheriff was appointed: E. Wilson (Bud) Purdy, a former FBI agent in New York and Florida who, among other jobs, headed Pennsylvania's state police for the three years prior to his Florida appointment. Purdy has a special interest in the movements of Santo Trafficante, Jr., and believes that every time Santo is picked up by police, there is a corresponding hole knocked in the Mafia's confidence in the Florida hood.

"Santo wants to have the confidence of the New York Mafia," Purdy told a reporter for *Time* magazine in April, 1967, "but how can he control this town when he can't even get past the Miami airport without being picked up?"

Purdy also seeks a boost in his department's $8.6 million budget. He would increase his 1,101 man force by 223 and raise salaries. He says he wants a "damn good" department—the best trained, best equipped, most efficient, and most honest anywhere.

Reflecting another facet of Florida's war on crime, quite apart from Sheriff Purdy's efforts in Dade County, was Governor Kirk's attempt, immediately after his January, 1967, inauguration, to establish a privately financed war on criminals. Kirk hired and utilized the men and files of a private detective agency known as the Wackenhut Corporation, headed by former FBI man George R. Wackenhut.

Wackenhut, according to reporter Jack Nelson of the *Los Angeles Times* bureau in Atlanta, met Kirk in 1964 when both men were staunch backers of Barry Goldwater in the presidential race, and the two became fast friends.

Kirk said that he personally solicited funds for the 1967 "private" crime probe from business and industry and that "money was pouring into the war chest" even before his solicitation began.

According to reporter Nelson, this particular war on Florida crime was called many names, such as "Gestapo, Kirk's private police force and Wackencops, among others," by persons who questioned its acumen. And, Nelson added, some Democrats in Florida, a state with few Republican office holders, fear that "if information developed by Wackenhut's men cannot be used to convict them in court, it can be used to convict them in political campaigns."

Claude Kirk is Florida's first Republican governor in ninety-four years, and the feeling was that his private probe could be a two-edged sword. However, on November 8, 1967, Kirk announced that the Wackenhut probe was ended. There was a $300,000 debt remaining, Kirk said, and the files that had evolved were being turned over to a new state crime-fighting agency, the Florida Bureau of Law Enforcement, which was created on October 1, 1967.

"My investigators are zero, zero, zero," Kirk said. "We don't have any money."

Consequently, when all the chips are down, Sheriff Purdy, along with the new state agency, may have the last word after all. But Santo Trafficante doesn't seem to be the least bit worried, in spite of the listing of forty-five Miami hotels and twenty-five restaurants as being Mafia-owned. The mob still finds its own kind of fun in the sun. And it will take more than a little effort to shift it.

7

BAHAMAS:
Hoodlum Sea

Columbus didn't know it, but he did find a pot of gold at the end of the rainbow when he steered his little ships into the heart of what has become one of the greatest crime syndicate enterprises since Al Capone left Brooklyn and discovered Chicago.

Capone had no connection with Columbus, of course, but their descendants share one thing in common: a place at a trough of gold where pigs and paladins are born, weaned, and grown to maturity —the West Indies. Laved on the north by the Atlantic Ocean and on the south by the warm waters of the Caribbean Sea, this ancient haunt of pirates is the new playground of the mob.

The Caribbean can be blue or green, according to weather conditions, but for the gamblers who rarely give it a second glance the sea generally glints gold. Just a scant ten years ago these almost tropical waters harbored a pearly string of tranquil islands, stretching from the Bahamas, seventy miles off the coast of Florida, to Barbados and Trinidad, off the northern coast of Venezuela, South America—a thousand-island crescent of peace and pleasure providing retreat for tired tycoons, wound-up executives, and more or less lethargic but happy natives, many of whom thought voodoo was the closest they could get to the devil. Places with names such as Bimini, Nassau, Virgin Islands, and Martinique were shrines dedicated to those who liked to take the sun every now and then.

If there was a devil in the area, he didn't make himself manifest until Fidel Castro unlocked the Cuban Pandora's box and drove out a segment of the American crime syndicate that had obtained a foothold in Havana—long a waystop, as we have seen, in the dope traffic that flows through the Caribbean via Florida and New

Orleans into the veins of addicts in the United States and, during the years of Batista's regime, a gambling hot spot as well.

Castro, who sought no piece of the action in the country he took over, banished the gambling operators, pimps, and dope pushers from the Cuban littoral. American law-enforcement officials were impressed by Castro's efforts to clean his nest, but Cuba's loss was America's unfortunate gain, for the hoods drifted back into the underworlds of the cities that had spawned them: Miami, Tampa, Biloxi, Gulfport, New Orleans, and Las Vegas.

Thwarted only temporarily by Cuba's rejection, the hoods soon regrouped, returned to some of the smaller islands in the Caribbean, and began to discover more riches than Columbus ever dreamed of. In outflanking Castro on the Spanish Main, they became part of a milieu that combined many talents—the know-how of financiers, lawyers, legislators, politicians, construction men, show-biz nabobs, gamblers, and plain "ordinary" greedy people—and came up with what in financial and real estate parlance is called a "real business boom."

There is little doubt that Castro has since taken note of this "capitalistic" influx of money just a few blue waves from the shores of Cuba, where, under his guiding hand, communism is making its play under a somewhat marginal economy. But one of the first to note the potential in the Bahamas and get the ball rolling for the entry of the syndicate boys was a man named Wallace Groves, "Boy Wonder of Wall Street." Groves did not throw himself out of a window when the financial crash of 1929 tumbled fat cats and golden calves throughout the United States, and he now has just about everything a man could want—a man such as Groves, that is—though he'd no doubt like to expunge from his record a 1941 conviction involving a $750,000 stock swindle for which he was sentenced to two years in prison. In fact, he served only five months in durance vile, in the federal penitentiary at Danbury, Connecticut, and was released in December, 1942.

The conviction arose through Groves's pyramiding company on top of company until he had built up $10 million in assets at a very small cost to himself, though this success could hardly have changed the flavor of the federal food allotment at Danbury. At the time of the conviction the Securities Exchange Commission said: "Almost all of the companies which came under the control of Mr. Groves suffered severe losses." Yet a friend said of Groves, who owned substantial pieces of twenty-three corporations, "He had a good reputation on Wall Street. He wasn't one of those sharpshooters."

In January, 1967, after trying to dig out the facts about Groves, *Parade* magazine reported: "There is one area in which Groves's friends and enemies agree: He is shrewd, quick and perceptive—'a natural genius at making money.'" Groves is also credited with having extrasensory perception when it comes to business deals and has said that he receives "vibrations" during business negotiations.

Groves's vibrations were apparently unhampered by his short vacation behind bars, for he went to Grand Bahama Island in the mid-forties to cut timber and found natural beaches, a frost-free climate, and convenient proximity to the tip of Florida—whence the scent of tourists wafted across the surging sea waters. Since then, the sixty-seven-year-old Boy Wonder has managed to wolf down half the island for himself with the help of two other men peculiarly suited to the task of helping him build up what is now a one-hundred-and-fifty-thousand-acre barony plus substantial pieces of outlying enterprises. The two associates have been fifty-six-year-old Louis Chesler, a 256-pound, blue-eyed son of a Lithuanian immigrant to Canada, and sixty-seven-year-old syndicate gambling chief Meyer Lansky.

Groves provided the land; Chesler, through his Canadian connections and financing, helped smooth the way for the construction of a beautiful hotel and subsequent permission for gambling therein; and Lansky came up with the syndicate know-how of casino operation to entice, cater to, and gauge the financial limits of the tourists—thousands of them—that was the main prerequisite to the money-making dreams of all three men.

In 1955 Groves managed to wangle property from the Bahamian (British) government for £1 per acre (at that time £1 equaled $2.80). Certainly, Groves couldn't complain. Some of the original $2.80-acres he purchased from the Bahamian government were reportedly later sold at $50,000 each. Critics of the Bahamian hierarchy say Groves was given a blank check. His domain on Grand Bahama Island includes a 211-square-mile slice of the 430-square-mile island.

All Groves's holdings are the legal property of various Groves corporate entities: the parent organization, Grand Bahama Port

Authority, Ltd., set up for the supposed purpose of creating a deep-water port to enable Groves to bring industrial and commercial establishments to his barony, which is named Freeport; the Grand Bahama Development Company, established for the management and sale of real estate; and Bahamas Amusements, Ltd., a subsidiary organized to take charge of the gambling casinos to be brought to the island.

No branch of the Bahamian government seems willing to tangle with Groves, yet the big man loathes descriptions of his operation as a "kingdom" or "dictatorship." "That's a lot of bunk," he scowls. Nevertheless, if you went to live—or play—in Freeport, you would use Groves's airport, Groves's harbor, Groves's roads, Groves's schools, Groves's land, Groves's supermarket, and Groves's electricity and water. The Port Authority is a private tax-exempt super-corporation, and its subsidiaries affect Freeport's twelve thousand residents from birth to death.

Freeport has no income tax, no profits tax, no real estate tax, and no sales tax. Indeed, Groves's long-term contractual guarantees build in these privileges, which are almost impossible to find elsewhere. Consequently, wealthy businessmen looking for business outlets are quick to take advantage of such favorable opportunities.

These advantages were probably what first attracted Toronto tycoon Lou Chesler to the sunny Caribbean. Chesler was no novice at the business of making a fast dollar. Starting as a customer's man for a brokerage firm, he had piled up $4 million on Toronto's version of Wall Street almost before he was weaned. With his $4 million he built up a paper profit of $70 million by stalking small U.S. companies with big potential. His perception was uncanny. For example, he accurately presaged the coming boom in electronics, Florida land, and leisure activities, including horse racing. In fact, he gave all such industries a boost up to the starting gate.

Chesler was also something of a *bon vivant*, building up a large and what, in June, 1964, the *Wall Street Journal* called "somewhat incongruous circle of friends and acquaintances." Among these, the *Journal* pointed out, were such respected business figures as publisher Gardner Cowles, investment banker John Weinberg, and bank president Gabriel Hauge, onetime economic advisor to President Eisenhower. Others listed were such former Eisenhower administration officials as Robert Anderson, who served as Secretary of the Treasury, and cabinet secretary Maxwell Rabb, who in 1964 was one of those trying to secure the Republican presidential nomination for Henry Cabot Lodge.

Chesler, who fed $12 million into the Bahamas before Groves ousted him with a clever squeeze play in May, 1964, has been a prime mover behind many important companies in the United States, including General Development Corporation and Universal Controls, Inc. Universal makes electronic equipment, and General Development is a huge mail-order merchandiser of Florida houses and lots. Banker Weinberg went on the General Development board of directors in 1959 at about the same time publisher Cowles became interested in the organization. Cowles later succeeded Lou Chesler as chairman and became the company's second largest stockholder.

Chesler's guiding hand has also functioned in Canada's Lorado Uranium Mines, Ltd., and in the entertainment complex called Seven Arts Productions, Ltd., which has made its mark on the Hollywood movie-making scene. Incidentally, it was Maxwell Rabb who, as a board member of Seven Arts, came to Chesler's defense in 1963, when the management was being attacked by stockholders for investing $5 million in Chesler's and Wallace Groves's Grand Bahama Development Company—a squabble resulting in an announcement that Chesler would liquidate his holdings in Seven Arts and resign as chairman and director of the board after Seven Arts had disposed of its investment in the Grand Bahama Development Company.

The circle of Chesler associates and friends was not limited to Wall Street or Capitol Hill. He had a well-known love of horse racing, which may have prompted him in 1965 to secure, with the help of millionaire cronies such as Baltimore Colts' owner Carroll Rosenbloom, an outfit known as Baltimore's American totalizator, which owns and leases most of the racetrack "tote" systems that figure odds and winnings based on bet totals of individual horse races. Another Chesler associate, who had no business connections with the Canadian but was a friend, according to the *Wall Street Journal*, was Trigger Mike Coppola, whose activities were detailed in the chapter on the Mafia in New York.

Looking back on his Caribbean adventure in April, 1967, Chesler classified himself as "probably the biggest loser in the Bahamas" and admitted that he had paid huge sums of money to the "Bay

Street Boys," the ruling clique at the time in Nassau, to buy permission to bring big-time gambling into the British colony. The story began in 1960 and 1961 when Chesler entered the picture as Groves's partner in the Grand Bahama Development Company, which was then selling real estate in Freeport.

Chesler arrived on the scene at a time when Groves's initial ideas were undergoing change. What had originally been planned, ostensibly, at least, as an industrial boom—seen in terms of harbor development, hotels, golf courses, shops, homes, and various private businesses—was beginning to take on a new aspect. The Groves enterprises apparently needed a few additional inducements for the growth their creator had envisioned, something to bring in the fun-loving, rather than just sun-loving tourists with money in their pockets. Gambling, therefore, was put on the agenda for the Grand Bahama Island, and in the winter of 1961 construction was begun on the lavish, 250-room Lucayan Beach Hotel—for which Chesler, as part of his agreement with Groves, had to raise and invest $12 million—containing, among other conveniences, a room with nine thousand square feet of floor space designed officially as a convention hall and privately as a handball court.

Since gambling was, and still is, specifically forbidden by law in the Bahamas, some legal maneuvering was necessary. But getting the needed certificate of exemption was easy, providing the right lawyer was on hand. And he was. Sir Stafford Sands—the leader of the Bay Street Boys and of the primarily white, long-standing governing party—had helped Groves all along the way in setting up his numerous interlocking firms in the island and was just the man for the job.

Louis Chesler, being a Canadian, would supposedly carry none of the onus of American gangster influence with him into the hallowed halls of a casino and thus was another essential party to the scheme. Finally, all was ready. In March, 1963, Groves and Chesler went to the Bahamian government to seek an exemption from the anti-gambling laws. They went specifically to the governor's executive council, and their case was presented by Sir Stafford, who just happened also to be a member of the council. The certificate of exemption made out in the name of Bahamas Amusements, Ltd.—whose shares were then split equally between Chesler and

Groves's wife, Georgette—was granted in April. The gambling license was ordered prepared for issuance, and the boys were in business.

The initial contract stipulated that casino employees be British, Irish—no one could have been more surprised than the Irish!—or European citizens and specifically excluded American executives and personnel. It provided that company casinos could be operated anywhere on Grand Bahama so long as they were in, or in the vicinity of, a hotel having at least two hundred rooms. What a happy coincidence that the newly built Lucayan Beach Hotel had not only the necessary guest rooms but also a sizable "convention hall," which could be, and was, quickly transformed into a casino!

The hotel opened in January, 1964, with all the glitter and gold its social director, Mrs. John McLean, could muster. The plan had been to operate gambling on the highest level—a white-tie-and-tails copy of the ornate gambling palaces of Monaco. But the great experiment proved a complete bust, at first, as the fickle phonies of the jet set failed to show. The Monte Carlo room remained as empty and cold as a pit boss's heart.

Chesler and Groves, however, quickly learned what the big-time operators of Las Vegas and Reno, Nevada, spent millions to find out: that a successful casino must in the long run grind its dollars from the pockets of little people, simply because there are so many more of them than jet-setters. Accordingly, plans were changed, and the boys in the know—Meyer Lansky and crew, who had made a lifelong study of gambling within the framework of the crime syndicate—were brought in. The avant-garde of the gambling fraternity, with the love of warm climes already in their blood, turned their hawk noses to the Spanish Main, and things began looking up in the Bahamas.

Early in 1967 Chesler blandly told a four-man investigative Royal Commisson of Inquiry headed by Sir Ranulph Bacon, former assistant commissioner of Scotland Yard, that he sought Lansky's advice on gaming potential in the Bahamas because he considered him a "dean of gambling." "It was no easy job," he told the probers, to organize a large-scale gambling operation, and he needed the advice of an expert.

A smooth and profitable route for the gaming industry always seems to require the Lansky types and their know-how, but sometimes you wonder what keeps their noses to the grindstone. Is it the result of a sort of force-feeding hoodlums have to put up with? Or perhaps the Lanskys of this world have nothing else to do with their days? Whatever the reason, apparently no one ever really *retires* in the crime syndicate, although a few have claimed to have done so when investigators were on their trail.

For example, witness the current career of eighty-year-old George Sadlo, time-honored gaming Sancho Panza for Lansky, who, it appears, thought nothing of launching a new project such as the Bahamian enterprise.

In the early days Lansky had been a murder partner of Las Vegas pioneer Bugsy Siegel when Siegel was strong-arming it for Louis Buchalter. Years later Lansky provided—through George Sadlo, his "insulation"—the wherewithal for the late gambler Marion B. Hicks and Cliff Jones when they decided to build the Thunderbird Hotel in Las Vegas. In fact, Jones himself is another example of how old friends stick together and of how men connected with the Mafia never seem to give up. A former Lieutenant-Governor of Nevada, Jones now has his fingers in various financial and gaming pies in and out of the Caribbean and is a good friend of top airlines officials, who also have a vast financial stake in that tropical playground.

But to return to Sadlo, Lansky thought nothing of bringing his old crony out of semiretirement. And when Louis Chesler was asked about Sadlo's duties by the investigative commission, he said: "George Sadlo was in complete control of the hiring and firing of employees" when the casino got started. In fact, Sadlo's activities in Grand Bahama merely illustrate the beginning of another operation featuring the competence and talent of the men who make up one side of the seemingly endless war of attrition waged by the syndicate against legal authority. There was, and is, a specific ban on the employment of American personnel in the big Freeport casino. Yet at first it was not enforced; it was forgotten, as is made clear by the following list, which appeared in the April 6, 1967, *Wall Street Journal*, of just a few of the syndicate workers, American born or naturalized, who moved in, along with Sadlo, as gambling aides in the Monte Carlo room of the Lucayan Beach Hotel:

Frank Reiter, alias "Frank Ritter"	credit manager
Max Courtney	general manager
Charles Brudner, alias "Charlie Brud"	floor manager
Dino Cellini	craps supervisor
James Baker	craps supervisor
David Geiger	craps supervisor
Al Jacobs	craps supervisor
Roy Bell	craps supervisor

Max Courtney and Frank Ritter first made their marks as close associates of Dutch Schultz, a leading bootlegger in the New York-New Jersey area who unsuccessfully plotted the murder of Thomas Dewey, prosecutor in Manhattan during the vicious Prohibition days of open gang warfare. When Dutch Schultz died —he was machine-gunned by his rivals—Ritter and Courtney decided to take up a less violent occupation. In the fifties they appeared in Montreal as operators of a huge layoff bookmaking operation. To relieve the pressure of large bets made in Las Vegas, Chicago, New York, and other fast-buck areas, the two men set up their operation in Canada outside the reach of U.S. law-enforcement agencies. But somebody must have snitched to the Royal Canadian Mounted Police, for they soon galloped into Montreal and arrested the two bookies. Expelled from Canada, Courtney, who is also known by his real name, Morris (Moishe) Schmertzler, and Ritter, who often moved around under the alias "Red Reed," spent a number of years taking bets in the salubrious atmosphere of various gaming centers in the United States, finally showing up as executives of the Monte Carlo room in Freeport. Which all goes to prove that though a good hood may be down, he's never out.

Cellini, Baker, Geiger, Jacobs, and Bell were eventually investigated by the Bahamian government and expelled from the Bahamas in March, 1964. Apparently it had taken some of the more conscientious officials that long to discover that the whole crew —including Sadlo and Lansky's brother Jake—had been the mainstem of the Lansky gambling combine in Havana under Batista's rule before Castro threw them out in 1959.

Ritter, Courtney, and Brudner, who also had done time with Lansky's gang in Havana casinos, escaped pressure in the Bahamas until January 15, 1967, when it became clear to the Bahamians that they were fugitives from justice in the United States, having been charged with evading income taxes while allegedly running a bookmaking operation in New York. But at least the three fugitives were still on hand when the new El Casino opened in Freeport on January 1st and had two weeks in which to give a high-level, graduate course in running the place to the new boxmen, stickmen, and pit bosses—also, of course, Lansky associates from way back.

Miami Crime Commission Director Dan Sullivan, on an "Open End" television program, said that Courtney and Ritter, before they left the country, were probably the "two biggest, heaviest bookmakers and sports bookmakers in the United States." Yet, though officially banned from the Bahama casinos along with Brudner, all three men have been granted asylum "as residents" in the Bahamas despite their fugitive status. In this connection, too, it is interesting to note that Sir Ralph Francis Alnwick Grey, Governor of the Bahamas by appointment of Her Majesty Queen Elizabeth II, said in relation to the hard lines tossed at the Lansky boys running the gambling details at Freeport: "The mere giving a dog a bad name ought not to be cause to have him hanged. If you go into the tourist business, all sorts of strange people with strange proclivities come in."

Testimony before the Bacon investigative committee revealed that banishment of Courtney, Ritter, and Brudner from the casinos did not exactly leave them out in the cold. An agreement was made that the three men will, over the next ten years, receive $2.1 million for a credit-card file they apparently brought to the island when gaming first began. Thousands of well-heeled American gamblers are listed on the cards, and Keith Gonsalves, president of Bahamas Amusements, Ltd., and former head of Barclay's Bank in the Bahamas, told the commission that the purchase was made so that the casinos would "continue to function smoothly." As Gonsalves said, the men "could have left us with a completely sabotaged organization."

While the hoods in the Bahamas have had to put up with certain inconveniences, the operators of the casinos cannot complain about their profits, although their initial expenses were not negligible, either. For example, in 1965, its first full year of operation, the Lucayan Beach Hotel casino on Grand Bahama Island laid out $490,000 for chartered flights to bring in free-loading "high rollers" from the United States, people with blue-chip credit ratings meticulously provided by Lansky and his associates. And, according to a *Life* exposé of the Bahamian gaming idyll, another $930,000 was spent to provide hotel and ship accommodations for the pampered guests.

Rumors are that close to $500 million have been sunk into Wallace Groves's island empire, and, according to *Parade*, Groves calls profits from his gambling casinos "peanuts." For Groves's information, Meyer Lansky has *never* settled for peanuts, and it is estimated that by 1970 more than half a million tourists a year will be visiting the Lucayan Beach Hotel and others like it, some still to be built. And syndicate ledgers prophesy that each tourist will leave at least $25 on the tables. Some peanuts!

The *Life* article went on to point out that U.S. lawmen are convinced the mob is getting a big cut of casino profits, so perhaps their harassment is not too onerous. In January, 1967, the El Casino, a new carpet joint also owned by Bahamas Amusements, Ltd., opened to swell the total take, and 30 per cent of the sum is going, *Life* claimed, to such Lansky confederates in the Mafia as Stephen Magaddino of Buffalo, Angelo Bruno of Philadelphia, Frank Costello of New York City—this is disputed by Mafia buffs in Manhattan—Santo Trafficante of Tampa, and Joe Adonis in Italy.

Newsman Clarence Jones of the *Miami Herald* reported in July, 1967, that so much money was being raked in by the casinos that "it had to be mailed, parcel post, to New York banks in cardboard beer cartons." He quoted records of the Royal Commission of Inquiry and said the cartons full of money also "hinted at wholesale skimming from the casinos."

If this is true, and there is little reason to doubt it, it is also true that the gambling operation is having a profound effect on the whole economy of Grand Bahama and neighboring islands. Some fringe "benefits" of wholesale gambling have already become manifest: the local, comparatively unskilled, and certainly confused police on Grand Bahama are, for the first time, up against organized prostitution and narcotics, traditional enterprises of the Mafia. Three Americans were recently deported for trafficking in whores and drugs. Two of them had police records and Mafia affiliations in New York City and used Las Vegas-trained girls in the old "badger game," housing them, according to the *Saturday Evening Post*, in the King's Inn, one of the island's plushest hotels.

The periodical also recounted the inauguration of a Mafia-type extortion enterprise in which local businessmen were threatened with physical harm if they did not pay protection money to the gangsters. To the Bahamian government it seems to be of little concern. In response to such allegations Sir Ralph Grey said: "We can't police the world. No one has yet shown me any clear-cut evidence of wrongdoing."

Evidence is, however, not unavailable. Under oath, Keith Gonsalves, who apparently was third in the Groves hierarchy before Lou Chesler moved out of his post as president of the Grand Bahama Development Company in 1964, named a dozen Bahamian government officials who had been receiving largesse from the Groves operation, and he pointed out that Chesler negotiated most of these deals. One deal Gonsalves referred to involved Sir Etienne Dupuch, editor of the *Nassau Tribune*, who took "5,000 or 6,000 pounds a year" for two years "to assist us with our public image," which "locally has always been poor." Gonsalves also testified that former Bahamian Premier Sir Roland Symonette had a road-building contract with one Groves company that paid him over $16,000 a year. Symonette's son, a jet-setter named Bobby whose yachting prowess got him on the cover of an issue of *Sports Illustrated*, was hired by Groves to act as adviser on marina construction at $14,000 a year.

The big man behind the men on the islands, however, was Minister of Finance and Tourism Sir Stafford Sands, the highest paid lawyer in the playground of pirates. Sands will deny it, but testimony indicates that his fees for guiding Groves through choppy legal waters over the years may run well over $1 million, so it was not surprising that Sir Stafford was said to be "ill in Spain" when the commission of inquiry first met in the Bahamas in May, 1967, and did not make an appearance.

When Gonsalves was asked by the commission about a $500,000 check reportedly given to Sir Stafford in April, 1964, the witness said it was an "omnibus fee," related to "obtaining an exemption certificate [to operate gambling casinos in Freeport] from the government." Gonsalves said the size of the check "didn't stagger me" and added that Sir Stafford performed many duties for Bahamas Amusements.

An additional $50,000 a year, for ten years, was promised to Sands, Gonsalves testified, for advice in "advertising, publicity and promoting all phases of the development company." In addition, Gonsalves listed "political contributions" by the Groves group to the United Bahamian party totaling $320,000, which were said to have been funneled through Stafford Sands as legal fees.

Thanks to the absence of a conflict-of-interest law in the Bahamian government, Sir Stafford and some of his other Bay Street Boys had functioned for years both as legislators and private lawyers, a combination that has enabled them to accumulate and manipulate considerable power and wealth.

Apparently 1964 had been a very busy year for all concerned. According to the *Wall Street Journal* of October 19, 1966, Lou Chesler "resigned" in May, 1964, because he and Groves "didn't see eye to eye." "There was a lot of emotion built up," Chesler stated. "It got to the point that I wanted out."

"Groves hates inefficiency," said one person who had worked in the organization, belittling Chesler's administrative abilities. "So he made it clear to Lou he'd have to go."

The exact circumstances of the split are somewhat clouded, but in the obvious clash of personalities Chesler was apparently the one to yield and allow himself to be bought out. And he did it at a time when the development company was apparently becoming financially shaky and the ownership of the Lucayan Beach Hotel was undergoing some complicated legal shenanigans—the understanding of which would take a battery of Philadelphia lawyers.

The hotel itself, a separate entity from the Monte Carlo room casino within its walls, has run in the red almost since its opening. Officially, this is the result of overstaffing and poor management; unofficially, of the usual "tax write-off" or "robbing Peter to pay Paul" reasons. At any rate, while being subsidized to the tune of $500,000 yearly from the Monte Carlo room, which is raking in the money hand over fist, the hotel has gone from Chesler's sponsorship through the hands of another Canadian entrepreneur into the control of a Canadian holding company that had numerous other investments in Freeport but defaulted on $104 million in debts in June, 1965, declaring bankruptcy and causing what was called an "international financial scandal." The hotel then went into receivership.

The story goes on and on. But it is enough to say that Louis Chesler played his part well, spent his, or somebody's, $12 million, and left his mark on Grand Bahama. He brought money, his "good name," and—despite the protestations of a Seven Arts publicist who said, in defense of his company's $5-million investment in Chesler's Bahama interests, that jurisdiction over the gambling licenses there had been given to Bahamas Amusements, Ltd.: "to make sure no improper elements infiltrated the operations of the exclusive gambling licenses"—the syndicate to the island.

The first competitive challenge to the Groves-Chesler-Lansky triumvirate came in 1963 from grocery-chain, model-agency, theater-arts magnate Huntington (Hunt) Hartford, who tried to fire a legal torpedo from his own little domain a few miles away across the blue sea at the Freeport empire a-building.

Hartford had control of a smaller island a short sail from Freeport on Grand Bahama Island, and just across the harbor from the Bahamian capital of Nassau. Hartford's island is listed on navigation charts as Hog Island, but, as a step to converting it into a tourist paradise, Hunt renamed his floating platter of earth Paradise Island. Between 1959 and 1963 Hartford said he poured $25 million into Hog, trying to change it into a silk purse, and originally he protested the introduction of any form of gambling to the Bahamas.

Hartford apparently assumed he had the right to speak for the islands, and he still had a substantial part of the A & P fortune to back him up. But he must have reckoned without the ABC's of modern economics, especially since his attempt to buck both the gambling-eating-sunning-carousing splendor of Las Vegas and other tourist traps and the rapidly developing Grand Bahama Island right in his own back yard was made from an off-the-track island: Paradise.

Finding that a marina, hotel rooms, golf course, and continental restaurant weren't enough of a lure to tourists, Hartford made an about-face in 1963 and said he would like to put a gaming casino on Paradise Island and build a bridge to get the tourists across the bay from Nassau. In a press release issued at the time, making a public plea for the issuance of a gambling license, Hartford declared that he thought it would be of benefit to the natives on Paradise Island because

> babies are occasionally being born blind, and worms and amoebic dysentery and tuberculosis are prevalent due to poor sanitation and

> overcrowding. If gambling would be permitted on Paradise, it goes without saying that there will be employment for thousands and I trust that my past record in giving employment will confirm the responsibility of my statement.

Hartford's seemingly good intentions, however, came to naught, for neither the gambling license nor the bridge-building permit could be secured. It appears that Hunt had failed to hire the able Sir Stafford Sands as his lawyer and, to add insult to injury, had even contributed $15,000 to the opposing political party: the largely Negro Progressive Liberal party, which scored heavily in the January, 1967, elections and gave the islands their first black premier.

The A & P heir eventually decided to bail out, and, in a flash, a buyer showed up for the former Hog Island. Hartford announced in January, 1966, that for $3 million in cash, the assumption of a $9-million mortgage by the buyer, and the retention of a 25 per cent interest in the entire operation (to include the building of a five-hundred-room hotel with casino), he had sold Paradise Island and its facilities to the Mary Carter Paint Company.

Since 1962 the Mary Carter Paint Company, a Delaware corporation recorded in October, 1958, with headquarters in Tampa, Florida, had been exceedingly active in swallowing up businesses, increasing her paper assets, and assuaging her thirst in various ways in the Caribbean. There were, by 1964, some one thousand Mary Carter dealer and company paint stores spread throughout much of the United States and in Puerto Rico and the British West Indies. A subsidiary operated National Biff-Burger System (drive-in restaurant) franchises together with a manufacturing plant that produced everything needed to operate one of the drive-ins, including the portable building-units themselves. Another subsidiary, Bahamas Developers, in 1963 acquired some thirty-five hundred acres of land within the Groves domain on Grand Bahama Island, part of which was developed in 1965 into a residential community called Queens Cove.

In 1966, therefore, when Mary Carter—she doesn't really exist, but it's a good feminine handle on which to hang one's company hat—made her deal with Huntington Hartford, she was no virgin in island commerce and already had a more-than-platonic interest in her future playmates. Shortly after Mary disposed of Hunt, she proceeded to make a marriage of financial convenience with the Groves group in order to accomplish something that Hartford had been unable to do: secure permission for gaming on Paradise Island. The Mary Carter Paint Company was able, through the representations of none other than Sir Stafford himself, to purchase for $750,000 the certificate of exemption covering the Bahamian Club, a conservative gaming parlor in Nassau owned by Groves's interests.

The agreement, according to *Life* magazine of February 3, 1967, called for the Bahamian Club permit to be transferred to the Paradise Island casino when it opened on condition that Mary Carter relinquish a reported four-ninths of the casino's profit as well as management of the entire casino to Wallace Groves's Bahamas Amusements, Ltd. Lansky and his crew, who were at the time managing the Bahamian Club for Groves as well as the Monte Carlo room on Grand Bahama Island, were slated to run the Paradise Island casino when the change of ownership was made, for a flat 15 per cent of the gross gaming profits.

In reporting the details of the arrangement to her jet-set readers, syndicated gossip columnist Suzy spoke of "nice fresh money" being brought in by Hartford's new partners to alleviate the $50,000 monthly losses he had been suffering. "That's expected to stop," she surmised, "because the new group has acquired the gambling permit once owned by Nassau's Bahamian Club. Now they can play with the big boys." How right she was!

Since then, Mary Carter's Paradise Island has joined hands with Nassau on New Providence Island via a $2-million toll bridge. It seems that, miraculously, Mary Carter was also able to get the bridge-building permit denied Hartford in 1963. The new $15-million Paradise Island hotel and casino was opened in January, 1968, in typical gala fashion. Columnist Earl Wilson reported that Lady Astor, Lady Sassoon, Carol Channing, Serge Obolensky, and Huntington Hartford—apparently still comfortably ensconced within his 25 per cent retained interest in what Wilson called the "Paradise Island, Ltd., Complex"—together with others of the jet set, made quite a night of it.

"It's all run by James M. Crosby, head of the Mary Carter Paint Co.," Earl reported, "and they tell me there never was any Mary Carter but this paint company thought it sounded like a sweet name."

Business on Paradise Island has been booming ever since, and plans are going ahead for the building of houses, apartments, a shopping center, and more hotels. Consequently, it is interesting to note that the Paradise Island casino is managed by none other than the brother of the ousted Dino Cellini, Eddie.

Dino Cellini, moreover, although out of sight is anything but out of action. After he was ousted from the Bahamas in 1964, he ran a school in London to train European croupiers for work in the Bahamian casinos. Then, when the British got wise and banned him at the same time as they gave George Raft his walking papers, Cellini returned to Miami to become a highly successful organizer and promoter of international gambling junkets—affairs involving the bringing in of planeloads of "high-rollers" to a hotel-casino, to be lavishly coddled, catered-to, entertained, and deprived of their money.

According to Keith Gonsalves' testimony before the Royal Commission of Inquiry, two-thirds of the Bahamas' casino profits come from junkets, each of which reportedly costs the casino operators about $50,000. It is therefore not too difficult to picture the brothers Cellini working hand-in-hand, "doing their thing" for the mob.

At any rate, it now would appear to be a toss-up between Groves, Lansky, Mary Carter, and the local Bahamian government—officially represented by its newly elected premier, thirty-eight-year-old Lynden O. Pindling, whose vociferous campaign against allowing the Bahamas to become a "lucrative center of international crime" had resulted in the royal commission—as to just who will roll the vital seven that loses the game and shifts the dice to the next man at the table.

Groves lives in a blue-green tile palace valued at $1 million; Lansky lives in a modest $25,000 house near Hollywood, Florida; and Mary Carter's J. M. Crosby is rather comfortably situated—when not in Paradise—in Great Neck, Long Island, where, cozily enough, Lou Chesler also maintains equally elegant lodgings. The question at the moment is what kind of residence Pindling is planning for himself.

Pindling's drawing boards are currently covered with designs for a new approach to the gambling free-for-all—for Groves and friends, that is—espoused by the former Bahamian administration. The new approach is somewhat obscure, however, because the Nassau-born, London-educated Pindling plans to reject the royal commission's ruling barring Americans from casino employment on the ground that "some taint" seems to cover anyone connected with organized gambling in the United States, even persons with no criminal records.

According to Pindling's enemies, his Progressive Liberal party has accepted money from syndicate sources; in fact, they say that the party must have received payments because gamblers always insure their bets. But Pindling is not alarmed at the reports or criticism, nor does he seem to have to be. Apparently, his philosophy is: if you're going to have a gambling casino, you need gamblers to run it. The skilled labor needed for such an enterprise will therefore stay.

Pindling has, however, stated that there will be no more certificates of exemption granted for new casinos—which eliminates the competition, at least—and that he will honor a previous law prohibiting Bahamian residents from playing the games. New schools and housing tracts are planned for the impoverished native residents, but Pindling is apparently moving toward ghetto-style living for his people—Negroes represent 80–85 per cent of the Bahamian population—through his efforts to keep the gambling environment off-limits to the local black electorate.

Appeasement, in the form of a flat $500,000 fee charged annually against each casino and increased taxes on a graduated scale for all revenues above $5 million, has done little to demonstrate that things will be easier for the locals. The cost of living has gone sky-high, and the Bahamian chamber of commerce has warned that a family of three needs about $10,000 a year to live reasonably, an altogether impossible prospect for the people who voted Pindling into office.

Regardless of politics and the changing of the guard, it would appear that the syndicate holds most of the gaming aces in the Bahamas. After his election Pindling, who demands the islands' eventual freedom from Britain, apparently not only changed his mind about the facts of gambling life and related aspects of international crime but also showed up in full dress at the January, 1968, opening of the Paradise Island hotel and casino with a big welcome for the guests. He danced a wild rumba with actress Janet Leigh and reportedly kept asking orchestra leader Meyer Davis for more of the same. It seems that Pindling, too, is "playing with the big boys," and it remains to be seen just who is hustling whom.

There are hundreds of sunny islands in the warm sea around

the Bahamas, and it could be that Lansky and his cohorts may one day spread themselves too thinly. The key point, perhaps, is just how far his associates in the States will let him go. A big head is an easy target, and the Mafia is not quite as racially integrated as it may seem. Meyer Lansky is still the kid on the corner who shines the shoes of the boys in the Sicilian brotherhood. They know without question that he handles the shinola with a dexterity second to none and that he takes a goodly cut for his services, but they aren't likely to let him climb to the top of the stool himself and pretend he's really one of them.

The Bahamas, however, do not stand as the only gemstones in the Caribbean crown of the syndicate; there are other diamonds in the rough operated by the slick-suited professional gamblers. To the south are numerous other islands, stretching down to Aruba in the Dutch Antilles, where the Mafia boys have decided to settle.

In Port-au-Prince, Haiti, the depression-ridden voodoo capital of the Caribbean, a gaming casino has been established by Mafia hoodlums. Run by the Canadian branch of the syndicate and controlled locally, according to U.S. Immigration Department files, by the Volpe brothers, Paul, Albert, and Eugene, the Carib-Haiti was established with the help of Haitian dictator François (Papa Doc) Duvalier.

Also connected with the Volpe operation in Haiti is John Pasquale Tronolone, alias "Salvatore Tronolone," also known as "John Rich," and intimately known to his Mafia colleagues as "Peanuts." Tronolone is known to have represented Mafia chieftain Frank Costello's interests in Las Vegas. Some of his more odious associates, in addition to Costello and the Volpes, have been syndicate hearties Joe Massei, John and George Angersola, Joseph DiCarlo, Fred Felice, and Frank Caruso.

Wherever you pry the lid off a Caribbean vacationland nowadays—with the possible exception of Puerto Rico, where government-run gaming casinos are in the experimental stage—you generally find that if there are casinos, the cashiers of the mob are in charge. An even more disturbing fact, however, is—as the next chapter shows—that Caribbean gambling is not just a syndicate operation. Representatives of the U.S. government, union officials, executives of American financial institutions, as well as Las Vegas gambling operators—all have set out on their own treasure hunt for the buried gold of the Spanish Main.

8

THE CARIBBEAN:

Las Vegas Sharks

Take Eddie Levinson, one of the country's top gambling entrepreneurs from Las Vegas and "leg man" for Joseph (Doc) Stacher, elder in the Jewish Mafia. Add Sam Giancana, Chicago underworld chief until recently, Cliff Jones, former Lieutenant-Governor of Nevada, and Bobby Baker, onetime handmaiden of the U.S. Senate. Stir them all together in the Caribbean. What you come up with is something less than a fragrant bouillabaisse, but it is somewhat fishy: a sort of Alliance for Progress syndicate-style.

Ed Levinson's involvement in the Caribbean first came to light in 1957, with the accidental discovery of two of his canceled checks made out to a casino in Havana totaling $50,000.

Bryant R. Burton, the Beverly Hills attorney then listed as secretary of Levinson's Fremont Hotel Corporation in Las Vegas and long a legal front man for Stacher, is usually an extremely cautious man. He always exercised great care in the protection of the private records of the hotel and the boys connected with it. But in November, 1957, he slipped up. As he boarded a plane at McCarran Field, port of entry and exit for the starry-eyed tourists who keep Las Vegas operational, he left behind a bulging briefcase.

Officials of the airport opened the briefcase in an effort to establish ownership, but what they found sent them scurrying to the FBI. Mob faith in the airport hierarchy began deteriorating from that point on. Among the more interesting items the investigators dug out of the leather case was a bank statement of Ed Levinson showing that he had a current cash balance of $24,582.33 in a local bank, but they also found several canceled checks recently written on the account, three of which were rather sizable. One for $350,000 was payable to the First National Bank of Nevada;

the other two totaled $50,000 and were payable to Compañía de Hoteles La Riverside de Cuba. All three checks were dated October 18, 1957.

Levinson remained calm when the find was announced. After all, it wasn't his fault. But Stacher chewed out everybody until the briefcase was returned to Burton. Whatever significance the FBI attributed to the findings was officially filed away, but it was apparent to those in the know—in Las Vegas and Havana—that the $50,000 represented Levinson's (Stacher's) share of expense money for the newly established Cuban hotel-casino.

The Stacher-Levinson relationship began in Las Vegas years earlier and resulted in Ed Levinson's becoming top dog in the multi-storied Fremont Hotel and casino in downtown Las Vegas. Levinson, in fact, had come a long way along the many-dimensional road of crime. From his birthplace in Detroit, he traveled to Las Vegas via the twin cities of corruption, Covington and Newport, Kentucky, and Miami, which he left after Kefauver's rousting of illegal gambling. Levinson finally arrived in Las Vegas in 1952 as part-owner of the Sands Hotel—a Stacher interest and the shrine of one of Frank Sinatra's best efforts to maintain status among gambling *aficionados* until he relinquished his 9 per cent "piece" after a hassle with Nevada gaming control officials over his close friendship with Sam Giancana.

Levinson's record of some forty years of hustling his way up through the world of illegal gambling already showed five arrests, four dismissals, and one $1,500 fine. But he had a wife and family, including a couple of grandchildren he adored, and apparently couldn't do anything about his own future. The mob had locked him in.

By 1955, Levinson had acquired interests in the Flamingo and Dunes Hotels but was ready to give them all up for his coming involvement—a 20 per cent interest in Doc Stacher's Fremont Hotel, which was built with the help of substantial Teamster loans.

Joseph Stacher is a former New Jersey gangster whose charmed life transcends all common concepts held by the public and even by law-enforcement officials about just how long a man in the business of giving the business to the law can survive. Little known, Stacher nevertheless has been in and out of trouble throughout his life and has more aliases than J. Edgar Hoover has enemies.

His police record, however, is scattered, its availability depending on where he has been able to have it expunged. But pick just one alias—such as "Joseph Rosen," the name under which he is listed in Newark, New Jersey—and in the six years between November, 1924, and November, 1930, you find ten arrests for breaking and entering, larceny, atrocious assault and battery, robbery, and interfering with an officer guarding a still for the federal government. Stacher's consistency in being arrested in those days was matched only by his consistency in securing a dismissal—or at least in avoiding a disposition. In nine of the above arrests he secured a dismissal; the only disposition was a $50 fine.

Using the same alias in New York City in 1931, Stacher, who put together the Jewish Mafia at about the time people were beginning to accept that the syndicate was a fact, was rousted from a hotel room in the company of eight other mobsters, including Bugsy Siegel, Louis Buchalter, and Harry (Big Greenie) Greenberg, who was murdered in Los Angeles eight years later. In fact, of the eight men in the room that day, Stacher is the only one still living, having survived the men who helped him along the way in his early days in New York.

Doc Stacher came to this country from Russia in 1912. As a youngster he shined shoes, sold newspapers, and peddled fruit from a pushcart. Settling in Newark, he met Longy Zwillman, New Jersey syndicate chief for many years, and was introduced by him to such men as Willie Moretti, who was murdered in a Palisades, New Jersey, tavern in 1951, and Jerry Catena, both of whom became Mafia leaders in New Jersey.

Stacher has what might be called a certain mystique. Certainly he has something that keeps him immune from punishment and was no doubt instrumental in his being left a criminal heritage by Zwillman, who was New Jersey's version of underworld Prime Minister Frank Costello. In 1965 Stacher left for Israel—because he chose to be deported rather than to serve a jail term for income-tax evasion imposed by a federal judge—where, apparently, he passed part of his heritage along to Jerry Catena, who was named in 1966 by the *Chicago Sun-Times* as a secret part-owner of the new Caesar's Palace in Las Vegas.

The Levinson-Stacher interest in the Hoodlum Sea was revealed at a time when the dope-smuggling activities of the Florida Mafia were being conducted through Cuba with the help of corrupt government officials operating with a free hand under Batista. Castro's subsequent take-over in 1959 resulted in the exclusion of syndicate gambling. However, New York City narcotics agents seized more Cuban cocaine in the fall of 1962 than in the entire year of 1961, which indicates that Cuba's liberator has increasingly had to fall back on the old system to raise money and is, through the well-used pipelines to Tampa and the Trafficante mob, reaping a harvest other than sugar cane.

It is interesting to note, moreover, that Cuban narcotics smugglers, within the framework of the Cuban Navy and the fishing fleet, have also been using Cozumel and the Isle of Mujers as smuggling bases. These Mexican islands, off the east coast of the Yucatan peninsula, are becoming popular American tourist areas. In 1965 native hotel proprietors on the islands complained to the Mexican government that Cuban seamen were insulting and beating up U.S. tourists, but all indications are that their protest was quietly filed away in Mexico City.

Whatever the current developments, Levinson had staked his claim in Havana with his $50,000 and probably much more, and after Castro's housecleaning apparently thought he still had squatter's rights in the Caribbean. He joined the other displaced gamblers and their Mafia associates—some of whom reestablished themselves in the Bahamas—who were soon to turn their Cuban failure into a monstrous success. And the monster is still growing.

The mob is firmly entrenched in the vast sweep of Caribbean islands and intends to stay there, using the time-tested techniques of bribery, graft, intrigue, and unkept promises. The boys make friends and promote goodwill among the local governments, whose island economies are in the developmental stage, by corrupting businessmen, lawyers, and politicians through the promise of wealth more easily acquired than through the dubious potential of milking U.S. development loans.

Part of the syndicate Caribbean money structure is represented by the Bank of World Commerce, Ltd., which was incorporated in 1961 under British law in Nassau, Bahamas, where, as has been pointed out, taxes are no problem. Ed Levinson and Nevada's Cliff Jones were listed as stockholders. Tied into the whole structure was an outfit known in 1961 as Allied Empire, Inc., formerly Allied Television Films, Inc., of Beverly Hills, California. At that time Allied Empire was listed as a corporate stockholder with ten thousand shares of Bank of World Commerce stock, and was the holding company for the bank. In 1964 Allied changed its name to Riverside Financial and moved its offices to Riverside, California.

The financial structure had myriad connections. For example, Jimmy Hoffa, through Allied Empire investments, and a score of Las Vegas gamblers and politicians were involved in the setup through Anjon Savings and Loan, Account Number 804, and Merritt Savings and Loan of Baltimore, Maryland, which was bought out by Anjon Account Number 804. By means of a bewildering network of American and British corporate laws, Account Number 804's list of depositor-stockholders (the complete list of names can be found in the Epilogue) includes not only the Bank of World Commerce—$23,000—but also a number of Las Vegans. And when all the records are put together, we find that the names of a number of individuals involved show up again and again in the complex web of gambling operations in various places on the North American continent—inland and offshore—and form compass points with which patient investigators are attempting to chart a course to the truth, and the enormity, of the operation.

Take, for instance, the persons holding office and stock in the Bank of World Commerce at the time of its inception. Corporate papers filed in Nassau listed the following officers: John Pullman, president and director; Edward Dawson Roberts, vice-president and director; Gerald Nelson Capps, secretary and treasurer; N. Roberts, director; Alvin I. Malnic, director; and Philip J. Mathew, director. In addition, stockholders and the number of shares indicating their initial investment were listed as follows—each share representing £1 British, or, at that time, $2.80 American:

Stockholders	*Shares*
Edward Dawson Roberts	1
Margaret Elizabeth Roberts	1
Alexander Pericles Maillis	1
Margaret Rose Malone	1
Gerald Nelson Capps	1
Philip J. Mathew	82,500
Thomas A. Shaneen, Jr.	30,000
James H. Adams	10,000
Joseph Fendel	10,000
Henderson, Holton & Company	5,000

Elwood Linde	5,000
Kenneth D. Mann	5,000
Harvey Glen Leason	5,000
Charles L. Holton	10,000
Sydney V. Levy	10,000
Leon C. Bloom, Jr.	10,000
Philip Nasser	11,786
Mr. and Mrs. Irving J. Leff	10,000
Clifford A. Jones	20,000
John Pullman	2,000
Irving Devine	1,000
Edward Levinson	1,000
Alvin I. Malnic	1,500
Aaron Magidow	11,800
Allied Empire, Inc.	10,000

On September 8, 1967, two of the individuals involved with the Bank of World Commerce and Anjon Savings and Loan, Account Number 804, were named by *Life* as "bagmen" for Meyer Lansky in the syndicate's far-flung gambling kingdom. A third, an alleged "bagwoman," is the wife of one of the Bank of World Commerce stockholders. Cash was carried by these people and others, the article stated, via the Bank of World Commerce into the financial arteries of an organization in the Bahamas known as the Atlas Bank, a working subsidiary of yet another financial institution, the International Credit Bank in Switzerland. All three of the boards of directors and staffs of these money entities were what *Life* described as "studded with both skimmers and couriers" for the mob.

Among the bagmen listed was Ben Sigelbaum (Seigelbaum), sixty-five years old, political adviser and a long-time associate of Ed Levinson in many of his business endeavors. Sigelbaum was also a business associate and confidant of Bobby Baker when the latter was secretary of the Democratic Majority in the U.S. Senate. Also named was John Pullman, sixty-seven years old, original president of the Bank of World Commerce who once served a prison term for violating U.S. liquor laws and gave up his American citizenship in 1954 to become a Canadian. He now lives in Switzerland. Another alleged bagman was Sylvain Ferdmann, a thirty-three-year-old Swiss citizen described as an international banker and economist and, by U.S. authorities, as a fugitive accused of interfering with federal inquiries into the skimming racket in Las Vegas and elsewhere. In addition, *Life* charged, Ferdmann was once approached by Teamster boss Jimmy Hoffa to raise money for union officials' surety bonds.

Ida Devine, wife of Las Vegas gambler Irving (Niggy) Devine, supposedly traveled with Sigelbaum from Las Vegas to Miami with skimmed money for Lansky; Ferdmann is said to have carried the skim from the Bahamas to Lansky; and Lansky supposedly counted the money in Miami, took his own cut, and dispensed other sums, via different couriers, to a few syndicate chieftains in the United States. At that point, the story went on, Ferdmann and Pullman carried the remainder of the funds to the International Credit Bank in Switzerland and deposited them in numbered accounts in the Swiss haven for secret-money banking.

The most mysterious part in the whole affair seems to have been enacted by Ferdmann, who organized the Atlas Bank as the Bahamas subsidiary of the International Credit Bank. *Life* contended that Ferdmann's contacts in this country included members of the Communist party in New York and functionaries of the Czech delegation to the United Nations. Probers are said to have drawn conclusions that the International Credit Bank enjoys strong ties with communist countries and that there was a flow of communist money coming to this country through the Ferdmann conduit. At least, his money bags seemed to be as full each time he returned to the United States as when he left.

Ferdmann made one blunder, on March 19, 1965, when he dropped a piece of paper from one of his pockets while loading satchels into an auto at the Miami airport. A parking attendant turned it over to authorities, who identified it as a letterhead of the International Credit Bank. The memo beneath the letterhead read as follows:

> This is to acknowledge this 28th day of December, 1964, the receipt of Three Hundred and Fifty Thousand ($350,000) Dollars, in American bank notes for deposit to the account of Maral 2812 with the International Credit Bank, Geneva, the said sum being turned over to me in the presence of the named signed below.

Life states that John Pullman was listed as a witness on the note and that the cautious Ferdmann had added the following postscript: "The above is subject to the notes being genuine American banknotes." Thus, here was a document not only proving the receipt of the syndicate's skimmed money by a Swiss bank but also identifying the account number under which it was deposited.

To sum up, it appears that the Hoodlum Sea is at present split into two areas of money-making syndicate endeavor tied into the mainstream by Meyer Lansky: the northern regions, which reach into the blue waters of the Atlantic, where the Groves enterprises hold forth in the Bahamas; and the islands to the south, which fall under the domain of Stacher, Levinson, Cliff Jones, and their associates.

In 1962 an attempt was made by another branch of the Mafia to "muscle" in on the Caribbean domain of the Trafficante-Lansky combine. Chicago's chief Mafioso, Sam Giancana, who was last reported looking after the shop from faraway Argentina, had watched Albert Anastasia's attempt to carve out some of the Caribbean for himself with great interest. Undoubtedly he thought that he would be more successful than the murdered head of Murder, Inc., and therefore, despite weak protests from the Florida branch of Cosa Nostra, which considered the Caribbean its private preserve in spite of the infiltration from Las Vegas, Sam and his associates began making overtures to government officials in the tropical islands.

Giancana first arranged to meet a top man from Dominica in a neutral area—France—to discuss gaming potential, but the FBI scotched the meeting by tailing Sam on an around-the-clock basis. Sam then invited a member of the Jamaican government to Chicago for discussions regarding gambling on Jamaica. An emissary, displaying an abundance of greed, perhaps, but a great lack of wisdom, flew to the Windy City to confer with Giancana. But since the Chicago boys demanded 70 per cent of the Jamaican take, the good people whose home is in the midst of the Hoodlum Sea decided instead to limit their tourist attractions to horse racing, steel drums, calypso singing, and tall rum and Cokes.

However, although Giancana was not wanted in the Caribbean, the syndicate members already entrenched were not averse to calling on people for help. Among those who contributed their talent to syndicate efforts in the Hoodlum Sea was Bobby Baker, the country boy from Pickens, South Carolina, who started as page boy in the Senate and ended as secretary to the Democratic Senate Majority. In his sixteen years in the Senate, Baker became an influence peddler par excellence, the most successful—while the going was good—since the days of Albert Fall, U.S. Secretary of the Interior under President Harding. Fall, who secretly peddled oil-rich lands at Teapot Dome in Montana to the highest bidder, was a piker compared to Bobby. Fall put his fist into only one honey pot before his exposure and downfall; Bobby was grubbing into many enterprises with both hands when he was finally caught. Baker was found guilty on January 29, 1967, on seven counts of tax evasion, larceny, and conspiracy and sentenced to serve one to three years in prison, but he is at present free on bail pending appeal. Among other things Baker was charged with stealing at least $80,000 from a fund totaling $99,600 that represented payment from some savings and loan companies in California, presumably to be used to influence Senate legislation to give tax benefits to savings and loan organizations.

The syndicate boys may have made a mistake when they chose Baker to help them in an attempt to strengthen their power structure in the Caribbean, but it could be called an "honest" mistake inasmuch as they couldn't have foreseen that he was headed for a fall. And Bobby was a persuasive man. He had a habit of running off at the mouth and dropping the names of important people he claimed could—and they often did—help him in his various moonlighting business deals, and he could produce glowing testimonials.

Senator Alan Bible (D., Nev.), for instance, coyly referred to Bobby as "Lyndon, Jr.," and Lyndon Baines Johnson, who was Senate Majority leader at the time, proudly claimed that Baker was his protégé: "One of my trusted friends, and a man who will go far." He was so right.

Baker took time out from his busy schedule in April, 1963, to charter a plane of Riddle Airlines to fly a group of eighty Washington lobbyists and congressional employees to Las Vegas to attend a $100-a-plate dinner at the Flamingo Hotel in honor of Senator Howard Cannon of Nevada. Later that summer Riddle Airlines, in what seemed to be an afterthought, billed Baker, but he made no payment. In January, 1964, after a Civil Aeronautics Board investigation, the airline offered to pay $750 as a compromise fine for failing to charge, and press collection of, scheduled fares—a violation of the Federal Aviation Act. The $750 was accepted by the

CAB after Riddle's veteran airline officials claimed a "misunderstanding" of CAB rules.

Two months after his Vegas charter junket, Bobby Baker began to concern himself with a chain of resort hotels that had three casino operations in the Caribbean. Bobby's interest had to do with the possibility of moving one or two friends in on two of those operations—and perhaps himself, as well, for later investigations showed that he had a habit of "taking his cut" when profitable business deals were made for buddies. He aimed his influence, and the know-how of his syndicate friends, at Intercontinental Hotels Corporation, which is a 100-per-cent-owned subsidiary of Pan American World Airways. Intercontinental operates twenty-three hotels in nineteen foreign countries, three of them resort hotels with carpet-joint gaming casinos located in Curaçao, the capital of the Dutch Antilles, Santo Domingo, in the Dominican Republic, and San Juan, Puerto Rico.

Incidentally, Puerto Rico has nine casinos in San Juan and five others throughout the island, all located in major hotels. The gaming is strictly regulated by government control, which includes security checks for all personnel, casino licensing by the economic development administration, and low bet limits. The government philosophy is, according to the head of its tourism department: "Gambling must only be another attraction for tourists and not a main reason for their coming."

The movement of Pan Am into the gaming business through its hotel chain was outlined to the Senate committee investigating Bobby Baker in 1964 by John Gates, chairman of the board of Intercontinental Hotels. For competitive reasons, Gates maintained, his company had to have casinos in the three Caribbean hotels as an attraction for tourists—the same people, of course, that Pan Am conveniently dropped into the lap of the tourist-hungry Caribbean community. The inference was that tourists—the "right" types, that is—just would not be enticed unless there was a crap table handy as a pleasant change from water skiing, skin diving, sunbathing, and the other usual approaches to fun in the sun.

Gates went on to explain that Intercontinental had no wish to operate the gambling casinos itself and that, while it was forced by law to do so in Puerto Rico as the owner of the hotel, the casinos in Curaçao and Santo Domingo were treated as concessions and let out to "acceptable" gamblers.

Pan Am was gearing to bring in thousands upon thousands of tourists and "grinds" a year to the Caribbean playground, and the responsibility apparently fell to Gates to help find the knowledgeable—yet acceptable—syndicate men who could handle the elite, "high-roller" clientele they hoped would be included among those seeking to lose their money with little effort.

What obviously was needed were men with years of experience in dealing with the credit end of gambling together with the knowledge of how to collect the "lost" money afterward. But such "inside" knowledge was manifest only in the experience of the men of the syndicate who meet and memorize a thousand faces and bank accounts every week.

For Bobby Baker, apparently, with his influence on Capitol Hill and important contacts throughout the Caribbean, the situation was fraught with wealth. He saw an unbeatable opportunity to squeeze himself into a big-time operation and wheeled his motive out into the open for all to see in the summer of 1963.

On June 20, the "101st Senator"—a title Washington newsmen often used when referring to Baker—appeared in the New York office of John Gates with an associate. The appointment had been arranged, at Baker's request, by Samuel Pryor, a Pan Am vice-president. Baker's associate that day was introduced to Gates as Ed Levinson, owner of the Fremont Hotel in Las Vegas, and John Gates was asked about the possibility of Levinson's becoming associated with either the Santo Domingo or the Curaçao gambling concession.

Gates, who had not previously met either of the men, asked Baker if he was interested for himself, or for both himself and Levinson, or what. Bobby quickly explained that he himself had no interest in the concessions. Levinson was his friend and client, and he was merely trying to pave the way for him as a favor. This was no more than the truth. Levinson, along with Ben Sigelbaum and others, had made substantial and complicated investments in various Baker enterprises, including stock shares in the District of Columbia National Bank and the Serv-U Corporation, entities that figured prominently in the Baker investigation.

Gates accepted Bobby's explanation, apparently unconcerned with a most unusual situation in which the Majority secretary of the U.S. Senate was openly representing a major gambling figure in a request for interests in two rather small casinos, and at the time when, in the words of Wallace Turner in *Gamblers' Money*, agents of the executive branch of the U.S. government "were watching Levinson's every movement and checking carefully on all his financial transactions." But, then, as Turner concludes: "The flood of money that powers the gambling empire in Las Vegas creates many ironies of this sort."

Levinson himself, a squat man with a strong jaw and heavily-lidded eyes, slow-moving except when Doc Stacher or one of his hirelings is on the other end of the wire, is supposed to have said little in Gates's office, evidently satisfied with Bobby's representations. At any rate, Gates explained that the existing lease on the Curaçao gaming concession would soon expire and that other potential bids were already under consideration for it—including one from Cliff Jones and his partner, Jake Kozloff, whose Caribbean American Investment Company, Inc., already had four small casinos in the Caribbean.

Ed Levinson assured Gates that the Jones-Kozloff bid created no problems by saying, "We're all very close," and indicating that they could all work together. As it turned out, Jones and Levinson were a great deal closer than Gates realized, and Bobby Baker must have known it from his previous relationships with the two gamblers. The meeting ended with Gates's agreeing to write the Curaçao hotel owners about another possible bidder on the casino lease, since the owners were responsible for letting out the concession.

A second meeting was held a month later, with Bobby Baker present, during which Gates told Levinson that if his brother, Sleep-out Louie, were involved, their bid could not be considered. At a third meeting, also in August, 1963, and again arranged by "Baker's office" but unattended by him, Levinson showed up in Gates's office with Jones and Kozloff in tow. According to Gates's testimony to the Senate committee, Levinson told Gates that he was dropping out of the picture but that Jones and Kozloff were prepared to submit their bid.

Oddly enough, the letter written by John Gates to the Curaçao hotel owners on August 13, the day after the above meeting, stated: "Messrs. Jones, Kozloff and Levinson called on me yesterday in regard to the casino contract. They are going to present a joint bid." The actual bid submitted to the Curaçao hotel board for its September meeting and decision was signed only by Jake Kozloff and Clifford Jones for the Caribbean American Investment Company, Inc., probably for the very good reason that Levinson, under a Nevada law passed in 1958—of which, one suspects, Mr. Gates must have been aware—would have had to give up his Nevada gaming license if he officially went into the gaming business in any other part of the world. Nevada claims its own with the fervor of a mother elephant, and Levinson was obviously not about to relinquish his 20 per cent interest in the Fremont Hotel setup or an additional reported 27 per cent interest in another downtown casino, the Horseshoe Club. But Jones and Kozloff, having officially divested themselves of any gaming interests in Las Vegas, were in the clear.

On September 12, after perusing the two bids submitted to the Curaçao hotel owners, Gates wrote them that the Jones-Kozloff bid would seem to be preferable "from a strictly objective, business point of view," in that it "provides a more favorable guaranty and the quality of their entertainment is well known." Gates went on:

> Apparently there is some problem about Jones and Kozloff insofar as the Government of Curaçao is concerned, and they may have compelling reasons for preferring Sweet [the former casino operator who was also bidding] but I am in no position to judge or evaluate the reasons since I do not know what they are.

In a postscript Gates added: "I have made inquiry in the United States regarding Jones and Kozloff because we have asked them to make a bid on our casino in Santo Domingo. Everyone I have contacted gives them a clean bill of health."

One of Gates's inquiries was directed at John Scarne, "gambling detective," so-called nemesis of crooked gamblers and staunch defender of Las Vegas gaming. Scarne replied that Levinson ran honest gambling. Scarne's concern apparently is only that the tourists get a fair shake. The government's share is of no interest to him, it seems: in 1968 Levinson pleaded no contest to charges of skimming in that eventful year of 1963.

On November 7, 1963, another letter was written by Gates to the Curaçao hotel owners, and he enclosed articles from New York papers regarding the Bobby Baker case, which was beginning to receive a good deal of public attention. With references to Ed Levinson's probable involvement with Baker, Gates said:

> As for Levinson, you will note that Jones is quoted as saying [in the articles] he is not involved. I recommend you write Jones asking whether Levinson is associated with him since my sources of information about Levinson may have been wrong.

Further inquiries were put to Jones at that point. Jones replied in the negative, but the Curaçao people kept postponing a decision on the letting of the new casino lease. On November 20, Gates wrote once more to Curaçao, pointing up Jones's explanation that Levinson withdrew his interest when it was learned his brother would not be acceptable and that "Levinson took the attitude he would not be a party to a bid against Mr. Kozloff and myself . . . In declining to bid, he did decline in our favor." Gates enclosed more newspaper clippings and added: "I believe this should be the end of any mention of the Bobby Baker episode so far as Intercontinental and Curaçao are concerned."

On February 27, 1964, when John Gates appeared before the Senate investigating committee, he said that the decision of the Curaçao hotel owners as to the letting of the new gaming concession lease had still not been made. In August, 1968, however, when questioned by the author, Gates revealed that four months after the Senate hearings, in June, 1964, the Jones-Kozloff bid for the Curaçao Intercontinental Hotel casino lease was accepted. In addition to the Curaçao concession, Jones and Kozloff have the casino leases at the Embajador Intercontinental Hotel in Santo Domingo, Dominican Republic, and the Quito Intercontinental Hotel in Quito, Ecuador—all three hotels being Pan Am affiliates. The two casinos in Puerto Rico, San Juan and Ponce, are run by Pan Am personnel with local help, in keeping with government regulations there. They are "not particularly profitable," according to Gates. Indicating that he was "alarmed" at the thought of a possible Jones-Kozloff tie-in with syndicate gambling elements, Gates said both men would be "further checked out."

Gates won't have to delve too far back into history to find the truth. In 1954 Clifford A. Jones, Nevada's Lieutenant-Governor and Democratic National Committeeman, was an 11 per cent owner of the Thunderbird Hotel casino. After the *Las Vegas Sun*'s exposure of connivance between the gambling fraternity and state politicians, the Nevada tax commission began proceedings against the Thunderbird, charging that it was unfit to hold a gaming license. Jones denied before the commission that Meyer and Jake Lansky had hidden interests in the hotel, in spite of the fact that his own law partner had told of Lansky backing in "bugged" conversations subsequently published in the *Sun.* The commission produced, for Jones's enlightenment, a copy of the federal income-tax returns of George Sadlo and Jake Lansky showing that the two of them had paid taxes on $200,000 worth of income from the Thunderbird. The hotel's gaming license was subsequently revoked by the tax commission, but the state Supreme Court then came to the boys' assistance by reversing the commission's decision. However, the proof of the pudding was in those tax returns. Perhaps the only question John Gates needed to answer for himself is whether or not a leopard can change its spots.

An interesting addendum to the Pan Am Caribbean story occurred at the end of 1968, when the Mary Carter Paint Company, under its new name of Resorts International, bought a sizable chunk of Pan Am stock. In May of the same year, Mary Carter had sold its paint division for approximately $7 million in cash and $2 million in 6 per cent notes. The new company, Resorts International, decided to limit its interest exclusively to land development in the Bahamas—probably for the very good reason that its earnings as a paint company had decreased steadily over a four-year period and then, in 1968, showed a substantial upturn after the January opening of the Paradise Island hotel-casino operation.

The Resorts International purchase of Pan Am stock, although not nearly large enough to give it control, gave certain Pan Am officials food for thought. Their concern was not only as to how much more stock might be picked up by Resorts International but also, and particularly, as to how much influence such men as Meyer Lansky might have on the future of Pan Am.

All these complications make one wonder what there was, prior to 1963, that had already made Bobby Baker an old hand on the Hoodlum Sea as well as in the murky waters of stateside political-business negotiations. The fact is that Bobby had been "pooping" around the Caribbean for some time, with Levinson and other pals, and had become involved with highly placed Puerto Rican and Dominican public officials in the process. Consequently, he had built for himself a tall ship and had a star by which to steer when he later plunged into more dangerous waters. The boys from Puerto Rico and the Dominican Republic were small and rather innocent fry, however, compared to the syndicate sharks for whom Bobby played pilot fish in the Pan Am-Intercontinental-Hotels caper.

One of Bobby Baker's first big deals in the Caribbean involved him in the highly lucrative import-export meat business. At the 1952 National Democratic convention in Chicago he became acquainted with a free-wheeling politician named Jose Benitez, who was the chairman of the Puerto Rican Democratic party. The friendship flourished, and Bobby soon became a part-time commuter to Puerto Rico—collecting people, as always, who would be useful to him over the years in the exchange of small favors. Thus by 1960, when Bobby was firmly entrenched as Majority secretary to the Senate, the Benitez-Baker exchange was in the making.

Benitez had discovered through a friend, Puerto Rican meat importer Andres Lopez, that there were many people in his country who had never tasted fresh beef, a luxury item only the rich could afford. Lopez explained to Benitez that the high cost of beef resulted from the necessity of having to buy it in Central America and then ship it to Puerto Rico, a fourteen-hour trip by air. The freight time plus the need for expensive refrigeration on the long trip put the cost of fresh beef beyond the reach of the poor people on the island.

Lopez, a shrewd businessman concerned over his limited market, had searched for other sources of supply and happily stumbled across the answer to his needs: a slaughterhouse and packing plant in Haiti barely two air hours from Puerto Rico. But there was a fly in the ointment: the U.S. Department of Agriculture had denied Lopez a license to import meat to Puerto Rico—an American possession—because of unsanitary conditions in the Haitian slaughterhouse. Lopez told Benitez that he was willing to give a finder's fee of one cent per pound of beef imported to anyone who could clear up the matter and secure for him a contract with the Haitian company. Benitez assured Lopez that he knew someone who might be just the man for the job, and within days Benitez was winging his way to Washington for a meeting with Bobby Baker.

This was when the seeds of influence Bobby had so carefully planted in earlier days effected a kind of cross-pollinization that resulted in hybrids that will probably haunt the ex-Senate version of Paladin and his pals for years to come.

The slaughterhouse and packing plant in Haiti's capital city, Port-au-Prince, were a new investment venture called HAMPCO—Haitian American Meat Packing Company—which had been set up by the Murchison brothers of Texas. The Murchisons' holdings in oil, construction, real estate, and cattle were so vast and complex that they maintained a staff of attorneys, public relations men, and lobbyists in Washington second to none. But the Murchisons and their lawyers were generous and made it a point to include Bobby in many opportunities.

Spurred to action by Benitez' story of a finder's fee for the solution to Lopez' predicament, Bobby Baker made one phone call and parlayed it into a substantial income for three years, manipulating the situation eventually to a point where he was in the unusual position of collecting dividends from both buyer *and* seller.

Bobby called the Murchison brothers' Washington attorneys, Webb and Law, explaining that he had an interested buyer in Puerto Rico for HAMPCO meat. They apparently indicated that if Bobby was interested in the deal, they were. Shortly thereafter, therefore, Benitez made another trip to Washington, with his wife and Andres Lopez. Baker referred them to the offices of Webb and Law, where, on the same day, according to Senate testimony, a HAMPCO-Lopez export-import deal was made. The agreement included Lopez' paying the one cent per pound finder's fee to Baker and Baker's subsequent distribution of the money: "one-half cent to Webb and Law and one-quarter cent each to Baker and Mrs. Benitez."

The deal, of course, hinged on obtaining Department of Agriculture approval for the shipping of meat from the Haitian slaughterhouse to Puerto Rico, or into the United States. Law, according to the Senate report, "thought the conferences with representatives of the Department were in progress when the first meeting was held with Mr. and Mrs. Benitez and Lopez and when the agreement was made about the compensation of the 'finders.' " At any rate, by the time the contract was ready to go into effect, the Department of Agriculture had found conditions in the slaughterhouse to be adequate. Everything was in order for a smooth operation. What voodoo couldn't do, Bobby Baker apparently did. He may even have made a second ten-cent phone call to earn his finder's fee.

By the end of 1961 Lopez was getting his meat from HAMPCO, and Bobby was happily counting his pennies and making distribution of same. Before the two-year contract was up, however, Lopez had become disenchanted with the deal and wanted out. Instead of the fine beefsteaks he wished to sell to his fellow Puerto Ricans, he complained of receiving inferior meat, some of which had to be disposed of back in the United States for conversion into bologna.

At this point Irwin Davidson, a registered lobbyist in Washington for the governments of Haiti and Nicaragua—and also for the Murchison interests—contacted William E. Kentor, an official of The Packers Provision Company, Inc., with headquarters in Chicago. Kentor's firm, which had been a buyer of some of Lopez' meat shipped to the United States, also had a meat-processing plant in Puerto Rico. Kentor subsequently made a deal with HAMPCO to take over the Lopez contract, importing the HAMPCO beef to the Puerto Rican plant for processing into bologna and sausages, mostly for local sale. When Kentor was informed of the one cent per pound finder's fee arrangement, which he was expected to continue, he balked. Then he made a compromise offer of one-half cent per pound—which, after much dickering, was accepted.

What Kentor didn't realize was that, as a result of his reluctance to pay the full one cent per pound, Baker and his co-finders had persuaded HAMPCO to give them 10 per cent—up to $30,000 a year—of HAMPCO's net profits from the Kentor contract. Thus Kentor, the buyer, and HAMPCO, the seller, were both paying off Baker and his pals.

Bobby Baker netted himself approximately $12,000 as a result of one or two ten-cent phone calls, and even those were paid for by his employer, the U.S. government. It would not seem too illogical, therefore, to assume that Bobby had clearly explained his finder's fee method of operation to the Levinson-Jones-Kozloff combine when making their representations to Pan American and John Gates in the summer of 1963.

Obviously, then, Baker was well known in the Caribbean, but his influence in the Hoodlum Sea may have been far greater than has yet been generally recognized. In fact, it may even have a bearing on some of the political upheavals in the Dominican Republic.

Diego Bordas, an exiled Dominican revolutionary whom Bobby

had met in 1956 or 1957 through Jose Benitez, had been exporting cement from Dominica to the United States with Benitez in a partnership arrangement. When a group of American cement companies complained to the U.S. Department of Customs that the pair were in violation of America's anti-dumping laws—especially at cut-rate prices, with which they could not compete—Benitez took his problem to his friend Bobby. The upshot was that Baker walked into the Department of Customs with his arm around Diego Bordas' shoulder while the matter was pending and pointedly announced: "This is Diego Bordas. He is a friend of mine." There is no record of any further consideration of the complaint.

Bordas and Baker began spending a great deal of time discussing the turbulent Dominican political situation. When Trujillo was assassinated in May, 1961, Bordas paraded for Baker's benefit his friend Juan Bosch, a historian and self-taught political scientist. Bordas told Bobby that Bosch could become the first freely elected president of the Dominican Republic in over thirty years.

It all happened as Bordas said it would, and, at the end of 1962, for his loyalty to President-Elect Bosch, Bordas was in line for a top cabinet appointment in the new administration. Before Bosch was inaugurated in February, 1963, however, Bordas suggested that he make a trip to New York to meet his friend and intimate associate of the then Vice-President, Lyndon B. Johnson, Bobby Baker. United States support for Bosch had to be won, and the Baker pipeline could be used.

In December, 1962, a meeting between Bosch and Baker took place in the luxurious Hampshire House Hotel, overlooking Central Park in New York City, and the following month Bobby received an invitation to the Bosch inauguration. He flew down to the ceremony in February with Johnson and the then senior senator of Minnesota, Hubert Humphrey. Pictures were taken of Johnson happily embracing Bosch, and Dominicans interpreted this as an official blessing of their new president by the United States.

Within a year, however, Johnson had become president through the tragedy of John Kennedy's assassination, Bobby Baker's situation of power and influence had greatly changed, and the 101st Senator had been publically dumped by many of his former friends, including Lyndon B. Johnson. Bobby was described as a wanton opportunist who used his Senate position for personal gain, and when he resigned from his job as secretary to the Senate

Majority in October, 1963, Baker's former business associates scurried to protect themselves from the publicity that was to come from the exposé of his wheeling and dealing.

That Bobby Baker's questionable elbow-rubbing with, and influence-peddling for, Dominican politicians and would-be politicians had a part in effecting a subsequent change of official U.S. attitudes toward the Dominican Republic is perhaps in the realm of speculation. Still, the complete turn-about toward Juan Bosch made by President Johnson, after the Baker scandal had erupted in Washington and all hands were being washed of him, makes for interesting reading and consideration.

Although the Kennedy administration had fully endorsed and supported Juan Bosch after his victory in the free elections of 1962, the Johnson administration, despite much criticism from Congress, sent U.S. marines into Santo Domingo in April, 1965. Presumably this was to protect U.S. citizens there, help restore order, and "avoid another Cuba," but it occurred at a time when revolutionary elements were trying to return Bosch to his rightful position as president, a post from which he had been ousted by a military coup in September, 1963, just seven months after his inauguration.

In commenting on this shift in policy, Senator J. W. Fulbright said:

> In 1963, the United States strongly supported Bosch and the PRD [Bosch's party] as enlightened reformers; in 1965, the United States opposed their return to power on the unsubstantiated ground that a Bosch or PRD government would certainly, or almost certainly, become Communist-dominated. Thus the United States turned its back on social revolution in Santo Domingo and associated itself with a corrupt and reactionary military oligarchy.

The role played by Baker and the syndicate in Dominican affairs is of course unclear. But almost certainly the Alliance for Progress that Bosch saw exemplified in President John F. Kennedy's inauguration gift to him—an ambulance for the use of the people—is dead. As Bosch said: "Although the machinery of the Alliance for Progress survived him, the vitality and spirit of reform with which he imbued it when he created it, died with him in Dallas on November 22, 1963." But a syndicate Alliance for Progress remains, solidly entrenched in the Caribbean under Meyer Lansky's watchful eye. And for Bobby, perhaps, it now makes little difference; he "has it made." According to an *Esquire* article in July, 1967, Baker still has considerable financial worth and shows few signs of tightening his personal purse strings to cut expenses. He also is said to command no small amount of attention and respect from headwaiters, hatcheck girls, restaurant proprietors, and like admirers in Washington, where, as the article says, "obviously, Bobby Baker is somebody."

While speaking to writer Milton Viorst about his reaction to the jury that found him guilty—the verdict is being appealed—Baker may well have voiced not only his own outlook and self-serving philosophy but also that of the syndicate itself when he said:

> I feel sorry for the members of that jury, even if they convicted me. They were all just little government workers, putting in their time, filling out their forms, waiting for their pensions. There's none of 'em ever made more than $7,000 a year in his whole life, maybe $10,000 at the most. They just couldn't understand how anybody who worked for the government, like me, could get his hands on so much money. They figured it had to be crooked. It just never occurred to them that it could be honest.

Bobby Baker's appeal could eventually reach as high as the Supreme Court, where justices receive an annual salary of $39,500. But it's just possible that even the justices would take a dim view of a man who apparently got more than an honest baker's dozen out of every deal he ever made.

9

NEW ORLEANS:

Bayou Buccaneers

"Oh, Billy, Billy, they have given it to me and I gave them back the best I could!"

New Orleans Police Chief Peter Hennessey had six chunks of lead in his body when he mumbled these words to a detective friend, Captain William O'Connor, at about eleven o'clock on the Wednesday night of October 15, 1890—a balmy, peaceful night filled with the scent of the flowers that strewed Hennessey's front lawn. He died in Charity Hospital after eleven hours of physical anguish.

It was a sweet night in New Orleans, but it signaled the advent of the terror, of the indelible hue that always comes with the Mafia, of the ground-color on a horror-splashed canvas that is never finished. And in the Bayou City it has been added to each year, each month, and each day since the night Hennessey put the key in the lock of his front door on Girod Street and a shotgun blasted him from behind.

Hennessey was a good policeman and a fine man but, nevertheless, a minuscule stopgap against an almost classic disease. In its essence the story of Hennessey is much like that of any town engulfed by the Mafia in those early days when no one felt the terror of the secret society—no one, that is, until Hennessey took six slugs in him.

Hennessey had been checking into several murders that had no validity, as ordinary murders go, from the standpoint of motive. And in boiling them down, he came up with an answer that sealed his doom. What the good police chief had stepped into was a feud between two Mafia brotherhoods, the Camorra and the *Stoppag-lieri*, whose U.S. contingents, dedicated to a way of life Hennessey would not have believed if the chapter and verse were thrust down his throat, had freshly arrived from Sicily.

Hennessey's death could have been a hallmark in the understanding of the criminal mind and what it can do with a little organization, but the truth is often hard to come by—especially when details have to be provided. Nevertheless, two grand juries in New Orleans studied the situation that had led to Hennessey's murder, and one of them came up with the fact of the existence of the Mafia, seventy-five years before Valachi's testimony.

The other grand jury returned indictments against nineteen persons in connection with the Hennessey murder. One of those indicted was a fourteen-year-old boy accused of running ahead of Hennessey as he approached his house on the fatal night and whistling, thereby earning himself the dubious title of "fingerman," one of the first in the history of organized crime in New Orleans.

All of the accused were put on trial for their lives on November 29, 1890, but, unaccountably, the state asked for an order of severance, with the result that only nine men were left in the dock facing what was to become a thoroughly confused and botched-up trial. The defense, among whom were some of the ablest attorneys in the city—chief counsel for the Italians was Thomas J. Semmes, former attorney general of Louisiana—drew on a $75,000 defense fund raised by the Mafia in New Orleans and other cities. Sixty-seven witnesses gave testimony for four days, and then, dramatically, one defendant, Manuel Polizzi, said he wanted to confess. Amazingly, the district attorney turned down the offer and proceeded with the prosecution of the nine defendants, including Polizzi, whose lawyers refused to handle his case further after the confession offer was made.

Local newspaper accounts of the trial told of Polizzi's testimony about a drawing of lots among the Mafiosi to see who would murder Hennessey. And the trial jury was shaken during the proceedings by reports that efforts had been made to bribe its members. These reports were so strong that a detective was given a seat behind the press table in view of the jury to discourage "telegraphing" between spectators and members of the jury panel.

On March 13, 1891, after nine hours' deliberation, the jurors found that in the cases of three defendants they were unable to reach a verdict and that the six others were "not guilty."

The citizens of New Orleans were jolted by the unexpected

outcome of the trial, and pandemonium followed. An investigation by yet another grand jury resulted in charges that one lawyer had indeed attempted to bribe panel members. An indictment was handed down, but nothing ever came of the charges. The people formed a "Vigilance Committee" and began the purchase of shotguns, rifles, and revolvers from the hardware shop of A. Baldwin & Company. A public meeting was organized and exhorted by concerned citizens to denounce an attorney for the defense as a "suborner and procurer of witnesses and a briber of juries."

The meeting on March 14, the day after the verdict was delivered, soon became a mob, and a horde of armed men rushed from the town square down Bienville Street to the local prison, where the Italian prisoners were still under custody. The captive Mafiosi gibbered in terror as they heard the roar of the approaching crowd outside. A giant Negro picked up a huge paving stone and smashed it through a wooden door at the side of the jail, about 150 feet from the main gate. The crowd was momentarily awed and stilled by this feat. Then thirty men rushed through the wooden shards of the door into the prison, like a wolf pack hunting its quarry. The leaders of the mob decided to bring the prisoners outside and hang them publicly. The boy who whistled and signaled Hennessey's doom was found and left unharmed, but the others were herded under a grove of trees. The first to meet his doom was a dark little man named Manuel Polizzi.

The *New Orleans Picayune*'s reporter on the scene quickly filed a story that reflected the goggle-eyed horror with which he watched the massacre. He later wrote that a "stalwart public official" had dragged Polizzi into St. Anne Street from his hiding place on the ground floor of the prison and carried him in one hand to the corner of Treme and St. Anne, where a rope lifted Polizzi off the ground to the top of a lamp post. A group of armed men were said to have riddled him with bullets, the power of the Winchesters jolting his body and making it wriggle "like an angle worm on a hook."

Some even were hanged from tree limbs and then shot. Finally, they hung limp in a pall of blue smoke that brought the stink of burning powder to the frenzied executioners, who screamed, again and again, "Shoot! Kill the Dagoes!" The crowd was estimated at eight thousand, and so tightly did it pack around the scene of carnage that there was scarcely room for the executioners to bring their guns to bear on the cowering victims. Eleven men finally lay dead, including two whose trial had been severed from the others' —of no matter to the mob. One man escaped by hiding in a barrel of trash in the women's quarters of the prison, curled up like a child about to be born.

One local newspaper, *The Item*, viewed the whole proceeding with satisfaction. Next day an editorial pronounced:

> The military precision, skill and rapidity with which the prison was stormed and taken, the care exercised to do no harm except to the guilty parties, the wonderful forbearance of the angered populace, all are commended: while no complaint is uttered against the officials for their failure to interpose resistance to the avengers of outraged justice.

The *St. Louis Post-Dispatch*, which many years later was to engage in a deadly editorial crusade against The Green Ones, scolded New Orleans with the words: "It is hoped that the leading citizens will get the same punishment they meted out to the Mafia."

The *London Times* declared that "Italy's indignation is shared by the whole civilized world." In Rome, the *Don Chisciotte Delta* said:

> Italy ought to demand that instant measures be taken to protect the Italian colony in New Orleans. . . . It is just also to recognize the fact that similar incidents would not occur if the towns on the Atlantic littoral were not infested with the ex-galley slaves of Europe.

A lot of hell was raised by Italian officials in the United States, and veiled threats to take some sort of action by deploying the Italian Navy in U.S. waters were voiced. Secretary of State James G. Blaine maintained that the protesters were off base and declared: "The Sicilian who comes here must become an American citizen and subject his wrongs to the remedy of the law of the land, or else there must be no place for him on the American continent."

Money was furnished by Congress for more ships, and the U.S. Navy was really the chief beneficiary of the squabble, for it was brought home that the Italian Navy consisted of twenty-two first-class ships while the United States had only one first-class battleship, and an uncompleted vessel at that. This realization led to a great deal of shipbuilding, so that seven years later, when the Spanish-American War broke out, the U.S. Navy found itself in excellent condition, with much new equipment.

In the meantime, the Italian government, which was having money problems, decided against war, and eight Italians suspected of complicity in the Hennessey murder were freed and promptly vanished. The stir caused by the Mafiosi massacre was smoothed out by time and some soothing words from President Harrison, who offered $25,000—the offer was accepted—to the Italian government as compensation for the victims of the New Orleans affair.

It is evident, however, that some of the descendants of the same Mafia factions that spawned the murderers of Chief Hennessey are today in control of the rackets surrounding New Orleans, so much so that the original $25,000 largesse from the U.S. government has multiplied a million-fold for the secret society.

The man currently spinning the syndicate wheel of fortune in New Orleans is hoodlum Carlos Marcello, Louisiana boss of bosses, the midget Midas of the Mafia who, upon the deportation in 1947 of Mafia chieftain Sam Corollo, inherited the bullet-drilled mantles of the men who died at the hands of vigilantes.

The story of Marcello can be recounted with the same kind of tedious but telling facts that typify the histories of others of the Mafia hierarchy who brought its terror to the United States and who siphon off the money in every direction and under every guise. Carlos Marcello, according to the considered judgment of top U.S. law officials, was born in Tunisia as Calogero Minacori on February 6, 1910, after having been conceived in Sicily. Tunisia was merely a way-stop in his parents' emigration to the United States, for they soon proceeded to New Orleans. During Carlos' childhood in New Orleans, the family shared its home with another Sicilian family. They, too, had crossed the ocean with the Marcellos, and they could, but for the Mafia code of silence, give witness to the fact of Carlos' Sicilian heritage, which he denies.

In his early days Carlos committed more obvious, though less sinister, offenses against society than now, one of the first being assault and robbery of a Chinese grocer. This caper he paid for, serving four years in prison. A practice skirmish, apparently, was a bank robbery a year earlier in the Algiers section of New Orleans. Carlos, then nineteen, his brother Peter, and his father

Joseph were arrested as accessories, but the charges were dismissed.

After his release from prison, Carlos tied up with the Frank Costello-Phil Kastel combine, which had moved operations to Louisiana after their slot machines had been outlawed in New York by Mayor LaGuardia. In 1935, at the relatively tender age of twenty-five, Carlos received a full pardon for the 1930 assault conviction from Governor O. K. Allen, stooge of the Kingfish of Louisiana politics, Huey P. Long. The record shows two more arrests of Carlos—for assault, beating, and attempt to murder and for violation of the U.S. Internal Revenue Code—in the same year. But the charges were again dismissed. Carlos had obviously learned well his lessons from his seasoned Mafiosi tutors and was entering into the more sophisticated echelons of crime where "the handcuff was replaced with the handshake."

However minor these charges may have seemed, at least in underworld circles, Marcello became a real target for lawmen when he pleaded guilty in 1938 to selling more than twenty-three pounds of marijuana in association with the largest narcotics ring in New Orleans' history. He had left himself wide open and was sentenced to a one-year stay in Atlanta's federal prison and fined $76,830—a sum that he was permitted to settle with a token payment of $400 on the plea he was a pauper.

The U.S. Immigration Department subsequently found that Carlos had never become a naturalized citizen. This fact made deportation for a narcotics conviction feasible, and in 1951, after Marcello had appeared as a reluctant witness before the Kefauver hearings and refused to answer questions, Senator Estes Kefauver recommended that he be deported. Thus, from 1953 until 1961, when Robert Kennedy finally turned the trick, Carlos was under a continuous order of deportation and had to do battle with every legal weapon available to him in order to stay in the United States.

When approached by U.S. immigration officials, both Italy and Tunisia turned thumbs down on taking Marcello back. It seemed no one was interested in the boy who had left town and made good. Besides, from Carlos' point of view these places were thousands of miles away, and he was the kind of man who liked to insure his bets. If he was to go away on an enforced vacation—and he hoped this would never happen—he wanted both a friendly welcome and a salubrious atmosphere.

Finally, therefore, Marcello dispatched an aide to Guatemala to dig up evidence that there, in a country of many friends, Carlos Marcello first saw the light of day. The attorney, ensconced in a chauffeured limousine thoughtfully provided by Guatemalan government officials, toured the country examining birth records in remote villages. Large document books are kept in these sparsely populated, mahogany-forested areas, and anyone handy—the parish priest, the local clerk, the farmer-mayor of the town—could and would make the necessary birth entry. Blank spaces were sometimes left between names and could well be used for the very purpose Carlos had in mind.

Finally, in a jungle city called San Jose Pinula, there was found the kind of blank space needed in the local record book. The name of Calogero Minacori was inserted, in water-mixed ink so that the scrawl would match those already there, and Carlos Marcello was born again—in Guatemala, a scant three-and-one-half-hour trip by air from New Orleans. To make doubly sure of his new identity, Marcello also succeeded in getting the best mob counterfeiter, who was at the time in jail—such is the power of Marcello—to make him a Guatemalan passport. If worse came to worse and Carlos had to take that "vacation," he would at least be in fairly close touch with his business associates.

Meanwhile, according to the New Orleans crime commission, which had compiled an extensive file on Marcello's past, Marcello has not been neglecting his affairs. At one time or another his varied business operations have involved banks, truck dealerships, motels, housing subdivisions, bars, restaurants, finance companies, linen-supply services—a traditional syndicate interest—beer and whiskey distributorships, shrimp fleets, shipbuilding firms, taxi and bus companies, souvenir shops, gas stations, ceramic-tile companies, phonograph-record wholesalers and shops, and electrical-appliance stores. The evidence points to the fact that Marcello interests are not confined only to Jefferson and Orleans Parishes (counties). His many enterprises are scattered through surrounding states and include thousands of acres of oil leases on federal land. In one section, Marcello purchased land for 50 cents an acre; a few years later, he sold a thirty-acre parcel for $7,500,000 for the development of a shopping center.

Marcello's financial successes, however, had little effect on the Justice Department. The Attorney General, Robert Kennedy, and his staff greeted with hilarity the news of Carlos' rebirth in Guatemala and decided that they would oblige.

On April 4, 1961, Carlos Marcello left his white marble two-story home overlooking a well-trimmed golf course in Metairie, a suburb of New Orleans, to make his quarterly visit to the New Orleans immigration department. Kennedy and his aide, Walter Sheridan, had already collaborated on the script. As Marcello extended his arm across the desk at the department's headquarters to sign a statement of appearance, instead of being offered the customary pen he was quickly handcuffed by two officers and hustled out of the office into a waiting car. Within thirty minutes he was the only passenger aboard a giant Immigration Department jet plane whistling its way toward Guatemala.

Apocryphal stories have been published about the great outcry Guatemalan citizens were supposed to have made over Marcello's presence in their midst. One such story relates that eight government secret agents "redeported" him by depositing him at the El Salvador border, the whereabouts of which have always been in dispute. In turn, the El Salvadorians are supposed to have taken him and deposited him on the top of a mountain in the wilderness on the Honduras side of the border. From here Carlos is supposed to have walked seventeen miles to the nearest village, fainting three times on the way. Actually, Carlos was wined and dined by the aristocracy of Guatemala. He was flown to the finest resort areas in the private plane of the country's president, Miguel Ydigoras Fuentes, who was forced to flee Guatemala in 1963.

Carlos' exile was short-lived. He was photographed at the Guatemala City racetrack with Felice Golino, once the biggest shrimp-boat fleet operator in the Gulf of Mexico and a long-time friend of Marcello sometimes identified in newspapers as his uncle and certainly a partner in various enterprises. Then in May, 1961, just one month after his abrupt deportation to Guatemala, Carlos was escorted from his "native land" to neighboring Honduras, then a British colony but claimed by Guatemala and therefore looked upon by Guatemalan citizens for immunity. And in Honduras, it is said, Marcello soon set off for home from the capital city, Belize, in one of Uncle Felice's shrimp boats. Carlos was supposedly taken to a spot off the Mexican port of Chetumal, a few miles to the north, where one of the shrimpers waited for him in the dead of night to carry him back to New Orleans.

This version of Carlos' return with Golino's help—given by Carlos himself to close friends—is somewhat discredited by lawmen, who say that Golino disposed of his shrimp fleet long before Marcello's deportation difficulties began. Golino, moreover, has denied any part in assisting in the reentry to this country of one of the underworld's brightest stars. However, both Marcello and Golino had connections with shrimpers and their boats, a connection that would have made both easily accessible to Carlos, and on a shrimp boat Carlos could have arrived in Louisiana via any number of the secluded bayous that weave mysteriously from the gulf coast almost into the heart of New Orleans.

In any case, on June 3, after getting his business affairs in order, Carlos surrendered voluntarily to immigration agent Bruce Hemstad, spent a few days at the federal alien detention center in McAllen, Texas, and was released on bond. He was subsequently indicted for conspiracy to commit fraud by obtaining a fake Guatemalan birth certificate, for committing perjury in swearing he had nothing to do with obtaining the fake certificate, and for unlawful reentry as a deported alien. However, nothing ever really happened to untangle the legal flim-flam. A conspiracy trial resulted in a not-guilty verdict, and Marcello went back to his men and his properties, and business went on as usual—except for one thing: the vendetta with the Kennedys, Robert in particular, was sworn.

Business as usual has meant dispensing income. And if a portion of Marcello's money has an eventual resting place in the pockets of mysterious and powerful higher-ups, or in the seemingly sacred vaults of the Alps-girdled Swiss banks, or in Panamanian money houses, he has spread as least some of the wealth among a huge and prospering family, many of whose members are planted in key positions in his Louisiana investment honey pot.

Most of Marcello's interests in illegal activities are carefully screened by the practice of having the businesses officially listed in the names of others, but his finger is in whatever pie he feels a fondness for at any given moment. The big questions are: Why does a family constantly pile up wealth when it already has plenty? And, who holds the big purse into which the net profits finally find their way?

Robert Kennedy may have been close to the answer when he was Attorney General, but even he must have been puzzled by Marcello's rapid climb to fortune up the ladder provided by the

Mafia—a criminal talent machine oiled by pure gold. To be sure, it is difficult to make too many mistakes when you have Mafia backing, especially when one considers its resources. Thus, a former collector for Marcello's music company, convicted in 1943 of bribing a witness to help two mobsters, was identified by *Life*, September 8, 1967, as being at that time a chief investigator on the staff of the district attorney of Jefferson Parish—a story confirmed to this author a year later by Aaron Kohn.

Perhaps the secret of Marcello's success lies in the fact that his organization is tight and laid out according to the oldest and, apparently, best Mafia tradition. In the opinion of Aaron Kohn, managing director of New Orleans' metropolitan crime commission, Marcello's underboss is his brother, Joseph Marcello, Jr., who operates handbooks and gaming casinos and has had minor brushes with the law. A *caporegime* in the outfit is Peter Marcello, another brother, who is blind in one eye but can see enough to be able to run strip joints such as the Sho-Bar on Bourbon Street. Peter has been arrested for crimes of violence and has served time on a narcotics conviction.

Marcello's six younger brothers—Peter, Joseph, Pascal, Vincent, Anthony, and Sammy—maintain control of many of the operations of the boss of bosses. Having been born in the United States, they, unlike Marcello himself, are not subject to deportation, which is usually a most helpful weapon in the armory of government lawmen trying to rid the country of pestilence. The brothers, according to the crime commission, are the guiding forces behind a variety of business partnerships, including a wire service, a music company operating slot and pinball machines and jukeboxes, and a gambling casino.

Marcello's lieutenants come and go, for it is apparently a rule that if one gets caught cold, he takes the rap and thereby, it is hoped, gets a little smarter. One such lieutenant is Nick Nuccio, for years a chief lieutenant with a $4-million-a-year bookie business. Like others of the Mafia hierarchy, Nuccio could not keep his hand out of relatively minor matters, and thereby he provided one more look at that baffling facet of the Mafia character. Nuccio was caught in the act of burglarizing the safe of a large dairy near Baton Rouge in 1963, captured after a gun battle with police, sentenced to ten years in the state penitentiary for the burglary, and fined for illegal possession of burglar tools and narcotics. Why risk such punishments when you are already a chief lieutenant to a boss of bosses? Perhaps because most Mafiosi have a fatally flawed character. They always want more.

Known in the New Orleans underworld as "The Little Man," Carlos Marcello stands only five feet four inches in his elevator shoes, but he is infinitely more polished than such slick Mafia worthies as Chicago's Sam Giancana and New York's Vito Genovese. He sets himself apart with the well-tailored $300 suits he has made with a triple-sized pocket sewn into one pants leg to accommodate the huge sums of cash he usually carries with him.

Crime fighter Aaron Kohn, an ex-FBI man, figured that in 1964 Marcello was directly providing the syndicate with about $400 million a year, of which $100 million came from Uncle Sam in the form of underpayment—or nonpayment—of taxes. Actually, the overall annual take for the mob in the city of New Orleans and environs is something like $1.114 billion in Kohn's estimate, and the sum compares favorably, from the viewpoint of Mafia accountants, with the calculated $2-billion racketeer rakeoff in Chicago, an area with more than five times the population of metropolitan New Orleans.

The local boys, under the astute guiding hand of Carlos Marcello, have become so adept at high finance that their combined annual income makes them and their business the state's largest industry. As if that weren't enough, they seem to have become the nucleus of an "investment center" for the whole Mafia organization. Their legitimate real estate acquisitions, together with partnership and other involvements in countless thriving businesses, add up to what is an unbelievable total worth.

Thus Frank Klein, chief assistant district attorney of Orleans Parish, has said:

> In fact, we think there's too much money here. We feel that it's flowing in from other Cosa Nostra organizations in other parts of the country for investment by the local mob. This could be their financial center, with a lot of nice safe places where campaign contributions and outright bribery have pretty well insulated them from the law.

The heart of Marcello's territory is Gretna, the "Cicero of the South," which lies directly across the Mississippi River from New Orleans in Jefferson Parish. New Orleans itself, in Orleans Parish, is comparatively clean, but of Jefferson Parish, wherein prostitution, gambling of all varieties, and narcotics are apt to be found with ease, Kohn has said, "Not even in Tangier was there ever a cozier arrangement between the mob and the law." The customers who throng to the many pleasure palaces in Gretna would seem to have a death wish, and Marcello has a ready-made guillotine for them. Louisiana's version of Las Vegas wears a suit that badly needs laundering, but it has the same big back pocket.

Possibly the fun seekers who troop to syndicate-provided pastimes, not only in Gretna and Las Vegas, but also in the hurly-burly of the casinos being built up in the Caribbean, feel somewhat as Lincoln Steffens suggested all Americans do:

> The American people don't mind grafting, but they hate scandals. They don't kick so much on a jiggered public contract for a boulevard, but they want the boulevard and no fuss and no dust. We want to give them that. We want to give them what they really want, a quiet Sabbath, safe streets, orderly nights and homes secure.

Steffens was quoting a Tammany Hall politician who operated in old New York at about the time Marcello was changing his diapers for real pants. The Tammany brand of serenity was fine for the politicians, but apparently it did not produce enough money for a group of killers who kissed your hand as they killed you. The mobsters therefore pushed south to Florida and Louisiana to find a breed of moneyed swingers who prefer a violent whore over and above a willing but indentured Lady Chatterley; for the swingers pay well for their fun.

Apparently immune from the law, Marcello cleverly operates with an arrogance that brooks virtually no opposition, and the good people of Louisiana appear to be unimpressed by the menace of his power. "Our biggest problem is the attitude of the people," New Orleans Police Superintendent Joseph I. Giarrusso has said:

> We closed up half of the mob-operated strip joints on Bourbon Street and elsewhere in the city because tourists were getting drugged or getting their heads bashed in and robbed in them. But we can't close up the rest because certain businessmen feel that, with no place to sin, the tourists won't come to New Orleans anymore. The bookies come across the line from their main base in Jefferson Parish, and we raid them; the prostitutes come across the

> line from Jefferson Parish on a call-girl basis, and our Vice Squad makes arrests nearly every night. But the courts tend to give out light, slap-on-the-wrist fines and they're back again. Our people just can't understand that what seems to them to be a little harmless gambling is really tied in with far more serious crimes. They can't understand that these are not just local boys they've known all their lives and that they really *are* tied in with the national crime syndicate.

Given such attitudes on the part of the people of Louisiana, it is not surprising that Marcello is not often opposed now by the so-called lawmen who back up the sovereignty of the people in the area, but reporter Bill Davidson tells of at least one rebuff given The Little Man by New Orleans District Attorney James Garrison, who is trying to remake the Warren Commission report by proving a conspiracy in the assassination of President John F. Kennedy. In the fall of 1963, Garrison is reported to have turned Marcello down on a $3,000-per-week offer for his help in opening up the city to hoodlum slot-machine operators. The idea was to have the district attorney seize two illegally placed slots so that a test case could be brought for the purpose of having the machines declared legal. And thereafter Garrison was to get $10 per machine per week for this favor.

Another reverse occurred on September 22, 1966, when Carlos Marcello was arrested in the company of twelve other Mafia chieftains during a luncheon meeting in a private basement dining room at La Stella's Restaurant in fashionable, tennis-oriented Forest Hills, New York, just across the East River from Manhattan. The thirteen Mafiosi, among whom were leaders of the Genovese, Gambino, and Colombo New York Mafia families, were charged with "consorting with known criminals" but had little difficulty in putting up the $1.3-million bail—$100,000 each—that set them free the next day.

Police theorize that the New York luncheon was merely one of a series of top-level Little Apalachin meets, one of which had taken place in Las Vegas two weeks earlier and another in Palm Springs in October, 1965. Among other items on the agenda, it has been suggested that one involved Santo Trafficante, Jr., who early in 1968 visited Singapore, Hong Kong, and South Vietnam and has had his eye on portions of Marcello territory in the South for some time. Since Trafficante lost a good slice of revenue when Castro dumped gambling in Havana and is being given a hard time by lawmen in Florida, he needs new ground. He made frequent trips to Louisiana prior to the La Stella meeting and may very well have been presenting his case for a piece of Marcello's rather substantial pie.

Upon his return to New Orleans after his arrest and release by the New York police, Marcello was met at the airport by inquiring newsmen and photographers and by FBI agent Patrick Collins. Apparently thinking this an invasion of his privacy, Carlos reportedly said, "Don't you know *I'm* the boss around here!" and took a poke at agent Collins. As a result of his action, Carlos was charged with, and found guilty of, assault in September, 1968, fined $2,000, and sentenced to two years in prison. Of course, Marcello is free on bail, and the sentence is being appealed.

After all his troubles, Marcello should know better, but he remains fond of using the telephone, and even his experience at the restaurant in New York did not prevent him from keeping in touch with the boys. The result was predictable. His calls were monitored. And in its issue of September 29, 1967, *Life* laid some details bare. Via a complicated series of "cheesebox" phones—used by bookies to hide their location—Carlos made calls until March, 1967, from his office in the Town and Country Motel near New Orleans, the first of two such motels built by the mobster. Some of these calls, *Life* claims, went into the governor's offices in the state capitol at Baton Rouge after being diverted from a nearby motel owned by a Marcello henchman.

Other calls, according to *Life*, outlined a plan for bribery in connection with an effort to spring Jimmy Hoffa from federal prison at the behest of syndicate and Teamsters Union officials in the East. The scheme was to offer $1 million to a Baton Rouge Teamster official, Edward G. Partin, in order to "encourage" him to change or recant his testimony as a prime government witness at Hoffa's trial. The bribe was turned down, according to *Life*, but the stench is still floating through the state capitol.

Marcello also used the phone to contact other Mafiosi. At least six Mafia figures—Mike Miranda and Thomas Eboli of New York City, Nick Civella of Kansas City, Joe Civello of Dallas, James Lanza of San Francisco, and Santo Trafficante of Florida—were called during the period the bribery deal was being considered.

And it is interesting to note that Miranda, Eboli, and Trafficante were all at the La Stella luncheon meeting.

Unfortunately, under the law it is impossible to use testimony derived from tapped telephone calls. While the listings of toll-call records can be secured, the resulting dialogue has been placed in limbo insofar as legal action is concerned. However, Marcello's protection is not without weak spots. Thus a surprising hole in his layer of criminal-activities insulation, which generally keeps his name from public mention, was made in August, 1968, in East Chicago, Indiana, when a thirty-three-year-old Chicago truck driver, who allegedly claimed to be representing Marcello, was picked up while collecting $6,500 from a Chicago stockbroker as part of what was said to be an extortion plot.

The victim, who worked with the FBI in setting up the arrest, admitted a legitimate debt of $2,000 owed to a former New Orleans business associate, but he said the young collector more than tripled the amount to be collected and threatened bodily harm, saying he was representing the New Orleans Mafia boss. If the truck driver did in fact represent Marcello, it is a good indication that the long reach of Marcello's power extends far beyond the bayou country he chooses to call home. Indeed, an incident that occurred at Churchill Farms, the plantation Marcello owns on a soggy piece of land near New Orleans, suggests that Carlos Marcello is mixed up in some extremely murky activities.

September, 1962: a great blue heron had just speared a frog from the pond beside a dusty road. The huge bird looked up suddenly, pumped its great wings, and sailed away as a black Cadillac bumped smoothly along the road that flanked the marsh, plowing furrows in the powder, tracks that filled in as fast as the bubble of air behind the car sifted the dust again.

The marsh is flat, and streaks of silver—seen best at evening—trace the waterways that thread the rough grass to the Mississippi, muddy pathway to the Gulf of Mexico traversed by shrimp boats, catfish, and waterfowl.

In the air-conditioned car were four men. At the wheel was Carlos Marcello, "the most powerful, most influential, most sinister racket boss in Louisiana." Carlos stopped the car outside a small shrimp packing plant. A man came out and handed him a crate of frozen, packaged shrimp, which was placed in the car. The signal was clear: no one had preceded Carlos down the lonely road. The car started off again, this time along damp ruts through the rank marsh growth, and in a few minutes two buildings came into view.

One was a typical country barn. It served as a shelter for chickens and goats. Swallows had plastered their light-gray mud nests against the angle of eaves around the barn. Bottle-green flies were everywhere. The other was typical southern lower-class Americana—narrow windows, a tiny porch, no pretense—but it served as a retreat and secret meeting place for Marcello and his business associates.

Carlos braked the car to a halt at the farmhouse. He led his guests into the kitchen, sat them down on comfortable chairs next to a refrigerator and large freezer, and poured Scotch all around.

The kitchen led into a hall flanked by sparsely furnished bedrooms. One door, however, opened onto a room about twenty-five feet long, completely alien to the simple farmhouse with its ramshackle façade. Down the middle of this room was a long table of polished wood, and placed around it were twelve executive-type, black leather chairs. It was a room set aside strictly for business, and the business discussed was not a matter of pigs and cows.

The conversation began with the usual badinage of men of the underworld—sex, money, sex, money. Later, as the Scotch brought more familiarity and relaxation, the dialogue turned to serious matters, including the pressure law-enforcement agencies were bringing to bear on the Mafia brotherhood.

It was then that Carlos' voice lost its softness, and his words were bitten off and spit out when mention was made of U.S. Attorney General Robert Kennedy, who was still on the trail of Marcello.

"*Livarsi na petra di la scarpa!*" Carlos shrilled the Mafia cry of revenge: "Take the stone out of my shoe!"

"Don't worry about that little Bobby son of a bitch," he shouted. "He's going to be taken care of!"

Ever since Robert Kennedy had arranged for his deportation to Guatemala, Carlos had wanted revenge. But as the subsequent conversation, which was reported to two top government investigators by one of the participants and later to this author, showed, he knew that to rid himself of Robert Kennedy he would first have to remove the President. Any killer of the Attorney General would be hunted down by his brother; the death of the President would seal the fate of his Attorney General.

No one at the meeting had any doubt about Marcello's intentions when he abruptly arose from the table. Marcello did not joke about such things. In any case, the matter had gone beyond being mere "business"; it had become an affair of honor, a Sicilian vendetta. Moreover, the conversation at Churchill Farms also made clear that Marcello had begun to plan a move. He had, for example, already thought of using a "nut" to do the job.

Roughly one year later President Kennedy was shot in Dallas—two months after Attorney General Robert Kennedy had announced to the McClellan committee that he was going to expand his war on organized crime. And it is perhaps significant that privately Robert Kennedy had singled out James Riddle Hoffa, Sam Giancana, and Carlos Marcello as being among his chief targets.

It is impossible to assert that any syndicate member organized the assassination of President Kennedy without further proof. But Lee Harvey Oswald did live and work for a time in New Orleans, could have been connected with Jack Ruby—a small-time ex-Chicago hood—and could well have contacted displaced American mobsters in Mexico during the crucial five "lost" days in September, 1963. Certainly many mobsters had every reason to want the Kennedys out of the way.

Of course, as District Attorney James Garrison is certain he can prove, other interested parties also had reasons for wanting to eliminate John F. Kennedy. Perhaps the truth will emerge one day. Meanwhile, Marcello remains in the country, no longer pestered by the Kennedy brothers. His fate is no longer in their hands. In fact, to return to his more "ordinary" affairs, whether he will be permitted to exercise continued control of the mob's money machine, in New Orleans and points north, east, and west, is up not to officials but to the citizenry that comprises the hoards of suckers who play the syndicate games in one back room while their pockets are picked in another.

10

CALIFORNIA:
Malice in Wonderland

The Mafia came to California almost as soon as the golden dawns had faded for the Spanish grandees and the Conestoga wagons of those who rushed westward had blotted out the sun. The pueblos and missions and land grants fell before the invaders who brought what was known as law and order—though the law was designed largely to make things easy for the new native sons.

The lawyers obliged and begat judges, the judges begat decisions, the decisions begat protection of a sort, for the Mafiosi, and the Mafiosi begat a monster of terror capable of hypnotizing anyone. The terror, of course, is not always needed, for the Mafia can also use another kind of enslavement—the enslavement wrapped up in the hallucinogenic and pacifying products that have begun to twitch the minds and bare feet of a generation of young people. But, in any case, a tea party has begun, and it may never stop in the Mad Hatter's personal preserve: California, U.S.A.

California's nine-hundred-mile littoral features archetypes who would almost make you believe Lewis Carroll had explored the American West for his material. It is as though the looking glass Alice stepped through was simply a doorway to California, for there can be found almost anything.

Almost everyone in California has his own looking glass, but deep in the heart of America's movieland-wonderland each finds himself being upstaged by Cheshire Cats, Red Queens, and such assorted bad men as Humpty Dumpty, the White Knights, and the Jabberwockys. Everybody seems to have gotten into the act, and some of the money-grubbers and their bosom-buddy, mob-connected politicians have never had it so ruthlessly good. As in the rest of the country, so in California: the men with the money are out to make more of it, and the men without it are hoping for a chance to make it. The Mafia casts a long shadow on what once was an Eden, and there appears to be few left to cry or care. There is little left of that garden, and that little will be saved only if a real effort is made to drive out the crooked businessmen-politicos and the syndicate boys who helped put them in their positions of power.

Police records show that by the turn of the century the Mafia had firmly entrenched itself in southern California, chiefly by using its dreaded terror tactics on those of the Italian element, within and outside of the secret society, who didn't go along with its demands. A review of suspected gangland murders and mysterious disappearances in this early era, prior to Prohibition, shows a consistent pattern to the method of operation used by "The Black Hand Society," as it was then called by lawmen and frightened citizens. Only the motives—intimidation, extortion, revenge, jealousy—varied.

The police investigation reports on these cases invariably contained such phrases as:

> Italian fruit peddler . . . shot in back on street. Believed to be long standing feud of Sicilian origin.
>
> Victim killed by shot through window of his barber shop. Definitely a "Black Hand" killing as a letter was found in victim's pocket written in Sicilian. Letter also bore crude drawing of a clown and a policeman, evidently referring to victim as a stoolie.
>
> Victim wounded after being shot by unknown person with shotgun on street . . . stated he did not see who fired as his back was turned (although he received wounds in front of his body). Victim stated he had received Blank Hand letters demanding money under threat of death. Letters later found in his room.
>
> Victim shot in back of head and hand. Aftermath of a Sicilian mob feud . . . believed at time to be Italian Black Hand killing.
>
> This killing was the outcome of bad blood between Italian elements and also from "muscling" of different factions.

The four words, "no prosecution to date," that terminate a large majority of these reports are a good indication of the high degree of skillfulness that the Black Handers had achieved.

A second era of organized crime began in California, as it did all across the country, with the enactment of Prohibition as of

January 29, 1920. The bootlegging of illegal liquor gave the Mafia an opportunity to make larger amounts of money in a shorter time than ever before. But simply because there were more profits to be made, Prohibition also initiated a divisive power struggle within the organization. Brother was pitted against brother, one faction of the society against another, in a joust for the plunder and the spoils. And while the Roaring Twenties became in one stratum of society the era of Flapper Girls, raccoon coats, and female emancipation, in another they were a decade of criminal violence involving smuggling, hijacking, and murder.

A typical twenties incident occurred in California on November 25, 1929: a person was reported missing to the authorities.

The incident was typical in that people were always being reported missing. However, this particular incident led to nailing into place one of the many rungs in the ladder of organized crime in California, and it also served to introduce the name of gangster Jack Dragna to California police files at a time when orange groves and vineyards were paving the hills with gold once again.

The official record can be found in a Los Angeles police department report entitled "Gangland Killings—1900–1951," a partial recitation of what is known of man's inhumanity to man in Los Angeles and environs.

The man in this case was Frank Baumgarteker. Baumgarteker, who was partly bald and about fifty years old, was a well-known winery owner, and he was also part-owner of the Western Grape Corporation, 279 North Avenue 19, and owner of the Union Motor Transport, 633 Gibbons Street, Los Angeles, three ranches, and the Cucamonga winery near that city.

Baumgarteker was suspected of large-scale bootlegging and transportation activities in connection with the bootlegging, and it was reported that he owed over $200,000 to creditors and that he was unable to pay them. It is almost certain that Baumgarteker's winery was being used to manufacture illegal alcohol, and it became apparent to investigators that the vintner did not exactly like the idea and wanted out. His debts were not being taken care of by the men who had forced him to use the winery to manufacture moonshine.

In September, 1929, Baumgarteker had an argument with the mob representative in charge of the "alky cooker," Jimmy (Schafer) Fogarty, whose true name was Zorra. Somehow Baumgarteker summoned enough courage to order the bootleg installation out of his winery. It was removed the same day, and on his way out of the office that evening the vintner made it plain to his secretary, a Mrs. Day, that the Italians could no longer use his winery for the making of illegal alcohol. And he added: "I have signed my death warrant."

Shortly thereafter three up-and-coming hoodlums—Jack Dragna, titular head of the Mafia in California and president of the Italian Protective League, Joe Ardizzone, treasurer of the League, and Eddie Rollings, about whom little is known—dropped in to talk to Baumgarteker. But the vintner was adamant, and the trio left the winery.

Baumgarteker was last seen on November 25, 1929. At 11:30 A.M. he finished eating lunch with his partner, Bob Demateis, and his attorney, Walter Hass, at the Hoffman Cafe, 743 South Spring Street, Los Angeles. He had also spoken that morning with John Vai of the Padre Wine Company, Los Angeles and Alameda. The vintner left the luncheon appointment in his purple 1926 Cadillac touring car after telling his friends that he was going to Wilmington, California, where his Union Motor Transport organization had an office. That night, at 10:50 P.M., his car was left at the Sixth Street Garage, 745 Sixth Street, San Diego, California, by a man described as being about 40 years old, weighing about 160 pounds, and wearing a short leather coat, khaki pants, and leather riding boots.

The missing man's wife received a letter from her husband postmarked San Diego, 7:30 A.M., November 26, and the handwriting indicated that the writer was under great mental strain. An intensive search made in southern California and Mexico yielded many leads, much publicity, and no results. A $1,000 reward was posted, to no avail. Baumgarteker's auto, lab tests revealed, carried the type of peculiar dust and dirt found at a place called Riverside County Wells—in those days a place of bubbling springs and deep mineral water where a skeleton would be washed free of its enclosing flesh in a matter of days, especially if weighted and lowered into the gushing water.

The last line in the missing man's folder at police headquarters reads: "To date, no indication or evidence of victim's whereabouts. No prosecution."

As Alice said, after she read the poem "Jabberwocky" in the

White King's castle: ". . . only I don't exactly know what they are: However, *somebody* killed *something;* that's clear, at any rate. . . ."

Jack Dragna had made his mark. And while he hadn't exactly established himself as the leader, at least he had impressed others that he was the man to look up to in the California underworld—a process that would require a great deal of neck-twisting under any circumstances.

The Italian Protective League, which had its offices on the eleventh floor of the Law Building in Los Angeles, was, according to police intelligence reports:

> strictly a "muscle" outfit, preying on various business activities, such as produce, cleaning establishments, barber shops, etc.; also had its fingers in gambling, bootlegging, smuggling, and was suspected of many "Black Hand" killings and some "sudden disappearances" of Italians, bootleggers and others.

And its president, Jack Dragna, was the man who, floating on a river of illegal alcohol, led the big-time Mafiosi into California by smoothing the way for Frank Costello's boy, Bugsy Siegel.

The story of Dragna's career and infiltration into the heart and soul of a great land should be documented even though it is a long and typical one. Dragna died in 1957. He stumbled out his last days in Las Vegas browbeating cashiers whose courage fronted for the fear of their bosses. He had even been ordered deported a couple of years before he died, but the order had never been carried out. Presumably it was on appeal. It is all a rather dreary story.

Dragna, whose real name was Anthony Rizzoti, was born in Corleone, near Palermo, Sicily, before the turn of the century. He came to the United States with his brother Tom about 1908. The family settled in California. Although arrested many times on various charges, Dragna served only one term in jail, going to San Quentin in 1915 on a three-year sentence for attempted extortion.

Released from prison in time to get into full swing with syndicate Prohibition activities, Dragna soon worked his way to the top of California's criminal hierarchy and, eventually, into the Mafia's ruling council. However, he was never all powerful. For example, even if he had wanted to, he was unable to prevent the disappearance in 1931 of Joe Ardizzone, his fellow officer in the

Italian Protective League who had helped him try to "muscle" Frank Baumgarteker two years earlier.

Ardizzone's fate also illustrates once again how the syndicate will use the vengeance on its own men, when necessary, that it uses on outside competitors. The police report on Joe Ardizzone, missing since October 15, 1931, reads as follows:

> Ardizzone shot and killed George Maisano, July 2, 1906 . . . was apprehended and charged with murder, but on February 9, 1915, case dismissed, insufficient evidence, no witnesses that would talk.
>
> Ardizzone was wounded in a gang war deal in February, 1931, when he was supposedly taking Jimmy Basile for a "ride." Friends of Basile saw them in a car in Downey and opened fire on Ardizzone, wounding him. It's always been a question of whether Ardizzone had already killed Basile or if the bullets intended for Ardizzone got Basile. Three men with sawed off shotguns did the job, but Ardizzone crawled away only wounded, and later while in the hospital another attempt was made to get him, but was unsuccessful.
>
> Ardizzone [had] had an argument with Jimmy Basile, "Little Jimmy," and his partner in the "bootleg" business, Domenico Di Ciolla, "Danto," a power in "Little Italy." These two men had invested $1,000 in a "still" to start making alcohol. Ardizzone tried to "muscle" in but was repulsed. Ardizzone is supposed to have told Di Ciolla that he [Ardizzone] had killed 30 men and he would make Di Ciolla the 31st, if the partners didn't "cut him in." Ardizzone suspected of killing Basile, by taking him for "a ride," and then putting Di Ciolla "on the spot" because of fear that Di Ciolla would "squeal."
>
> Ardizzone was known as one of wealthiest of local Italians, and was mixed up in the bootleg wars between local factions and Eastern gangsters who were attempting to "muscle" into local territory . . . [He] was called "Iron Man" because he wanted to be king of the Sicilian gang; he claimed to be the "strong man." . . . [He] was a suspect in the disappearance of Tony Buccola and Joe Porrazzo and others, as he was trying to gain control of the local scene, the "bootleg wars" having disrupted the status quo of the local Sicilian Mafia. He had made many enemies, and many there were who would like revenge.
>
> In 1926, Ardizzone was listed as an executive officer of the "Italian Protective League."
>
> Ardizzone left his residence at 6:30 A.M. on October 15, 1931, to go to Joe Cuccia's ranch near Ettiwanda, California; never arrived. At time was driving a 1930 Ford Coupe SR W7653 and carrying a 41 Caliber Colt Revolver #323. Victim was a cousin of Frank

> Borgia . . . and was going to pick up another cousin Nick Borgia, who had just come from Italy, at the ranch.

On December 3, 1931, four suspects were arrested. "All were released; insufficient evidence; no prosecution."

Thus goes the last memory—on the police blotter, anyway—of a missing person last seen October 15th at 6:30 A.M. at his home, 10949 North Mount Gleason, Sunland, California. It was not for Joe Ardizzone that the sun shone brightly that day. What matters the year?

The repeal of Prohibition on December 5, 1933, came, in the words used to summarize the Los Angeles gangland killings report,

> as such a shock to the Los Angeles underworld that for half a dozen years, an uneasy peace prevailed. Many of the big shots of the Twenties went legitimate and bought into wineries, distilleries, and other comparatively respectable businesses. To their great surprise, they found going legit could be as profitable as bootlegging. Others just couldn't face respectability and went in for other violent pursuits which marked the underworld's reconversion period. It wasn't long, however, before the cagiest of the racket boys struck it rich with the biggest bonanza in the history of crime—organized gambling. It wasn't long before the guns came out, professional killers were again taking rubout orders from here to Brooklyn, and organized crime introduced sound business doctrine at gunpoint into what had been a penny ante racket.

Again, it was Jack Dragna who set up the gambling operation when Prohibition went down the drain and the Mafia bosses began to seek diversified sources of income. In the process, however, he had to deal with Benjamin Siegel, reputed West-Coast representative of the eastern gang, Murder, Inc., who arrived on the Los Angeles scene in 1937.

Bugsy Siegel was a graduate of the "Bug and Meyer" mob, which was formed when he joined forces on the Lower East Side of New York with Meyer Lansky to execute "contracts"—murders—for the New York and New Jersey gangs during Prohibition. Siegel and Lansky, who were friendly with all of the top eastern syndicate mobsters, traveled across the country doing their "jobs" and eventually sat as equal members on the board of directors with Lucky Luciano, Frank Costello, Vito Genovese, and others.

While at the zenith of his power in New York, where he lived in a suite of rooms at the Waldorf Astoria Towers two floors above Luciano, Siegel was "given" California during the division of territory undertaken by Costello and other gang bosses in 1931. His mission was to form a coalition of the top West-Coast mobs, which previously had no working arrangement between them, and to help Mafioso *capo* Jack Dragna establish, for the use of bookies, the Capone-controlled Trans-America wire service in California and, later, in Nevada.

Bugsy's reign in California, with Dragna as his chief lieutenant, blossomed as he played around with George Raft and many other of Hollywood's early stars, including Jean Harlow, who was having a Pygmalion-type romance with Longy Zwillman, one of Joe Adonis' mentors in New Jersey and political fixer of note. Siegel was handsome, liked sharp clothes, and found it necessary to have his initials monogrammed on everything he wore or carried, even down to his tailored silk shorts—which put Bugsy, in his own mind, in the echelon of real class.

There was, however, nothing foppish about his power or the syndicate weight he brought with him from the East. In September, 1937, the year in which he arrived on the West Coast, Siegel held a meeting of the top mobsters he was about to organize and laid down the rules of the game. Only one hood stood up to protest: Les Brunemann, a Redondo Beach gambler who had hopes himself of controlling gambling activities in southern California. Less than a month later, on October 25th, Brunemann, who was still recuperating from gunshot wounds inflicted during a previous attempt on his life, was shot to death at the Roost Café in Redondo Beach by two gunmen, who also wounded his nurse and others and killed a bystander.

There is some difference of opinion in law-enforcement circles about the relationship between Bugsy Siegel and Jack Dragna. To talk in terms of elegance about two people with few social graces may seem stupid, but Dragna needed Siegel in the overall plan the mob had worked out ultimately to get deeply involved in the free-gaming town of Las Vegas. Dragna was a "plug-ugly" who needed a silk purse, and "Glamour Boy" Siegel provided the come-on for the Hollywood-Beverly Hills crowd who were the first to rush to Las Vegas and be "busted out." On the other hand, Siegel needed Dragna as his California contact man, especially at first. Perhaps it was a marriage of convenience in which both partners thought himself the leader.

In any case, many authorities believe that Bugsy was the first one to recognize the mother-lode potential of Las Vegas. It was Dragna, however, who unintentionally moved big-time gambling into Vegas when he attempted to "muscle" into the bookmaking activities in Los Angeles of the then Los Angeles police department vice-squad officer Guy McAfee and his gambling partner, Tutor Scherer.

"Who the hell is Jack Dragna?" McAfee wanted to know. He soon found out. Stick-up men raided his books, runners were roughed up, and the Italians demanded in. McAfee folded his gambling tent, took Tutor by the hand, and went east to Las Vegas, where together the two put together the Golden Nugget, two blocks from the railroad station at the north end of Fremont Street.

Charlie King, auditor for the Golden Nugget, told the author that McAfee was not driven out of Los Angeles by Dragna. "McAfee saw a great opportunity in Vegas and decided to get in on it," said King, formerly a group chief for the IRS in southern California. But however it happened, McAfee and Tutor soon were reaping such a golden harvest that Jack and his pals began blinking their eyes.

Perhaps engulfed by his unexpected good fortune, Tutor Scherer, who affected flowing white locks, married a Las Vegas girl and had a son by her. For some reason, he named the child Lord Bacon Scherer, and everyone figured that Tutor was a secret devotee of the art of poesy. Scherer, however, was far less flamboyant than the first legitimate "California" Italian Mafioso in Las Vegas, Antonio Cornero Stralla. Tony, a sort of maverick member of the brotherhood who was born in Italy at the turn of the century, had made a million dollars as a bootlegger before he was thirty years old. He therefore went to Las Vegas looking for money and trouble, and the extravagance of his dreams made even Siegel's look like two-bit nightmares.

Tony started a place called the Green Meadows and staffed it with girls, slot machines, and waiters. It was actually the first "class" joint in Las Vegas, and he built it after he had served two years on bootlegging charges arising out of his arrest when his gambling ship, the S.S. "Lilly," was boarded by the Coast Guard off Long Beach, California. Four thousand cases of bootleg liquor were found on board. Bad luck seemed to follow Tony, in fact. The Green Meadows burned down one hot night. Cornero then sold out his remaining piece of interest in Las Vegas gaming, a chunk of the Apache Hotel casino at the corner of Second and Fremont Streets operated by the Silvagni family.

Tony Cornero died on July 31, 1955, while shooting craps at the Desert Inn in Las Vegas. Before he had his fatal heart attack, he had begun work on the Stardust Hotel, a glittering place that he thought might cater to the little people, and the plan called for hundreds of rooms for them. It remained for many other people to complete the Stardust, and today the glittering façade of the hotel is his tombstone. Everyone remembers.

Cornero's dream came true some years after Siegel started construction on the Flamingo Hotel, drawing on the Frank Costello-Joey Adonis bank in New York and New Orleans. It was evident that Siegel had the proper formula in spite of many troubles: he was the elected, true, and legal representative of the syndicate in Las Vegas, by way of California.

Since Siegel enjoyed such backing, Dragna was stuck with him. Left with what he could dig out of California, Dragna found that the boys had sent him, in the person of Siegel, someone he couldn't even understand. In fact, the golden age of gambling in Las Vegas left Dragna far behind, and in so doing, it unglued the eastern mobsters. The big men of the East suddenly realized that many people had moved into Los Angeles, along with the kind of industry they had feasted off for many years in New York City. Las Vegas was a lemon-cream pie. Even when dished out in small wedges to members of the Cosa Nostra families, there were suddenly more relatives coming to the tea party than anyone could imagine. But California was a different matter. In Los Angeles and the other cities were pickings for many jackals. Consequently, eyes turned back to California. There one could await the call to Las Vegas and yet still get immodestly—if not filthy—rich.

Some of the first to try and move into Los Angeles were garment racketeers from New York City's garment section. Supposedly, a fellow named Louis (Scarface) Lieberman led the assault, and the records indicate that John Ignatius Dioguardi, the hood believed by the FBI and others to be at the bottom of the conspiracy that resulted in the blinding of labor writer Victor Riesel, followed Scarface into California.

The suave Dioguardi, who escaped a conspiracy conviction in the case involving the acid-blinding of Riesel after prosecution witnesses refused to testify, was, in September, 1957, sentenced to two years on conviction of extorting money from an employer in return for labor peace. In pressing his case against Johnny Dio in the Riesel blinding, U.S. Attorney Paul S. Williams said that a twenty-one-year-old thug named Abraham Telvi had, for a fee of $500 from Dio, splashed sulphuric acid on Riesel's face. Incidentally, in the way of many mobsters, Telvi signed his own death warrant by going back for more money and by talking too much. After receiving another $500, according to Williams, Telvi was shot and killed on Dio's orders.

Scarface Louis Lieberman, alias "Louis Green" and "Louis Martin," has a criminal record that started in 1931, when he was sentenced to a prison term of fifteen years. The prison term lasted the legal minimum period, and it was followed by a long series of arrests and convictions. Finally, on February 20, 1951, Lieberman was sentenced to Sing Sing for a term of three to four years for attempted extortion. Shortly after the completion of that sentence, which marked his graduation from the lower to the higher echelons of the mob, Lieberman migrated to California, where his internship began. He started something called the Lucky Trucking Company.

Among the mass of testimony in a 1959 report of the Senate committee on rackets concerning organized crime in California is one most inviting morsel. The Lucky Trucking Company, it seems, was financed by the sale of two kilos of heroin, apparently provided by a prospective partner, Louis Fiano, who eventually wound up in a federal penitentiary after conviction on July 18, 1958, on a charge of selling the heroin. No conviction has deterred Lieberman, however. His interest in the garment trade has not altered. Bombings and acts of violence have been directed against legitimate garment firms such as the D'Amico Coat Manufacturing Company of Fullerton, Vogel and Weiss of San Gabriel, Jack Kramer of Los Angeles, and Mike Silvers, a dress manufacturer in Los Angeles.

At Mike Silvers' place on November 17, 1953, Gene Burg, a U.C.L.A. student and member of the varsity football squad, helped two thugs break up the machinery with crowbars. Burg eventually pleaded guilty and served a three-year sentence in a state penitentiary. He was "hooked" on narcotics, it was learned, and refused to answer questions put to him by the state rackets committee.

One of Burg's two accomplices in the wrecking of the plant was Rocco Guiliani, who although only twenty-four at the time already had a long criminal record, both in New England and California. A few weeks after the Silvers incident he was convicted of grand theft in San Francisco and sentenced to a ten-year penitentiary term. Later he was brought from the penitentiary to Los Angeles to plead guilty in the Silvers case and received a three-year sentence. The third accomplice has not been apprehended.

Guiliani, a smug, smirking hoodlum, was interviewed at San Quentin but would give no information beyond saying that he "got Burg into the deal—Burg does not know the persons" who hired them to do it. This could have been a grandstand play to impress officials with Guiliani's importance, for it had been established that Burg had called James Fratianno and his long-time associate, John Battaglia, alias "Charles Batts," many times before the Silvers incident.

The late Captain James Hamilton of the intelligence division of the Los Angeles police department called Guiliani a lieutenant or "right-hand bower" of Battaglia prior to the incident. Therefore, it would appear that the action was not an independent act of Burg and Guiliani but an ordered job by the Fratianno-Battaglia combination.

The East Coast-West Coast connection enabled the boys in Three Finger Brown's section of New York to try their luck in California, and the new association was cemented at a meeting between Louis Lieberman and Louis Tom Dragna, nephew of the now-deceased Jack Dragna, held in Room 101 at the Sands Hotel in Las Vegas on January 18, 1957. Louis Fiano and other soldiers were present, and the future of the Lucky Trucking Company was mapped. The target was to secure for the company the delivery work in the Los Angeles garment section.

It would reasonably be deduced that such an array of experienced talent from the East was not welcomed by the relatively untrained hoodlums of California, especially by the young ones who had been shouldered out of the lush Las Vegas melon patch by such elders as Emilio (Gambo) Georgetti, who moved from San Mateo

County, California, to Las Vegas in 1947 when his friend, San Mateo County Sheriff James McGrath, was defeated after a twenty-six-year tour at the helm of the county law-enforcement office. Their jealousy is understandable. Georgetti bought a piece of Benny Binion's Westerner Club in Las Vegas and in six weeks controlled the whole operation.

The garment boys had high hopes of breaking into Las Vegas when Jack Dragna took over in Las Vegas after Georgetti died of cancer. But despite Dragna's ties to Johnny Dioguardi in New York through a mutual friend, Sam Berger, the boys in the garment rackets on both the East and West Coasts made very few dents in the behind-the-scenes Las Vegas economy. Legalized gambling seems to have fallen primarily into the hands of the Jewish element of the mob—the old-time gamblers from the Detroit, Cleveland, New York City, and Chicago areas who, in later years, were accused of sending a share of the skimmed profits back east to their Italian Mafiosi brothers-under-the-skin.

While it is true that the mob looked increasingly to other money-making opportunities after the repeal of Prohibition, the liquor industry remained a fruitful source of Mafia funds. In addition, the mob's involvement in liquor shows how the boys exercise, with the help of their friends in office, political power. The story of the California alcohol beverage control board, born in 1939, might well be a case in point, for it came into being after the syndicate's Prohibition dream had gone down the drain and many former bootleggers had become legitimate distributors.

The Alcohol Beverage Control Act gave the control board and the state board of equalization responsibility for the licensing of every cocktail lounge, liquor retail store, and restaurant or nightclub serving wine and the headier stuff. Appointed by the governor, the members of the board were given the authority to determine not only who should be licensed but also which licenses should be suspended or revoked.

Meanwhile, during the rather turbulent aftermath of the state of California's attempt to get a grip on the liquor industry, a man named Artie Samish became top dog in the dark halls that house the lobbyists who plague the state capitol in Sacramento. Samish often called himself the "unelected governor of California" and represented himself as the man who controlled the state board of equalization while fronting for major breweries on the West Coast. Certainly, in his heyday Samish was immensely powerful in California.

The portly Samish had a number of clients for whom he lobbied, including the California State Brewers' Institute, which paid him $30,000 a year in salary and expenses and gave him control of a $153,000-a-year slush fund. In addition, merely for being "on call," Samish received $36,000 a year from Schenley Distillers in New York. Samish's brewery funds, which were supplied by the eleven-member Institute "for so-called political purposes" and "to establish good will" or protect the industry, totaled $953,943 over a six-year period—all in cash, a fact that later led to problems with the tax men. And lack of information was not confined to the IRS. In 1951 the Kefauver probers had trouble getting at the facts of the Samish operation. Finally, however, the big man admitted that the special funds given him by the Institute were spread around among "good, honest, outstanding officials that subscribed to the temperate use of beer, wine and spirits."

If that is the case, it is equally true that mobsters Mickey Cohen, Joe Adonis, and Phil Kastel were among the seamier people Samish called friends. Telephone company records indicate that Cohen, former non-Mafia operating member of the syndicate's bookmaking and strong-arm departments in California, called Samish frequently.

Samish was fond of saying that he was "the governor of the legislature and to hell with the governor of the state," and he made no bones about thinking he was the power behind the political throne in California. Perhaps he was—for a while. But in 1956 the federal government clipped Artie's wings when he was sentenced to three years in prison and fined $40,000 for failure to pay taxes on income of $90,000 between 1946 and 1951.

Samish served twenty-six months on McNeil Island and was released on March 17, 1958. A stockily built man weighing over three hundred pounds when he went to prison, Samish emerged much slimmer, insisting that the "stretch" was good for his health. Samish had always had a Lucius Beebe-like instinct for fine meals and a very real understanding of the value of good food even at the bargaining table. In his lobbying days he believed more in plying a man with succulent wild ducks flown a thousand miles to a well-placed table in a fine restaurant than in confounding him with mere words. An army travels on its stomach, and Samish was an army.

The year Artie Samish decided really to swing with the pendulum of the power he claimed was 1947, when he decided to promote a man named Fred N. Howser for the post of state's attorney general. Samish thought his boy Howser would be a shoo-in because his lobbying cabal would be able to trade on the good reputation of a man with a similar name: Fred Houser, who had been elected Lieutenant-Governor of California and was remembered for his great integrity.

The stratagem, however elementary, was successful. In January, 1948, Howser took office as attorney general under Governor Earl Warren, now Chief Justice of the U.S. Supreme Court. Fortunately, however, the results were not all bad for California. Because there were rumors of a certain lack of ethics in the conduct of Howser's campaign, Warren established a commission to study organized crime in the state, with the initial request that Howser investigate bookmaking organizations operating with the use of Western Union wires in Palm Springs, a sunbathed winter resort basking not only in the direct rays of a cruel orb but also in the reflected heat of the limestone slopes of 12,000-foot Mt. San Jacinto.

Howser sent to this palm-fringed clot of desert one Wiley H. (Buck) Caddel, who was to be aided by an investigator named John Riggs. Riggs did his job. But it was found that doctored, negative reports had been sent to the commission, and Riggs in defense said he had been ordered to do so by his chief, Caddel. Warren then ordered that his group send their own investigator to Palm Springs. The new findings resulted in a ruling by the state Public Utilities Commission that when a telegraph or telephone company was notified by law-enforcement units of illegal use of its wires, it must immediately cancel the leases involved.

The rule set up by the Warren group was first used by Pat Brown, California's governor from 1958 to 1966, who was then district attorney of San Francisco County. A publicity release announced that "bookie drops," the places where bets are made, had been shut off from service by the telegraph and telephone companies. Apparently District Attorney Brown had located a network of bookies in short order and really surprised the more conservative elements in San Francisco, who wondered why the bookies had been allowed to operate for so many years. The final scenes were played out later when Howser's Wiley Caddel was convicted in 1948 on charges of bribery and conspiracy to violate gambling laws. The case and the details eventually disappeared in a flurry of appeals, but the point had been made. The bookmakers would no longer have such an easy time.

What did not appear at first, however, was Samish's part in the affair. Those details appeared later. In July, 1956, Bernard P. Calhoun, executive secretary of the Southern California Spirits Foundation, was charged with others of conspiring to collect illegal political funds from liquor dealers. In reply Calhoun said that $5,000 was contributed in 1950 to Howser, who was defeated in the June primaries that year for reelection as attorney general, and an additional $5,500 was paid the same year to "various candidates." Several other politicians were named by Calhoun, who also recalled that a check for $5,000 was sent to the Los Angeles Jefferson-Jackson Day dinner in 1954. It seems almost certain that Samish was the channel for those moneys, and there is no doubt that Howser was Samish's man.

In fact, as is well known, the 1950 election resulted in Democrat Pat Brown's defeat of Edward C. Shattuck, who had defeated Howser in the Republican primary election. And of course Brown went on from attorney general to become governor, without the overbearing influence of Artie Samish but with the ever-present specter of corruption in the liquor and illegal-gambling industries plaguing him—which brings us back to Western Union.

It seems that California gamblers, and those to the east in Las Vegas, received a little better service from Western Union than did honest citizens. John Doe came second to the gambling nabobs who leased lines from Western Union. This was made clear when a small plane attempting an emergency landing near Bakersfield, a San Joaquin Valley town later to be included in the investigation by Howser, tore down the Western Union hot line to the bookies and other salient points and wiped out itself and its crew. Within half an hour all the leased wires of Western Union in use by bookies were in operation, but the U.S. Army Western Defense Command had to wait more than two hours before service was restored to one of its lines.

The story of liquor-bookmaking interests in California is interminable. But one more brief interjection into the California history is worthwhile since it brings the chain of corruption closer to a current analysis and the inevitable conclusion that things are getting worse instead of better.

In March, 1949, a grand jury in San Bernardino was convened to hear the testimony of a Mrs. Earl Wilson. Mrs. Wilson flatly accused State Senator Ralph E. Swing of soliciting an under-the-table cut for using influence to obtain a midget-auto racing concession for her and her husband at the San Bernardino County National Orange Show.

Swing was a director of the Orange Show, which turned into a real lemon for Mrs. Wilson when another 5 per cent kickback for the concession was demanded by W. C. Shay, then chief agent for the board of equalization, which Artie Samish boasted he controlled. Denials of any graft were quickly voiced by the accused. But the accusation remained.

The total cut demanded by Swing and Shay was 20 per cent, 15 per cent to Swing, 5 per cent to Shay, and negotiations for the graft came, according to Mrs. Wilson, through a Mr. Edward J. Seeman, known throughout southern California as the slot-machine king of San Bernardino.

Checking records for the grand jury, probers discovered through the California division of corporations that Seeman and Senator Swing were two of four partners in a liquor business known as Alfred Hart Distributing Company of San Bernardino and Riverside—an association confirmed by C. H. Palmer, Los Angeles attorney for the Alfred Hart Distillers, Inc. The third partner was Al Hart, who has since divorced himself from the liquor business and now is head of City National Bank of Beverly Hills. The fourth partner listed by Palmer was a Miss E. Mack, who helped organize the liquor outlets.

Apparently all the male partners were on good terms with Artie Samish. Profits of hundreds of thousands of dollars had resulted from an initial capital investment of $2,000, through know-how and know-who, the testimony revealed. But the grand jury apparently found nothing amiss and returned no indictment. The testimony, however, is on the record. And though it was shortly after these revelations that Attorney General Howser announced he would run for reelection, he was probably aware that both he and Samish might soon be found out. And so it came to pass. Even the bad guys finish last occasionally.

Today, rule of the burgeoning Mafia in southern California is vested in several men who have long histories of criminality. They are, in the order of their importance: Nick Licata, an elder whose advice is much sought after to settle quarrels among the Mafiosi in most of the western states; Louis Tom Dragna, a much younger man and nephew of Mafia West-Coast pioneer Jack Dragna; Frank Bompensiero, former strong-arm man for the San Diego organization; Anthony Pinelli, an elder facing possible deportation who often hosts Mafia chieftains at his home in Sierra Madre, near Los Angeles; John Roselli, former labor racketeer who also may be deported; and James Fratianno, "muscle" and "trigger man" who supposedly was the "hit" man involved in the last of the big Mafia murders in Los Angeles—the still unsolved 1951 murder of two toughs, Anthony Brancato and Anthony Patrick Trombino, killed in an auto on North Ogden Drive in Los Angeles following their holdup of a Flamingo Hotel cashier in Las Vegas.

Nick Licata, whom *Life* magazine has labeled "one of the top leaders of criminal groups in California," lives in Torrance, California, and his position as chief don is not exactly of his own doing. He became top man on January 10, 1968, on the death following a heart attack of the California boss, Frank DeSimone of Downey, California, who had taken over southern California after the 1957 death of Jack Dragna.

DeSimone, convicted of conspiracy to obstruct justice in connection with the 1957 Apalachin meeting, was sentenced to four years in jail, but the conviction, along with those of two dozen other Mafiosi at the meeting, was later reversed. DeSimone, in fact, was a strange man. Apparently he exemplified the terror that has played such a large part in the viability and success of the Mafia.

The hoodlums have always prided themselves on their respect, not only for their family boss, but also for the women of the family. There are, however, any number of exceptions to the rule. And one such occurred in 1956, when DeSimone, according to a police informant, raped the wife of Girolamo (Momo) Adamo in the presence of the shocked husband, who had served the Mafia longer and in more diverse capacities than DeSimone.

DeSimone's action, according to the informant, was undertaken to show Adamo who was boss. The outraged and disillusioned Adamo seriously wounded his wife shortly thereafter, then shot and killed himself with a .32-caliber pistol in their home in

San Diego. DeSimone had broken a primary Mafia law relating to the inviolability of the women within the society, but there is no record that he was ever brought to task for it.

Incidentally, children find no protection, either, when they can be used to further the terror that permeates the Mafia structure. Thus, an eleven-year-old boy was killed by the mob to silence his brother, a government witness in a narcotics case in Kansas City. The witness, Carl Caramussa, was a member of a narcotics ring, and despite the terror of his brother's murder he later testified against hoodlums associated with the tough Kansas City Mafioso Joe (Scarface) DiGiovanni. After he had testified, Caramussa tried to elude his former associates and start a new life. But in June, 1945, while attending a wedding party, his head was blown off by a shotgun. City detective Louis Olivero also was shot and killed as he probed the ramifications of the Kansas City dope ring.

DeSimone's underboss and family heir had been Simone Scozzari who also was at the Apalachin meeting, until Scozzari's deportation to Palermo, Sicily, in 1962. Scozzari reportedly still receives large sums of Mafia money from the United States, and he is apparently trying to arrange for his reentry to the country.

Meanwhile, Nick Licata not only has the last Mafia word from San Diego to Los Angeles and points north, but his domain also reaches Dallas, Texas, where he shares the rule with Joe Civello. In Dallas, Licata and Civello have replaced a hood known as Sam Maceo, the iron hand in the velvet glove who ruled the southern tier of states for many years with Carlos Marcello of New Orleans and Santo Trafficante, Jr., of Tampa, Florida.

Born in Camporeale, Italy, in 1897, Licata presumably took over the California business interests of another Mafioso, Tony Mirabile of San Diego, who was murdered in 1959 and left control of twenty-seven bars and taverns to Licata and the organization. Mirabile, who came from Alcoma, Sicily, typified the father-type don whose hands are kissed and to whom the Mafiosi genuflect when they come to pay court. He operated a club known as the Midnight Follies in Tijuana before establishing permanent residency in San Diego. He set "true" Mafia patterns of conduct: over the years he was arrested on various charges, including one of assault with intent to kill—a charge dropped when a prosecution witness took fright—and one of grand larceny—which was not pressed.

Mirabile's interest in bars served a good purpose. He sought control of the local bartenders' union in San Diego through the simple process of hiring men for his union shops, then firing them and hiring others to increase union membership. Finally, the weight of the votes was carried by employees and former employees who knew and feared the don.

The San Diego locale is most useful to syndicate members because of its proximity to the border, where illegal crossings, into and out of Mexico, can be implemented with relative ease.

For all his advantages, however, Licata seems to be more penurious than Mirabile, who maintained $50,000 in the San Diego Security Trust and Savings Bank for the use of friends, who merely had to say, "Tony sent me," in order to get a loan.

Licata's record includes a small fine for refilling liquor bottles. And he was also questioned about the murders of the two Tonys, Brancato and Trombino. Later, during a probe of California racketeering by a state assembly subcommittee, Licata denied any knowledge of the Mafia and was cited for contempt upon refusal to answer other questions, but charges were dismissed in November, 1959.

Despite his silence official police records indicate that Licata's interests have included gaming operations in Mexico with hoodlums Joe Sica, Pete Licavoli, and a couple of relatives of noted Mafioso Frank Garofolo; gold and silver smuggling from Mexico City; and a variety of legitimate businesses including fruit-juice vending machines and dairy-products companies. Licata has also invested in subdivision developments near Los Angeles, which reportedly involved James Fratianno and Jack Fox, a Chicago hoodlum. Mortuaries and such mundane businesses as delicatessens have also attracted his organizational zeal.

In 1949 Licata was associated, according to law authorities, with Louis Tom Dragna, the late Girolamo Adamo, and three others in the operation of the Prairie Club in Hawthorne, California, just outside Los Angeles, and he also controlled bookmakers in nearby Burbank with tough Mafia enforcers.

Licata's sense of decorum and adherence to the old-time principles of the Mafia have won him a revered position in the secret society—insofar as the criminal society may be said to understand reverence—but, at seventy-two, he is perhaps too old to last much longer in the highly competitive world of the Mafia.

Louis Tom Dragna of Covina, who was listed by the McClellan committee as a "criminal associate" of hoodlums, seems gradually to be grasping the reins of ultimate, supreme rule of the California Mafia. Forty-eight years old, Dragna is directing his racketeering efforts with the help of the clan, which sees a potential gold mine on the West Coast.

Dragna, according to McClellan committee records, is closely associated with Harold (Happy) Meltzer, a product of the New York City rackets who has been tracked on various occasions, during weird but apparently profitable wanderings, through New England, Canada, Mexico, Cuba, Hong Kong, Japan, Hawaii, and the Philippines, to mention but a few way-stops. Meltzer, who, like Meyer Lansky, the ex-husband of his wife Doris, is Jewish and therefore a non-Mafia syndicate power, has two federal narcotics convictions. The McClellan committee called him "an international drug trafficker closely allied with top Mafia racketeers," an associate of top labor organizers, especially those affiliated with Dragna —who owns or has interests in a number of dress-manufacturing concerns in Los Angeles—and "head of a large bookmaking and prostitution syndicate in California."

The McClellan report also listed Dragna and Meltzer as partners in the California Sportswear Company of Los Angeles. And it was no doubt Meltzer who, along with Jack Dragna, helped Louis Tom Dragna's climb up the ladder of Mafia hierarchy in the early 1950's when police records point to the latter's involvement in bookmaking and a wire-service operation—Trans-America—to provide betting information to bookmakers.

Louis Tom Dragna has had many brushes with the law, including arrests on charges of burglary and conspiracy to commit murder, and he was picked up for questioning in 1941 about a ring that counterfeited $10 bills. In 1959 he was indicted with four other men for extortion; they were allegedly attempting to shake down welterweight fighter Don Jordan. Subsequent conviction, however, was reversed as Dragna's lucky charm held.

Louis Tom is not without influence in Las Vegas, either, having in October, 1967, according to police intelligence files, placed an associate as a pit boss in the Thunderbird Hotel casino in Nevada's sanitized, legitimatized, and glamorized version of Sin City.

Frank (The Bump) Bompensiero of Pacific Beach in San Diego is sixty-three years old and has an impressive roster of past and present criminal playmates. A paragraph in the listing of Los Angeles gangland killings indicates that on February 28, 1938, Bompensiero and a fellow hood forced one Phil Galuzo

> into an automobile and drove him to the vicinity of 1674 E. 83rd Street where he was severely beaten, pushed out of the car and shot several times. Victim taken to Maywood Hospital and on March 7, 1938, died. Frank Bompensiero was arrested on June 21, 1941. However, as there was insufficient evidence to prosecute on kidnapping and murder charges, suspect released. At this time Bompensiero was wanted for three felony counts of robbery by San Diego police. Disposition unknown. Bompensiero is now located in San Diego operating a cafe bar and poses as a legitimate businessman. He is a partner of Tony Mirabile and an associate of Jack Dragna.

By 1955 Bompensiero was reported by informants to be the head of the Mafia in the San Diego area, "an organizer . . . feared by all who know him." But in April of that same year he was convicted on three counts of bribery and sentenced to serve five years in the state prison—a slip that may have prompted Mafia elder Anthony Pinelli three months later to call Bompensiero a "dumb hoodlum."

Paroled in May, 1960, The Bump, whose wife, Marie, is rumored to be Momo Adamo's widow, apparently remained on relatively good behavior until his release from parole in June, 1965. Since then police surveillance records indicate that he "has become increasingly active in the bar business in the San Diego area" and that he has been observed on numerous occasions in the company of such former hood buddies as James Fratianno, Louis Tom Dragna, Leo (Lips) Moceri, Joe Matranga, and Detroit's Papa John Priziola, Joe Matranga's father-in-law. The *El Centro Press* believes him to be the "head of the Mafia in San Diego." Bompensiero's messenger boy appears to have been Julio Petro of Van Nuys until Petro was shot and killed in the front seat of his car at Los Angeles international airport the night of January 12, 1969. The forty-six-year-old Cleveland-born safe burglar received a twenty-five year sentence in 1952 for a $71,000 bank robbery and was released on parole in 1966. Petro was considered by police intelligence to be the southern California contact man for eastern hoods, and his murder added more fuel to the Mafia fire developing in California.

Anthony (Tony) Pinelli was born in 1899 in Calascibetta, Sicily, and came to New York in 1913 as an immigrant. He has never applied for citizenship and years later was named by the U.S. Senate rackets committee as "a top figure in the Cosa Nostra and associate of Anthony Accardo, heir to Al Capone's Chicago crime empire." Madeline, Pinelli's wife of forty-three years, was born in the United States. They have five children and twenty-two grandchildren. Pinelli has a business record that, as outlined by his attorney, would raise no eyebrows whatsoever:

> He has lived in Sierra Madre since 1949, headed Century Distributors, a juke box business, from 1956 to 1962, and was in the grape business for 16 years as Northside Grape Distributing Co., which operated in the Chicago area. Pinelli sold out in 1963 and has since been in retirement.

In fact, Pinelli has kept out of the limelight for the most part, but in 1960 he was intimately linked by the Senate rackets committee with the gambling, prostitution, and other rackets around Gary, Indiana, as a sort of absentee landlord. Robert Kennedy, the committee's chief counsel, charged that Pinelli used profits from the rackets to acquire valuable real estate in southern California.

The Senate committee's chief investigator at the time was Pierre Salinger, later press secretary to President John F. Kennedy and an unsuccessful candidate for the U.S. Senate in California. According to Salinger, Pinelli used profits from gambling and other rackets activities in Gary and Chicago to acquire $443,000 in real estate and to set up his son in the motel business.

Salinger charged that Pinelli—in a kind of reverse version of the skimming operations recently charged to Las Vegas casinos—often exchanged thousands of dollars in cash for checks issued to him by Las Vegas gambling casinos, making it appear the money came from legal dice-game winnings. Salinger introduced as evidence a series of canceled checks from the Desert Inn, ranging from $5,000 to $15,000 and totaling $74,000 up to December 31, 1958. Obviously, this kind of procedure merely returned Pinelli's own money to him, but instead of being illegally gotten syndicate money, it became legitimate gambling winnings, which merely had to be included on his income-tax report. Moreover, the casino was able to show the same amount as a business loss, thereby lowering its reported income.

Eventually, however, tax men caught up with Pinelli. On June 17, 1960, he was fined $1,470 and placed on two years' probation for failing to file a California State tax return on earnings from 1955 to 1958.

Pinelli's home has often been used to entertain rackets figures. And when, in the past, Tony Accardo of Chicago went to Las Vegas via Los Angeles, it was Pinelli who met him at the Los Angeles airport. One of Pinelli's special pals is Gabriel Mannarino of New Kensington, Pennsylvania. A labor racketeer and gambler who was at the Apalachin meeting, Mannarino owns slot-machine, vending-machine, and jukebox privileges in New Kensington and was formerly part-owner of the casino at the Sans Souci Hotel in Havana.

In July, 1966, the government began making efforts to deport Pinelli by arresting him at his home on grounds of "moral turpitude." The charge was based on a record of two convictions in connection with defrauding the government of alcohol taxes (bootlegging) and of two income-tax convictions. He pleaded guilty to evading $4,315 in federal income taxes for the year 1959 and was fined $2,000 and put on probation for two years. Pinelli won a delay in the deportation case, however, by filing with the Immigration Service an application for permanent residence and was released on $10,000 bail.

John Roselli, sixty-three-year-old Italian-born Mafioso, is "right-hand bower" of the fast-rising Louis Tom Dragna. In fact, he might have been top man in California but for a threatened deportation —which may yet come off—and a recent court case involving him in a card-cheating ring at the "members only" Friar's Club in Beverly Hills, where he was sponsored for membership in 1963 by Frank Sinatra and Dean Martin.

Roselli arrived in the United States under his real name, Filippo Sacco, with his mother on September 16, 1911. They were to join his father, who was then living in East Boston. In 1921 Filippo Sacco was arrested by federal narcotics agents in Boston. Released on bail, he left town, and it was probably at that time that he changed his name to John Roselli.

Through his early associations with the Longy Zwillman mob

in Brooklyn and Newark, and later with Al Capone, Roselli became prominent in bootlegging and illicit liquor, and by 1936 he had a percentage of Nationwide News, the only bookmaking wire service at the time.

After Prohibition was repealed, Johnny Roselli went west from Chicago and, as an associate of Jack Dragna, became known as a labor racketeer and "muscle" for the movie studios. These activities, however, led to his conviction in 1944 on charges of racketeering and conspiracy to interfere with interstate trade in connection with the 1941 Bioff-Browne movie extortion case. Sentenced to ten years in prison, he was released on parole forty-three months later, on August 13, 1947.

After his stint in prison, Roselli was given the green light from the eastern boys to run Jack Dragna's wire service while using his position as "public information and contact man" with the Eagle-Lions movie studio as a front. Roselli began spending a lot of time traveling between Los Angeles, Palm Springs, and Las Vegas, associating extensively with Mafia members. In 1951, in fact, he testified at the Kefauver hearings that he knew Jack Dragna, Momo Adamo, Tony Accardo, Frank Costello, Joe Sica, Bugsy Siegel, Joe Adonis, Anthony (Little Augie Pisano) Carfano, Joe Massei, Meyer Lansky, Louis (Little New York) Campagna, Frank Milano, Joe Profaci, Sam Maceo, and Lucky Luciano, among others.

Although he answers to Meltzer and Dragna, Roselli is reputed to be a *capo*-Mafioso and the Mafia's western power and mouthpiece in Las Vegas. He lives in Beverly Hills and is said to have among his closest associates a man once employed by the Sands Hotel as "muscle man" to collect bad debts from debtors living in the Los Angeles area, a onetime public relations man for the New Frontier Hotel who has arrests for bookmaking and was once in the bail-bond business, and an attorney who has a lengthy and rather successful record of defending pimps, gamblers, and hoods.

On October 20, 1967, John Roselli was indicted by a federal grand jury on one count of failing to register and be fingerprinted as an alien and five counts of failing to notifiy the U.S. Immigration and Naturalization Service of his address for the previous five years. The indictment charged that Roselli is really Filippo Sacco, born in Esteria, Italy, in 1905, although Roselli has always maintained he was born in Chicago. It is interesting, too, that Roselli claims that he is a Los Angeles-Las Vegas real estate developer, and that he has nothing to do with former gangland associates.

United Press International Photo

Jackson Township, New Jersey, March, 1967: a state policeman looks at the remains of one of the two bodies found in what the FBI claims is a Cosa Nostra graveyard.

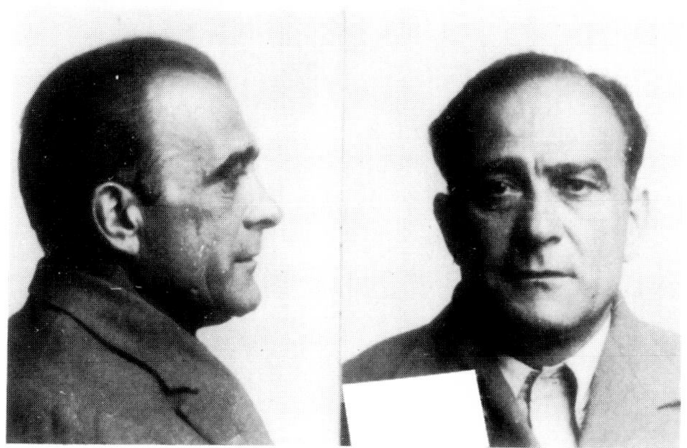

Vito Genovese, top Mafia hoodlum, currently serving a 15-year term in Atlanta federal penitentiary.

Five of the 13 Mafiosi arrested on September 22, 1966, return with attorneys to the site of the arrest: La Stella Restaurant, Forest Hills, Queens, New York. *Clockwise:* Joseph Marcello, Jr. (back to camera), attorney Jack Wasserman, Carlos Marcello, Santo Trafficante, attorney Frank Rangano, Anthony Corollo, Frank Gagliano.

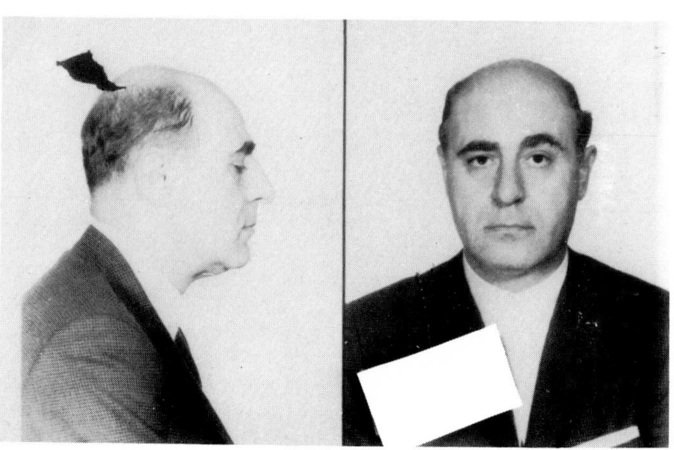

Thomas Eboli, acting boss of the Vito Genovese family, who attended the first La Stella luncheon.

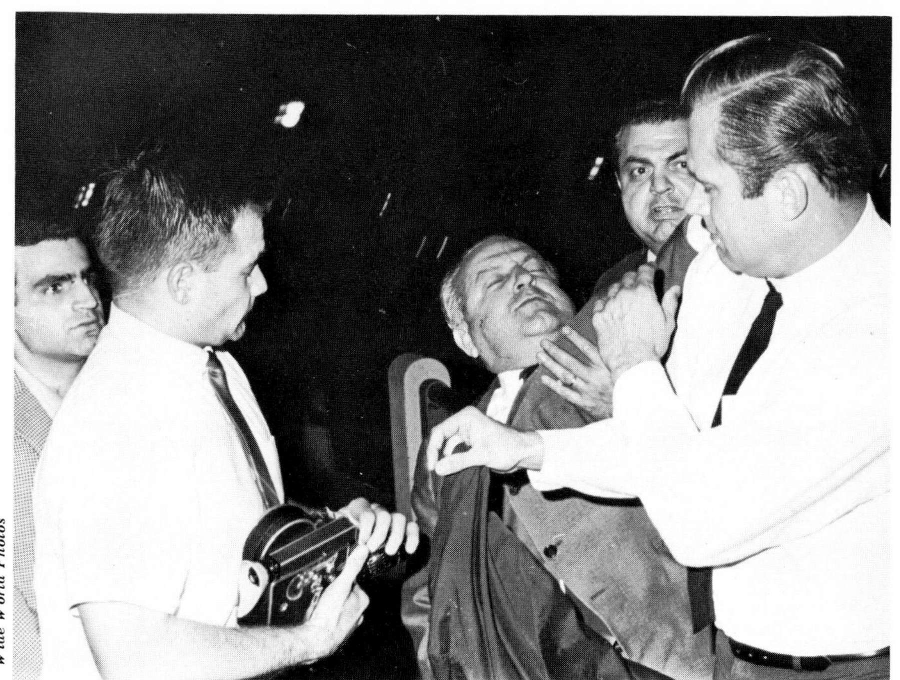

Wide World Photos

New Orleans Mafia boss Carlos Marcello lets fly at an FBI agent at New Orleans airport, October 1, 1966. Behind Carlos is his brother and family underboss, Joseph, Jr. Both men were among the 13 Mafiosi arrested at the La Stella restaurant.

Carlos Marcello, one of the most powerful Mafia figures alive today, absolute boss of the New Orleans area and much surrounding territory.

Virginia Hill and Major Riddle, owner of the Dunes Hotel in Las Vegas, during his earlier Chicago days when he was linked romantically with Bugsy Siegel's girl friend.

Antonio Cornero Stralla, the first Californian to grasp the potential of the Vegas gold mine.

During a 1952 fund drive, Francis Cardinal McIntyre was photographed with members of the Vegas gambling fraternity after receiving a pledge of $7,500, to be spread over five years. *Left to right:* Elias Atol, Gus Greenbaum,* Monsignor Empey* of Las Vegas, Jake Kozloff, Bishop Dwyer* of Reno, Israel (Icepick Willie) Alderman (a former Minneapolis hood who used to boast that he had murdered 11 men), Cardinal McIntyre, Monsignor Sibon, Benny Binion, Sam Genis,* Ben Goffstein.*

** now deceased*

Las Vegas—Zoom Town U.S.A., 1962

Even the Vice President — Tommy knows 'em all.
From left — Vice President of the United States, Lyndon Johnson, Tommy and Mrs. Johnson.

Lyndon B. Johnson, at the 1959 opening of the Stardust Hotel and Casino. ***Photograph published in 1962.***

Chicago's American

Anthony Accardo, currently one of the two top Chicago Mafia figures.

Chicago's American

Paul Ricca, with Accardo the present boss in Chicago.

Chicago's American

Sam Giancana, until his one-year jail term and his subsequent flight to South America the boss of Chicago's Mafia.

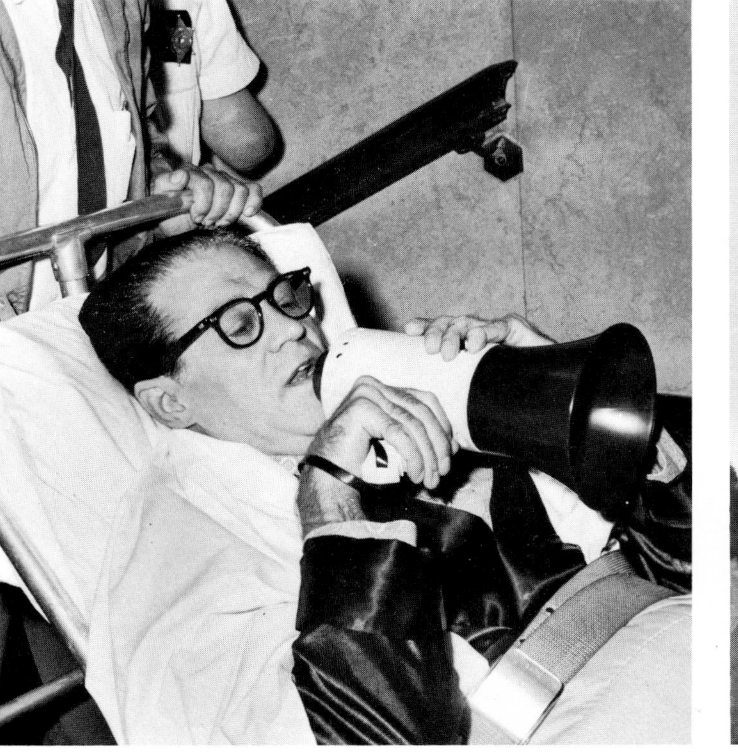

Sam DeStefano, a leading Chicago Mafia figure, using a bull horn to accuse the police of harassing a "sick" man while being carted off to jail.

Chicago's American

Sam DeStefano and his wife, Anita, at one of his court appearances. The strain that must be felt by all Mafiosi wives is apparent on Mrs. DeStefano's face.

Wide World Photos

Teamsters Union President James R. Hoffa, talking to newsmen on March 7, 1967, before he began serving his eight-year federal jury tampering sentence.

Roselli took the Fifth Amendment in declining to answer the questions put to him by U.S. District Judge Warren Ferguson in Los Angeles. Mrs. Barbara Crosby, wife of singer Gary Crosby, was more talkative, however. She told the grand jury investigating Roselli's citizenship status that she knew of him as "a nice man. He has been like a father to me."

"Dear Old Dad" Roselli took a trip to Washington, D.C. in November, 1967, and upon his return was quoted as saying that the purpose of his visit was to make contact with certain influential persons who could help him win his case with the U.S. Immigration and Naturalization Service. He did not identify anyone by name but made the statement that he had many friends in Washington, "including two ex-FBI agents who are now practicing attorneys, an inspector of police who accompanied him to the airport on his return trip and several senators, one of whom he described as an elderly statesman with a great deal of experience." Roselli reportedly said he had been told by his friends not to worry, that everything would be taken care of.

Nevertheless, Roselli lost out to the government in his attempt to prove he was born in Chicago and, as a result, may face deportation plus a fine of $2,000 and eleven months in prison. Oddly enough, if he had admitted to being an unregistered alien and then registered within thirty days after his indictment, the government probably would not have had a case, according to an Immigration Service spokesman. But if he was so advised by his attorney, James Cantillon, Roselli apparently paid no heed, trusting his luck to his eastern contingent.

The Friar's Club incident arose out of a summer, 1967, Los Angeles federal grand jury probe into charges that electronic devices were being used by a ring of conspirators to cheat wealthy club members who had a penchant for gin rummy and used the exclusive show-business hangout for their card playing.

The roster of disgruntled losers who testified about their mysterious losses and their suspicions of peepholes in the ceiling included the following: Harry Karl, millionaire shoeman and husband of actress Debbie Reynolds; singer Tony Martin; television's famed Sergeant Bilko, Phil Silvers; Zeppo Marx of the Marx Brothers; Ted Briskin, former camera manufacturer and onetime husband of Betty Hutton; Richard Corenson, real estate investment banker; and Hollywood actors' agent, Kurt Frings.

There were obviously no problems of poverty among the players. Subsequent testimony brought out evidence of individual losses for one day's play ranging from $5,000 to $50,000—with one individual's total loss over a period of ten months going as high as $220,000. One key witness who participated in operating the cheating apparatus—peepholes in the ceiling that allowed the observer to signal a confederate player with an electronic shocker attached to the player's leg and concealed by his trousers—testified that the swindlers took in "about $400,000 in a period of less than a year."

The grand jury investigation led to the indictment in December, 1967, of five members of the club, including Johnny Roselli, who allegedly participated in a five-year conspiracy of card cheating, primarily at the Friar's Club. All five faced charges of conspiracy to violate federal statutes, punishable by five years in prison and/or a $10,000 fine; interstate transportation to aid racketeering, five years and/or a $10,000 fine; and interstate transportation of funds obtained by fraud, ten years and/or $10,000. Three of them faced an additional tax-violation charge of failing to report what they won in the crooked games.

The four men indicted with Roselli were Maurice Friedman, onetime part-owner of the New Frontier Hotel in Vegas whose application for a 2 per cent share in the casino ownership was subsequently turned down by the Nevada gaming commission; Manuel (Ricky) Jacobs of Beverly Hills, a professional gambler; Benjamin J. Teitelbaum, manufacturer of movie-studio equipment and owner of an art collection valued at $3 million in 1962; and a prominent Beverly Hills physician whose name was later dropped from the list. A sixth indictment named a nonmember of the Friar's Club, T. Warner Richardson of Las Vegas.

Included among nonindicted "co-conspirators," whose testimony at the trial gave them immunity and helped put the others on the spot, were Beverly Hills restaurateur Al Mathes and ex-convict George Emerson Seach. Seach manned the peepholes and gave the necessary signals to the card players down below. Edwin N. Gebhard, the Miami electronics engineer who allegedly installed the cheating devices in the club, was convicted on fifteen counts of perjury during the grand jury hearings that led to the indictments.

The card-cheating trial, held in U.S. District Court in Los Angeles, makes rather interesting reading—if you don't have a sensitive stomach and want to see to what lengths some men will go to "make a buck." On December 2, 1968, four defendants in the conspiracy case—Roselli, Friedman, Jacobs, and Teitelbaum—were found guilty on 49 felony counts. Richardson was acquitted. A later date was set for sentencing and hearing arguments on motions for acquittal. Whatever the outcome for the others, it would appear that Filippo Sacco (or John Roselli, or "Don Giovanni," as he is known in the Mafia family) may have an opportunity—at government expense—to return once more to the old homestead in Esteria, Italy, in the not too distant future.

James Fratianno is last, but possibly not least, among the top Mafia powers in southern and central California. Based in Sacramento and named in California's 1959 Assembly committee report as the "West Coast executioner for the Mafia," Fratianno may even rank in syndicate hierarchy above his pal Frank Bompensiero. If so, however, it is probably only because of his ability to reflect and transmit the terror on which the Mafia feeds and profits. At any rate, his press notices are not improving, unless he takes pride in newsmen's frequent references to him as "The Weasel."

Captain James Hamilton credited Fratianno with at least sixteen gangland executions, including the 1951 mob execution of Tony Brancato and Tony Trombino. Hamilton, as well as others, was convinced that The Weasel was the calm killer who fired four shots each into the heads of the two Kansas City thugs who had the audacity to pull off the only successful armed robbery of a Strip casino in Las Vegas history. Fratianno was arrested and questioned regarding the murders. But later he was reluctantly released by the police for lack of witnesses and evidence.

Fratianno was subsequently sentenced to five years in prison for extortion and, after his release, resumed associations with his former Mafiosi playmates. But he was not forgotten by at least one member of the fourth estate. On July 8, 1966, *El Centro Post Press*, a little newspaper in the lettuce belt at the foot of California's Imperial Valley, broke a story by reporter Mike James. James reported that James Fratianno, alleged gangland executioner, and his buddy, Frank Bompensiero, had started a trucking firm in Sacramento, the Fratianno Trucking Company. The story also noted that the firm had "managed to obtain a contract to haul fill for the last 15 miles of freeway into Las Vegas" and was in the process of zeroing in on El Centro, where Fratianno and Bompensiero had taken up residence in a local motel.

Both men, wrote reporter James, became interested in the Imperial Valley, the most fertile in California, after a meeting in 1965 at the Beverly Wilshire Hotel in Beverly Hills with Frank Liparoto, alias "Frank LaPorte." James pictured LaPorte as a mystery man who lives in a closely guarded home worth $100,000 in Flossmoor, Illinois, and is reported to control mob-ridden Calumet City, Illinois. Frank LaPorte was identified at the McClellan hearings as a "terrorist once in the employ of Tony Accardo" and listed by the U.S. Attorney General as one of the top ten Mafia figures in the United States.

The Fratianno-Bompensiero trucking gimmick was that the Fratianno firm leased tractor-trucks to drivers as subcontractors on an earth-removal project on two sections of Interstate 8, south of El Centro, totaling 12.3 miles. Reporter Mike James claimed that the unusual leasing deal included eventual purchase of the equipment and stipulated that the driver "agrees to lease tractor exclusively to the Fratianno Trucking Co., Inc. Driver and tractor to be under complete control of Fratianno Trucking Co., Inc. Buyer agrees to work whenever and wherever jobs are offered by Fratianno Trucking Co., Inc." But as it turned out, none of the drivers was ever able to make enough money to cover all the monthly payments, and upon default each forfeited to the Fratianno Trucking Company his equipment and any equity he thought he had built up in it.

The *El Centro Post Press* story named Leo Moceri, former member of the Detroit Purple Gang and a convicted blackmailer, as a big Mafia power in California and an associate of Fratianno who had accompanied The Weasel on several mysterious trips to Mexico. The *Post* article also states that Moceri was present at the 1957 Apalachin conference—although this has never been verified—and charged that the Mafia is seeking control of "all trucking operations from San Francisco south."

Reaction to the James story followed quickly. Fratianno and Bompensiero, among others, threatened to sue the *El Centro Post Press* unless a retraction was made. The *Los Angeles Times*, playing it safe, waited a month to pick up the story and then did so only after Fratianno, the Fratianno Trucking Company—owned in the name of Fratianno's wife, Jewell—Bompensiero, and several associates were charged with fraud by Imperial County District Attorney James E. Hamilton, who had been investigating the matter.

A month prior to the *Post*'s story, a Fratianno associate, forty-three-year-old Nick Diacogianis, who has a record of convictions for auto theft, burglary, forgery, and white slavery, had been convicted of assault. He had slugged a truck driver who had complained about the system. The Mafia implications in the trial of Diacogianis were on the record for all to see, but it was left to a relatively tiny paper, one of a small chain, to brazen it out with the boys.

The felony case, based on twenty-eight counts, against Fratianno almost went out the window when Imperial County Superior Judge Victor A. Gillespie dismissed charges because of "lack of evidence and jurisdiction." However, Hamilton and the state attorney general's office appealed, and on January 11, 1968, the Fourth District Court ruled that Fratianno, his wife, and the Fratianno Trucking Company must stand trial on sixteen counts of "conspiracy and aiding and abetting the making of false reports on payrolls" during the 1966 period of highway construction. The Merced trucking firm, which shared Fratianno's contractual responsibility and had been accused of overloading dump trucks—apparently one reason drivers could not meet their quotas of two loads per hour—paid a $25,000 fine after the initial charges had been dismissed.

A month after their convictions on June 28, 1968, of conspiracy to defraud the federal government through false statements, Fratianno was fined $10,000, and his wife and the Fratianno Trucking Company were ordered to pay fines of $4,016 each. Although the maximum penalty could have included five years in prison, U.S. District Judge Edward Schwartz handed down no prison sentence for Fratianno but placed him instead on three years' probation.

In the meantime, on July 8, California Democratic floor leader George N. Zenovich presented a bill to the state Senate that would, in the words of the *Los Angeles Times*, "remove dump truck operators from State Public Utilities Commission regulation and control while working on state public works projects such as highways." The bill is supported by the California Trucking Association and the Teamsters Union. Opponents say that, if enacted, the bill "could directly benefit Sacramento trucking contractor James Fratianno," who faces yet another trial, in Los Angeles County, on several charges stemming from public utilities' violations.

Fratianno's troubles continue. On July 19, 1968, James and

Jewell Fratianno (and others) were sued for $645,000 in Sacramento Superior Court by the Mercantile National Bank of Chicago. It was charged that the defendants "fraudulently transferred and hid assets and used various subterfuges, including the corporate form, to veil individual dealings, to prevent [the bank] from securing proper payment." In addition to the $645,000, the bank is asking 7 per cent interest on the money and the return of seven truck-tractors.

All in all, 1968 may well have been in Mafia circles, "The Year of The Weasel." Then, in January, 1969, Fratianno was found guilty of conspiring to commit petty theft and to violate the state public utilities commission and labor codes. He was sentenced to spend one to three years in prison and his company was fined $85,000.

Not all things go well for the Mafia all the time. But in California the Mafiosi have spread their poison widely. The rootlets of the good things in California are slowly dying. And like barracuda circling a swarm of anchovies, the mob follows the public with a cradle-to-the-grave malevolence.

Consider the arteries of the airlines, crisscrossing the country, dropping customers by the millions at every important city. The International Airport Hotel, located on Century Boulevard, the gateway to the Los Angeles airport, would seem to be a product of the malevolence that is reaping a harvest for the boys.

Two of the individuals who appear to be involved in the hotel corporation out of which the Los Angeles hotel developed are Ed Levinson, whom we have already mentioned as a front man for syndicate vice king Joseph Stacher, and Benjamin Sigelbaum, partner of Levinson in numerous business deals, truly one of the mystery men in the Levinson entourage, and, as reported in the Caribbean chapter, an alleged "bagman" who carried skimmed money for the mob.

When the airport hotel corporation decided to go public in 1962, the names of Levinson and Sigelbaum probably would have made a stock offering somewhat unattractive for several reasons: Sigelbaum had declared bankruptcy many years ago in Florida; Levinson was associated with Las Vegas gambling interests; both men were deeply involved in financial transactions with the fast-stepping Bobby Baker, whose downfall was already in the making.

In any case, Levinson's name was not listed among the officers and directors of the company when the Los Angeles International Airport Hotel saw the light of day. Nevertheless, he is reported to have been able to keep an eye on his interests, and to make some pocket money on the side as well, through his control of the drugstore concession there.

The airport hotel system originally got under way in Miami in 1958 as Airway Hotel, Inc., and in 1959 it obtained a lease from the Dade County Port Authority and constructed a 264-room hotel atop the Miami International Airport terminal building.

The green light from the flight-control tower was apparently activated by Jimmy Hoffa, for the company received a $2-million loan from an "institutional lender," which was quickly assigned to the Teamsters' central states, southeast, and southwest areas pension fund. This, of course, occurred in the early days of Hoffa's power climb up the ladder of Teamster pension fund loans, well documented by Gene Blake and Jack Tobin in a series that appeared in the *Los Angeles Times* in the summer of 1962.

One of the next jumps on the flight schedule of the airport hotel boys, who in 1961 changed the company name to International Airport Hotel System, Inc., was the leasing from the city of Birmingham, Alabama, property within the airport compound. From Birmingham, the same company made a fast move to Houston, Texas, which was to become one of the best-known airports in the country when the N.A.S.A. program was based there.

Almost simultaneously, the hotel group made application to build airport hotels in Minneapolis, Minnesota, and at the Dulles International Airport in Chantilly, Virginia, which serves Washington, D.C. In February, 1961, it negotiated an agreement for a Dulles hotel, including a forty-year lease, between Airway Hotel of Washington, Inc., a wholly owned subsidiary, and the director of the Bureau of National Capital Airports, Federal Aviation Agency.

The Justice Department is said to have expressed great shock upon learning that Airway Hotel group, several of whose members were under the probing eye of congressional committees, had managed to obtain the Dulles Airport hotel lease. The Minneapolis lease application had been short-circuited, at last reports, inasmuch as a preliminary check into the reputations of some of the corporation directors gave pause to the city officials who authorize such leases.

In Houston, however, the airport boys were successful. And

while the Houston operation was under way, the company pushed westward in a frenzy of activity, and the hotel at Los Angeles airport began to take shape in 1962.

In its efforts to raise money to purchase the land for their Los Angeles hotel, the company decided to offer stock for public sale. Securities division officers in California and Illinois, however, had some serious reservations about sanctioning the stock offering. They questioned in particular the company's showing no profits for the previous three years of business. Other misgivings concerned the proposal that the stock price to the public be $10 to $12 per share while the directors, officers, and promoters of the company would continue to hold their 68.8 per cent of total shares acquired at anywhere from 2¢ to 34¢ per share. The applications for public sale in those states were eventually withdrawn, and the shares sold instead to a group of seventeen underwriters.

In the corporation's 1962 annual report, the following officers and directors were listed:

President	Saul S. Cohen
Executive Vice-President	George M. Simon
Vice-President	Bryant R. Burton
Secretary	Burton M. Cohen
Treasurer	Solomon Levine
Director	Bryant R. Burton
Director	Burton M. Cohen
Director	Saul S. Cohen
Director	Solomon Levine
Director	David Lubart
Director	Roy Perry
Director	Maxwell M. Rabb
Director	George M. Simon

Not listed, but reported to be behind the company along with Levinson and Sigelbaum, was Jack Cooper, a former vice-president of the Miami Marlin's Baseball Club and the West Flagler Kennel Dog Racing Club. Certainly, Cooper's wife, Gertrude, held considerable stock in the airport hotel firm.

A sort of Miami-Los Angeles-Washington, D.C. axis seemed to be in the making. A probe of the city officials involved might be very revealing, and it might also provide an embarrassing, or at least interesting, contrast to their more conservative counterparts in other cities where similar proposals by this company must have been turned down. After all, the officers and directors of the International Airport Hotel System, Inc., do have interesting backgrounds.

Bryant R. Burton is a Beverly Hills attorney who pops up periodically in many deals involving big money and the mob boys, like a pit boss watching out for the house dough. Burton, who was secretary of Ed Levinson's Fremont Hotel, Inc., in Las Vegas, is also an acknowledged representative of Levinson's boss, Doc Stacher. In fact, Burton made the association official for any disbelievers when he testified in February, 1962, before a federal grand jury investigating underworld gambling figures that he managed properties for Stacher, including the Moulin Rouge Theater-Restaurant in Los Angeles.

Solomon Levine figured in the 1959 Senate committee hearings on improper activities in the labor or management field. As a vice-president of the Manhattan News Company in New York, wholesale distributor of magazines, he took the Fifth Amendment when asked whether he had made payoffs to a union official representing fifty union drivers employed by Manhattan.

In 1959 Levine also held stock in the Manhattan News Company in trust for the children of his brother-in-law, Henry Garfinkle, president of the American News Company. And Garfinkle's Union News Company, a division of American News, has an exclusive lease for the restaurant and cocktail lounge concession in the Miami Airport Hotel.

Maxwell M. Rabb is a New York City attorney. He served as secretary to President Eisenhower's cabinet from 1953 to 1958 and as special assistant to the controversial Washington Svengali, Sherman Adams, Ike's political mentor for many years. In 1956 Rabb was accused of leaking confidential information about the cabinet to a writer, much to the chagrin of Senate investigators who had previously been unable to get the same information. Rabb declined an invitation to come in and tell the probers about the situation.

In 1962 Rabb was listed as a director in the Gotham Bank, the American News Company, Seven Arts, Ltd.—of which we have previously spoken—and other corporate entities. An interesting addition to his circle of business influence and affluence was his appointment as a director of the Struthers Wells Corporation, a company licensed in Maryland. On April 26, 1966, George E. Reedy, onetime press secretary to President Lyndon B. Johnson who in July, 1965, had been moved for reasons of health over to the post of Special Assistant to the President, announced that he would be leaving to take a job as an executive in private industry, though the name of the specific firm was not mentioned. *Standard and Poor's Annual*, which lists industrial corporations throughout the country, had in its 1966 edition a listing of the Struthers Wells Corporation officers and directors showing George Reedy as a director.

Struthers Wells and a subsidiary, Titusville Iron Works of Titusville, Pennsylvania, manufacturers of welded carbon and alloy products and of high-pressure vessels, have been on the receiving end of numerous U.S. government contracts for equipment to be used in its space and underwater research programs.

Max Rabb, born in Boston in 1910, took a law degree at Harvard in 1935. He is now a partner in the firm of Stroock, Stroock, and Levan at 61 Broadway, New York City. He lives at 145 Central Park West, one of the few places in Manhattan where you can see trees from your front window over the tops of luxury cars, cabs, and ambulances transporting the strained heart and bleeding ulcer cases in that odd suburbia of New York's financial district.

Two years after acquiring his law degree, Rabb became administrative assistant to Henry Cabot Lodge and served in varying capacities to that wandering minstrel of several administrations. He served with Lodge from 1937 to 1952, then jumped to the White House in 1953, where he became right-hand man to President Eisenhower until 1958.

Finally, in 1965, Rabb became Chairman of the Board of Directors and the Executive Committee of the International Airport Hotel System.

George M. Simon is the accountant for Levinson's buddy, Sigelbaum, and for the International Airport Hotel System, Inc. It was he who testified before a congressional committee about Bobby Baker and a junket Baker took with Jack Cooper, Levinson, and Sigelbaum to the Dominican Republic. Together, Simon and Cooper invested $91,889.30 in Baker's controversial Serv-U Corporation at the request of Eddie Levinson, who invested some $64,000 in the company himself.

As of December 31, 1965, the International Airport Hotel System listed the following officers and directors, indicating a slight shuffle in the three-year interim, but the mixture was much as before:

President and Treasurer	Solomon Levine
Vice-President and Secretary	Burton M. Cohen
Vice-President and Director	Bryant R. Burton
Director	David Lubart
Director	William Ash
Director	Jerome Molasky
Director	George M. Simon
Director	Maxwell M. Rabb
Director	William Levine
Director	William Werfel

William Levine figured in the McClellan rackets committee testimony. There it was revealed that American News Company president Henry Garfinkle set Levine up in the trucking business in Queens County to force a competitor out of business—almost in the fashion of Detroit's Joe Barbara, Jr. Of course, Levine was in good company in Queens. There Jimmy Hoffa ran things, with the cooperation of his enforcer, Tony Corallo, a noted mobster who helped get a New York State Supreme Court justice into trouble as well as the assistant U.S. attorney in Brooklyn and later a commissioner in Mayor Lindsay's administration.

Jack Cooper was revealed on the company's stock prospectus as a promoter, having been paid $75,000 for his services in connection with securing the lease and construction financing, through the $2-million Teamster loan, for the Miami airport hotel. His name would hardly be ideal on the roster of officers and directors, however, inasmuch as in 1962 he was convicted of income-tax evasion totaling $259,000 for the years 1953–1954, sentenced to three months in prison (plus nine months' probation), and fined $15,000. He was thus, in the lingua-Vegas, "eighty-sixed" out of corporate respectability.

Cooper, who is in his fifties, is a short man, a product of the Oak Street section of New Haven, Connecticut. He can often be seen visiting the come-as-you-are places in Las Vegas in black mohair slacks and matching shirts and slippers with red linings.

During his tax-evasion trial in federal court in Miami, Cooper admitted that he and Rafael Trujillo, Jr., son of the dictator, garnered $744,000 from the Dominican Republic in an airplane deal involving the purchase of U.S. fighter planes delivered to Sweden and resold to Papa Trujillo's country. When Cooper was later summoned to the Bobby Baker hearings, however, he lost his tongue, took the Fifth Amendment, and admitted only to having been born in New York City.

Cooper is the happy tour conductor for the airport hotel group, arranging charter flights that scoop up gambling men from all over the country and drop them down on the rather hard sod of Las Vegas, where the routine of booze, twenty-four-hour-a-day companions, and the eternal sound of clicking roulette wheels somewhat softens their landing. Silver dollars in Vegas are passé; plastic chips and souvenir coins enthrall at the moment. But the gold is still there—for the bosses, who find its keening command in paper money, a rare gift of hearing, indeed.

These then are the sort of men who run International Hotels. Why? Why do they involve themselves in such affairs? Perhaps we can find an answer by looking at Ed Levinson, the man behind numerous operations across the country, some yet to be detailed. Very possibly Levinson is the heir apparent to Doc Stacher and the dynasty, now spread across the United States, that Doc took over from Bugsy Siegel and Jack Dragna. What makes him tick? Certainly not a vibrating spring in a commanding hoodlum clock.

Are the men of the Mafia in the thumbscrews of a power that overwhelms them, that promises only two variations: a life of happiness if they are capable of achieving it under the conditions that prevail, or a life that becomes nothing the moment they slip out of the vortex of mob influence that pushes them on? Are they truly the other side of the coin that matches the sucker prototyped by Phineas T. Barnum when he said, "There's one born every minute!"?

Who are the suckers? The suckers themselves, or the men born to bleed the suckers white? Perhaps the answer lies in a simple concept: the mob boys have reduced their lives to such common concepts of eating, drinking, and sleeping that they go along with each day, doing the accepted job but really serving as slaves to bigger people about whom they know nothing, like so many ears of corn in a willing windrow ready to be chopped down at the first sign of insurrection or ripeness.

Who really bosses the crime syndicate?

Maybe Eddie Levinson is a product of his time. Not yet ready to die, he lives each day hoping that it will bring one more good thing—a step up on the ladder of the next day. But believe it, *he* is getting *his* orders, too!

Obviously, the presence of large numbers of men of Levinson's ilk in California and elsewhere has a considerable effect on ordinary citizens. In California, in fact, the citizen can find anything he wants in the long state that encompasses and supports the flora and fauna of every known level of geologic time—and many things he may not want. But there are signs that an enormous lethargy is setting in, while very few of the public officials who have the power to act seem to care that the state is being undermined from within.

Take the case of ex-Governor Edmund G. Brown, for example. Of the Samish-Howser-Brown trio, only Brown remains on the public scene. And Brown has very carefully avoided trouble ever since 1947, when a body was found in the trunk of a new convertible.

The body in the trunk was that of Nick De John, who had been killed in the basement of the Alouette Restaurant in San Francisco. There was a hemp rope around his neck, and the car was parked in a quiet corner of the Marina, a sacrosanct section of town noted for its tidy lawns and very fine view of the steel harp that is the Golden Gate Bridge.

The auto Nick's body was found in could be considered a hearse, for he wasn't placed there by choice. His killers had apparently planned to take the corpse across the bridge and leave it on a lonely mountain back-road, where play miniature iguanas and the small blue butterflies such as *Brephidium Exilis*, the smallest of them all, which floats on gossamer wings over the driest of salt flats and loves it when the tide goes out.

As the murderers neared the approach to the bridge, however, a motorcycle policeman warned them against speeding. Taking fright, they left the body in the car at the Marina, and as the tide went out for Nick, they found no butterfly hovering over him. Instead, a penny—that's all it was worth to his killers—had been stuffed into his rectum: a Mafia mark of derision for a double crosser.

Nick De John was a member of the Chicago mob who tried to become a big shot too fast. After being threatened on several occasions by some of the mob's tough guys, he suddenly took off for the San Francisco area. He left in such a hurry that his wife had to remain in Chicago to make arrangements for packing their household goods while De John tried to find a place for them to live in California.

One theory behind his hurried exit was that he had squandered mob money on extracurricular gambling and betting on the races—things that had no relation to mob economy. But in any case, he hardly had time to settle down and contact a few of his Mafia friends before it was all over for him. The San Francisco police, answering a citizen's request to remove a parked car, opened the trunk and discovered De John's mutilated body.

Two dedicated inspectors of the San Francisco police department, Frank Ahern and Thomas Cahill, began an investigation of the murder and soon had narrowed a long list of suspects down to a very important few. Leading the list was Leonard Calamia, alias "Benny Leonard," who had served two terms for narcotics peddling. Calamia admitted to having been with De John and, in fact, proved to be the last known person to have seen De John alive.

Calamia denied any knowledge of the crime and insisted he was merely an employee of the Sunland Oil and Cheese Company of San Francisco. The car he drove was registered to Frank Scappatura of the oil and cheese company. Scappatura was a native of Italy and had served two years in federal prison for counterfeiting. Two other Italian-born men were also partners in the olive oil business: John Franzone of Tunisia and Italy and Michael Abati, a part-time bartender.

At this point Ahern and Cahill had a lot of evidence tying their suspects to Nick's death, but not enough to make an airtight case against them. Then, from out of nowhere, came a big break. A local woman who was an admitted abortionist complained to the two police officers that she was being shaken down by a former bootlegger in the Bay area named Gus Oliva. In return for protection, she calmly announced to the amazed policemen that she had overheard the plot to kill Nick De John.

The woman, Anita Venza Rocchia, said she was willing to testify in court that she had been in a basement card room in the Italian North Beach section of San Francisco, and that the men playing cards—Barbuta—were Scappatura, Abati, Tony Lima, a food broker from Lodi, California, and Sebastiano Nani, an international dope smuggler born in Sicily. Anita said she had heard the complete details of the plan to murder De John; when the news of her evidence sifted down to the underworld, all four of the men mentioned disappeared.

Scappatura hid out in Seattle until the case cooled; Lima, who was convicted in 1956 on charges of grand theft and embezzlement, took off for Johnstown, Pennsylvania, but is once again very active in the produce business in California's Napa Valley. Calamia was picked up in Albuquerque, New Mexico; Nani was arrested in New York; and Abati was arrested when he tried to return to San Francisco.

The San Francisco grand jury voted indictments for murder against the men, and on February 1, 1949, the trial of Calamia, Nani, and Abati began. The case went through the usual court procedures, with testimony from, among others, Anita Venza Rocchia, and finally went to the jury on March 8. Then, when the jury was still undecided after more than thirty hours' deliberation, District Attorney Brown asked that the indictments be dismissed without prejudice. Brown told Cahill and Ahern that there were implications of perjury and that it would be better to drop the case at this stage rather than take the chance of losing it and closing it forever. Brown said he would aid them in the case and resolved also to reopen it as soon as they were ready. That was twenty-two years ago, and it has never been mentioned since.

In the interim, Pat Brown became governor of California and made his prosecuting attorney in the case, Tom Lynch, state's attorney general. Both have moved up many places, like the Mad Hatter, to get to cleaner cups. Frank Ahern and Tom Cahill did likewise. Ahern was jumped over dozens of other officers with seniority into the top spot as chief of police, and Cahill moved nearly as far to become his assistant.

The point, of course, is that everything went down the drain. But perhaps another point is that when Frank Ahern died, Cahill inherited the mantle of a very important job along with the responsibility for the safety of many people.

When legal action on the De John murder was pulled out of court, Ahern and Cahill said to Pat Brown: "We'll keep working on the case. Nobody is going to get away with murder on our beat"—an ironic statement, in view of later events. But those very events make clear the reasons behind Cahill's failure to return the phone calls the author made in 1966 to inquire about progress in the case.

Somebody got away with murder, and Pat Brown never mentioned it again. Perhaps he felt no different from one witness who became fearful and dropped out somewhere along the line. No names were ever put into the hands of newspapermen, but Ahern dropped a few hints about the frightened man:

> He was afraid of them. They are Sicilians. He is a Sicilian. They stated they wouldn't only get his wife. They would get his family. He got down on his knees; he said he would do anything but tell. He doesn't mind facing anybody, but he would be walking down the street someday and somebody would step out of a dark doorway—and they would all get it.

Of course, it did all happen a long time ago, but even twenty-two years can't erase the memory of a job unfinished.

As governor of California, Pat Brown had an annual salary of a mere $44,100, knew a lot of people, and seemed bitten by the celebrity bug. His political and moral acumen may be challenged on many fronts.

For instance, the *Los Angeles Times* of April 11, 1966, turned out a very fine story about the governor's spending a quiet Easter with his family at a desert estate near Palm Springs, "despite demands that he meet striking grape workers at the end of their 300-mile march to the state capitol in Sacramento."

The grape workers staged a protest rally in downtown Palm Springs—to be accommodating, no doubt—but failed to budge the governor from his previously announced "family" commitments. Imagine their surprise, then, when it developed that Governor Brown and his wife, their four children, and eight grandchildren had spent most of that Easter Sunday at the home of singer Frank Sinatra, six miles southeast of Palm Springs.

Frank Sinatra lost his gambling license at Lake Tahoe and relinquished his points in the Sands Hotel in Las Vegas because he was overfriendly with Sam Giancana, alias "Sam Mooney," alias "Sam Flood," etc. But the governor apparently dismissed the implications of the association, which had been monitored through every step of the way by the FBI, as a bad dream, the nightmare of the Nevada gaming control board.

To grab the throne once occupied by Al Capone, Giancana, who became boss of the Mafia's Chicago fraternity and one of a dozen members of the grand council that controls syndicated crime in the United States, had to work his way through the ranks of pimps, burglars, bootleggers, dope pushers, and varied assassins. This was and is Sinatra's buddy, along with numerous other known mobsters, and Sinatra apparently had Governor Brown's approval —or was it vice versa?

Behind most organized crime is not only the thinking, the buying of votes, and the allegiance of learned lawyers with dubious morals, but also the lack of any real comprehension of the problem on the part of the public—the people who call the shots on their own future, depending on how they think in the voting booth. California voters seem not to be aware of the soaring crime rate in their state. Thus, when in 1965 a fighting assemblyman, George Deukmegian (R., Long Beach), introduced bills to put into effect the demands of a Republican crime task force to increase the minimum penalties for armed bodily-injury crimes, the governor used his veto. Likewise, Brown's successor, Governor Reagan, has yet to come to grips with the problem of organized crime, though current legislative efforts may soon put him on the record.

Perhaps Governor Brown's indifference to organized crime and influence peddling and their repressive effects on his constituents' lives can best be illustrated by an incident having to do with the alcoholic beverage control board.

As has been mentioned previously, the board was created to probe the characters and records of applicants for liquor licenses, determine the true ownership of prospective licensed premises, and see that license fees are collected. Late in 1965, however, while presumably performing the above duties, two investigators from the A.B.C. were lavishly wined and dined by certain notorious members of the Matranga family of San Diego, California, who are part of the family of Mafioso John Priziola of Detroit.

The Matrangas were having difficulty in obtaining a liquor license for their La Mesa Bowl, the bowling alley in which Teamster President Jimmy Hoffa sank $1,250,000 of his union members' pension funds. The original license had been revoked on the grounds it was obtained by subterfuge: a dummy corporation had been set up. Probably the Matrangas thought a party was a good way to win friends and influence people. Unfortunately, for the Matrangas, publicity given to the dinner for the A.B.C. men resulted in the investigators' resignations. Governor Brown hastily assured the press that he thought there was nothing wrong with the situation and that he felt the men had merely made a mistake. In getting publicity?

The result of the whole affair shows that justice is occasionally allowed to rear its head. On April 8, 1966, the financially troubled owners of the Bowl lost a court fight for their liquor license. A writ was sought by Frank (Big Frank) M. Matranga, president, Leo M. Matranga, vice-president, and Joseph Matranga, secretary-treasurer of the bowling alley, but without success.

Troubles mounted. The Teamster loan was in default—as are, at present, a number of similar loans throughout the country. But in July, 1967, a company headed by prominent San Diego land developer Irving J. Kahn used a $1.2 million loan from the Teamster pension fund to bail out the bankrupt bowling alley, which was already in debt to the union for $1.1 million.

Kahn's group could afford to be generous, for seven months later the outfit received a $35-million loan from the pension fund, the largest in the union's history. The loan did not list as a trustee Teamster President James Hoffa, who has been convicted of conspiracy to divert $1.7 million from the union's pension fund. But the Teamsters have invested a total of $55 million in Kahn enterprises.

Meanwhile, Frank Matranga has succeeded in getting himself in trouble by violating the probation order he had acquired as a result of a 1965 fraud conviction. On February 15, 1968, he drew a sentence of from one to ten years in Superior Court, San Bernardino, California, after adding insult to the fraud injury by getting indicted in nearby Orange County late in 1967 on charges of grand theft, conspiracy, and obstruction of justice.

Indicted with Matranga was Robert B. Salerno, former City of Commerce councilman. They were charged with taking $3,500 from a Newport Beach man on a promise they could arrange for his acquittal in a case involving the use of an electronic device to circumvent telephone toll charges. Upon hearing the case, Superior Judge George Dell said: "I think Mr. Matranga and Mr. Salerno perpetrated a 'con' job on a 'con' man." Judge Dell found Matranga guilty as charged in June, 1968, and scheduled Salerno's trial for later in the year.

Big Frank Matranga is another example of a hood who stooped for pennies in the shadow of millions—in terms of syndicate operations—and got himself caught. And his confreres in the secret society have surely written him off by now as having fallen from grace.

It is one thing for a mobster to overreach himself. It is, however, quite another for him to be apprehended by law-enforcement agencies before he overreaches himself. And in California the latter seldom happens.

The lack of consideration for the citizens' protection on the part of public officials found in so many offices in the state is not paralleled by a complete indifference to all things, however. The officials give great care to some things. Recently, for example, a committee of the Los Angeles city council recommended salary increases ranging from 47 to 85 per cent for 18 city officials, including: mayor, from $35,000 to $52,592; city attorney, from $32,000 to $47,333; city controller, from $25,000 to $36,814; and city councilman, from $17,000 to $31,555.

Los Angeles should not be singled out over much, however. In San Francisco, where the elite meet to eat, police intelligence has determined that packages of cash are finding their way from syndicate strongboxes right into well-manicured fingers at City Hall itself—as usual via a circuitous route. The couriers are said to be a long-time Cleveland hood now based in Los Angeles and an associate who is a convicted safe cracker. The two have been observed carrying the money more than once, and some careful police work could put on the record the name of the ultimate beneficiary and the reason behind the transfer of funds.

The outlook is not entirely bleak, fortunately. Announcements made recently by California Attorney General Thomas C. Lynch and his chief deputy, Charles O'Brien, seem to indicate an increasing concern over organized crime, their prime targets being the boys who are investing racket money in legitimate businesses through the state. According to O'Brien:

> These fellows are not making their money in California. They make it from rackets in New York and New Jersey and from gambling in Nevada and other places. Then they "wash" the money or invest it in legitimate businesses here. That way they can put the profits on their income tax reports.

Although the businesses may be legitimate, O'Brien explains, the methods of operation used by the boys seldom are:

> For example, recently crime operators have invested in the vending-machine business. Instead of asking a bar owner or a cafe owner if he wants a vending machine in his store, they tell the proprietor he will be roughed up if he doesn't install a machine.

In June, 1967, announcing the formation of a special unit within his Department of Justice to study organized crime, Attorney General Lynch said: "Our state has become the favorite investment area of the veiled finance committee of organized crime." And he went on to point out the following major danger areas of such activity: hidden interests on state licenses; the intrusion of criminal cartelists into our sensitive world of finance; the layoff of huge sports bets into the Los Angeles area; loan sharking and the reported moves of remnants of the old Mickey Cohen mob to control it, together with some new tough boys; and the conspiracy of silence that so often meets enforcement agencies, grand juries, and courts when investigations are undertaken.

It will be interesting to see what inroads are made into these "major danger areas" by law-enforcement agencies when the flames fanned by such enthusiastic announcements have died away. In July, 1968, just one year after the new crime fighting unit went into operation, Charles O'Brien, its overall chief, told the author that slow progress was being made and that a larger staff and budget were needed, and that there was much to be done.

In the meantime, the land of milk and honey curdles day by day, racked by scandals that arise through abuse of responsibility the perpetrators should never have been given—from some of the corrupt city assessors in the north (three have been convicted to date for taking bribes on behalf of clients of tax consultants) to the mob boys and their bankers who prefer the crowded cities in the South while on the waiting line for Las Vegas, killing time and doling out dollars to developers who chop down the land into squat, house-crowded obelisks with chipped-in terraces going up to nowhere.

Meanwhile, too, another matter is becoming even more important and occupying Mafia interest to an even greater degree: drugs.

One cannot annihilate the image and importance of a big city or of the state in which it exists by bewailing the moral degradation of a segment of its youth. It is a fact, however, that over the past few years the people who have swept across the United States into California—only, like jewels in a strongbox, to be trapped against the backstop of the Pacific Ocean—have tolerated thus far the growth of a new morality. And by this concept, born of a new revolutionary spirit in youth and moving in a direction that is as baffling as it is unprecedented and dangerous, is the reputation of the state imperiled. How so? Because the Mafia is able to use the art workings of this morality to penetrate, in yet another way, the armor of the people inhabiting our largest state.

The Mafia in California has had its successes in the past. But until recently free and easy gambling in Nevada has served as a safety valve against Mafiosi greed. While in the past many hoodlums have merely waited on the Coast for an opening in the gambling structure of Nevada, recent events in the big coastal cities may have changed the direction of their interest. Youngsters queuing up in ever-lengthening lines for a dip into the fast-rising river of dope flooding across our southwest borders provide a tempting prospect.

The police in California like to say that there is no true Mafia organization operating on the West Coast. In Los Angeles, for instance, the belief that a known lawbreaker, Mafia member or not, will call the police before he visits the city to see whether he would be stepping on any toes is enough for them. Perhaps their faith is justified. But it is hard to say what is gained by such social amenities; possibly the hood is only out to protect himself from enemies.

In 1967, in a speech given in Los Angeles, U.S. Deputy Attorney General Warren M. Christopher made a statement to the effect that organized crime had not gained a foothold in California "because of the quality, honesty, and integrity" of law-enforcement agencies in the area, and he added that those organized crime figures who do live on the West Coast do not have major ties into the secret organization.

While this writer has no wish to question the quality ascribed to California's law-enforcement agencies—particularly in Los Angeles, where the late Police Chief William Parker built up a superb department—it would seem that the host of names, associations, and activities outlined in this chapter refute the accuracy of the remainder of Christopher's statement. But perhaps Christopher was the victim of ignorance.

A lack of cooperation between police and intelligence units throughout the country, at the local, state, and federal levels, is certainly one of the reasons for the scattered and incomplete knowledge about organized crime in California. And while ignorance may be bliss, the facts indicate that the bliss could be short-lived: the criminal syndicate on the West Coast is perilously fluid and quite capable of becoming one of the largest organisms in the whole structure of North American crime.

If the revolutionary spirit in California is typified by its bearded and beaded hippies and their miniskirted molls, as the news media imply, then the populace is being offered a dangerous and comic approach to what must be considered in a more serious vein in areas of the country such as Chicago, Cleveland, and Detroit, where blood rather than just youthful spirit is beginning to bubble to the surface. The widespread and growing use of drugs is a door to unlimited ecstacy—for the Mafia. And they are quickly learning to make the most of it.

If one assumes that no gangster organization now operates in Los Angeles, San Diego, and other southern California cities despite the some-fifty documented gangland killings in Los Angeles alone in the first half of the century—not to mention other syndicate activities—how can one dismiss with total equanimity the fact that while in 1964 only two tons of marijuana were seized by customs officials at the Mexican border, in the year ending April, 1968, twenty-four tons were seized? And, it must be remembered, these quantities must represent a very small percentage of what actually got through.

There are as many methods and kinds of couriers—"mules"—used in bringing the stuff into California as there are varieties of youthful users. Often the mules are solicited below the border to drive a car containing hidden marijuana into California, park the car at a designated spot, and leave it. They never meet the pickup man, who has been forewarned that the shipment is on its way, and are therefore unable to identify him for California lawmen. One U.C.L.A. student used this system, with the help of some good contacts below the border, to bring in one hundred kilos of marijuana a week for a number of months (for profitable and widespread distribution) before he was finally caught and sent to prison.

Another young man, newly arrived in San Francisco's Haight-Ashbury hippie haven and anxious to help his roommates pay the rent on their pad, passed around the hat for contributions to buy some marijuana in order to sell it at a profit for rent money—saving just enough to keep everyone hazily happy for a time. He drove down to Tijuana, where it's as easy to get marijuana as it is to get a girl, but was caught by border guards while bringing the stuff back. He doesn't have to worry about rent money anymore.

California's braceros, the agricultural workers who go back and forth across the border with relative ease, can be used for smuggling. American tourists, too, are sometimes victimized while unknowingly carrying marijuana or other narcotics in the hubcaps and other hard-to-get-at places of their cars. No, mules are not hard to come by.

Along with an ever-increasing volume of marijuana being brought across the border, there has been a corresponding increase in the amount of heroin seized by authorities. Over thirty pounds of Mexican-manufactured heroin fell into the hands of customs men in the year ending April, 1968—again, just a fraction of the heroin that must have been smuggled in. This potent, chocolate-colored dope made of poppies cultivated in hidden fields on the Mexican mainland is so powerful, and therefore so profitable, that the lighter-colored heroin made in Red China, Europe, and South America is often tinted with powdered coffee to give it a darker color and make it more salable here.

Thirty pounds of heroin will go a long way, depending on how it is cut, and its increased flow over the border indicates that the marijuana users are probably moving on to the more potent dope. And there lies the danger. There is scarcely a single victim of the strong heroin-derivative drugs who did not start on the dope kick by experimenting with marijuana.

Most of the Mexican contacts who handle heroin and marijuana—weed, tea, pot, as it is variously called—are well known to U.S. authorities and Mexican lawmen as well, but they operate with almost total immunity south of the border. As one U.S. narcotics agent told the author: "It almost seems to us that arrests down there are made only to impress upon the peddlers that control can be exerted upon them, control that is then translated into 'mordeda' or graft paid to certain Mexican policemen to keep hands off the traffic."

The apparent lack of Mexican law-enforcement cooperation is not the only difficulty, however. The U.S. Treasury Department has only forty customs agents to do the job of curtailing the circulation of marijuana and other drugs in eight western states, and the intrigue used by the smugglers together with the necessity of coping with vast numbers of people crossing the border every day make detection a chancy kind of thing.

The fact is that California is the victim of a poverty of body and spirit in the area just south of the boundary between the United States and Mexico, where the demarcation has left geography behind and the black lines representing latitude have come to mark the smudge of dope spreading across the southwest.

The Mafia has moved in on every source of easy money to be found in America, and the dreamers who see social revolution in the smoke curlicues of marijuana cigarettes offer a perfect opportunity to the patient artisans of the Mafia. Mafiosi are always looking for a larger foot in the door—whether it be the entrance to a college dormitory, an expensive split-level home in one of the finer suburbs, or the rat-chewed egress to a hovel in a ghetto.

Official awareness of the seemingly sleepy cat that is the Mafia in California has always been manifest in a low key. The men of the syndicate have rarely been sought behind the façade of so-called legitimate business or even official corruption. One statement made by San Francisco's Mayor Joseph L. Alioto in July, 1968, however, at least indicated official recognition of the existence of organized crime in the illegal business of peddling narcotics.

After one of the hippie riots in his city, the mayor said that the long-haired, blue-jeaned youths and their female counterparts were inspired to go on the rampage because the mob was taking over the sources and distribution of marijuana and making things tough for the flower children. He clearly inferred that the hippie influx had created a huge market for pot and heroin and that the increasing revenues were being diverted to the pockets of mobster narcotics vendors.

Two murders in August, 1967, in the Haight-Ashbury district of San Francisco have been attributed to the new "muscle." The victims were John Kent Carter, aged twenty-five, and William E. (Superspade) Thomas, aged twenty-six, both known narcotics dealers. Thomas was found in a sleeping bag at the bottom of a cliff. He had been stabbed in the heart and shot in the back of the head. Carter's body was found in his apartment. He had been stabbed many times, and his right arm had been cut off above the elbow. Missing was about $3,000 in cash he was known to have been carrying. The arm was later found, wrapped in a suede cloth, in a car belonging to a twenty-three-year-old motorcycle racer who said he killed Carter in self-defense after having been cheated in the sale of some L.S.D. during a "bad trip."

A hippie newsletter put out by a group called the Communication Company deplored the killings and said that "the dope business has been like that lately. Lots of burns. Lots of guns. Lots of power games." The newsletter went on to state that some of the most "beautiful" people in the San Francisco hippie community are moving out, and it also reported that Negro gangs have begun to attack hippies despite the operation of a free store for the blacks and the staging of weekend festivals with free food, rock music, and flowers.

The Mafia's role in promoting the importation and distribution of narcotics in the United States has been well established and documented over the years. Anyone only vaguely aware of the existence of a criminal syndicate knows that profits from narcotics have always been one of the basics of mob economy and have helped finance their more recent entry into the so-called legitimate fields of endeavor that are proving even more lucrative.

In refuting rumors of organized crime's infiltration into the mushrooming marijuana traffic across the Mexico-United States border, police authorities regularly fall back on such standard arguments as:

> It takes no talent, no organizational ability, no brokers, no middlemen to drive to Mexico to arrange for a purchase of drugs. Anyone who has an automobile and ambition to be a peddler can drive to Mexico and pick up narcotics. These people who peddle in California are private entrepreneurs.

These arguments could be applied as well—and even better, in fact—to prostitution, where some talent may be needed but certainly no organizational ability, no brokers, and no middlemen. And you don't even have to drive to Mexico! Yet organized prostitution in its heyday undoubtedly put enough money into syndicate coffers to rebalance the current national budget.

The Mafia has the power and the means to organize *any* kind of activity and will do so if there is promise of sufficient return to make the effort worthwhile. And although California's marijuana traffic may have been little league a few years back, all reports indicate that marijuana is continually reaching greater numbers of users and filtering down into younger age brackets. And all of these pot smokers are potential buyers of the syndicate's stronger stuff a few months or years hence; for while the smoking of marijuana does not *necessarily* lead to drug addiction, it does, in the words of the McClellan subcommittee report on the investigation of narcotics, "tend to cultivate the 'fertile soil' of addiction—the state of mind and the environmental influences that lead to the use of addictive drugs." As if to substantiate this theory, narcotics officials are currently checking the suspicion that, in some cases, heroin is being mixed into marijuana by the pushers to "hook" people who might otherwise not go on to the stronger stuff.

In short, it would behoove all those charged with the responsibility of keeping an eye on the activities of organized crime in California to recognize the possibility that the criminal syndicate may have, or take, a hand in pushing the use of marijuana to proportions that represent an even greater menace to the citizenry than that already reached by private entrepreneurs.

At the same time, law-enforcement authorities should also look to another drug source: the Chinese. Though powerful and well-entrenched Chinese "families" exist in San Francisco and elsewhere on the West Coast, probably some of the disparaging remarks made about the California Chinese can be attributed more to the opium-oriented legends of the early Chinese tongs, which flourished in New York City at the turn of the century, than to any substantial participation in this generation's narcotics picture. But a real Chinese interest in narcotics can almost certainly be found in the mind of Red China's ruler, Mao Tse-tung, whose heroin factories are turning out the white powder in wholesale lots.

In May, 1968, for example, six Chinese seamen believed involved in a huge heroin ring were arrested in Long Beach, California. Federal agents discovered heroin worth $12 million in concealed pouches strapped about four of the seamen. The Dutch-registered cargo ship, S.S. "Zeeland," on which the seamen had arrived in this country, was searched, but no more heroin was unearthed. Narcotics agents determined that two of the seamen were natives of the Kowloon district of Hong Kong and that the other four came from Kwangtung Province and the city of Canton in

Red China. They carried what was called the "very finest type of Far Eastern-grown heroin."

When Harry J. Anslinger, who served for thirty-two years as U.S. Commissioner of Narcotics before becoming U.S. representative on the narcotics commission of the United Nations, testified at the McClellan hearings, he presented evidence, according to the subcommittee report, to show that

> the Soviet Union believes the Red Chinese are actively engaged in fostering the narcotics traffic as a national economic measure. An article in *Pravda*, dated September 15, 1964, charged Red Chinese officialdom with active support of the growth of opium poppies in Yunnan Province. The newspaper's correspondent, on an official tour of the Province, saw vast fields of poppies under cultivation. The article made the following charge: "About half a billion dollars every year comes into the hands of the present leaders of China from the illicit sale of narcotics." The article stated that the traffic was encouraged in order that the resulting opium would find lucrative dollar markets outside Red China.

Drugs, corruption, gambling—syndicate activities seem to reflect the eventual ending of California's reputation as a recreational and dwelling area. The politicians have demonstrated their ineptness, corruption, and lack of interest in minorities and have invoked a sense of frustration in the people who crowded west with their dreams. The fine, tall trees that once blanketed the surrounding mountains are mostly gone—leaves, conifer needles, wilted by a host of automobile exhausts and the gaseous dregs of careless industry, by people who already outnumber the struggling saplings in the summer campsites of California's national and state forests. Soon, possibly, the people themselves will be driven out.

In the long history of California's involvement with the Mafia there is precious little on the record about anyone or any local group really trying to lock horns with the secret society, although Los Angeles police department's Captain Hamilton could have claimed much of the credit for thwarting the attempted take-over of the garment industry by the invaders from New York and for harassing Mafiosi in his domain whenever, wherever, and however possible.

Even the famous shakedown of the Hollywood movie industry

in 1941, which saw half a dozen mobsters, including Johnny Roselli, go to jail for conspiring to extort $1 million from Loew's, 20th Century Fox, and Warner Brothers, was a cross-country affair. Arrests, indictments, and prison sentences were arranged by the government, not by the state, with the help of informers Willie Bioff and George Browne.

The ancient code of *omerta* still holds, and any infraction of the rule of silence is followed by the old Mafia terror tactics that reinforce the meaning of *omerta* for others. Thus Bioff was killed November 4, 1955, when he stepped on the starter of his pickup truck at his Phoenix ranch and a load of dynamite blew up under his seat. Or take the case of Chicago hood Gerald Covelli. Covelli made a deal with law authorities in 1962. In exchange for a short prison sentence on a major charge, he exposed mob secrets to federal officials. Later he was quietly released from an obscure Texas prison, given a face-lift that was supposed to throw any pursuers off his trail, and moved with his family to Encino, California, just outside Los Angeles. However, there, on June 18, 1967, forty-five-year-old Gerald Covelli was blown in half when a bomb exploded under the front seat of his aquamarine Thunderbird.

Yet the mob, in California as elsewhere across the nation, is changing. The post-Prohibition era, which saw the syndicate turn its efforts from bootlegging to gambling and bookmaking, is now itself giving place to a new approach to illegal activities, involving infiltration and subversion of seemingly legitimate business. This new sophistication represents a change from the forceful, often violent seizures of the past, but it is change of technique, not of philosophy. No matter what color you try to paint it, the Mafia story always comes up red—blood red.

11

LAS VEGAS:

Teamstertown, U.S.A.

The beginnings of Las Vegas are found in the land itself—split open in a cataclysm that an aeon ago produced a gigantic spring of water athwart a wide, mountain-rimmed valley, gouged out by the turbulence of mountain storms that snapped gigantic whips of white foam and rocks down across the desert, smoothed clean by howling winds, and haunted on hot sunny days by dust devils swaying in their own weird ballet as they twist, counterclockwise, forever to the northeast.

Vegas itself had its beginning at about the time the Declaration of Independence sounded the death knell of British rule in the American colonies. In 1776 a small band of Spanish soldiers carrying the banner of King Charles III camped beside the sweetly flowing spring around which Las Vegas later sprouted.

The Mormons further tamped down the dust in 1855, when Brigham Young sent a mission from Salt Lake City to the area to convert the Indians and cutivate the land, a dream that disappeared as quickly as water in the hot sun. The Indians idled away the hours stealing and starving and almost ate the Mormons out of house and home, and the experiment was abandoned.

A reputed cannibal, Bill Williams, a Baptist preacher turned mountain man, organized a band of Indians and made Las Vegas and other western "spas" the headquarters for a group of horse thieves that terrorized ranchers from Cajon Pass, near Los Angeles, to the big spreads in Arizona.

Williams had guided the explorer General John C. Fremont through California's Mojave Desert and the country split by the Grand Canyon of the Colorado. On one occasion a detachment of men was threatened with starvation, and it was during this rough time that Williams was thought to have had a fling at "long pig," much as had members of the ill-fated Donner party in the Sierras. Of him, Kit Carson is reported to have said: "In starving times don't walk ahead of Bill Williams."

Carson himself fought the horse thieves and Indians and made a reputation in the country with Jose Antonio Carillo, who once led a posse from San Gabriel mission toward a lair of horse thieves and routed them, seizing clothing, saddles, and cooking utensils. Fifteen hundred horses dead from lack of food or water were counted during the chase.

Squaw men by the hundreds wandered the countryside, and every settlement had its gambling halls. Everywhere gamblers used their skills and their special type of squaws to lift the pokes of the horse thieves, who, in turn, retrieved their losses by charging exorbitant prices to the prospectors and ranchers for the very nags that had been stolen from them.

Fortune-hunting miners drilled still-to-be-seen stopes and holes into the rocky mountains around Las Vegas, branching out to every point of the compass and taking the "high grade from the grass roots" until it was all gone. Thirteen million dollars came out of one major lode in Searchlight, Nevada, to the south of Las Vegas. That was real success, and today a couple of gaming joints maintain the high-grading tradition there, moving tourists, however, instead of mountains.

The Union Pacific Railroad threw spurs into the gold country, extending one to Las Vegas in 1905 and maintaining service until the gold disappeared. The line was renewed when Las Vegas came to life again, but automobiles and airlines now supply the gold-plated maw of the gambling town with the necessary tourist grist for its money mills.

In 1931 Nevada legalized gambling, and the gaming parlors, which had run openly though illegally since 1910, really began to flourish. The next decade saw Las Vegas' Fremont Street become the still-touted Glitter Gulch, with its carnival atmosphere of flashing neon lights, block after block of open-doored casinos, and a beckoning din of frenetic merriment.

In the process, gambling became refined. Sawdust joints gave way to multi-hued, carpet-swathed halls of chance flanked by tiers of handy rooms, flickering numbers of Keno games, mahogany-and-walnut-veneered crap and 21 tables, and crystal glasses laced with amber booze doled out to the players by sleek cocktail waitresses. Cheering sections comprised of pay-as-you-go broads stacked around the tables lent simple solace to winners and losers alike.

The gamblers' playground soon expanded from Fremont Street to a strip of land lying conveniently just outside the Las Vegas city limits on Highway 91—the Los Angeles-Las Vegas artery that for years has carried to and from Las Vegas a steady stream of weekend players who are about as talented at the game of chance as they are at dodging one another in the traffic lanes.

Appropriately called the Strip, the gamblers' mecca had its beginning in 1941 with the building, right on the county line, of El Rancho Vegas. Legend has it that the owner stopped to water his horse at a windmill there, liked what he saw, and stayed on to usher in what was to become the Golden Age of Las Vegas gambling. The Last Frontier Hotel followed, adding to El Rancho's western flavor, which lent a come-as-you-are invitation to fun-seeking travelers.

However, the present-day flashy counterpart to the coruscating mountains that parallel the Strip was really pioneered by hoodlum Benjamin Siegel, a Jewish Don Quixote in reverse who faced many strange windmills in the new land, aided by Tony (Hard Way) Cornero, of California gambling-ship fame. Siegel and Cornero came into Las Vegas from two different directions but with the same objective. Tony had even bigger dreams than Bugsy, but his money-making dreams were largely for the benefit of himself and a few of his hoodlum-gambler associates back in California. Bugsy, on the other hand, was obviously bringing mob organization from the East to the do-it-yourself gaming entrepreneurs who had arrived in Las Vegas ahead of him.

In 1941 Bugsy, who was getting his California business pretty well in hand, sent a disciple to Las Vegas to extend the Siegel barony via the wire service, which was in ever-increasing demand as the state of Nevada began licensing casinos with a free hand. In fact, many of the downtown casinos had "race books" for bettors, to attract daytime patronage, while the nearby gaming tables provided a handy pastime between races. A year later Siegel himself paid a brief visit to Las Vegas and "sewed up" his cut from all the casino bookmaking operations using Trans-America's wire service —a total take for Bugsy of something like $25,000 a month.

Ben Siegel—his friends never called him Bugsy—soon began

to dream of bigger things. He envisioned himself as *the* impresario of American gambling, with a luxurious gambling casino surrounded by a plush hotel with all the elegant trimmings: nightclub, restaurant, bars, swimming pool, fine service, and exotic landscaping. Finally, he packed his bags and went to Las Vegas in 1946, taking with him not only his dreams but also the backing, financial and otherwise, of the syndicate bosses from New York, Florida, Louisiana, Detroit, Cleveland, Illinois, and points west such as Minneapolis and Kansas City.

Bugsy hired the Del E. Webb Construction Company of Phoenix to build his hotel—the "fabulous" Flamingo—on the Strip, out in the open spaces beyond El Rancho Vegas and the Last Frontier. After he had experienced numerous troubles in getting not only the building materials he wanted but also additional funds to cover the ballooning costs—he sold hotel "stock" to hoodlum pals in the East and raised $3 million—Bugsy finally had a white-tie opening of the still-unfinished hotel on December 26, 1946. The casino went into the red from the start, with few of the expected Hollywood celebrities showing up. Within two weeks $100,000 had gone down the drain, so Bugsy closed the hotel until all construction could be completed.

In the meantime, the Capone mob had taken over its wire-service competition in the West, Continental Press Service, after killing its owner, gambler James M. Ragen, in Chicago in June, 1946. With the extensive apparatus of Continental Press in its grasp, the boys no longer needed Trans-America, and they so informed Siegel. But the budding impresario's ego had become so inflated by then that he talked back to the mob, informing them that his hard work in California—with Jack Dragna and Mickey Cohen—and in Nevada, and the efforts of his pal, Gus Greenbaum, in Phoenix, had together made Trans-America vastly profitable and that it could therefore only be bought off for $2 million.

Bugsy went ahead with the completion of his hotel. But the conflict was still unsettled, and bookies in Los Angeles began to scream at the $150 weekly charge for each telephone of both the wire services they were now forced to use.

The Flamingo reopened on March 27, 1947, and after three nervous weeks, Bugsy was somewhat calmed as the money began to roll in. His little domain was graced by a number of women, chief among them being Virginia Hill, busty messenger for the syndicate and former sweetheart of Joe Adonis. Ensconced by Bugsy in the Flamingo's penthouse, Virginia helped work things out for him through the troublesome times and probably kept him alive longer than the mob thought necessary. But Bugsy seemed unaware of the favor and attributed his syndicate seaworthiness to his own talents. By early 1947 Bugsy was still deep in debt, and he had been told by Lucky Luciano in Havana, during a hasty visit there to plead for time, that the $3 million he owed the boys was long overdue and that the wire service had better be turned over to them in a hurry.

On the night of June 20, 1947, in the Beverly Hills home of Virginia Hill, the matter was settled—in a way the secret society has been settling such disputes for years—when Bugsy was shot to death through an open window by an unknown killer.

Bugsy's dream, the Flamingo Hotel, was entrusted by the syndicate to the care of Gus Greenbaum, who soon put the hotel in the black. But seven years of gambling, booze, and women—all of which interested him personally—took their toll on his health, and Greenbaum tried to bow out in 1955. He moved back to Phoenix, but a new Strip hotel, the Riviera, had opened in March of that year and was losing a lot of money. Gus still owed a large debt to the Chicago mob from his high-living Flamingo days, and he was compelled to return to Las Vegas to put the Riviera on its feet. He did his work, and the old habits were taken up once more. His gambling debts increased along with his liquor and drug consumption, to the point where his backers wanted him out. The casino books were showing unexplained losses, and Gus was suspected of doing some skimming on his own. But by then he was well hooked on Las Vegas ways and had no intention of retiring. He hired a couple of bodyguards and stood his ground.

In November, 1958, Gus Greenbaum went home to Phoenix for the holidays. The mob permitted him a pleasant Thanksgiving dinner with his family, but on December 3, the society did its work once more: Gus and his wife, Bess, were found at home, their throats slashed with a butcher knife from their own kitchen.

It is significant—if anyone cares about *why* the mob murders its own—that both Siegel and Greenbaum were thought by the syndicate to have misused funds entrusted to them. Gus, perhaps, had little excuse when he got his mob deserts—his wife, apparently, just happened to be there at the time—but Bugsy was up against a stone wall of postwar priorities in the building of the Flamingo and was "stolen blind" by dealers in supplies and by the unions. Consequently, the costs of the Flamingo had risen, and so had Bugsy's dollar demands on the boys back east.

In the period following Bugsy Siegel's glorious entrance to Las Vegas, the mob had pretty much of a free hand. Its emissaries thronged the Strip. In ten years there was built an equal number of luxurious hotel-casinos, with the building splurge taking a temporary halt after the completion in 1957 of the Tropicana Hotel, which was backed by Frank Costello and his pal, Phil Kastel of the Louisiana mob.

The Lansky-backed Thunderbird Hotel opened in 1948; Cleveland's Mayfield Road Gang opened the Desert Inn in 1950; Doc Stacher's Sands Hotel made its debut in 1952; the same year the Sahara Hotel, which had its backing in the Portland, Oregon, gambling-horsebook organization headed by Al Winter, opened its doors. The year 1955 saw the opening of the New Frontier Hotel, which was the Last Frontier, restyled and renamed, with a strictly "non-pro" by the name of Warren (Doc) Bayley at its helm. Later, Bayley, who has since died, built the Hacienda Hotel at the far end of the Strip, and it, too, was a kind of amateur operation—by mob standards. Three other hotels opened in 1955: the Riviera, which Gus Greenbaum took over for the Chicago boys; the Dunes, backed by Rhode Island's Mafia boss, Ray Patriarca; and the Royal Nevada, which went broke and closed on New Year's Eve, to be taken over later by the Desert Inn crew as a convention center.

The Las Vegas entrance of Moe Dalitz and his Mayfield Road Gang buddies, whose notoriety has been detailed in *The Green Felt Jungle* and other places, signaled an era of predominantly Jewish operation of *the* Mafia's money business: legalized gambling. Dalitz and his pals bailed gambler Wilbur Clark out of debt and made possible the completion of "Wilbur Clark's Desert Inn" by cutting themselves in for 74 per cent of the take. They arranged financing, satisfied gangsters elsewhere who wanted "in" on hidden percentage points, and greased the palms of various local politicians who had their own two-way-stretch scoops in the money pot. The only remaining barrier was the Nevada tax commission, which had declined to issue licenses to Moe and his boys because of an alarming report from Virgil Peterson of the Chicago crime commission.

In spite of Peterson's detailed outline of the previous criminal activities of Dalitz and his friends, opposition began to melt away when Mafioso Sam Maceo, top syndicate man in Texas at the time, showed up at the Riverside Hotel in Reno to talk things over with Nevada's Senator Pat McCarran. The necessary licenses were issued post haste. With a Sicilian running as quarterback and an Irishman providing interference, the game was a pushover for the Cleveland team. Today both McCarran and Maceo are dead, and most of the Mayfield Road Gang have limped away, their ranks somewhat thinned by punitive government measures and by the greenback offerings of Howard Hughes, the walking Fort Knox, to take over their holdings and lure them out of Las Vegas.

A perusal of trends in Las Vegas, and of the vanishing powers behind various thrones, shows that the Jewish members of the syndicate, who lived through and brought about the Strip's Golden Age, have been edged slowly, very slowly, out of the picture. Meyer Lansky stands today as perhaps the last of the big-time Jewish gambling racketeers with a vested interest in the Vegas Temples of Mammon, though he long ago abandoned his belief in the moral concepts that have shed greatness through the centuries on the race that produced him. Needless to say, his turn will come when he stops producing.

If the barbarians conquered Rome, then it could be assumed their descendants built today's Las Vegas Strip and have withstood the onslaught of the millions of Americans who for years have rushed headlong with rubber-tired, gasoline-propelled chariots toward a financial cancer that happily consumes their purses at about the same speed as that with which it divests them of their reason.

There are two dooms in Vegas, doomsday and doomsnight. The latter is merely an artificial extension of the former occurring when the sun goes down. If, however, you can manage to stick it out in a casino for twenty-four hours—Nick the Greek did it once for seventy-two, betting on the no-pass line at a crap table, without ever going to the men's room—you begin to wonder what are the normal waking and sleeping hours. One thing is certain: the doom is inevitable, whatever the hour.

There is no point in going outdoors at night since it is opthalmological suicide to expose the delicate retina of the eye to the didactic rhythm of the incredible, blinking spectrum that burns up desert moths long before they get to the alluring electric inferno. When daylight comes, the gambler finds he is handcuffed, a prisoner of the heat and the bright flame of the sun, which crawls into his head and drives him back to the air-conditioning, the pastel-tinted cards, and the polka-dotted dice.

So it was with a considerable amount of squinting and brow-wiping that a slight, fiftyish, balding man, dressed more for the Kriendlers' "Club 21" in New York than for Kit Carson's sandy acres, looked out one day in 1958 over a mesquite-lined dry wash jutting north from U.S. Highway 91 and decided that he was going to be a really big man.

The name of the dreamer was Max Field. He was a laundromat distributor in Los Angeles. He placed machines in stores, hired a couple of hostesses, and then sold or leased the properties to people who figured soap and water and a little bluing was a clean way to make money.

As he looked out over the sand and mesquite and even beyond to the geological phenomenon that is Mount Charleston, Field visualized a highrise hotel to be called the Tower. He could see it, even taste it: a pristine white mass of air-conditioned cubicles that would give shelter to thousands of tourists and joy to the least inhibited of them, greenbacks fluttering to the floor of the counting room where a man could stand hip-deep in security.

Field's vision was shared by other people with more violent histories and ideas—by men such as Joe Sica, scion of a multi-murder family that has been the scourge of California since Joe and his brothers, Fred, Frank, and Angelo, went west from New Jersey and boiled a pot of hell for one and all.

Another visionary was Roger Leonard, a partner of Joe Sica with somewhat less vision than either Sica or Field. Leonard once trotted around Mexico under the name of "Kallman de Leonard" but was booted out as an undesirable, probably because of a U.S. arrest record that included charges of rape, burglary, robbery, murder, and assorted bookmaking that he had racked up in thirteen years of activity starting at the age of twenty.

Leonard won a lot of popularity with the right people, one of whom was Mickey Cohen, pal of Joe Sica in many forays where knuckles and muscles played a counterpoint to demands made on Los Angeles businessmen by racketeers. Leonard, in fact, had some winning ways. For example, he tickled Cohen's risibilities by laughing fit to bust when Mickey draped his pet bulldog with a napkin in Rondelli's restaurant in California's San Fernando Valley and fed the beast ground round.

Roger Leonard and Joe Sica tickled Max Field's back with a gun and declared themselves in on his desert dream. What can a man do under these circumstances? Field probably knew that a man once walked into Cohen's favorite private kennel club in Rondelli's and all of a sudden crumpled up, stone dead, with a bullet in him. The bullet ended the life of bookmaker Jack (Jack Whalen) O'Hara, and it was discovered that a man who called himself Kallman de Leonard had purchased the murder gun in a pawnshop in Phoenix, Arizona.

The start of what appears to be a troubled existence for the little strip of Max Field's desert seems to have been initiated the day Sica and Leonard tried to move in on the dreamer. But the mobsters at least got results. Today, a concrete pterodactyl called Caesar's Palace stands astride the sands, financed by an army of partners and $10 million from Jimmy Hoffa's Teamsters. Caesar's Palace is Las Vegas' latest entry in the ever-running hotel derby, and though its wings—unlike the desperate arms of the crap shooters within its gold-spangled, statue-flanked casino—do not beat the air, Max Field may have provided for it the beginnings of the same kind of continually eroding extinction that erased the flying reptile aeons ago.

Perhaps Field should not have erected the giant sign on his property, calling attention to the fact that the Tower Hotel would be built on the spot and outlining a few of the coming attractions. Perhaps he did make a mistake, but it was an honest one. He just hadn't counted on the two gangland minstrels, Sica and Leonard.

Of course, to attempt to do what Field's new partners tried required an okay from the boys who give the okay to come into Las Vegas. This permission has nothing to do with the governor's office, the gaming control board that operates out of the state capital, or the local county offices encompassing the sheriff and county commissioners. Consequently, Field could turn nowhere. Everywhere he was told that Sica and Leonard had the "fix" in with the politicians who run Nevada, and the heartless racketeers milked the little man dry with the promise that his gambling license was a sure thing.

The fleecing of Max Field did not go unnoticed. Captain James

Hamilton of the Los Angeles police heard the story, and when Sica, Leonard, and Field stopped at the Sands Hotel during a visit to Las Vegas, the Clark County sheriff's office stepped in and arrested both mobsters. Sica was on a list in a "black book" issued by the gaming officials in Nevada and was therefore "eighty-sixed" out of all Vegas casinos. In the pockets of the two mobsters were found checks made out by Field for hundreds of dollars plus credit cards with Field's name on them.

Incidentally, use of a man's credit card is a tried and true racket with Mafiosi. Instead of asking for cash from businessmen who are "under the muscle"—cash for which the businessmen must account—the mob boys take their credit cards and bleed them for all they're worth. Indeed, the syndicate is involved in a thriving trade in stolen credit cards.

Sica and Leonard soon dropped their relationship with Field when they found they had drained his resources and that he had, in fact, not even enough money left to pay for the sign he put up on the Strip in Las Vegas to announce his dream.

Las Vegas, then, is a constant source of misery for others than the "busted" gamblers. And in particular an aura of sadness and doom seems to curse what were to become the future Caesar's Palace grounds. An especially haunting episode concerns one Myford Irvine, heir to a multi-million-dollar estate in Orange County known as the Irvine Ranch which was originally a Spanish land grant, contains 88,256 acres, and includes the posh, oceanside city of Newport.

Irvine somehow became involved with Vegas gamblers who had their eyes on his millions. They pointed him toward the same property Max Field had woven his illusions around a few months earlier, and they had high ambitions late in 1958, when Irvine's gilt-edged two-reeler began.

No one who will tell knows what really happened to cause Myford's death "by suicide" on January 11, 1959. We can, however, piece together some of the story. Irvine apparently had made commitments to a gambling group in Las Vegas. The result was that the sixty-year-old protagonist in one of Las Vegas' oldest and most repeated plays got deeply involved and had to produce a fantastic sum of cash, in a hurry. Irvine could have done it, given time. He was president of a vast trust left to him by his father, and a brother who could have shared it with him had died of tuberculosis in 1939. However, at first he tried to buck the pressures placed upon him. Then, it seems, he suddenly decided to go ahead and provide the money that would transform everybody's dream into reality.

But by then it was too late. He asked the men who helped him administer his trust to give him the money he needed—reportedly about a million dollars—and for some incredible reason insisted he had to have it almost instantly: on Saturday, January 11, 1959. It was not possible, and Myford cried, "Too late, too late!" when he learned that his trustees would not be able to meet until the following Monday to vote the funds. His niece, Joan, tried to speed the loan but failed.

According to the Orange County police files, on Saturday, January 11, Irvine went into the den of his home on the estate and fired a shotgun blast into his body. Then he is supposed to have secured a .22-caliber pistol and finished the job with a shot in the temple. Why?

Part of the answer to the Irvine mystery may have come in a disclosure made by U.S. Judge Thurmond Clarke and his wife, a former sister-in-law of the dead man whose death was finally listed by law officials as a suicide. Judge Clarke recounted that "Irvine approached Mrs. Clarke and her daughter [Joan Irvine Burt] and said he needed $5 million right away. He said he had to have $400,000 of it by Monday morning.

"He said he was 'sitting on a keg of dynamite' and had been trying to sell some stock to friends," Judge Clarke continued. "One was interested but decided he couldn't set up a company to take the stock in time for Irvine's needs."

Judge Clarke said he asked Irvine why he didn't go to a bank for the loan, and the man replied: " 'I've never had to borrow from a bank before and I don't want to start now.'

"We never did find out what the keg of dynamite was," Judge Clarke concluded.

After his death, Irvine's estate was estimated to be worth in excess of $10 million and his yearly income $100,000. He also had a $325,000 home under construction at Corona del Mar. And although there is some confusion about the total amount of money Irvine needed and the date he had to have it, he evidently needed the kind of money necessary for entree into the more select circles of Las Vegas' gaming gentry. Relatives are still trying to figure it all out, and the answer may lie in the sands of Las Vegas, under dunes flattened by the weight of Caesar's Palace and the pressure of unhappy and unholy memories.

The parcel of land that supports the Palace has been an "in and out" bit of property. Owned and claimed by an assortment of people at one time or another, it was finally wrapped up by one Kirk Kerkorian, a sort of ham-sandwich Howard Hughes. By the end of 1968, Kerkorian had sold his Trans International Airlines, which he had started with the purchase of one war-surplus DC-3 for $12,000, gained control of and was running the Flamingo Hotel, and was planning the building of another hotel and casino near the Strip. He and Hughes were competing for headlines and confusing readers by their respective bids for control of Western Air Lines and Air West.

According to a local magazine, Kerkorian's landlordship of Caesar's Palace was frequently interrupted by his disappearance "in his private jet ($620,000 cost—$15,000 monthly maintenance) to Europe and the Caribbean." It was further stated that Kerkorian negotiated and closed the land deal for Caesar's Palace over a weekend.

An even more important figure in Las Vegas, however, and one who received a great deal of local publicity when Caesar's Palace stuffed the customers into the amphitheater on its opening was a relative unknown, the prime owner of the casino, Jay Sarno, who had a 10 per cent interest.

It was supposedly Sarno's imaginative talents in the architectural world of marble and concrete-over-chicken-wire that helped pace the tourists' path past fountains—replicas of classic originals such as the Rape of the Sabine Women by Bologna, Apollo and Daphne by Bernini, the Aphrodite of Melos, Hebe (powers of rejuvenation were attributed to this young lady) by deVries, and the Three Graces by Antonio Canova in Italy in 1757—into the casino. But then, if Martin Stern, the prominent Los Angeles architect who designed the Sahara and the new façade of the Aladdin (formerly the Tally-Ho) in Las Vegas, will check his files, he may discover that Mr. Sarno has marvelous extrasensory perception. The design of Caesar's Palace is remarkably similar to Stern's own renderings for the aborted Tower Hotel and of a dream once held by a man named Max.

Sarno, however, takes no small amount of credit for the marble and mammary trappings of the Palace. As he told a *West* magazine writer coyly:

> So I don't look like a designer, but see that block outside there through the window, that design that covers the front of the building? That's the Sarno Block. I've had it patented and anybody wants to use it, they got to come to me! . . .
>
> The new convention hall we're building will be my version of a Roman circus—elliptical. [It opened in October, 1968.] I dreamed up the idea for this whole place, and I designed or supervised everything. It was a team project with Melvin Grossman of Miami Beach and Jo Harris who's an architect and interior designer. I was like the quarterback. I'm a builder and I've always been very impressed by Roman architecture. It's very romantic.

The first of Las Vegas' resident caesars, Sarno added that he has a "fine Roman head" that would "look very good on a bust." But comic Alan King may have said something not nearly as funny as it sounded when, while playing the Sands Hotel in Las Vegas, he joked about Caesar's Palace: "I wouldn't say it was exactly Roman—more a kind of early Sicilian."

Sarno, who owns fourteen hundred shares in the Desert Palace, low-key name for the holding company that controls Caesar's Palace, has a real talent for knowing where the money is. He and his partner, Stanley Mallin, are not new to the hotel game. They put together a chain of plush motels called Cabana, starting in Atlanta, Georgia, and spreading out to Dallas, Texas, and Palo Alto, California. An interesting story behind the Cabana concerns the business merger of two fairly well-known names: Doris Day, America's Number One screen virgin, and James Riddle Hoffa, America's Number One purveyor of labor's pension funds. Doris, with Cabana partners Sarno and Mallin, has benefited greatly from loaned Teamster pension greenbacks, $5 million worth.

Mallin, who lives at 130 Alden Avenue, N.W., in Atlanta, owns a mere 3.9643 per cent of the Caesar's Palace casino end of the deal but is in for a whopping 17.55 per cent of the hotel operation.

In fact, it appears that the real caesar is Jimmy Hoffa. Although he must now reign from a prison cell, his suite at the Palace is lavishly furnished in modish ebony and white. Even the Teamsters' famous "Taj Mahal" headquarters in Washington, D.C. can boast no finer accommodations.

Los Angeles society columnist Cobina Wright could not make the three-day opening celebration of the Palace in August, 1966, but printed a lengthy guest list of the "beautiful people" who attended. On hand, among the bejeweled celebrities, were Governor Grant Sawyer, who later attacked the FBI for trying to pry into the secrets of skimming in Las Vegas and Reno casinos and carried his complaint all the way to the President of the United States; Nevada's junior senator, Howard Cannon; and Andy Griffith, Joe Louis, Prince Puchartra of Thailand, and Melvin Belli, San Francisco legal eagle and onetime defender of Jack Ruby. Belli's nine-year-old son, Caesar, was given a pair of gold-plated dice by the Palace president, Nate Jacobson, owner of a 4.6429 per cent interest in the casino. The boy gave them to his dad, who went down in local history as having rolled the first pair of bones at Las Vegas' newest pleasure dome.

Jimmy (Caesar) Hoffa, wielder of the $10.5-million money mace that kept everyone in line, took the occasion of the opening—and made it official a few days later—to announce that he was tossing another generous $5.5-million loan at Las Vegas' principal phallic symbol, the Landmark Hotel, then a silo-shaped shell. The structure resembles an atomic explosion at the moment that the mushroom cloud umbrellas out. The shaft houses the rooms; the umbrella encloses the gaming casino and restaurant that goes around and around—but slowly, so that the gourmets can enjoy 360 degrees of Las Vegas between soup and nuts, achieving a gastronomic empathy with all the roulette wheels in town.

With the loan to the Landmark, Teamster participation in Las Vegas, which extends to four other hotels, a hospital, two golf courses, and some hoodlum-connected downtown business property, totals over $50 million.

Clearly, the lines are now drawn between Hoffa and his union, the mobsters who fawn upon him, and the people who figure that Las Vegas should be contained and not stretch across the trail of East-West travelers. The route gets longer and fatter along Highway 91, a dollar-studded booby trap operating for the mob, which roars like a lion through the electronic verbocity of coruscating signs and bleats like a lamb when it is asked to come up with a little extra tax money for the benefit of the stable residents of Nevada and their children.

The laurel wreaths assumed by the management at Caesar's

Palace wilted a bit in January, 1967, when a Miami bookmaker named Ruby (Fat Ruby) Lazarus was summoned by a federal grand jury and declined to answer any questions. He was ordered to jail the following March by U.S. Judge A. Andrew Hauk, who alluded to the biblical story of Lazarus who died and was entombed but was resurrected by Christ.

"He had no control over his death," the judge said. "Mr. Lazarus here has control over his fate. He has the key to his own resurrection."

The judge meant that if Lazarus talked about a Little Apalachin meeting held in Palm Springs in October, 1965, he would be let out of jail. Among questions Lazarus refused to answer, even though granted immunity from prosecution, was whether conferees at the Palm Springs meeting—held at a home rented by two Las Vegas showgirls—discussed how ownership of Caesar's Palace was to be divided.

Those in attendance at the Palm Springs meeting were identified in grand jury questioning as Vincent Alo, Anthony Salerno—eastern gangsters—Jerome Zarowitz, and Elliott Paul Price. The latter two assumed positions later at the Palace, Zarowitz as credit manager and Price as a host.

Lazarus, if he did not talk, could have stayed in jail for one year or until the life of the grand jury expired. However, after eight months in jail Lazarus decided to talk and, as a result of his testimony, was indicted for perjury. Sentenced on May 28, 1968, to thirty months in federal prison, he is at present free on a $10,000 appeal bond.

A dramatic aside to the federal probe was an alleged attempt by one of the showgirls, Natalie Loughran, to commit suicide by jumping out of a car on Wilshire Boulevard in Los Angeles in December, 1966, after her initial appearance before the grand jury. Judge Hauk later told her she need fear no person, "whether he comes from the underworld of New York or the overworld of Caesar's Palace." The girl, who uses the stage name of Vickie Lockwood, later told what she knew about the Palm Springs meeting in a secret deposition given to the U.S. attorney in Los Angeles. Two psychiatrists stood by in an adjoining room.

Earlier scandals in Las Vegas, however, are nothing to the furor that erupted in Nevada just before the Palace opening. In July, 1966, Sandy Smith stated in the *Chicago Sun-Times* that

Caesar's Palace, among other hotels, was owned in part by gangsters. Named by Smith were Jerry Catena, a protégé of the late Longy Zwillman of New Jersey, Vincent Alo, boss of the Bronx, Ray Patriarca, New England boss and former money man behind the Dunes Hotel in Las Vegas, Chicago's Tony Accardo and Sam Giancana, and a number of assorted "muscle men" such as Jerry Angiulo, Henry Tamello, and Joseph Anselmo—the latter three members of Patriarca's branch of the Mafia. Anthony (Fat Tony) Salerno and Joe Palermo, supposedly racket bosses in New York City and across the Hudson in New Jersey, also received notice and are probably Alo's soldiers.

Smith also asserted that the take on skimming—the hiding of part of the profits before they are counted for the benefit of Nevada's tax men—totaled $6 million in one year in six Vegas casinos.

The reaction to the skimming exposé followed the normal lines of alarm in Nevada—probably the last state in the Union in which Indians regularly raided the settlers. Governor Grant Sawyer, in a taped interview that appeared on N.B.C.'s inquiry into organized crime a few weeks after Smith's article appeared, came up with a gem:

> Las Vegas, behind the glitter and the glamour that many people see—and that's all they see—happens to be a very stable town that involves a lot of people who are doing all the same kinds of things people in other towns do.

Nobody thought to ask the governor, "Such as what?" And if what happens in Las Vegas happens in towns all over the country, then what could possibly be the great attraction there?

In response to public pressure after the nationwide publicity, Sawyer did order the five-man Nevada gaming commission to conduct hearings into the charges of skimming, although little apparently was said about the even more damning charges of hoodlum ownership. But the hearings didn't get off the ground until three and one-half months after FBI testimony in Denver, which resulted in an attempted extortion conviction for one Las Vegas casino owner, clearly indicated that "bugging" in some casinos had produced evidence of skimming for the benefit of undisclosed interests.

The governor's foot dragging is perhaps understandable in view of the fact that Sawyer was facing a reelection campaign for his third term as governor of a state whose main industry—which is gambling, despite Sawyer's claim that it is tourism—reportedly grossed $330 million in 1965, employs 35,000 of its people, and provides in the way of gambling taxes alone 30 per cent of its general fund revenue. But in any case, nothing happened.

The closed-door hearings, which themselves led, even in Nevada, to criticism of the commission for not inviting elected representatives of the people or the press or the public itself to sit in, produced nothing unexpected. Chairman Milton W. Keefer dutifully called in some of the boys representing ownership of various casinos, asked them a few unrecorded questions, and said at the conclusion that they were "very cooperative and friendly" and that all "categorically denied they have been involved in any skimming whatsoever."

Attorney General Nicholas Katzenbach clamped a lid on the FBI's more than nine-hundred pages of so-called bugging records —which would have set Las Vegas and other cities right in the lap of the Mafia-guided gambling syndicate—although the records could have been used at Keefer's hearing since it was not a prosecutive inquiry. Katzenbach claimed "executive privilege" in buttoning down the records, but they were very important. Dean Elson, Las Vegas FBI chief, stated candidly that his agents hid an electronic listening device in at least one plush hotel-casino to pick up information on "criminal activities."

"In this connection," Elson said, "I would refer to ownership which is not officially recorded with the state of Nevada."

The suspicion that the FBI, who almost certainly "leaked" their records to Smith out of frustration, really did have evidence that would embarrass casino operators led Chairman Keefer to indulge in almost Byronesque semantics to defend the Nevada gamblers: "If the Federal agents have any information we do not have, they are unable to produce it. Hence, we cannot in any manner proceed upon any unverified public expression by people not in public capacity."

However, allegations aside, it is a fact that conspiracy-seeking wiretaps were found at the Fremont Hotel in April, 1963; at the Desert Inn in August, 1963; at the Sands Hotel on July 2, 1963; and at the Stardust and Riviera Hotels. Don't take the word of the FBI for this; take the word of Fremont chief engineer John Grandi who filed a taxpayer's suit, along with several Strip hotel nabobs, against the FBI and the telephone company when the taps, involving twenty-five phone lines, were discovered.

Former Nevada Lieutenant-Governor Cliff Jones claimed that he, too, was tapped by somebody. According to Jones, on August 15, 1965, he found a microphone and radio transmitter, powered by his own phone lines, hidden in a wall telephone well in his office.

So the hotelmen complain, recalling perhaps the incident of undercover man Louis Tabet. Tabet came to Las Vegas in 1954 and caught key officials with their money pockets open. The men he interviewed talked freely into Tabet's hidden microphone as the author and then Assistant District Attorney Gordon Hawkins worked the tape recorder in a closet. Quoted at hearings later in Carson City were an embarrassed Cliff Jones and various county officials who recommended allocation of gaming licenses. The state of Nevada has the authority to give gambling licenses, but it acts on the recommendations of the county or city that houses the proposed casino; without the approval of these entities, the state is somewhat helpless. One unit has a veto over all the others, which splits up the graft potential into many fine hairs.

While the FBI was never given a chance to lay its facts before the public, casino owners were given full opportunity. And when they were asked if they were skimming and cheating the state out of taxable dollars, they smiled benignly—there were no hurt countenances—and said of course not. That's apparently the way the questioning went—no records were made—just a query into "the truth and nothing but the truth."

An eight-page report by the gaming commission following its "inquiry" indicated, among other things, that: (1) the only discernible results to come from the skimming charges were "indictments by newspapers"; (2) Robert Kennedy was responsible for starting the stories; (3) it had failed to uncover evidence that substantial amounts of money were being skimmed by casino owners and channeled to the syndicate; and (4) it would try to devise a means of keeping a closer eye on Nevada gambling, possibly with closed-circuit television and other electronic devices.

The state, however, has its own anti-wiretapping statutes and has claimed that it lacks the authority to deputize federal officers for the purpose of keeping an honest count in the casinos. It has thus pretty well hamstrung itself, perhaps conveniently so.

But the proof of the inquiry pudding lies in the suppressed

records of the FBI, the lack of public access to the state hearings, and the political maneuvering—hurried conferences between Nevada officials, Attorney General Katzenbach, and President Johnson, followed by the public outcries of Democrat Governor Sawyer to the federal government to "Give us your evidence, or call off your dogs!"—necessary to send the damning electronic canaries into orbit, out of sight and sound.

Shortly after Governor Sawyer's "Call off your dogs" cry, grim federal officials decided to try for a jackpot themselves. The result was an investigation by a U.S. grand jury in the gaming town, and in May, 1967, three officials of one Las Vegas hotel and four former officials of another were indicted and charged with conspiring to skim money from gaming profits in order to evade corporate income taxes.

Named in one indictment were Ed Levinson, whose age was given as seventy-one, former president of the Fremont Hotel; Edward Torres, fifty-two, former vice-president; P. Weyerman and Cornelius Hurley, former stockholders and employees of the same hotel located in downtown Las Vegas. Defendants in the other indictment were Ross Miller, chairman of the board of the Riviera Hotel; Frank Atol, a stockholder and employee at the Riviera; and Joseph Rosenberg, a stockholder and casino manager at the same hotel for many years.

This was the first time indictments had been returned for skimming money. All four former officials of the Fremont were named in one count of conspiracy. Another count accused Levinson, Torres, and Weyerman of aiding in preparation of a false tax return. A third count accused Levinson of making a tax return he knew to be untrue. All defendants pleaded innocent in June, and U.S. District Judge Roger Foley said the trial date would not be set for at least three months.

A surprise came late in March, 1968, when Levinson and Rosenberg pleaded no contest to the charge they skimmed money in that they "wilfully aided and assisted in the preparation of false corporate tax returns for the fiscal year ending in 1963." But the real blockbuster came when Judge Foley accepted the pleas, despite government objections, and fined Levinson a mere $5,000 and Rosenberg $3,000. The government then moved to dismiss the other charges against Levinson and Rosenberg as well as the five other men originally named in the two indictments.

Just two days later papers were filed in Nevada State Court by Levinson's attorneys dismissing his suit against four FBI agents who had allegedly invaded his privacy by placing "bugging" equipment in his Fremont Hotel office. A related suit against the Central Telephone Company for supposedly aiding the FBI's wiretapping was left pending, but one can safely assume that this matter will be settled out of court.

The swift court action ended a government case that was almost two years in the making and encompassed a six-month long federal grand jury probe during which over one hundred witnesses, including singer Frank Sinatra, were called.

Federal racket busters were "shocked and demoralized by the sudden and unusual end of a major tax evasion case against Las Vegas casino operators," according to the *Los Angeles Times*, which noted that even Henry E. Petersen, chief of the Justice Department's organized crime and racketeering division, didn't know the skimming case was being ended until it was all over. When a reporter later tried to question Petersen about the case, he replied: "I refuse to talk because I don't know anything about this."

Judge Foley's handling of the matter is reflected in a study of tax cases brought before him in the past six years, the *Los Angeles Times* pointed out, quoting Mitchell Rogovin, assistant attorney general in charge of the tax division. Rogovin evinced dismay at Foley's record: only one jail sentence had resulted from fourteen tax cases in six years.

There was much private questioning as to whether the criminal cases were in any way related to the FBI "bugging" suit. And although many denials were made, some Justice Department and IRS people are not convinced, contending, according to the *Los Angeles Times*, that "it is 'just too coincidental' that the suit against the FBI was dropped the day after the criminal case ended."

Nevertheless, Edwin L. Weisl, Jr., assistant in charge of the civil division responsible for defending the FBI agents, said that the government's handling of the case was proper and that Attorney General Ramsey Clark and Petersen's boss, Fred Vinson, who was in charge of the criminal division, knew in advance of the government strategy. The case "served notice that skimming will have to stop," said Weisl, and that "the government is aware and watching."

At least one skeptic remains, however. A "lesser official," reported the *Los Angeles Times*, "noted that the investigation cost the government more than $100,000 and thousands of man-hours." His conclusion: "Now the gamblers and the mob think they're immune from attacks on skimming."

Possibly this official and others took hope, however, from a new investigation into skimming reportedly charted at a June, 1968, meeting in San Francisco of fifteen IRS and Justice Department officials. The new probe was expected to take a different approach, with attention being directed at "credit play" operations. This would involve locating players who would admit to losing in casino play large amounts of money given to them on credit. Then, once the loss had been paid off to the casino by the player, a perusal of casino records would reveal whether or not that loss had been reported as taxable casino income, the suspicion being that a number of these debts are reported as uncollectable and written off casino records although they actually are collected "on the outside" and thereby skimmed.

It might also be noted that money could be handed out as credit to a so-called player who actually is a management stooge. He need not bet on the tables at all, yet the money could be written off as a casino gambling loss while most of it finds its way back into the pockets, if not the records, of the casino operator.

Skimming is, without a doubt, the name of the game that has kept most of the syndicate boys in Vegas, and their Mafia pals elsewhere, so well fed for so many years. And there are more variations to this game than a poker player ever heard of!

However, while skimming is the most profitable pastime in Vegas, every once in a while "skamming" occurs. A skam at the Riviera Hotel participated in by almost every dealer in the casino over the Fourth of July holiday in 1958, just a few months before owner Gus Greenbaum was murdered, milked him of over $250,000. Chips were stashed away in "subs"—secret pockets in the clothing of the house men—until they bulged. The mobsters backing Gus were short a huge sum, and it could be that Greenbaum was framed by deliberate thievery. He certainly wasn't able to answer for the dishonesty of his subordinates, and it could be that he trusted too many people, too many times.

Least known or publicized of Las Vegas' legal money-making schemes are the coins minted by many of the casinos to take the place of scarce silver dollars. They cost the casinos about seventeen cents apiece, and in order to gamble with them you have to put down a dollar for each one. The proposed statute to cover their use at the time of the first minting in 1966 read that they were to be used only in the casino where issued, whose name appears on them, but tourists use them throughout the town in the dollar slot machines and on the gaming tables. The tokens were also used in over one hundred new automatic blackjack machines, until the machines were banned from casinos in December, 1967, by the Nevada gaming commission. And the coins quickly became "legal" tender for tipping cocktail waitresses, bellboys, etc.

So here is a town minting its own money—this time in metal instead of the clay chips used normally. The gimmick is that tourists, in the first few months after the initial minting of the coins, took home with them some $6,000,000 in so-called silver souvenir chips, leaving a profit for the casinos of about eighty cents apiece, depending on the deal they made with the minters.

Somehow the phony dollars tie into a statement made by Palace chief Jacobson, who said that the "nut"—the dollar intake necessary every day to pay running expenses—would be $40,000. He pointed out that gaming would not take over the whole load, as it did in the now-nostalgically-referred-to "old days," so that rooms, food, and beverages would have to pay a profit. In such an atmosphere it is still anticipated that the good gray tourist cannot win at the games; otherwise the hotel would soon go out of business. So what's in it for the tourist? Expensive broads, expensive gambling, and expensive booze.

Jacobson's quarrel with the government was that the federal government levies $250 a year and the state $300 for each slot machine operating in the casino. But if such demands are too great, why not take the dollar slot machines out, since it is illegal, anyway—in the partnership agreement the gambling fraternity has somehow worked out with the federal government—for the machines taxed by the United States to absorb phony money? The rules state clearly that only genuine coin of the realm be used in the machines.

What's behind it all? Maybe Mr. Katzenbach did not want his men too involved in the intricacies of the gaming in Nevada. There were—and are—after all, more important things, such as the "ten most wanted men" and all those Communists, to catch.

Of course, the men of Las Vegas don't always confine themselves to their gambling interests. For example, Caesar's Palace president Nathan S. Jacobson, an insurance company executive from Baltimore, is also interested in sports. According to a story in the *Los Angeles Times* of July 4, 1966, he was one of the original owners of the Baltimore Bullets basketball team. In this respect, Jacobson's credit manager at the Palace, Jerome Zarowitz, would seem to reflect his boss's interest.

Zarowitz, who attended the Little Apalachin meet in Palm Springs, served nearly twenty months in jail in 1947–1948 on a conspiracy conviction growing out of an attempt to "fix" a National Football League championship game in 1946. In recent years, according to gaming commission files, Zarowitz has operated as a sports bookmaker in Miami. But that is not of much concern in Nevada. Chairman Keefer, in admitting that the gaming commission was aware of Zarowitz' background when it granted Caesar's Palace a license, shrugged and added: "Many licenses are granted to people in bookmaking."

Another money gambit, possibly rather incomprehensible on the part of the men in Las Vegas, was that of Mike Singer, labor racketeer and convicted extortionist who built the International Motor Inn in Palm Springs, California, a few miles south of Palm Springs. In 1965 Singer, a former business agent of Teamsters Local 626 in Los Angeles and close friend of Jimmy Hoffa, paid for a series of advertisements in the Los Angeles papers stating that any guest at his motel would receive a 10 per cent reduction in his bill if he paid in silver dollars.

Then, in the summer of 1966, Singer ran ads in the *Wall Street Journal* offering five million silver dollars for sale at $1.50 each. Singer said that the silver was stored in a Swiss bank because he could not find space in U.S. banks.

Possibly Singer's advertisements were ill-advised, for in September of that year the IRS filed a $72,927.63 tax lien against him involving undeclared income for 1965. But in any case, Singer died in March, 1967.

Until his death Singer had been active in savings and loan groups. He was listed as a founder of Allied TV, which split up and became Allied Empire and is now known as Riverside Financial of Banning, California. He was also connected with Waikiki Savings and Loan of Hawaii, in which Bobby Baker, Cliff Jones, and their associates invested heavily when the move into the Caribbean was made.

In fact, few things have really changed since the author's last visit to the green felt jungle as far as the general trend of Las Vegas life is concerned. But there have been substantial changes in ownership.

For example, the Fremont Hotel, formerly operated by Ed Levinson, seems to have undergone a financial face-lifting. The hotel was originally financed in part by San Francisco's fabled real estate operator, Lou Lurie, with some substantial help from the Teamsters. But in 1966 an announcement was made that the Parvin-Dohrman Company of Los Angeles was negotiating to buy the Fremont. The company, however, had one minor problem. It was issuing stock to be publicly held, and the Securities and Exchange Commission could find no precedent for granting a permit to a gambling casino—which was one of the stumbling blocks that Tony Cornero ran across when he tried to juxtapose legal gambling in Nevada with other legal concepts in Washington, D.C.

If, as has been boldly proclaimed, casino operators skim money off the top of their winnings, how would a shareholder ever know the true value of his stock or receive a fairly representative dividend check?

IRS agents offered to be helpful and said their department would check around Las Vegas to ascertain just what yardstick could be used to establish the worth of a share of common stock, in any casino. But, strangely, the gambling fraternity was appalled and took appropriate measures to curb any such investigation. Parvin-Dohrman had seemingly rolled boxcars. It was, of course, all straightened out eventually and the government let the matter drop.

Months later, when the Fremont sale had finally gone through and Parvin sat in the driver's seat, his vice-president and treasurer Harvey L. Silbert explained to stockholders at their annual meeting just how the complicated acquisition was arranged.

Silbert said that purchase of Las Vegas gaming casinos by publicly held companies is, in effect, prohibited by Nevada law, so that for the purpose of purchasing the Fremont Hotel a dummy company was set up, with the approval of Nevada gaming officials. The dummy was owned by the Parvin-Dohrman Company, whose officials would be the gaming license holders and would collect profits from the "fictional" company as "rent."

The precedent for this kind of operation had been set when

the Del E. Webb Corporation moved into Las Vegas in 1961 with the purchase of a downtown casino, the Mint, and the Sahara Hotel on the Strip.

Obviously such moves were profitable. Silbert described the $10-million deal with five of the Fremont Hotel owners as "so good it's almost frightening."

"Tonight," he told financial editors, "we pay $1.5 million [15 per cent of the purchase price] to Fremont owners and they pay us $1.7 million for 125,000 shares [in the Parvin-Dohrman Company] and thus we get the Fremont and a surplus right away of $170,000." The remainder of the payments on the Fremont were due, he added, over coming years.

Midway through the meeting at the Beverly Hilton Hotel in Beverly Hills, California, a stockholder stood up and asked: "If it's such a good deal for us, why did the Fremont sell?"

"I couldn't answer that," Parvin said. "It's the way the ball bounces sometimes. It amazes us, too."

One reason the Fremont went on the block might be found in the impending government tax action against Fremont officials that ultimately resulted in the indictment of Levinson and others. Silbert said that a $5-million contingency fund had been set up in case the government proved that casino income had been understated. "It could be as much as $3 million," Silbert said of possible government findings. In fact, as has been shown, the actual penalties meted out at the skimming trial of Levinson and the others were puny.

To add to the tax woes of all casino operators, the new governor, Republican Paul Laxalt, has increased taxes on the state's principal industry by 18 per cent to raise $3.7 million in 1969. In addition, he is trying hard to mend Nevada's gambling fences after former Governor Sawyer's blasts at the FBI and the Justice Department for what he felt to be a campaign of harassment aimed at the state. But Parvin was no stranger to the seething gaming pits of Las Vegas and therefore knew what he was letting himself in for.

In 1955 Parvin, formerly an interior decorator, purchased the controlling interest in the Flamingo Hotel. Five years later he dumped it into the laps of a group of Miami Beach hotel operators, including one Morris Lansburgh.

The Flamingo history is one of constant change. On January

13, 1967, it was announced that a Japanese hotel firm had purchased the former Bugsy Siegel ménage for at least $20 million—subject, of course, to approval of the casino deal by the Nevada gaming commission, recently restaffed by Nevada's new governor, and other local agencies. The Fujiya Corporation did their negotiating with Flamingo major stockholders Morris Lansburgh, who shortly thereafter returned to his Eden Roc Hotel in Miami Beach, Sam Cohen of Miami, and Al Parvin.

However, the Japanese bid for the Flamingo Hotel was turned down by the gaming commission. And one therefore wonders if there is any connection between the gaming commission's authorization of Howard Hughes, former owner of Trans World Airlines, to purchase the Desert Inn Hotel and Casino and the seizure by its Japanese owners of Conrad Hilton's Tokyo Hilton Hotel—because of their objection, they said, to the Hilton merger with T.W.A. Hilton's hotel company has been eyeing with interest the profits being made by Las Vegas hotels every day.

Another incident that may have helped trigger the Flamingo upheaval occurred on December 8, 1966. Morris Lansburgh and a group of syndicate-connected men from the Philadelphia, Pennsylvania, and Short Hills and Trenton, New Jersey, areas were called before a New York federal grand jury probing gambling sprees on chartered trips from New York to London. Nothing really came of the probe, but the Flamingo was eventually taken over and is being run by Kirk Kerkorian. And so the trail goes around and around. But if there is a mystery man in Las Vegas now, it could well be Al Parvin.

Among the directors listed in 1966 for the Parvin-Dohrman Company are names that indicate interesting relationships. Along with Parvin, the directors' list shows: Harvey Silbert, Maxwell Rubin, and E. Parry Thomas.

Harvey Silbert was in 1954 an attorney for the group of Miami businessmen who built Las Vegas' Riviera Hotel, the first high-rise hostelry on the Strip. The Miami men went broke—or were "busted out," whichever you prefer—and Harvey acted as their representatives when Gus Greenbaum took his old group from the Flamingo to the Riviera. In fact, Greenbaum headed the men who had sold the Flamingo to Al Parvin. For his work in representing the Miami group, Silbert wound up with a fairly good-sized chunk of the operating side of the Riviera.

Silbert's name didn't show up at first on the gambling license of the Riviera, but he nevertheless maintained an expensive suite at the hotel and took part in many executive, usually secret, meetings there, and to give him an official, but harmless, title—so he could keep an eye on things—he was made chief "talent buyer" for the Riviera shows. Now that the Fremont has changed hands, moreover, Silbert's position at the Riviera seems solid. He is a four-thousand-share stockholder.

It was in the Bank of Las Vegas that the Teamsters placed their security when they first loaned money to the Fremont Hotel, and E. Parry Thomas, vice-president of the bank, also appeared as a director in the Parvin-Dohrman Company, which was supposedly going in as a brand new owner. Until Levinson's suit was dropped, Thomas was under federal subpoena, along with Levinson and others, to answer questions concerning the multi-million-dollar wiretap suit brought by Levinson against the FBI and Central Telephone Company.

The link between the Teamsters, Levinson, and Parvin has always been clear. And Max Rubin, a director in Parvin-Dohrman, held two points in the Sands Hotel along with Parvin.

While on the subject of Parvin, it is interesting to note that, as the *Los Angeles Times* revealed on October 16, 1966, Supreme Court Justice William O. Douglas has received $12,000 a year since 1962 from the tax-exempt Albert Parvin Foundation, which in turn gets its proceeds largely from a share in a mortgage on the Flamingo Hotel.

Stated purpose of the foundation is the support of fellowship programs for students from underdeveloped nations to study at Princeton University and the University of California at Los Angeles as a means of promoting international understanding.

According to the *Los Angeles Times*, the foundation's board of directors includes two of the nation's best-known educators, Robert F. Goheen and Robert M. Hutchins. Goheen is president of Princeton, and Hutchins, former president of the University of Chicago, now heads the Center for the Study of Democratic Institutions in Santa Barbara. Douglas, as president and adviser to the Parvin Foundation, is the only official to receive regular compensation, which, in his own words, is given him "largely as an expense account" for trips in this country and abroad in connection with foundation interests.

Parvin, who laid most of the rugs in the gaming casinos of Vegas and did a good job—by Las Vegas standards—of decorating the interiors of many of the plush hotels in that community, put his foundation together in 1960 when he sold the Flamingo to the Lansburgh group. Although Parvin held the first mortgage on the hotel to cover payments owed his interior-decorating company for furnishings, Justice Douglas told the *Los Angeles Times* he thought the foundation's interest in the Flamingo has been disposed of. In any event, it appears that everyone decided to bail out of the S.S. "Flamingo," torpedoed while on a goodwill mission to Princeton and other ports.

Another recent development in Las Vegas is the reentry, on the wings of a billion dollars or two, of mystery man-industrialist Howard Hughes. Always the recluse, but perhaps feeling that being in Las Vegas puts him in show business, Hughes now employs a makeup man to give him various disguises so that he can prowl the Strip incognito. A Lon Chaney he is not, but few people have recognized him thus far.

The local officials who once tried to discourage Hughes's making the local scene by boosting land taxes on thousands of acres of his desert real estate northwest of Vegas are now sweating out his return to the gambling mecca via the acquisition of several Strip hotels and casinos as well as numerous other properties.

Among announced Hughes's purchases thus far are the following: Desert Inn (hotel and casino), with a leasehold on the hotel land, and Desert Inn golf course where the celebrated Tournament of Champions was held every year until he took over in 1967; Sands Hotel (with casino) and golf course; Castaways Casino (directly across the Strip from the Sands); Frontier Hotel property (across the Strip from the Desert Inn), making him landlord for the Frontier Hotel and Casino, which have long-term leases; Alamo Airways (adjacent to McCarran Field, in which Hughes is extremely interested); North Las Vegas air terminal; 518-acre Krupp ranch; KLAS-TV, the C.B.S. affiliate formerly owned by Hank Greenspun, publisher of the *Las Vegas Sun;* and Silver Slipper Casino.

A sixth casino purchase, the Stardust, was arranged in June, 1968, for $30.5 million, but Hughes granted a private government request that he delay announcement of his acquisition for ninety days. Attorney General Ramsey Clark wanted "an opportunity to consider the implications of the purchase," according to a Hughes spokesman, with the implied possibility of an antitrust suit being filed by the Justice Department. Had Hughes succeeded in acquiring the Stardust, he would have become Nevada's top gaming operator; the taxes collected from his casinos would have made up about 14 per cent of the state's total take from legal gambling. But apparently wanting to leave well enough alone and not stir up a hornets' nest, Hughes announced on August 15, 1968, that "the Stardust Hotel and Hughes Tool Company have terminated any existing plans for purchase of the hotel."

Finally, an October, 1968, announcement that Hughes had purchased the twenty-eight story Landmark Tower Hotel and Casino for $17.3 million and an announced agreement two months later to purchase 67 acres of Strip property, including the fire-scarred El Rancho site, for about $11 million in cash, indicate that he has run out of neither steam nor money.

These purchases, along with offers being made on countless other properties and the unimproved desert real estate he already owns, are giving pause to all of those with a vested interest in Vegas. Two schools of thought exist. According to a chamber of commerce official, who was quoted in the *Los Angeles Times:*

> There's an underlying fear that Hughes will build a fence around the town, call it Hughesville, and paint it green. Then there's the other school, people who think Hughes will eventually bring some much needed industrial diversification to Las Vegas.

One positive clue to Hughes's intentions is seen in his hiring in September, 1968, of Los Angeles airports manager Francis T. Fox, ostensibly to help build up a jet airport complex in Las Vegas. Fox, who leaves a $45,000-a-year job to take what is said, unofficially, to be a $150,000-a-year position, built the regional airports of the Los Angeles area into the world's largest. Through Fox, Hughes, who owns thousands of prime acres to the northwest of Vegas, could develop a built-in tourist communications link with the gambling empire he has acquired.

Hughes himself talks—through press releases, no one sees the man himself—of industrial diversification, which is the best thing that could happen to Las Vegas. And Nevada, which has no state income tax, no inheritance tax, and no inventory tax on items manufactured there to be shipped out of state, could look good and green to many a businessman with an eye on his pocketbook.

The big question is whether or not such industrial diversification can coexist with gambling, and this is what worries the powers that be. Can *they* get to Hughes and those who surround him? Or have *they* already done so?

One thing is certain: his buying spree has increased property values in Las Vegas—some say to the tune of about 10 per cent—after a couple of years of real doldrums. But there is also concern, voiced by one businessman thus: "Where else could you get control of a state so cheaply as Nevada? If you have economic power you have political power, and in this state you could elect both senators for about $500,000."

And so, as always, there are the questions of how much power a man will have and of how it is to be used. In Nevada, where money talks with a loud voice, this is the question of the day with regard to Howard Hughes.

The ring-around-the-rosy goes on and on in Las Vegas, but as Swifty Morgan once said: "Ashes, ashes, all fall down." We think he made it up at that.

The literary model for Damon Runyon's unforgettable "Lemon Drop Kid," Swifty is court jester to the sporting crowd, lifelong crony of comedian Joe E. Lewis and a host of entertainers who walk on the fringe of the set made up of the people who have it made, put on a few airs, and like to be amused. He is a pleasant, irascible, charming, and vulgar character—all at the same time.

Swifty, who carries a cane and sports a dapper old-time golfers' cap and a goatee, both gray, once tried to sell a stolen watch to J. Edgar Hoover. He is on the long side of sixty but looks and acts the part of a frisky young colt. And that's how he wants it to be, for Swifty Morgan has spent his life and his money betting on frisky young colts. He has followed the horses across the country, giving a lot of questionable betting advice to Joe E., who has always said that he "follows horses that follow horses."

Swifty has rubbed elbows with every top mobster in the country, as well as a few of those somewhat lower down, and can talk for hours about them—but only for laughs, not for lawmen. He knew Bugsy Siegel well and was always a welcome guest at the Flamingo. He was never allowed to pay for a meal, or even a cup of coffee, at whatever odd hour he chose to visit the dining room. So when Bugsy was murdered, Swifty mourned—and why not?

A few years ago, Swifty made a small killing at the races and decided to visit his old haunts in Las Vegas. Warm with memories of the old days, he paid a visit to the Flamingo, which at that time had just been purchased by the Miami hotelmen. The men who *really* ran the casino—Sam Cohen, with 42.75 per cent, Chester Sims, casino manager with 3.75 per cent, and Danny Lifter with 22.5 per cent—welcomed Swifty, and Sims walked with his pink-cheeked guest to the restaurant. The conversation soon drifted to Bugsy, and Swifty regaled one and all with stories that will never be printed.

Swifty soon noticed a man—Morris Lansburgh—walking around the room, saying hello and bowing to the guests. The new secretary-treasurer, 14.6 per cent owner, and major domo at the hotel was a pleasant, smiling fellow—in the latest Las Vegas image of "respectable" ownership—who had made many bucks in surplus government property after World War II, especially in instruments and jewelry, and somehow got in with the hotel crowd that saw Miami fading and Las Vegas coming to the forefront of the tourist trade.

Swifty looked and looked at Lansburgh making the rounds, and he squinted as he did so. In a little while Lansburgh made his way to Swifty's table, and Sims introduced the two men, mentioning that Swifty had been one of the first guests at the Flamingo. At that moment a waitress brought the check for Swifty's lunch to the table. Swifty cocked his head and checked the prices, though he knew Sims would sign for the check. He noticed that a ham sandwich and a cup of coffee—his lunch order—was over two dollars, and his squint deepened into a frown. Lansburgh made no move to take the check. Instead, he looked Swifty full in the face and, in his best hotel voice, asked one of the greatest con men in the world what he thought of the great changes he—Lansburgh—had made in the "Fabulous Flamingo."

For a minute Swifty looked Morris straight in the eye. Then, without a glimmer of expression he picked up his cane and rapped three times on the floor of the dining room. Looking down, away from Lansburgh's beaming face, he said, in a hushed and sepulchral voice: "Come back, Bugsy, come back!"

The rest was confusion.

So you see, Vegas has changed little except externally. The once-vivid personality evoked by the sometimes less than blue-blooded but often colorful characters who peopled its shallowed halls has been watered down. All that's left is a bigger-than-life, gaudy-and-bawdy image of a cow-town that made the big time—with the help of a few thousand flocks of sheep in men's clothing.

12

CHICAGO:
The Loch Michigan Monster

The face of Chicago is the face of a clock with a million numbers around its rim, and each of its people is a fraction of a second ruled by a mob that says: "You live, you die; you prosper, you fail. We sift the sands of the hours through our fingers."

The story of Chicago, in fact, must necessarily be the story of its people, who curtsy to the mobsters—probably fearing them, sometimes profiting from their depredations, appalled by the idea, yet displaying an indifference that permits the monster to feed at will.

> Yes Chicago. First in violence, deepest in dirt; loud, lawless, unlovely, ill-smelling, irreverent, new; an overgrown gawk of a village, the "tough" among cities, a spectacle for the nation;—I give Chicago no quarter and Chicago asks for none. "Good," they cheer, when you find fault; "give us the gaff. We deserve it and it does us good." They do deserve it. Lying low beside a great lake of pure, cold water, the city has neither enough nor good enough water. With the ingenuity and will to turn their sewer, the Chicago River, and make it run backwards and upwards out of the lake, the city cannot solve the smoke nuisance. With resources for a magnificent system of public parking, it is too poor to pave and clean the streets. They can balance high buildings on rafts floating in mud, but they can't quench the stench of the stockyards. The enterprise which carried through a World's Fair to a world's triumph is satisfied with two thousand five hundred policemen for two million inhabitants and one hundred and ninety-six square miles of territory, a force so insufficient (and inefficient) that it cannot protect itself, to say nothing of handling mobs, riotous strikers, and the rest of that lawlessness which disgraces Chicago.

Thus did Lincoln Steffens in October, 1903, excoriate Chicago, though he put St. Louis at the top of his list and said that "grafting" in Chicago was petty by comparison and, after Philadelphia, "most unprofessional."

Steffens was profoundly affected by a reform movement in Chicago led by John Maynard Harlan, George E. Cole, and Martin B. Madden, among others. They organized the Municipal Voters' League and tried to fight crime. "The very name was chosen," Steffens said, "because it meant nothing and might mean anything." The group went out after the board of aldermen, sixty-eight in all —fifty-seven of them "thieves," the league stated, promptly and plainly—and proceeded to defeat most of them.

Harlan, who was on the board of aldermen and fought for reform, used to tell "ghost stories" to his fellow aldermen, who together formed what was also known as the city council. Said he: "You may wake up some morning to find street lamps are useful for other purposes than lighting the streets." Or: "Some night the citizens, who are watching you, may come down here from the galleries with pieces of hemp in their hands."

The city lawmakers would fidget. "I don't like dis business all about street lamps and hemp—vot dot is?" said a German boodler —"boodler" is a word coined by Steffens to denote a "grafter" who accepts money for political favors—one night. "We don't come here for no such a business."

Carl Sandburg came up with an idealized concept of Chicago, which was, in his eyes, "Laughing the stormy, husky, brawling laughter of Youth, half-naked, sweating, proud to be Hog Butcher, Tool Maker, Stacker of Wheat, Player with Railroads and Freight Handler to the Nation." He called Chicago the "City of the Big Shoulders," but no big shoulders got there, really, until the mob and the Mafia moved in with Al Capone in 1919. Steffens had come too soon.

Capone, who is supposed to have belonged to the murderous "Five Points Gang" in New York City, was really a product of Brooklyn and the docks in the South Brooklyn and Red Hook section where Albert Anastasia came up through the ranks. Control of the piers in the harbor means control of numerous rackets. Even the big sea crabs that tear the calcium covers off the barnacles of the pilings that are laved by the sea have a racket of their own. They waltz sideways no faster for a man dumped into the river than for a dead fish. The barnacles are merely a constant buffet, always there for the taking. The only competition for the sea crabs are the shiny eels. They swim really fast.

Al Capone sealed the power of the Italian mob in New York when he killed an Irish gangster known as "Peg Leg" Lonergan, a disciple of the notorious Owney Madden. Capone was then scarred by a hoodlum named Gallucio in a street fight. What eventually happened to Gallucio is not known, but shortly thereafter, in 1919, Capone was brought to Chicago by Johnny Torrio, who took the purple mantle of crime overlordship from James (Big Jim) Colosimo. Little is known of Torrio, or of the man he deposed, except that Colosimo had married a woman who was the best known madam in Chicago and kept records of customers known to have both influence and affluence.

The Colosimo pattern has been followed since that mythical temptress, Circe, turned Ulysses' seamen into a herd of swine, but Circe never profited to the extent Mrs. Colosimo did. In fact, part of the initial financial structure of the Sahara Hotel in Las Vegas rests on the Colosimo concept, inasmuch as one of its backers from Oregon married the top madam in Portland and thereby derived much financial wherewithal. There is no record, however, that any of the Sahara's customers, like Ulysses, ever put wax in their ears to drown out the sweet voices of siren temptresses.

It is possible that Capone murdered Colosimo as a favor to Torrio. But in any case, Big Al lined up gambling and prostitution for Torrio, who had become top man on the totem pole of vice in Chicago and its northern and western suburbs by 1924.

Torrio owned three breweries and had an interest in many others, and Capone was quick to see that Torrio was not able to hold the organization together. Capone therefore moved to take the insulation away from the man who had promoted him into the big money. There is no evidence that Torrio went down the drain because of anything Capone leaked to the federal government, but when Chicago police raided a brewery in May, 1924, Torrio's immunity suddenly ended. He was prosecuted by the government and sentenced to nine months in jail. An attempt was made on his life before he began serving sentence, but he was merely wounded and fled Chicago for New York. He wound up in Florida and retired from active mob duty—one of the few lucky ones.

Officials and judges still serving today attended the Colosimo funeral. Some are so old they must eventually die on the bench, for the mob won't let them quit. Once "in" with the boys, you can't get "out," and you pay back dearly every nickel and dime of mobster largesse.

Since 1919, when Capone came to Chicago, there have been over one thousand mob slayings in the city, and only two have been solved. On the other hand, about 62 per cent of all run-of-the-mill killings—murders committed by "average" people—are solved. The free-lance murderers are the ones who are caught, and their nervous paranoia is very different from the cold-blooded type of mental aberration that exemplifies the syndicate executioner. And the mob executioners, usually called in from far-flung parts of the country, are very clever.

Occasionally Albert Anastasia used a garrote to strangle personal victims, but more often someone else was brought in, someone such as "Big Greenie" Greenberg of Murder, Inc., Anastasia's private firm. For example, Greenberg killed maverick longshoreman Peter Panto, one of the few waterfront workers in Brooklyn who cried out in 1942 against various dockside evils.

When contractor Anastasia was going strong and Capone called on the firm for "hits," an unusual method was worked out by Phil Straus, a member of the killer team from Brooklyn, who has since died. Phil's forte was a switchblade knife and a moving picture theater. Phil would follow his victim until the future corpse settled himself comfortably at a local picture house. Then Phil would take the seat behind him and at the proper time thrust the steel blade of his knife through the back of the chair into his unfortunate human target.

Capone's henchmen had a variety of ways of disposing of victims, but the cruelest of all his practices—which had nothing to do with death but was worse because of the humiliation involved—concerned his dealings with the prostitutes who worked in his brothels. Capone, who ultimately died of paresis (motor paralysis of the body caused by syphilis), delivered punch cards to his brothel managers. They were much like the round cardboards given to patrons of the old fun place, Steeplechase Park in Coney Island, Brooklyn. About fifty numbers edged the cardboard disks, and these were punched as soon as a girl had finished with a customer. Often two lacily fringed disks a day were turned in by some of the more skilled whores.

Capone's inherited empire had a valuation that cannot be figured accurately since no books were ever kept, and nobody, not even the public officials, would quarrel with that. However, one raid on the gang's headquarters in April, 1925, indicated that Capone and his henchmen, Tony Arasso, John Patton, Joe Fusco, and Frank Nitti, were receiving millions of dollars from illegal activities involving beer, gambling, and prostitution. Also uncovered were customers' names and the names of federal and local officials who were being paid off.

Patton, who later became the mayor of Burnham, Illinois, was known at the time as the "Boy Wonder of Burnham," but soon after his appointment as mayor he slowly began to fade into the murky depths of time, along with Tony Arasso. Frank Nitti committed suicide, but Joe Fusco is still going strong, listed 'way down in the mob echelon as Joseph Charles Fusco. Fusco, in fact, helped build the Sands Hotel in Las Vegas along with Mack Kufferman, Mal Clarke, Ed Levinson, Meyer Lansky, and Jerry Catena.

The raid on Capone's headquarters in Cicero, where he had moved in 1923 when Bill Dever became mayor, was unusual merely because it happened and because some honest lawmen were behind it. There followed the killing, on April 27, 1926, of William McSwiggin, an assistant state's attorney, and two companions. The murders indicated Capone's utter contempt for established government, although he claimed later his gunmen meant to murder people bucking him in the beer trade.

McSwiggin was the son of Sergeant Anthony McSwiggin, for thirty years a policeman. On September 9, 1926, the father named Capone and his gang aides, Frank Rio, Frank Diamond, and Bob McCullough, as the men responsible for the machine-gunning of his son. Willie Heeney, a Capone roustabout, was named as the "fingerman" who flashed word to Capone at the Hawthorne Hotel in Chicago that McSwiggin, or whomever Heeney mistook him for, was wide open for the strike.

William McSwiggin, known as one of the ablest prosecutors of his time, was digging into the affairs of Capone and the mob and had informers who were close to the syndicate. The tumult and the shouting died in a few months with nobody in the lockup. Capone's claim of mistaken identity was considered to be quite valid by many Chicagoans.

Capone reached the peak of his power in 1927 when William (Big Bill) Thompson became mayor of Chicago. Thompson had run on a "wide open town" pledge—to the horror of reformers and the quiet apprehension of the good people of the city who generally accepted the corruption because they imagined it could not touch them. Capone's prestige soared to wild heights. He was included among those in the greeting party to welcome Commander Francesco De Pinedo's "round the world" fliers representing Italy's boss, Benito Mussolini. Official explanations for Capone's presence have a familiar echo today in the rioting in various cities in America, especially Brooklyn, where, in the summer of 1966, quasi-official authority in the form of the New York City youth board admitted to hiring gangsters to maintain order in riot-ripped areas of the city. Chicago officials said they believed Capone's presence would prevent possible anti-fascist demonstrations, implying that Capone could maintain order where the responsible authorities could not.

How close a city could come to complete criminal dictatorship cannot now be computed, but the fact is that lawmen admit it could easily flourish in what U.S. Supreme Court Chief Justice Warren has called a "Sea of Ethics," as long as a counter-sea, the "Sea of Hypocrisy," thins it out and nullifies its potency.

So Capone's star rose. The whores paid. And the cops were paid. And the numbers gangsters raked in the dough, and they paid. And the politicians were paid by the "alky cookers" in a general roundelay of corruption that made the old Tweed Ring in New York look like a polite game of musical chairs. Ultimately, however, Capone's power was built on the flesh-and-blood fact of murder, the ultimate power if an organization is willing to go that route. In 1926 twenty-nine gang killings occurred in Chicago. In less than six months in 1928 there were sixty-two bombings in the Windy City. Millions of dollars were milked from poor people by numbers racketeers, and when newsmen asked Mayor Thompson's police captain to explain the existence of such wide-scale gambling, he answered: "I am not going to interfere with policy unless I get orders from downtown. I am not going to be sent to the sticks." A few months later he became commissioner of police.

A contemporary of Capone was the storied Dion O'Banion, who ran a flower shop in Chicago and was a purveyor of roses, not a few of which had thorns that scratched Al's hide. It is not a matter of serious history that O'Banion was ultimately wiped out by Capone, but it is interesting to note the quality of loyalty inspired by the boss. For example, O'Banion, like Brooklyn's Joe Adonis, liked to ride horses and indulged his fancy whenever time could be spared from the more strenuous business of crime. It happened that one spring morning O'Banion went a-cantering, and his horse threw him, resplendent in his customary garb of a stylish horseman, into the bridle path, with all of its secondhand oats and hay. Several hours after the unfortunate accident, a group of O'Banion's cohorts went down to the stable that housed the luckless horse and shot the animal dead.

Incidents surrounding O'Banion illustrate not only a peculiar kind of honor among thieves but also how mobsters use odd businesses as legitimate fronts, as though perhaps each is pacing a troubled conscience as well as providing cover for his more nefarious activities. Flower shops and undertaking parlors were once the rage, the latter providing a convenient means of stashing an unreported dead body beneath the false bottom of a coffin housing the "legitimate" corpse.

Mortuary work was, in fact, a favorite pastime of the practical mobsters in bygone days. Now there is a newer way of burying a dead man. Used car lots mash together the steel cubicles of what once were automobiles. The compressed steel is taken by railroad to rendering plants and melted down into ingots. And some ingots contain the remains of missing bad boys of the mob.

Al Capone's reign was punctuated by many things that were disquieting to the men at the top of the Mafia, which was just beginning to be put into a nationwide operation by Frank Costello. The formula worked out at the Apalachin-type meeting in Atlantic City in 1929 contained no place for Capone; somehow he was tipped the black spot and permitted to go by the board. The Depression in 1931 saw Capone tried and convicted in federal court for evasion of income taxes, and the men who directed the syndicate—the real bosses behind Capone, no matter what he thought—let him go down the drain. History records that the federal attorneys did their work well in the jobbing of Capone, but unwritten history may yet show that Capone's day was over, anyway. The money men in the Chicago-New York axis had so decreed. In fact, he had been driving nails into his own coffin in his mistaken idea that he could not be beaten: the murder of a newspaper reporter, Jake Lingle, by gangsters; the death of the motorman on a passing streetcar, killed by a bullet intended for a hoodlum leaving police headquarters in the protective custody of a police lieutenant; the bombing of homes of State Senator Deneen and John Swanton, a candidate for state's attorney; the invasion of polling places, to kidnap election officials and steal ballot boxes, by armed thugs; the machine-gun murder of seven men, who were lined up against the wall of a garage during a bootleg liquor war—the Saint Valentine's Day massacre; and the murder of William McSwiggin.

After his 1931 conviction Capone went to jail and never again returned to Chicago. The syphilis bug was beginning to get in its effective work, and Al was put out to pasture in Florida upon his release from prison. But the organization he welded together remained intact.

Meanwhile, the criminal syndicate, which had sent Capone into exile, found itself without a steady source of revenue when the Eighteenth Amendment was repealed and the citizens of the country could purchase intoxicants without reciting the time-worn phrase, "Joe sent me." So the boys went legitimate and bought into breweries, beginning with 3.2 per cent beer and branching out into control of legal distilleries and distributorships such as Seagrams, Gold Seal, Galsworthy, Canadian Ace Brewery.

The new strategy for the organization backed by the Mafia, in Chicago and elsewhere, was simple: You lose the "alky" money, so you make it up somewhere else. There was gambling, including a host of variations. There were labor unions under duress for the wherewithal to enable them to put up a fight; it was easy to work both ends against the middle.

In Chicago, moreover, it was "more of the same." The top men after Capone's departure were Paul (The Waiter) Ricca, Frank Nitti, and Louis Campagna. But one new area of operation was the movie industry.

The first step that led to the infamous movie shakedowns in California started when the mob took over the International Alliance of Theatrical Stage Employees and Motion Picture Operators. The head of the local motion picture operations, Tom Maloy, who opposed the hoodlums, was murdered, and a few days later a

Capone henchman took over the union and extorted thousands of dollars from Chicago theater owners. Operators from coast to coast were victimized.

George E. Browne, business agent of the union, and Willie Bioff, a panderer, labor racketeer, and Capone mob bully-boy, built up the drive for extortion funds and decided to take over all of Hollywood. A few movie men resisted, and in 1941, with the help of testimony from Browne and Bioff, who made a deal with the law, and, the mob suspected, from a strong-arm man named Nick Circella, nine racketeers were indicted, convicted, and sent to jail.

It is an old story, but, like a snowball rolling downhill, it picks up facts, half facts, and pure rumor as the years go by. Louis Campagna, Paul Ricca, Phil D'Andrea, Charles (Cherry Nose) Gioe, Ralph Pierce, John Roselli—reputed top Mafioso in the Las Vegas-Los Angeles axis at the moment—and Louis Kaufman were among those sent away in 1943.

Paroles were forthcoming as soon as the boys had served one-third of their time and after some had had their delinquent taxes paid by the mob and generally made their fiscal peace with Uncle Sam. But there remained the matter of vendettas against those who had put them in their iron cocoons.

Frank Nitti had committed suicide after being indicted, and the mob was shocked. But an even stranger aftermath was the continued payment of money to Nitti's widow, Annette, by Johnny Patton. Amounts totaled over $30,000. Such dedication to relatives of Mafiosi who die in "the line of duty" points to part of the strength of the syndicate. When a mobster or his wife can get a guaranteed pension from the mob after the boys have been served long and well, it is easy to understand that something besides terror holds the organization together.

What shocked law-enforcement agencies more, however, was the killing of Estelle Carey, cocktail waitress, in Chicago during the incarceration of her boyfriend, Nick Circella, member of the movie extortion ring. The boys felt Nick might talk too much in jail and sent a killer with a penchant for arson over to Estelle's apartment. The killer—authorities believe that Marshall Caifano, top Capone mob lieutenant and "muscle man" may have had something to do with it—tied Estelle to a chair in her apartment, poured gasoline over her, and set her afire. Her pet poodle, cowering in the corner of the room, was the only witness to the crime. Nick never talked much after that. Caifano is currently serving time for attempting to extort $60,000 from oil millionaire Ray Ryan.

Ryan himself was indicted by a federal grand jury in December, 1968, and accused of conspiracy to defraud the government and obstruct justice. The indictment alleged that in 1967 Ryan destroyed records showing that New York bookmaker Frank Erickson, now deceased, had given gift memberships in Ryan's Mount Kenya Safari Club to Mafia leaders Jerry Catena, Tommy Eboli, and Pasquale Eboli. Unindicted co-owners of the club with Ryan are actor William Holden and Swiss banker Carl Hirschmann. To date there has been no disposition of the case.

So the widow of Frank Nitti, who dealt death to himself, was paid off with cash, and the sweetheart of Circella was paid off in another grisly way as death moved in two directions for two different reasons.

Cruelty, however, is not new to the mob, as has been demonstrated in this book and elsewhere. And cruelty is just as effective a bond as kindness. Typical of the simple, amoral cruelty practiced in a conscienceless way by the hoods is the story of Chicago's Sam (Big Juice) DeStefano and his late chief enforcer, William (Action) Jackson.

DeStefano, currently serving a three-to-five-year sentence on a 1966 conviction, holds the reins of the loan-sharking business and has a habit of always being "sick" when the police come looking for him. On past occasions, while being carried off by police on a stretcher from his very nice suburban home, he has shouted to curious bystanders, through a battery-powered bullhorn, of his travails and mortifications of the flesh, all supposedly brought on by the oppression of the law. He is then usually taken to the barred ward that Cook County jailers reserve for pestiferous people who keep each other awake with their ravings as long as they think someone is listening.

Jackson, an incredibly untidy hood, would visit the home of a recalcitrant borrower from his boss's high-interest money hoard, break in when the man's wife was at home, strip her, and inflict on her grave indignities, most of which cannot be recounted here: unusual forms of punishment even in the hardened areas of Mafia enforcement where only the men are generally worked over. Once, for example, Jackson bit the nipples off the breasts of the wife of a nonpaying borrower and spat them out on the floor.

Action, who eventually got to weigh 340 pounds, must have astounded DeStefano by his porcine proportions and sadistic proclivities. And DeStefano realized he was too dangerous to keep around; Jackson was therefore eliminated by mob killers.

Like a pig in a slaughterhouse, Jackson endured a short and swift demise, but the engineers who deal out death to Mafiosi fallen out of favor are not as good as the butchers staffing the packing plants in Chicago. Police records show that in August, 1961, Jackson was taken to a cellar and stripped naked. A barbed steel hook was then jammed into his rectum, and he was lifted, howling, to the cellar roof and left to hang there until he died. When he was later taken down, his bowels came out with the barbs as the hook was pulled free. He was later found in the trunk of a Cadillac on Lower Wacker Drive in Chicago. He still had his nipples.

Lincoln Steffens said that "Chicago is a city that wants to be led," and he lashed out against the politicians who gave away city franchises to the highest bidders, politicians who had the authorized city contracts and were paid off to steer the compass readings with a little personal magnetism. But while the syndicate makes use of such corrupt officials, the level of sophistication it is able to reach can be more closely gauged by its ability to put its victims on the spot and ripen them for extortion and payoffs, a far more effective method than that of going to the trouble of stalking them and catching them in some unlawful activity. The syndicate as a whole is not often caught doing the former, preferring to "muscle" a victim out of his bankroll. However, one case in Chicago certainly shows a certain finesse, and it is probable that the Mafia gave a grudging acquiescence to the action.

On June 24, 1966, a former Chicago police officer, John J. Pyne, was arrested and charged by the FBI with being the mastermind of a multi-million-dollar sex extortion ring operating across the nation. It was claimed that Pyne issued phony police badges to members of his gang to extort money from men accused of being homosexuals. Pyne's racket had been extremely profitable for two years until the FBI nipped it in full bloom. In May, 1967, for example, a jury in the courtroom of Judge Hubert L. Will in the U.S. District Court in Chicago heard evidence regarding the extortion of $10,000 by Pyne and two of his men from a Provo, Utah, contractor.

In the spring of 1964 the contractor was at a convention in Chicago. While walking on a Loop street, he was approached by Robert Schwartz, aged twenty-seven, of Bellmawr, New Jersey, who identified himself as a salesman for a heavy-equipment firm. He asked the contractor to return to his hotel room to discuss business. There, Schwartz made an indecent proposal, and the contractor said he would call the authorities. Schwartz then exhibited a police badge and left. Ten days later, on March 9, 1964, Pyne and a third man, Edmund Pacewicz, went to Provo with papers that purported to include a Chicago warrant charging homosexual conduct by the contractor and documents supposedly asking for his extradition to Illinois to stand trial. The contractor handed over $10,000 to Pyne and Pacewicz and then advised the FBI of his experience.

On May 5, 1967, Pacewicz, aged forty-five, entered a plea of guilty before Federal Judge Hubert L. Will in Chicago, and Schwartz and Pyne, the other two defendants in the case, were found guilty by a jury on May 18, 1967. All three received sentences of five years in jail.

The contractor's unwillingness to be a patsy for the ring paid off in the above case, and the resulting investigation saw seventeen other persons indicted for cross-country extortion activity. It was revealed that victims included a congressman from an eastern state, who was shaken down for $40,000, a U.S. general, who paid off $2,000, and an admiral, who gave the blackmailers $5,000. One man, who held an important post in the U.S. armed services, was approached in his office in the Pentagon by ring "detectives." He subsequently committed suicide. The sex ring also operated across international lines, another victim being a British producer who paid up $3,000 in England.

What happened to the Utah contractor obviously demonstrates more finesse than the mob usually applies to its basic rackets. Perhaps a change is in sight. Certainly, Cicero mob boss Joseph Aiuppa, powerful Chicago hoodlum who dates from the Capone regime, is trying to achieve at least what he considers to be a modicum of respectability. He and his hoodlum cronies established the Yorkshire Quail Club in Kankakee County with a special permit that allowed shooting for five months a year instead of the usual forty-five days. The Illinois conservation department had approved the Yorkshire Quail Club as a state game-breeding area, but it was used as a site for hoodlum hunting parties, membership of which included well-known fixers and gamblers. However, in October, 1968, Aiuppa, whose gangland nickname is "The Doves," had his wings clipped by the then governor of Illinois, Sam Shapiro. Shapiro revoked the permit "in the public interest" after local newspapers reminded their readers that Aiuppa was convicted in Fort Scott, Kansas, in June, 1962, for killing between nine hundred and fourteen hundred migratory birds, mostly doves, when the legal limit was twenty-four. A federal judge termed Aiuppa's bag of birds "unconscionable slaughter."

Evidence shows that the Aiuppa gang likes sitting ducks as well as quail. In August, 1968, the Chicago crime commission spotlighted an incident that indicates to what extent the mob is capable of impressing its will on the public, whether it be a Utah contractor or a visiting fireman.

The report stated that vile conditions "have long prevailed in Cicero night spots dominated by Joseph Aiuppa." It gave as a case in point a visit to Chicago made in August, 1967, by a medical doctor from Sandwich, Illinois. The doctor, on a business trip, completed his work and drove to Cicero. There he entered a night spot called the Show of Shows on South Cicero Avenue shortly after midnight. He downed a drink and then walked to the Town Revue, a nearby club. He ordered one drink and remembered nothing else until about 9:00 A.M. the next morning, when he regained consciousness and found himself in a room at the Karavan Motel, two blocks away. He was nauseated and had a splitting headache.

Sitting beside him in the room, the crime commission report states, was George Hyland, aged thirty-six, who had been a worker at the Shoo-Shoo-A-Go-Go club in Cicero, described by the commission as a mob establishment.

Later the doctor told police that Hyland said: "You owe me $500 for the room and the woman; come up with the $500." At that point Joseph Aiuppa's nephew, Simone (Mike De Rose) Fulco, entered the room armed with a revolver. According to the doctor, Fulco raved like a madman and "demanded that I produce $1,600 or I'd be put into a trunk. He said I had signed blank checks for girls in a number of Cicero lounges."

Fulco displayed five blank checks allegedly bearing the doctor's signature and demanded, "I want this money in an hour." Fulco threatened him with death as an alternative.

The doctor went to the police and filed charges, following up with testimony before a Cook County grand jury, in spite of telephone threats. One caller said: "Drop the charges and you won't owe us anything."

On December 19, 1967, the grand jury handed down an indictment charging Fulco and Hyland with attempted robbery. On September 12, 1967, the Illinois liquor control commission revoked the Shoo-Shoo-A-Go-Go license. The Show of Shows and the Town Revue, managed by mob-connected flunkies, also were forced to yield their licenses, although the liquor control commission indicated that the latter club voluntarily surrendered its permit.

Jumping up the ladder of syndicate power from Aiuppa to the Capone gang leader Paul Ricca is jumping quite a distance. If ever the entire treasury of the Chicago mob is earmarked for defensive action, it will be expended toward keeping Ricca in this country. To this end a seemingly endless battle is being waged, going to every extreme. Thus in the fall of 1966 Jack Wasserman, Ricca's attorney, filed a petition in Rome asking that the Italian government declare Ricca not a citizen of Italy, and the Italian government has given indications that it might oblige. Yet it is interesting to note that in June, 1967, the Italian government nullified a murder conviction outstanding against Ricca for forty-five years, which means that Ricca would at least not have to be imprisoned if, in the event of some legal catastrophe in the United States, he is ordered deported to Italy.

Although he is over seventy, Ricca, whose real name is Paul DeLucia, give or take a few aliases, is still, with Accardo, at the top of mob hierarchy in Chicago. Ricca was born in Naples. In 1917, when nineteen years old, he murdered Emilia Parillo, one of his sister's suiters. He was convicted and sentenced to prison for two and one-half years. Upon his release, Ricca murdered a witness who testified against him in the Parillo trial, Vincenzo Capasso. He then fled Italy, was convicted in absentia, and sentenced to prison for eighteen years for the second murder. This was the conviction that was recently nullified by the Italian government, but despite this act of legal clearance, the Italians do not want him. In fact, Ricca has been so far turned down by forty-seven countries, largely because he has made a habit of mailing abroad newspaper clippings that outline his vicious career as an American gang leader.

Ricca is definitely not a dumb hood. One notable courtroom appearance by the mobster came about when he was placed on trial for perjury in Chicago's U.S. District Court in November, 1967. It was charged that Ricca had lied while testifying at deportation proceedings in 1965 about the source of $80,159 reported as "miscellaneous income" on his 1963 tax returns. Ricca said he made the money by betting at pari-mutuel windows at various Chicago racetracks. FBI agents found evidence enough to warrant an indictment for perjury, and Ricca set about explaining how his winnings were achieved.

He presented a chart showing that he placed eighty-six wagers on thirty-seven races in 1963. In each case his horse came in first. Assistant U.S. Attorney John J. McDonnell sniffed a successful prosecution at this point. How was such complete accuracy possible? "Utterly ridiculous," said McDonnell. "His horses never came in second or third. They always came in first. Isn't that the silliest thing you have ever heard of?"

The jury heard testimony for five days then acquitted Ricca. It seems that he had accomplished not one but two miracles, one at the races and the other in a Chicago courtroom.

Once in a while the underworld stops to count noses, as if to see who is still around, and these tabulations usually take place at "social" gatherings held at swank clubs or hotels. Newspapers in Chicago faithfully report the names of those present, if this determination can be made. License plates on parked autos are also checked out for the identities of party-goers.

One such gathering took place on the night of March 25, 1967, at the Edgewater Beach Hotel on North Sheridan Road in Chicago. Over one thousand persons, including two hundred important crime syndicate members attended the $25-a-plate dinner dance sponsored by the Santa Fe Saddle and Gun Club, located near Hinsdale, Illinois. The club has served as a favorite haunt for gang leader Fiore (Fifi) Buccieri and his lieutenant, James (Turk) Torello, a Cicero loan shark. The Chicago crime commission told the rest of the story in its 1967 report on Chicago crime compiled by its executive director Virgil Peterson, a former member of the FBI, as follows:

> Preceding the dinner dance at the Edgewater Beach Hotel was a cocktail party which started at 6:30 P.M. on March 25, 1967. Arriving about five minutes early was the guest of honor, Fiore Buccieri, and following him in rapid succession were Joseph Aiuppa, the crime

> syndicate boss of Cicero, Illinois, and Chicago near north side mob leaders Ross Prio, Joseph (Joey Caesar) DiVarco, Dominic DiBello, and William Goldstein alias Bill Gold. Other early arrivals included syndicate loan sharks William (Wee Willie) Messino and Chris Cardi as well as such underworld characters as Mike Glitta, Lawrence (Larry the Hood) Buonaguidi, Joseph Grieco, Donald Grieco, Irwin S. Weiner, Sam (Sambo) Cesario, a First Ward gambling boss, and Lawrence Rassano, a former operator of a strip tease establishment in Cicero and once a suspect in a west suburban bombing.

The crime commission report went on to name literally dozens of figures and also stated that "Chicago police officers described the dinner dance at the Edgewater Beach Hotel on March 25, 1967, as the largest assemblage of mobsters ever staged in Chicago."

A covering blanket must have been woven around the operations of the mob, and for years that blanket would seem to have had the warp and woof of its pattern outlined at least in part within the confines of a modest office building located at 134 North LaSalle Street in the heart of downtown Chicago, a building that has earned not a little scrutiny from law officers.

In 1962 the building directory in the lobby of Number 134 showed offices for the firm of Korshak, Rothman, and Marshall. Next to the Korshak outfit were the offices of California Life Insurance Company president Bernard Nemerov. The concrete, lime, and pecky cypress structure also sheltered one Mr. Sam Tucker. And the mystery of the building was that many of the occupants seemed to have more than a passing acquaintance with one another.

Sleep must have been a difficult thing to come by, though, for some of the great hearts that worked out of Number 134. What could they possibly have in common that would have brought them to the attention of lawmen? Very few people know, for nothing much has happened outwardly, but one spoor of legal manuscript led to evidence of the occupants' great proclivity for doing business with Jimmy Hoffa and the Teamsters he commands. Another pugmark trails across a dry desert to Las Vegas, where every press agent tries not to, but has to, explain why Hoffa and the Teamsters' pension fund generally provide the big guns and the ammunition necessary to justify not only his existence but also the continued existence of Las Vegas.

How does all this fit in with Chicago? A lot. Forget a microscope; take just an ordinary reading glass and focus it on the firm of Korshak, Rothman, and Marshall. Top legal figure is Sidney Korshak, a tall, black-maned, poker-faced man with an ace up his sleeve where mob connections are concerned. Korshak, whose brother, Marshall Korshak, a former Illinois state senator, is now city treasurer of Chicago, limited his practice to Chicago in the early days of his career and maintained a residence at the Seneca Hotel, then a notorious gangster hangout. But how does he fit in with the syndicate? It is often difficult to trace connections, but consider Korshak's career.

Sidney Korshak, termed by the *Los Angeles Herald-Examiner's* labor editor in 1966 as a man who "seldom stops long enough in one place to get a wrinkle in his suit," began to call for reservations quite regularly in 1959 at the Desert Inn Hotel in Las Vegas. His neighbor at Number 134 perhaps saw to it that Korshak was never turned away, for Sam Tucker—who gave his address to the Nevada gaming control board as 1437 Eighty-Eighth Street, Surfside, Florida—owned 13.2 points in the sweaty jackpot that is the Desert Inn's gaming casino.

Korshak's "guest" tenure at the Desert Inn coincided with a move by Cleveland's racketeering Mayfield Road Gang, which during Prohibition spawned most of the Desert Inn partners, to buy their next-door neighbor, the Riviera Hotel. The gaming commission denied the application on the basis of dual ownership; nevertheless, important gaming personnel from the Desert Inn began to show up periodically in the pit of the Riviera to keep a brotherly eye on the currency.

Korshak's reputation shaded not one bit as a result of this symbiotic merger, and within a short time he had trudged a trail through the sticky clay of Hollywood show business as an effective negotiator for really large talent—not that Dinah Shore is large, but she made her Las Vegas debut at the Riviera, as did Debbie Reynolds and Tony Martin, the perennially youthful singer for whom it was actually a "second" debut, as he had previously been a Desert Inn regular. These Korshak clients became stars in the Riviera stable, and interestingly enough, it was at about this time that the Justice Department began looking into the West Coast jukebox-talent-agency tie-ups and their controls over the entertainment industry.

A later Korshak foray into the labor-management field came to light in June, 1967, in the midst of a campaign by three unions to control the twenty-eight hundred dealers, box men, stick men, change girls, and others who police the one-way tables that siphon money from gamblers' pockets into the counting rooms of Las Vegas casinos.

Flaunting membership blanks were the American Federation of Casino and Gaming Employees, the Seafarers International Union, and the Hotel and Restaurant Workers—the latter two being AF of L-CIO affiliates. Most of the workers in Las Vegas gaming houses and hotels are already union members, but those who actually handle the green stuff have been excluded thus far.

Seafarers Union chief Paul Hall is head of a mere eighty thousand members, but he is regarded as a possible successor to AF of L-CIO President George Meany. He minces no words in describing the bosses in Las Vegas as men who do not hesitate to "use Chicago and Cleveland mob tactics."

Speaking for management, Sidney Korshak, who said he was "certainly not anti-union," claimed management sees the dealers as part of management. Korshak was speaking of the so-called elite of the gaming pits, the men who play for the house and are counted on to give their bosses an honest count. Actually, of course, "eye-in-the-sky" one-way mirrors hide the watchers who check the dealers, and the watchers have watchers who watch them.

Korshak believes that management would not fight so hard against unionization of dealers "if something could be worked out to make certain that the management people were fully in charge of employment." Las Vegas ownership obviously wants to maintain its own little Utopia, and Korshak has apparently been chosen to see that the job gets done.

Sidney Korshak's record of accomplishment for his clients once prompted Chicago newspaperman Irv Kupcinet to state that he was undoubtedly the highest paid attorney in the United States. Today Korshak resides in style in West Los Angeles and has become a party pet of movieland's social set, but there is no record of his ever having taken the California bar exams, nor is he listed in any of the California law directories. However, there is no fracture of the law, apparently, where simple bargaining and agenting are the prime concern. He also shows up on the West Coast as labor-relations man for Max Factor, the Hollywood cosmetics tycoon, and a whole string of racetracks, in addition to his other role as talent and Teamster negotiator. His numerous capabilities have so impressed Dan Swinton of the *Los Angeles Herald-Examiner* that he called Korshak "the man to move the mountains." And Swinton could be right.

Take, for example, one of the many pieces of available information about Sidney. *Life* magazine, September 1, 1967, charged that a Giancana lieutenant, Gus Alex, has "an especially warm relationship with Chicago city treasurer, Marshall Korshak, and his brother Sidney." On Alex's 1957 application for an apartment on exclusive Lake Shore Drive, he described himself as a $15,000-a-year employee of Marshall, then a state senator, and the magazine quoted a prominent mobster's testimony from a witness stand: "A message from him [Sidney] is a message from us."

At the 1963 McClellan hearings Captain William J. Duffy identified Gus Alex as a "nonmember associate" of the Chicago Mafia, and in 1967 Alex was labeled publicly by the Chicago crime commission as a "member of the Chicago crime syndicate" whose major area of influence was the Chicago Loop. After the Swiss government slapped a ten-year ban on him in 1965, following numerous visits in previous years, a letter of intercession signed by Illinois Senator Everett Dirksen was sent on Alex's behalf to Swiss officials. Dirksen, however, according to the *Chicago Sun-Times* on July 31, 1967, denied knowing Gus Alex or intervening for him.

"Such a thing might have been handled by my Chicago office as a routine matter," said Dirksen, "but I have no knowledge of it."

The umbrella of legality provided by Sidney Korshak concerns even such oddly located individuals as the workers in the vineyards of California, who, in the spring of 1966, struck against their little old winemaker bosses. Speaking through the mellifluous tones of Korshak, Schenley Distilleries announced on television that an agreement had been reached with the grape workers. A week later the Teamsters tried to "muscle" in on the AF of L-CIO, which represented the winery employees. Despite Teamster threats, name-calling, and pure muscle, the sun-drenched workers in the vineyards voted, the following September, to stay with the AF of L-CIO.

There must have been a lot of action at 134 North LaSalle, or maybe there was none if a fellow has to take time out to worry about West-Coast vineyard workers. But close to what action there was, was a man named Bernard Nemerov, president of the California

Life Insurance Company. Nemerov, who owned four points in the Riviera Hotel in Vegas in 1963, came up through the ranks from Minneapolis, Minnesota, after getting to know Paul Dorfman, Hoffa's favorite insurance agent, and wound up with his own insurance company based in Oakland, California. It's strange how so many of the Number 134 roads lead in similar direction.

The association typified by some of the names of the office index at 134 North LaSalle Street goes on of course, even though some of the figures have moved away to other buildings in the city. And many of the details remain unclear—except perhaps to law-enforcement officials in Chicago and elsewhere who for one reason or another are unable to act. The convenient and unobserved meetings, in hall corridors and coffee shops—not to mention men's rooms—still take place. Locations change, but it's still business as usual.

An interesting meeting of minds, for instance, must have taken place in July, 1968, at the Teamster-pension-fund-financed La Costa Country Club—currently *the* V.I.P. spa in southern California—when a gathering was observed by law-enforcement officials. Among the cloistered participants were Moe Dalitz and Allard Roen, former executives of the Desert Inn, Allan Dorfman, of the California Life Insurance Company, Sidney Korshak, and Mrs. Jimmy Hoffa. Another attendant at the meeting, from seemingly far afield, was the Bahamas' Big Daddy himself, Wallace Groves, who could also have an interest in Teamster moneys.

There will never be a beginning of the end for Chicago, but there will perhaps be an end to the beginning, and lawyers will be the pallbearers. Meanwhile, it is difficult to leave the continuing caprices of a modernized version of the old Capone gang in Chicago and travel across the country without stumbling upon part of the overall chain of command that seems to point to that city as being a kind of command post where anything can happen.

It should be noted that the mob boys pay strict attention to what is known—especially in Chicago—as "business." Broads and booze are more or less taboo, except in the wide-open town of Las Vegas and some of the more shadowy places in New York, New Orleans, Dallas, and Palm Springs. And even the latter city is off-limits to the lesser hoods who go in for stick-ups, assaults, and the more juvenile proclivities of mob button men who are still wet behind the ears.

A case in point in Chicago occurred on May 2, 1962, when the police received a report that a suspicious automobile was parked in front of 1750 Superior Street. They checked and found a 1962 Ford sedan at the specified location. Crouched on the floor of the car, curled up like twin fetuses and caught literally with their switches down, were two notorious Capone syndicate hoodlums: Philip (Milwaukee Phil) Alderisio of Riverside and Charles Nicoletti of Melrose Park. The two hoods informed the investigating officers that the car did not belong to them and that they had no idea who owned it. It was 1:00 A.M., and the boys were promptly taken into custody and just as promptly released on $2,000 bail.

The car was registered in the name of a man who later proved to be nonexistent at an address that just wasn't there. The interesting thing, however, was that the car's dashboard hid three switches, two enabling the operator to disconnect the taillights, making it difficult to be followed at night, and the third turning on a small electric motor that opened a hidden compartment in the backrest of the front seat. This compartment was fitted with brackets to hold shotguns and rifles. It was also big enough for a machine gun, and the cops labeled the automobile a "hit" car—a "vehicle," as lawmen say, used to drive killers to their rendezvous with death, generally somebody else's.

Nothing ever came of the incident, and the failure to make something of the arrests proves that if you work at a thing long enough, as the mob does, you can wear down your opposition to such an extent that soon there are no disputed barricades. The Mafia has been doing just this for several hundred years, and for the past generation it has been building up insulation in this country in the form of judges, courts, and cops who are "bought" and then owe the mob something. And there lies one of the chief faults of a system whereby political selection dictates who chases what hoodlum down the street. Alderisio and Nicoletti had it made, and they knew it. They were going to stay on the job, and they knew the law-enforcement official—or whoever was in charge—wouldn't. If they were caught, they would pay bail and leave. Name the crime, and both of these men have had it tatooed on them where it won't wear off, so much so, in fact, that Alderisio's 1966 extortion conviction, now under appeal, represents merely one more step up the crime syndicate ladder.

Only one of the Chicago mobsters has ever angled tuna, a huge mackerel-like fish that courses both coasts of the United States: a silk-suited—especially for courtroom appearances—alligator-shoed, genial man who generally wears a Windsor knot in his smoothly draped tie. His name is Tony Accardo, but he is also known as "Joe Batters." "Big Tuna," which he is also called, is perhaps a better name, for the waters off Nova Scotia have been traversed many times by one of the country's leading gangsters and his trolling rigs, which have lured many a giant blue-fin tuna into close proximity.

Record catch for this species was a monster of 977 pounds, landed off St. Ann Bay, Nova Scotia, on September 4, 1950, by a lucky Izaak Walton named Hodgson. Tony, who once served as bodyguard for Al Capone and recently came out of "retirement" to reassert his control after Sam Giancana left for the Argentine, would like to beat this record, but he may have to get out that old machine gun and convert his fishing launch into a gunboat to do it.

There is really no point in trying to assess the position of Accardo, or even of Giancana, in the national crime syndicate, since these men and those who follow them and kiss their hands in the traditional greeting of the Mafia are but the rootlets of a growth so much bigger than themselves that it is difficult to understand. Certainly no public official who devotes but a few years of his life to an attempt to figure the mob can ever hope to cope with the solid core of criminality that is beyond all the common and duly regarded concepts of law and order. There is no law for the Mafia except its own.

Something must be said, however, about the princelings of the Chicago mob, the worst criminal conspiracy on the face of the earth, powered and financed by—and financing—men whose names are editorial way-stops in the columns of every newspaper across the country and abroad, but only for their social and business activities, not for their profitable dealings with Mafia underlings. The gang is hundreds of years old, but somehow its whiskers never get gray.

One of the top men for years in Chicago, pal of singer Sinatra, patron of the arts as represented by thrush Phyllis Maguire, who has long been a companion—except during a recent year's dry stretch in a Chicago jail because he wouldn't talk to the grand jury —is Salvatore Giancana, alias "Giancani," "Albert Mancuso," "Sam Mooney," "Sam Flood." Giancana is a sharp man who misses no tricks. Thus Anthony Tisci, his son-in-law, was in 1963 both a $900-a-month secretary to U.S. Representative Roland Libonati (D., Ill.) and an adviser to Mafia chieftain Giancana in a legal battle to halt FBI surveillance of the mobster.

Giancana's "at home" address in Oak Park, Illinois, is too unimportant to mention inasmuch as Tony Accardo's pad probably represents the real Fort Knox of the Chicago gang. Accardo once lived at 915 Franklin Street in River Forest, Illinois, where he was reputed to have had a vault sunk into the solid concrete of his basement and loaded with all the money he didn't know what else to do with. But by the time of the McClellan hearings in 1963, Accardo had apparently moved out, undoubtedly taking his underground valuables with him as well as his black onyx bathtub with its solid gold fixtures.

In Brooklyn, in 1950, when police officers were arrested in an investigation that sank a flock of bookmakers and sent Mayor Bill O'Dwyer's personal frigate, "Bill-O," to the bottom of the East River and Bill himself south of the border, the men sought by the grand jury used to shovel the greenbacks into cellar furnaces. If Tony Accardo didn't have his rumored basement vault, then the excess money went somewhere else—possibly pressed into a lot of campaign buttons.

After Giancana, Accardo, and Ricca, you come mostly to unimportant figures, and there is no guarantee that any of them will be alive for any length of time. But outstanding among them seems to be Marshall Caifano, alias "Johnny Marshall," also "Shoes" and "Heels," quaint appellations stuck on him by lawmen who have called him many other things, many other times.

Caifano is the hoodlum suspected of being connected with the torch death of cocktail waitress Estelle Carey, and he could be the mobster who eventually takes over in Chicago, not only to reap a harvest for himself, but also to serve as insulation for mobsters such as Ross Prio of 1721 Sunset Ridge Road, Glenview, Illinois, who has an arrest record dating back to 1929. But at present Caifano is in jail, having been convicted of fraud in 1967 and given a twelve-year prison sentence to run concurrently with the ten-year sentence he was already serving as a result of the Ryan extortion case.

The only man on record who ever really stood up to Caifano was Beldon Katleman, the owner of the El Rancho Vegas who, in 1960, had Caifano put out of the hotel because he was blacklisted by the Nevada gaming control board. Katleman's questionable reward for kicking Caifano out may have come two weeks later when the El Rancho casino was burned to the ground.

The issue of who will take over in Chicago is probably more important than the workings of civic and social groups out to improve the city, and it is no secret that the man currently being groomed for the role of gangster-guru—whatever Caifano's hopes—is Anthony J. Spilotro, protégé of Felix (The Weasel) Alderisio.

Something of a world traveler, Spilotro, a tough with a penny-polish gleaned from no school that can be found in his record of lawbreaking—which goes back to 1955—flaunts the colors of the U.S. Mafia throughout Europe with the aid of a red Mercedes. Points of call have been Amsterdam and Antwerp, where diamonds and breakfast salami are sliced, and solid gambling places and casinos in Monaco, Nice, and outlying places.

On August 2, 1964, Spilotro and a companion were picked up at the Hotel de Paris, Monaco, and questioned about the theft of $137,500 worth of jewelry from the visiting wife of a New York City oil company executive. Later, on a visit to Antwerp, Spilotro was relieved of two large cut diamonds and a switchblade knife. Although he was extensively questioned, no charges could be pressed against him, but Spilotro was—and is now—under a surveillance thumb that might keep the kettle boiling in Chicago while he goes to grade school and works his way up the long ladder to mob dominance. Others have done it before him, without the red Mercedes.

Chicago is full of hoodlums, and many of them tie in with the "licit" businessmen already mentioned. However, it also seems that wherever you turn in Chicago, you come across Jimmy Hoffa and his fountain of Teamster gold. Take the case of Guiseppe Glielmi: "Joey Glimco," as he is called.

Glimco, who lives at 629 Selbourne Drive, Riverside, Illinois, and has a total of thirty-six arrests—for larceny, robbery, assault with intent to commit murder, and auto theft—has served only twenty days in jail. But then Glimco is a Teamster man. For example, Glimco arranged an astounding deal in the operation of Teamster Local 777 having to do with the rebate of Teamster Union dues to the Yellow Cab Company and the Checker Taxi Company in the amount of $327,491.46. The companies said the rebates over a period of twenty years ending in 1959 were made in order for them to pay the additional help necessary to operate the union checkoff system for collection of employees' union dues. Glimco, beloved of Hoffa, who attributes Joey's troubles to "bad headlines," didn't object when the union paid for his house: $26,000 in Teamster dues money. But Hoffa wasn't around in February, 1969, when Joey was fined $40,000 for violations of the Taft-Hartley Act.

Glimco is only one example of Hoffa's Chicago connections. One can, however, be sure that there will be continuous syndicate and Teamster action as long as their cooperation is profitable.

A fuse was lit for a spell—a brief candle in the darkness that usually shrouds investigative processes where hoodlums are concerned—when Henry Peterson, chief of the Justice Department's organized crime and racketeering section, spoke out during an informal panel discussion at the National Conference on Crime Control in Washington late in March, 1967.

Peterson claimed he knew for a "moral certainty" that "in the upper echelons there is an amalgamation" between the Cosa Nostra and the Teamsters Union and the International Longshoremen's Association. He also said the Justice Department had "identified about 5,000 persons in the nation as members of Cosa Nostra."

Peterson's unexpected bombshell of testimony was cut off by the moderator of the panel, deputy director of the President's Crime Commission Henry S. Ruth, who said: "We're going to move on to another subject." And top officials of the I.L.A. and the Teamsters challenged Peterson to prove his allegation, perhaps secure in the knowledge that the man would have to go through many channels to be able to do this.

Actually, testimony taken by Senator John McClellan's rackets committee and the hearings into organized crime underscore Peterson's contentions, and public statements made by Jimmy Hoffa on behalf, for instance, of Joey Glimco bear Peterson out. The expressed friendship, evidenced by appearances at social functions and, more important, gangster funerals, of Hoffa and I.L.A. lieutenants indicates ties that run deep and wide. The FBI, which questioned Joe Valachi for a year before he testified to the McClellan committee on organized crime, has all the evidence necessary. All Peterson needs is a chance to talk.

There have been other indications of government suppression of damning evidence. For instance, while praising the work of the Chicago crime commission at a civic gathering in October,

1967, during Chicago Crime Prevention Week, George P. Hunt, *Life* magazine managing editor, deplored what he called censorship of an official document linking Chicago politicians to the mob. Hunt, who also declared that "the present organized crime program of the federal government is a colossal failure," charged that a sixty-three-page report, ordered by the government and prepared by J. Robert Blakey, Notre Dame law professor, was "reduced to four footnotes" by the White House in the final report of the President's Commission on Law Enforcement.

One thing is certain: while Hoffa doesn't wear long hair, he *is* "bigger than Jesus" to certain people in many parts of this country and the world. His crucifixion may start another religion, or end a really bad kind of faith, for the almost two million truck drivers who are helplessly hooked one way or the other by the syndicate—though they must admit there will never be a Cloud Nine or a harp for any of them if they follow the Hoffa-Glimco-Ricca-Accardo-Giancana Chicago recipe.

Meanwhile, in spite of murders ordered over the years for the benefit of the Mafia, not enough has been done to secure successful and lasting convictions; yet as recently as September, 1966, after an almost four-year moratorium on capital punishment in California, there sat in San Quentin over fifty men awaiting execution. These men waiting to die may be slobs, but their pictures and records indicate that few if any of them ever wore a silk suit in his life or had his nails manicured or had enough money in the bank to hire a lawyer. Certainly not one of them is allied in any way with the Mafia killer-types who have spilled more blood in Chicago since Capone's time than that shed by the average Latin-American revolution or the charge Teddy Roosevelt led up San Juan Hill.

In this connection, moreover, not a little of the blame must be placed on the shoulders of the congressional chefs in Washington who have for years placed the mob's culinary monstrosities before the noses of their hungry, but unknowing, constituents. Lift the top of the Capitol dome and sniff for yourself the aroma created by the questionable recipes of a host of questionable minds.

EPILOGUE

The men joined together today in what is known as the syndicate live quite differently from, and play a game that is incomprehensible to, the average citizen. Their claim is already staked out on the moon, you can be sure, and its future waxing and waning will be measured against what the mob can get out of it: whether the profit can be derived from earth or from the Mafia's presence—in absentia, as usual—behind the forces that create the machinery necessary to put flesh and blood in just another position to make a profit for them.

These apes no longer toss coconuts out of trees; they have now pledged themselves to a complete abortion of the law that has given them unlimited power.

The mob boys have exchanged their kinky coats for the very sharp splendor and protection of legal garments designed by men far removed from them intellectually but, for the most part, bound to them by the fear of death. And while the apes themselves seem not to worry about death, in their ultimate winding sheets there are always legal threads—at God knows what cost.

There are silk suits for the boys at $400 apiece, silken girls at a trifle more, and suckers galore, but most of all, there is the pervading, remembered atmosphere of what once was their own poverty—in Palermo, Sicily; in Boyle Heights, Chicago; in South Brooklyn; in the back streets and unwashed, hot alleys of Everytown that spawned the Bugsy Siegels, the Lepke Buchalters, and the people who served them out of fear and fond hope.

These people have put their pennies into hot hands and nickel-plated slot machines over the years, and the machines, like the silken girls, have acquired a patina of social respectability. The fingerprints on their shiny surfaces are those of a host of captive gamblers. The whole state of Nevada lies in chains, and the people who live there *and can change things* seem happy to be forging the links of their own perpetual imprisonment.

The joy of compulsive gambling springs, perhaps, from its very lack of joy, but the proprietors who rake in the money have no need for laughter. Joe E. Lewis once said, "Las Vegas—the only place you can have a good time without enjoying yourself!" and that goes for any gambling joint. But the big question is: "Where does the dough go?" "Who gets it and stashes it away?"

Most people work eight hours a day for their security, but the mob works twenty-four, and there is no man in the world too big for the boys to take on. Take the savings and loan saga, for example.

It appears that a funnel for funds to be siphoned out of the country by racketeers was fashioned in 1960, when it was discovered that Maryland was a honey pot for investors. It took only three incorporators with a total risk of $30 to form a savings and loan association and send out a milk train to investors with a promise that pure cream would be delivered in return. We have named a few of the mob men, and their apologists, who moved in fast. And it is therefore interesting to note that on January 8, 1966, Mayor Sam Yorty of Los Angeles demanded an investigation of "lame duck wholesale handing out of savings and loan charters" by the outgoing administration of Governor Pat Brown, and that in a letter to Attorney General Thomas C. Lynch, the only leading elected officer in Brown's official family to be reelected, Yorty minced no words. He charged that "a sudden speedup of pending applications" came about following pressure on Brown's savings and loan commissioner by top politicians.

On December 31, 1961, Laurence M. Stern of the *Washington Post* asked: "How was it possible for men with major criminal records and dubious financial backgrounds to go into Maryland and traffic in millions of dollars worth of savings drawn from an unsuspecting public?"

Stern stated that part of the answer lay in the fact that Maryland, until late 1961, had no controls over the "phenomenally burgeoning savings and loan business." Savings accounts in Maryland associations were, he said, in institutions that were federally regulated and insured and that state officials were "not worried" about the solvency of these firms or their ability to make good on losses.

Cited also were some four hundred additional associations with a combined $250 million in savings that are either uninsured or privately insured. And Stern concluded: "Official suspicions are that some of these associations have served as funnels for hot or dirty money."

Stern didn't say where the money came from or went to—which perhaps indicates a lack of liaison with the FBI—but he did ask how a stolen $100,000 treasury note made its way from a New York broker's office to the safe of the First Continental Savings and Loan Association of Chevy Chase.

It would seem that the high interest rates granted by many savings and loan groups—"Give us your savings and we will loan them"—represent earnings made possible by the mob's usage of "your savings" in "front" enterprises and by the accumulated gratuities acquired through the use of mob money, bastard currency that has to be legitimatized.

In fact, several of the savings and loan groups sanctioned by Maryland failed, and investors were left holding empty money bags. Consequently, a Department of Building, Savings and Loan Association was set up in Maryland to police operations of the non-federal segment of the industry, and to keep in check such excesses as practiced by at least one private savings and loan insurance company, Security Financial Insurance Corporation, which at the time was headed by Maryland House Majority Leader A. Gordon Boone. Boone had been provided with $450,000 to establish the company by a Chicago attorney, Henry McGurren, and a cast of prominent fellow Democratic politicians backed the venture too. Then it was discovered that with less than $1 million in surplus the firm was insuring on one policy a $12-million Utah association!

Before the lid was clamped down, however, people from all points of the compass got in on the honey pot. For example, there was the Las Vegas-inspired account in Anjon Savings and Loan whose history has already been referred to. Anjon Account 804 was apparently established, at least partly, for the purpose of gathering funds to purchase stock of the Merritt Savings and Loan Association. But it is curious to note the names and pedigrees of the Las Vegans and others who banded together where there was money to be made:

Charles D. Baker, former mayor of Las Vegas	$ 5,000
Edward J. Barrick, point owner in three Las Vegas casinos	10,000
George R. Bieber, Chicago attorney	5,000
Irving Blatt	10,000
C. R. Bramlet	2,000
Irving Devine, Las Vegas gambler whose wife was named by *Life* as a mob courier	25,000
M. J. DiBiase, Las Vegas contractor	5,000
James Genlert	5,000
J. E. Hazard	5,000
Herbert H. Jones, Las Vegas attorney	5,000
Clifford Jones, former lieutenant-governor of Nevada	10,000
Harry B. Lahr	5,000
Floyd Lamb, state senator of Nevada	5,000
Edward Levinson, hotel operator and Doc Stacher's man	12,500
Wayne G. Osborn	5,000
John Pullman, onetime president Bank of World Commerce	5,000
Preston A. Parkinson	10,000
M. A. Riddle, head of the Dunes Hotel	5,000
Emanuel Schwartz	5,000
B. E. Seigelbaum, friend of Levinson	12,500
Michael Silvagni	5,000
Sav-Way Investment Company	5,000
Charles Turner	5,000
L. Schofer	1,000
Joe Wells, Las Vegas contractor and onetime owner (in name) of the Thunderbird Hotel	10,000
Paul Weinert	5,000
Sam Ziegman	5,000
Bank of World Commerce	23,000

So there you have the lineup of depositors in a savings and loan association that is, in a very large way, a class above that of the three-member, $30 type that plagued investors with Maryland charters.

The names are indicative of the current trend in America's financial morality, and a lot can be gleaned by studying them. On the list are politicians who make the laws, attorneys who oversee them, labor leaders on both sides of the fence who use them, and gambling men—gambling men with underworld connections who like to take advantage of them if they can. Put them all together and they don't exactly spell mother; it's something more like smother, and the innocent public is the victim who is fast running out of air.

The influence of gangland in the field of money lending, and that business' rise from the obviously insufficient nomenclature and violence associated with the "juice racket" has been outlined by crime reporter Ray Brennan, who pointed out that the syndicate operation utilizes Illinois state laws that authorize acceptance agencies to deal in stocks, bonds, warehouse receipts, bills of lading, and other commercial paper. Such agencies could also be used for disposing of merchandise hijacked from interstate trucks. Three financial agencies under recent investigation in Chicago were incorporated under Illinois charters, Brennan said. A gangster known as Charles (Chuck) English is president of two of the companies, the Lormar Acceptance Company and the B. & D. Acceptance Company. "A third is bossed by Frank Padula, 55, known as the king of the jukeboxes in Chicago and downstate Illinois," according to the *Chicago Sun-Times*. Probers, the paper said, have uncovered evidence that such companies are apparently used to transmit huge sums of money between criminal mobs located in cities from coast to coast.

The disclosures came as a result of investigations by the Illinois crime commission, then headed by Charles Siragusa, who formerly spearheaded U.S. Treasury Department probes into narcotics smuggling from illicit, Mafia-controlled drug centers in Europe.

Said David E. Bradshaw, Chicago lawyer and member of the state crime commission: "Racketeers can feed tainted money, stocks, bonds and warehouse receipts for stolen goods into one end of such an apparatus and the paper would come out the other end, scrubbed and cleaned and ready to be put into legitimate banking channels."

Both English and Padula, who have long arrest records but have never spent a night in jail, are prominent in operations of a jukebox monopoly with estimated gross profits of $18 million a year, all of which is ladeled out to the crime syndicate, the newspaper charged. And such activities are not confined to the United States. In October, 1967, *Life* editor Hunt told Chicagoans of the mob's apparent move into Brazil, where the boys were supposedly trying to persuade the government to authorize the minting of $9 million worth of new coins to be used in syndicate slot and vending machines thoughtfully flooded into the country by Charles English and Jackie (The Lackey) Cerone. English and Cerone, who was indicted in February, 1969, on gambling charges, were said to be running the operation, but it is interesting to note that the report arose when Sam Giancana was working his way down to the Argentine.

Such, and other, foreign adventures mean that syndicate profits eventually have to be taken out of the country, not only to be away from the prying eyes of the IRS and, in some cases, to be washed clean for legitimate reentry, but also to be worthwhile to the foreign branch of the Mafia. Lucky Luciano used an order of Catholic nuns to transport money to him from Brooklyn. When the nuns, who had been conned into the act by a man named Balsalmo, traveled to Italy every so often, the cash was left in Rome.

And so it goes. The information has been available to the FBI for decades, but it is stymied at the eighteenth hole every time—whenever the government is called upon to make a choice.

The answers to the mystery of the crime syndicate in America—and around the world, for the boys all know each other—lie, most probably, in the vast sums deposited in Swiss and other foreign banks. Many of the top gamblers in the United States own interests in such banks, and it is not always a question of transferring hard cash. Sometimes merely letters of credit change hands, which indicates that U.S. bankers are lending full cooperation.

So the Mafia law of *omerta* is observed by the respectable banker families, some of whom in Switzerland are so rich that it is not unusual for them to discourage the placement of a deposit of less than $100,000.

Take the Mafia money out of these banks, and you would see a financial panic that could displace quite a few governments. The American dollar supports the economy of Europe in many ways, the least known of which is perhaps through the billions tossed into numbered bank accounts by the mob. And yet it all boils down to the beginning: a two-dollar bet made on a street corner in Anytown, U.S.A.

And everywhere the prospects for the mob widen.

Dollar-poor governments around the world desperately need an international shot in the arm. And instead of the usual loan from the United States, they sometimes look to an influx of U.S. gambling men to help get the tourists to visit. The new countries of Africa and the private American bankrolls that finance hotels in the strangest places all have their eyes on the potential gaming take. And the Mafiosi are willing to accommodate them—on their own terms.

Freetown, Sierra Leone, built a casino overlooking the Atlantic Ocean, and clicking roulette wheels and the whap of playing cards sound a counterpoint to trumpeting elephants and talking drums. A European-style casino is run in the government-owned Federal Palace Hotel in Lagos, Nigeria, by an outfit that also operates two casinos in Egypt. The Club Africana in Accra, Ghana, has assorted games of chance, and another casino is opening near Victoria Falls in Rhodesia, and may finance a large part of the cost of that country's abdication from the British Commonwealth.

All this may have been adding to the perturbation of Croesus, Aristotle Onassis, who in 1966 challenged Monaco's Prince Rainier on ownership of the legendary gambling house at Monte Carlo, a casino that long ago "busted out" many of Europe's aristocrats. The story is that Onassis threw all his shares in the outfit on the open market and that, under the law, the state was compelled to buy them. Possibly Onassis "cashed out" on what looked like a bad deal. The casino was very much out-of-date and quite without customers. At any rate, in March, 1967, the government of Monaco announced payment of close to $8 million for Onassis' 500,849 shares. Perhaps Rainier, who reportedly wants to modernize Monte Carlo, may know of a couple of Las Vegas-type fellows who can come in, throw a new rug on the floor, and really make a fast buck for the place. Anything can happen, but the handwriting seems to be on the wall for Monte Carlo as more and more tourists are heading for Las Vegas, Freeport, and Paradise Island.

Ultimately, of course, the trouble lies at home: the two-dollar bets at one end of the scale and the attitude of the Supreme Court at the other.

The wiretapping conflict is not as complicated as it sounds, but the mob lawyers realize that in the computerized electronic world of today their clients would not stand a chance if the full power of the law could also use the full power of science to aid it. Hence the clamp-down on "bugging" devices and the mob-directed publicity campaign to frighten the American public into believing that it is being spied on at every turn. And since everyone seems to be trying to get the better of the government where income taxes are concerned, there exists a *sub rosa* pricking of the conscience. Has everyone, all of a sudden, identified with the likes of the Accardos, the Giancanas, the Costellos, and the assorted dope-smugglers, counterfeiters, and other criminals the lawmen are *really* after?

The really hard fact of the case for and against wiretapping—which could be called "delousing"—is laid out clearly and voluminously in a report made by G. Robert Blakey, Notre Dame professor of law and contributor to a treatise called "Task Force Report: Organized Crime," a 1967 publication of the President's Commission on Law Enforcement and Administration of Justice. Among other things, Professor Blakey said:

> The most sophisticated use of these techniques—where the goal has been a criminal trial—has been made by the Office of the District Attorney of New York County. It has been testified that without electronic surveillance techniques, specifically wiretapping, this office could not have achieved the convictions of James "Jimmy Hines" [Tammany power for many years] John Paul "Frankie" Carbo, Charles "Lucky" Luciano and Anthony "Little Augie Pisano" Carfano.

Yet in spite of his well-publicized "all out war on crime," even former President Johnson came out against eavesdropping of any kind except in the extreme case of tracking down a plot to assassinate the president. He thereby eliminated one of the most lethal weapons lawmen have against the criminal syndicate and, in effect, cast the protective cloak of the presidency over the machinations of the mob. One cannot help wondering if Johnson's motivations might not have included the fear of similarly garnered evidence exposing other Bobby Bakers.

It is not beyond imagination that if the decline in law enforcement goes too far, vigilantes will take over again—it's an old

American custom. The Constitution, where the enforcement of anti-criminal laws is concerned, contains the seeds of its own destruction. The alternatives are clear: either we get the mob, or it gets us. If the latter process is allowed to continue unhampered, the Constitution will be valueless.

APPENDICES

APPENDIX I

Phi Beta Mafia

Anthony Accardo: FBI #1410106, also known as "Big Tuna" because of his proclivity for tuna fishing. Born April 28, 1906, in Chicago. A bodyguard for Al Capone. Developed the technique of carrying machine guns in violin cases in the early days of the Prohibition era. Reported to have become boss of the Chicago criminal syndicate in 1943, coming up through the ranks with an assist from Sam Giancana. From 1957 to 1966 relinquished control to Giancana. Probably reasserted control after Giancana's disgrace in 1966—an event still to be nailed down by police intelligence. Wears silk suits and likes fancy bathtubs with gold fixtures. Defied, with the help of syndicate-oriented lawyers and judges, every attempt to wipe out his underworld prestige.

Vito Agueci: FBI #889944D. Emigrated from Sicily to Canada during the early 1950's. Became, with his brother Albert, part of an underworld operation that set up outlets for heroin smuggled into Canada from Italy. In Toronto the brothers used a bakery as a front for their illegal activities, thus bringing themselves into contact with Stefano Magaddino, top Buffalo racketeer and friend of Mafia kingpin Vito Genovese. The vendetta killing of Al Agueci in 1961 indirectly led to the revelations of Joseph Valachi and details concerning the Cosa Nostra conspiracy in the U.S.

Ismael Barragan: FBI #455305. Born Jan. 15, 1914. Lives in Tijuana, Baja California, and Los Angeles, Calif. Associate of Juan and Roberto Hernandez in the narcotics smuggling racket and, according to the U.S. Bureau of Customs, is responsible for bringing tons of marijuana across the border into the U.S. Criminal record includes arrests for murder, narcotics violations, and, in Feb., 1968, possessing 1754.498 grams of heroin. Source of marijuana probably is the Guadalajara area; of heroin, the Sinaloa area on the Mexican mainland. Owns the Rancho Los Palmos, 20 miles south of Tecate. Is known to accept merchandise, guns, and jewelry in exchange for narcotics.

Anthony Joseph Biase: FBI #36521. Born Sept. 6, 1908, in Omaha, Neb. Lives at 2207 Mason St., and probably is leading Mafioso in Omaha. Frequents the Owl Smoke shop at 610 South 16th St. Arrested for burglary, theft, and, numerous times, bookmaking. Criminal associates, according to authorities, include his brothers Sam, Louis, and Benny and Samuel Carollo of Kansas City, Mo. Also tied in with Louis Ventola, listed by the police as a onetime resident of Las Vegas, Nev. Associated with Anthony Marcella, now serving a 40-year term for narcotics trafficking in Los Angeles and San Francisco, and Louis Fiano, and through him with top Mafioso Vito Genovese.

Frank Bompensiero: FBI #337240, also known as "The Bump." Born 1905. Lives at Pacific Beach in San Diego, Calif. Has a formidable roster of friends among the hoodlum element, among them James Fratianno and Louis Tom Dragna, but his importance in the California syndicate is a matter of debate by authorities. Yet to live down being called a "dumb hoodlum" by Anthony Pinelli after being sentenced to state prison in 1955 for 5 years on a conviction of 3 counts of bribery. Put in the spotlight, probably by informant, in 1955, when, police records indicate, declared to be head of the Mafia in the San Diego area, a perhaps erroneous assumption.

Joe Bonanno: FBI #2534540, also known as "Joe Bananas." Born 1905 in Sicily. Identified by Joseph Valachi as head of a family of Cosa Nostra members that included narcotics smuggler Carmine Galante. Business interests throughout the U.S. Criminal record includes arrests for grand larceny, possession of a gun, and obstruction of justice. Highly independent operator within Mafia ruling council.

Russell A. Bufalino: FBI #691589. Born Oct. 29, 1903, in Montedoro, Sicily. Lives at 304 E. Dorrance St., Kingston, Pa. Criminal record goes back to 1927 and includes arrests for vagrancy, petty larceny, receiving stolen goods, and, as a result of attending the Apalachin meeting—

which he, according to McClellan committee records, arranged—conspiracy to obstruct justice charges. On the latter count sentenced in 1960 to 5 years in jail and fined $10,000 though his appeal was successful, as were those of all who attended the Apalachin meeting. According to McClellan committee records, "one of the most ruthless and powerful leaders of the Mafia in the United States." Also engaged in narcotics trafficking, labor racketeering, and dealing in stolen jewels and furs. Frequents the Medico Electric Motor Co. in Pittston, Pa. Owns the Penn Drape and Curtain Co. of Pittston, and has an interest in other Pittston and New York City dress manufacturing companies. According to McClellan committee records, associates with Santo Volpe, Sam Mannarino, Frankie Carbo, James Plumeri, etc., many of whom are labor racketeers. Fond of prizefights, rarely missing a heavyweight championship contest. Left thumb and index finger amputated.

Leonard Calamia: FBI #366116, also known as "Culanis." Born Jan. 2, 1911, in Kansas City, Mo. Many arrests on record. Served one year in jail on a narcotics-law conviction in 1936. Questioned in 1945 regarding the murder of a government witness, Carl Caramussa, in June, 1945, in Chicago. In 1966 named by government as one of 15 most important narcotics violators. In 1967 lived in San Francisco, Calif. On Dec. 23, 1948, arrested in Albuquerque, New Mexico, and charged with the murder in California of Nick De John, a Chicago hoodlum who had migrated west. Three other men were also indicted, but all defendants were subsequently released when then San Francisco District Attorney Pat Brown called off the prosecution.

Gerardo Vito Catena: FBI #144036. Born Jan. 2, 1902, in Newark, New Jersey. Has lived at 21 Overhill Rd., South Orange, N.J. Owns or controls many business firms in New Jersey, where he has concentrated his criminal activities with such men as the late Lucky Luciano, Joe Adonis, Frank Costello, Anthony Strollo, and Charles Tourine. Since 1923 arrested on charges of robbery, hijacking, bribing a federal juror, and suspicion of murder. Used strong-arm methods to gain control of vending machines in northern New Jersey, aided by Abner Zwillman, late underworld political fixer in that state.

Nick Civella: Listed by the McClellan committee with brother Carl as criminal associate of important, though lesser, men in the Mafia setup in Kansas City. Despite denials, was at the Apalachin crime conclave, according to federal authorities. With Carl and an associate, Max Jaben (Motel Grzebienacz), a top enforcer in the Kansas City underworld, was among 11 men forbidden by the Nevada gaming control board to enter casinos in that state. Others from Kansas City reputed to be close to Civella are Michael and Joseph Lascoula, who have long criminal records.

Anthony Corallo: FBI #269969, also known as "Tony Ducks" because of his skill in dodging process servers. Good friend of labor leader Jimmy Hoffa. Involved in rackets that include gambling, labor racketeering, extortion, strong-arm, and other gangster activities. In June, 1968, convicted in New York City of conspiracy to commit bribery after 10 days of testimony that linked the Mafia with City Hall and sent several individuals to jail including James L. Marcus, a city commissioner and close friend of Mayor John V. Lindsay. Principal territory has been Queens County in New York City, where he has used an automobile agency as a front.

Frank Costello (Francesco Seriglia): FBI #936217, also known as "The Prime Minister" of the national crime syndicate. Born Jan. 26, 1893, in Calabria, in the Italian "boot." After coming to the U.S., for years resided at 115 Central Park West, New York City. Naturalized in 1925. Criminal associates include every known racketeer in the U.S., if not the world. Criminal history goes back to 1908 and includes arrests for assault and robbery, concealed weapons, conspiracy, contempt, and income-tax evasion. Has valuable real estate holdings in New York City and interests in at least one Las Vegas casino. For years was an influential factor in the selection of many candidates for public office who were associated with Tammany Hall in New York City. Derived much of his early income via gem smuggling from abroad: one of his carriers, killed in an airliner crash while on a mission, was carrying $600,000 worth of gems, which were scattered far and wide over a southwestern area in the U.S.

Louis Coticchia: FBI #1427493, also known as "Lou Brady." Born Feb. 25, 1920, in Cincinnati, Ohio. First arrested in 1936 in Ohio for robbery. Other charges filed in Miami and in Hot Springs, Ark. In 1938 sent to jail in Cleveland for 4 years on charges of assault with intent to commit rape. Later received 5 years in jail in Baltimore for receiving stolen goods. Wide range of activity and friendship with top Mafiosi such as Santo Trafficante, Jr., perhaps fitted him for the job of Mafia courier. Confidence vested in him by the gambling element was reflected by jobs he held as pit boss in casinos in Las Vegas, Nev., and Havana, Cuba. Arrested in Tampa in 1963 on suspicion of grand theft and found to have previously visited a motel in Miami under the name "Luiz Paulino Bailey" from Rio de Janeiro, Brazil. Missing for several years.

Frank Cucchiara: FBI #4477, also known as "Frank Caruso," "Frank Russo," "Frank the Spoon." Born March 29, 1895, at Salemi, Sicily. Lives in Watertown, Mass. Naturalized in 1931 at Boston, despite arrests in 1925 in Boston for possession of morphine and dynamite. Rapidly came up the ladder of crime to a position of rackets importance in that city, working hand in glove with Ray Patriarca, New England boss, and important members of the Mafia throughout the East. In 1932 picked up on suspicion of murder. Attended the Apalachin meeting in 1957. Named by the McClellan committee as an operator of gambling joints in the North End of Boston and a financier of narcotic transactions. Interests in Watertown in restaurants and a cheese company.

Joseph J. Di Carlo: FBI #286967, also known as "Jerry the Wolf," "Joe the Gyp," and "Joe DeCarlo." Born Nov. 8, 1899, in Vallellunga, Sicily. Acquired a derivative citizenship in the United States. Associated for many years with the Magaddino brothers of Buffalo, N.Y. Confidant of Mafia chieftain Joseph Massei of Detroit; believed to be currently engaged in illegal gambling in the greater Miami area, where Massei has long been a power. Criminal record dates from 1920 and includes arrests for assault, coercion, intimidating witnesses, and violation of federal narcotics laws. Has been utilized as a killer by the Magaddinos, according to McClellan committee records, and is now in Florida after having been forced to leave the Buffalo area by police.

Louis Tom Dragna: FBI #4677209. Born July 18, 1920. Nephew of the late Mafioso Jack Dragna, once boss of bosses in California. Seems to be reaching for the syndicate crown in that state. Lives in Covina, Calif. Second-in-command now under Nick Licata, venerable clan elder. Has surrounded himself over the years with men known to police from coast to coast as hard-line criminals, both Mafia and non-Mafia types, including his lieutenant, Harold Meltzer, Joe Sica, and boxing racketeers Frankie Carbo and Frank Palermo—the latter three of whom are all now serving time in Leavenworth for extortion in the shakedown of a well-known fighter. Has influence in Las Vegas, according to police records, where he has placed friends in position of influence in several casinos and is friendly with men involved in skimming operations.

Carmine Galante: FBI #119495. Born Feb. 21, 1910, in New York. Known as one of the most ruthless criminals in the U.S. Many aliases and an arrest record that lists crimes since 1921. Many associates in Montreal, Canada. Considered to be a prime candidate for the world Mafia throne, ranking with the late Charles Luciano and Lucky's superiors in Sicily. Is a confidant of Vito Genovese, Joseph Bonanno, and others and was a major factor in the successful plot to murder Carlo Tresca, the anti-fascist editor, in New York in 1943, according to testimony before the McClellan committee. Has traveled to Palermo, Sicily, for consultations with world Mafia leaders. In July, 1962, was sentenced to 20 years for conspiracy to violate the narcotics laws.

Joseph Gallo: FBI #120842A, also known as "Joe the Blond." Born April 6, 1929, in Brooklyn. A member of the so-called Young Turk group in the Mafia. With brothers Larry (now dead) and Albert ("Kid Blast" Gallo), once challenged—unsuccessfully—the might of the late Joseph Profaci, the Brooklyn don. Power has waned, although he is considered to be a "comer" in the Brooklyn Mafia barony. A good friend of Carmine Lombardozzi, a *capo* in the Carlo Gambino family of New York City. Criminal record dates from 1947 and includes arrests for burglary, kidnapping, attempted sodomy, and felonious assault.

Carlo Gambino: FBI #334450, also known as "Don Carlo," "Carlo Gambrino," and "Carlo Gambrieno." Born Aug. 24, 1902, in Palermo, Sicily. Attended the Apalachin meeting as representative of a powerful Mafia faction in New York City. Involved with his brother Paolo in large-scale narcotics and alien smuggling, according to McClellan committee records. Served 22 months in prison on income-tax evasion charges. Criminal associates have included Lucky Luciano and Thomas Lucchese (both now dead) and gambling chieftain Meyer Lansky. In the paper-products business in Brooklyn, N.Y., and owns a "labor consultant" firm in Manhattan. Married to his first cousin, Vincenza Castellana. A son, Tom, married Frances Lucchese, daughter of Thomas Lucchese.

Vito Genovese: FBI #861267, also known as "Don Vitone." Born Nov. 21, 1897, in Naples, Italy. For years maintained a home in Atlantic Highlands, N.J. Reputed head of the Mafia organization in the United States. Now serving time in a federal prison for narcotics violations. Criminal record dates back to 1917 and includes arrests for burglary, concealed weapons, auto homicide, and murder. Attended the Apalachin meeting in 1957. An intimate of former New York Mafia boss Frank Costello and the late Lucky Luciano as well as top-ranking officers in the U.S. armed forces during the occupation of Italy in World War II.

Sam Giancana (Salvatore Momo): FBI #58437, also known as "Sam Mooney Giancana," "Sam Flood," "Albert Mancuso." 60. Currently in the Argentine after a flood of publicity knocked him off the syndicate throne in Chicago. An ex-convict: arrested and rearrested in three murder investigations before he was 20 years old; served time for auto theft, burglary, moonshining, and refusing to tell a federal grand jury of syndicate operation. Arrested over 60 times on various charges. Boss of Chicago crime syndicate from 1957–1963, when he paid a forbidden visit to a gambling lodge known as Cal-Neva, on Lake Tahoe's Crystal Bay and was entertained by Phyllis McGuire of the McGuire sisters. Adverse publicity about the visit to the lodge, which was partly in California and partly in Nevada, sent his fortunes tumbling. Later, in Mexico City in Dec., 1966, before moving onto the Argentine, renewed his romance with Miss McGuire, who was driven from the airport by Richard Cain, real name Richard Scalzetti, onetime chief investigator for former Cook County Sheriff and now Governor of Illinois Richard B. Ogilvie.

Vincent Gigante: FBI #5020214, also known as "The Chin." Strong-arm man and suspected killer for the Vito Genovese family. A former professional boxer. Better known as the prime suspect in the attempt to kill declining underworld chief Frank Costello in May, 1957. Two years later found guilty, with Genovese and 13 others, of violating the federal narcotics laws and sentenced to 7 years in jail.

Anthony Giordano: FBI #1624141. Born June 24, 1914, in St. Louis, Mo. Rise in the syndicate underscored by arrests dating back to 1938, including charges of carrying concealed weapons, robbery, holdups, income-tax evasion, and counterfeiting tax stamps. On the latter charge sentenced to 4 years in prison in Sept., 1956. Inherited a sinister mantle dating back to the initial influx of Mafiosi into St. Louis in 1916. Criminal associates include Ralph Quasarano of Detroit and Frank Coppola, supposedly now in Sicily but known to be a frequent visitor to Mexico, where he meets with syndicate buddies from the U.S. Has ties to New Orleans through Sam Vitale and others.

Joey Glimco (Giuseppe Glielmi): FBI #238623. Born 1909 in Salerno, Italy. After making three applications, naturalized in 1943—despite a police record that showed 34 arrests—when he was assistant business agent of the Taxicab Drivers Union of Chicago, Local 777. Has served no time in jail or prison, but has been charged, at one time or another, with larceny, disorderly conduct, vagrancy, murder, attempted murder, and robbery with a gun. Recently fined on a federal indictment with having accepted gifts from two Chicago businessmen—who were indicted with him—in violation of the Taft-Hartley Act. Hoodlums named as his associates during a Senate hearing in 1959 were Tony Accardo, Paul Ricca, the late Jake Guzik, Gus Alex, and the late Louis Campagna, whose last will and testament was witnessed by Mrs. Glimco.

Leroy Jefferson: FBI #2028068. Born Feb. 1, 1919, in Warran, Ark. Long considered to be "the largest individual narcotic trafficker" and a "source of supply" for other top-echelon Negro traffickers in California, Oregon, and Washington. Made his first rackets money as a pimp. Handled heroin deliveries throughout the U.S. and Mexico and was able to get his hands on such vast quantities that, according to McClellan committee records, "several New York Italian groups were actually 'fighting' to get him as a customer." When arrested by the Los Angeles police on June 2, 1958, was carrying $32,430; common law wife, Delores Mitchell, had $5,765. Police claim to have broken up the Jefferson organization with convictions in three conspiracy cases involving Jefferson and his crew.

Meyer Lansky: Nearly 70. With his brother Jake rules the gambling roost of the crime syndicate and may be the direct link between unknown moneyed nabobs who stash away mob dollars in foreign banks and the cash vaults of the U.S. criminal cartel. Ran gaming houses for the syndicate in Havana, Cuba, under the Batista regime, then moved operations to British-owned Bahamas and thence to other islands in the

Caribbean. Served with mobster Benjamin Siegel as enforcer for Louis Buchalter, industrial racketeer in New York's garment section. Lives and flourishes by respect for the Sicilian element in the mob, as exemplified by a remark he made when notorious Las Vegas gambler "Russian Louie" Strauss disappeared after a card game while in the company of hoodlums Jack Dragna and Marshall Caifano: "That's the last time a Jew will cheat a Sicilian in this town."

James V. Lasala: FBI #690454. Born June 4, 1904, in Brooklyn. Operates as a wholesale distributor of narcotics on the West Coast, maintaining ties in New York City for "business" purposes. Considered one of the most important dope traffickers in northern California, obtaining huge supplies of heroin from the Mafia's eastern branch. Uses extreme caution while making contact with other traffickers or customers, but fell afoul of the law in Feb., 1954, when he was sentenced to 4 years in prison for selling narcotics obtained from Christoforo Rubino of New York City.

Nick Licata: FBI #2585380. Born Feb. 20, 1897, in Camporeale, Tampani, Italy. Probably the most influential syndicate member in the Southwest. Came to the U.S. in 1913, and worked his way up into Mafia ranks with an amazing ability to dodge interference, if not surveillance, from the law, despite association in one form or another with syndicate subchiefs Louis Tom Dragna, Frank Bompensiero, James Fratianno, and others. Lives in the Royal Arms Apartments in Torrance, Calif., and has been associated over the years with every important gangster in the West. Record includes a small fine and a 30-day suspended sentence for refilling liquor bottles in 1945. During a probe of California rackets by a state assembly subcommittee, said he knew nothing of the Mafia and was cited for contempt for refusal to answer other questions. Charges were dismissed in November, 1959. Became boss in southern California after the death on Jan. 10, 1968, of Frank DeSimone, of Downey, Calif., who represented the southern California branch of the Mafia at the Apalachin meeting and was considered a top enforcer. Interests reach Dallas, Tex., and Detroit, Mich., where he is related by marriage to William Tocco.

Peter Licavoli: FBI #237021. Born in St. Louis; therefore immune from deportation. Rules Detroit's Mafia hierarchy with Joseph Zerilli, John Priziola, Angelo Meli, and William Tocco—though all are answerable to Joseph Massei, retired elder of the Detroit complex now in Florida. Owns the Grace Ranch in Tucson, Ariz., and was associated with narcotics trafficker Nicola Gentile and, through Gentile, with Luciano. Legitimate business interests are legion, and a fair chunk of the Las Vegas Strip is reputed to be in his hip pocket.

Peter Joseph LoCascio: FBI #986365, also known as "Mr. Bread." Born June 10, 1916, in New York City. Lives in Copiague, Long Island, N.Y., frequenting the Lower East Side (Little Italy) section of Manhattan. A vicious and feared hoodlum. Criminal associates include Joseph and Pete DiPalermo, John Ormento, who attended the Apalachin meeting, Rocco Mazzie, James Picarelli, and Sammy Kass. Since 1935 arrested for federal liquor-law violations, conspiracy, and New York State narcotics-law violations. Business interests in the Ennis Construction of Lindenhurst, Long Island, N.Y., and Peppi's Restaurant in Forest Hills, N.Y., according to McClellan committee records.

Carmine Lombardozzi: FBI #290869, also known as "The Doctor." Over 50. Has been involved in gambling, shylocking, labor racketeering, vending-machine and jukebox rackets, extortion, strong-arm action, and murder, according to records provided by New York City police. Member of Gambino family in New York. Frequents cafés in the Flatbush and Coney Island sections of Brooklyn, where he orders cheese and prune Danish pastry and coffee in the wee hours of the morning. Was given a "suspended" underworld sentence for mismanagement of a jukebox concession in Brooklyn after the late Joseph Profaci interceded for him with Mafia chieftains. Has served less than 5 months in jail since his first arrest in 1929 and has the kind of record his bosses like—1 incarceration out of 22 pinches.

Joseph Paul LoPiccolo: FBI #790022 C, also known as "Joe." Born April 28, 1918, in Chicago, Ill. Considered by authorities to be an important member of the Mafia. Arrested during an investigation in Miami. Convicted on a federal narcotics charge in Aug., 1958; sentenced to 20 years. Lives, when not in jail, on East 69th St., New York City, and at 621 44th St., Miami. Frequents both the Vesuvio Restaurant and the Paddock Bar, 50th and Broadway, in New York City, according to McClellan committee records, and is a partner in the Rock Creek Fluorspar Mining Co., in Hardin County, Ill. Often travels to Philadelphia and Chicago and friendly with hoodlums Santo Trafficante, Jr., and Joseph DiPalermo.

Stefano Magaddino: FBI #7787220. Born Oct. 10, 1891, in Castellammare, Sicily. With his brother Antonino controls syndicate operations in the Buffalo-Niagara Falls area of New York. Lives on Dana Drive, Buffalo, and for years operated a funeral parlor and other "legitimate" fronts, including a linen service and the Power City Distributing Co., of Niagara Falls. Arrested in 1921 in New York as a fugitive from justice (homicide) for the Avon, N.J., police department. Provides a link in the chain of Mafia influence that stretches from Boston across the Great Lakes area to Minneapolis. Is believed to have been at the Apalachin meeting, escaping the police raid there across nearby fields and woodland.

Carlos Marcello (Calogero Minacori): FBI #292542. Born Feb. 6, 1910, in either Tunisia or Guatemala, depending on whose word you take. Mafia chief of New Orleans. Barony extends across the borders of states adjourning Louisiana, and owns vast tracts of land and myriad "legitimate" businesses. Also has a stranglehold on every racket and racketeer in Louisiana—even the shrimp, through his many boats. Has spent time in the penitentiary for selling marijuana, but has not been incarcerated as long and as many times as the authorities would like. Received special political favors over the years, including a full pardon by Governor O. K. Allen, then a political ally of Huey Long, for an assault conviction. Efforts to deport him reached a climax in 1961 when he was "dropped off" in Guatemala—where he had claimed he had been born—by U.S. immigration officials. Promptly returned to the U.S. and has been here ever since. No other country wants to take him. Helping govern Louisiana fief are six younger brothers. Adheres to Mafia principles perhaps more fervently than any other boss of bosses in the country.

Harold Meltzer: FBI #113017, also known as "Happy." Operates large bookmaking and prostitution syndicates in California and is associated with the more important labor organizers on the West Coast. Confidant of California gangland figure Louis Tom Dragna. Appears to be a world traveler for the organization, having visited Canada, Cuba, Hong Kong, Japan, Hawaii, and the Philippines in recent years. In 1951 pleaded guilty in a conspiracy case following a probe by the Federal Bureau of

Narcotics and was sentenced to 5 years in prison. Has associates in Oklahoma, Texas, Baltimore, Miami, Las Vegas, and Boston, and ranks with gaming chieftain Meyer Lansky in the syndicate hierarchy.

Michele Miranda: FBI #91524, also known as "Mr. Big," "Mike," and "Frank Russi." Born July 26, 1896, in San Giuseppe Vesuviano, Naples, Italy. Attended the Apalachin meeting as a leader from the New York area. Is one of the most feared and ruthless Mafiosi in the country, concentrating his attention on New York City's garment industry—inherited in part from the notorious industrial racketeer, Louis Buchalter—and on rackets once shared with Thomas Lucchese. Last known address: 167 Greenway North, Forest Hills, N.Y. Travels to Florida, Canada, and Italy and has an interest in Cuban enterprises. Has spent much time in jail with a record dating from 1915.

Salvatore Mussachio: FBI #191344, known also as "Sally the Shiek." Related by marriage to the family of the late Giuseppe Magliocco, who headed one of New York City's larger families before he died of natural causes in Dec., 1963. Now nominal head of the family, may be superseded by a *caporegime* in the Magliocco empire named Joseph Colombo. Has 22 arrests and 1 conviction on his record sheet. A suspect in the slaying of two people in 1938. Friend of Frank Livorsi and Livorsi's associates such as Vito Genovese, John Stopelli, and members of the Tocco and Meli families of Detroit. Claims to be in the fish business and to be a barber and a baker. Also probably a social lion: had two tables at the Tocco-Profaci wedding in Brooklyn in June, 1955.

Raymond Patriarca: FBI #191775. Born March 17, 1908, in Providence, R.I. Began his criminal career as a bodyguard for bootleggers and led a charmed life, for was known to have planned the hijacking of many shipments of alcohol he was hired to guard. Long enjoyed the favor of top mobster Frank Costello. Controls the lotteries, bookmaking, dice games, and wire services in the New England area, particularly in Boston and Worcester, Mass., and also in Broward County, Fla. As one of the many gangsters involved in the makeup of the gambling complex in Las Vegas was very influential in the affairs of the Dunes Hotel. Inherited his criminal empire from Mafia chieftain Phillip Bruccola, former boss in New England now residing in Italy. Convicted on March 8, 1968, for conspiracy to commit murder, is now free on bond, appealing a 5-year prison sentence and $10,000 fine. Latest sentence raised his conviction record to 6, for a variety of offenses including violation of the Mann Act.

Anthony Pinelli: Also known as "Tony." Born 1899 in Calascibetta, Sicily. Came to New York City in 1913 as an immigrant. Has never become a citizen. Has entertained top Mafia figures at his home in Sierra Madre. Revered by his syndicate friends. Presently is the object of deportation proceedings as a result of his 1966 guilty plea to charge of evading federal income taxes for the year 1959. In 1960, despite the fact he did not live in his "district," monopolized gambling and other rackets around Gary, Ind. According to the late Robert Kennedy, former chief counsel of the Senate rackets committee, used profits from the rackets to acquire valuable real estate in southern California and was put in charge of Gary-East Chicago gambling in 1954 by Tony Accardo and Sam Giancana. Has been reported linked with two known mobsters who attended the Apalachin meeting: John Sebastian LaRocca and Gabriel Mannarino.

Al Polizzi: FBI #118357, also known as "The Owl." Arrived in the U.S. from Siculiana, Sicily, on March 15, 1900. One of the "most influential members of the underworld in the United States," according to U.S. Senate investigators who also point out, in a review of underworld statistics compiled by the McClellan committee, that he somehow managed to retire and get away from the action in Cleveland, Ohio, before it became the bailiwick of the Mayfield Road Gang headed by Moe Dalitz. Shaped the course of syndicate events for years in Cleveland and has a police record that starts in 1920. Lives in Coral Gables, Fla., and is a buddy of Frank Milano of California, *caporegime* of an area that embraces southern California and includes operations in Mexico.

Raffaele Quasarano: FBI #736238, also known as "Ralph," "Gino," "James Quasamoni," and "Jimmy Q." Born Dec. 20, 1910, in Mauch Chunk, Pa. Lives in Grosse Point Woods, Mich. Is considered a top-level Detroit underworld member and narcotics trafficker. Criminal record dates from 1931 and includes arrests for disorderly conduct, armed robbery, shooting, wiretapping, gambling, and violation of federal narcotics laws. Owns a barber-supply business, a furniture company, a housing development, and a gymnasium in Detroit. Father-in-law Vito Vitale is an underworld leader in Italy. Listed as criminal associates by authorities are most of the principal members of the Detroit underworld including Angelo Meli and John Priziola, and a fair smattering of New York City characters including Frank Costello, Frank Livorsi, and Frank Coppola, narcotics dealer deported to Italy.

Vincent John Rao: FBI #792086C. Born 1898. Considered a *consiglieri* in the Mafia structure of the family of the late Thomas Lucchese. Appeared at one time to be in line as successor to the throne. Has real estate holdings in East Harlem and currently lives in Yonkers. "Legitimate" interests include paint companies, housing projects, and parking lots. Is the owner of, or has an interest in, the Parkway Motel at Elmsford, N.Y., according to McClellan committee records. Has five arrests, one for homicide, but has never been convicted. Named by John F. Shanley of the New York City police department as an associate of mobsters Mike Coppola, Joe Rao—no relation—and Willie Moretti, a New Jersey gambling kingpin until his slaying in a tavern in Palisades, N.J., in 1951. Also according to Shanley, is interested in gambling, using Nunzio Arra, also known as "Frank Arra," a business agent for a lathing union, as a lieutenant.

Paul Ricca (Paul DeLucia): FBI #832514, also known as "Felice DeLucia," "Paul Viela," "Paul Villa," "Paul Salue," "Paul Maglio," "Paul Barstow," "Paul (The Waiter) Ricca," and "The Porter." Born 1898 in Naples. Apparently has resumed his leadership of the Chicago mob, sharing the throne with Anthony Accardo. A favorite of certain factions in the Teamsters Union. Arrest record dates back to 1927. Served time for conspiracy and income-tax evasion. Arrested twice in his native Italy for murder; convicted once. Is up for deportation, but is undeportable because no foreign country will grant him residency. With Accardo took the Fifth Amendment almost 200 times during questioning before the McClellan committee, dodging questions concerned with an illegal attempt to seize control of the Chicago liquor industry. Once bodyguard to Al Capone. Became boss of bosses in Chicago after Capone died, until income-tax troubles—solved at one point when the Teamsters Union "bought" Ricca's home for $150,000, far above the appraised value—created so much publicity that Accardo, then Sam Giancana, took over.

John Roselli (Filippo Sacco): FBI #333986. Born 1905 in Esteria, Italy. Claims Chicago birth, but was recently found guilty of falsifying his birth record in the U.S. In 1968 faced deportation and a fine of $2,000. Also, along with several other men, charged in 1968 with conspiracy to cheat members of the Friar's Club in Los Angeles through the use of electronic devices during gin-rummy games. Arrived in the U.S. on September 16, 1911. In 1921 arrested by federal narcotics agents in Boston and released on bail. Jumped bail, somehow wangled his way out of the charge, and changed his name to Roselli. Early associates included Abner Zwillman of New Jersey and Al Capone in Chicago. Convicted in 1944 as one of the principals in the Bioff-Browne movie extortion case, sentenced to 10 years in prison, and released on parole on Aug. 13, 1947, after serving 3 years and 7 months. Close associate of hoodlum chieftain Louis Tom Dragna in California. Seems to be in charge of the Los Angeles-Las Vegas gambling axis. Dresses in the latest fashion. His steel-gray hair, thin face, and bright piercing eyes are well known in almost every Las Vegas gambling casino, but prefers the Desert Inn.

Joseph Sica: FBI #343378. Born Aug. 20, 1911, in Newark, N.J. Considered an extremely rough and hardened criminal. Lengthy criminal record includes arrests since 1928 for robbery, murder, extortion, narcotics, and other serious crimes. Now serving time in Leavenworth for extortion. Connections extend coast to coast and criminal associates include his brothers Alfred, Frank, and Angelo. Well known to all racketeers in southern California. Listed in McClellan committee records as an important Mafia leader who is known as a killer, travels with a bodyguard, and has dipped his fingers in the narcotics trade. In early 1950 with 15 other gangsters was indicted in California for conspiracy to sell narcotics, but the case was thrown out when the principal government witness, Abraham Davidian, was shot to death while sleeping in his mother's home at Fresno, Calif.

Anthony C. Strollo: FBI #4282858, also known as "Tony Benda" and "Tony Bender." Born June 18, 1899, in New York City. Is mystery man of syndicate. Disappeared on April 18, 1962, from his home in Fort Lee, N.J., during a family ruckus with the reigning Brooklyn don Joseph Profaci. For years was one of the most powerful racketeers in the U.S., concentrating his attention on the northern New Jersey dock area. An intimate of most of the top racketeers. Arrest record dates back to 1926. A hoodlum known as Joseph Lanza was his enforcer for many years.

William Tocco: FBI #534742, also known as "Black Bill." Born in Terrasina, Italy. A member of the board of reigning Mafia dons in the Detroit area. Related by marriage to Mafiosi throughout the country. Said to share the rule in Detroit with Joseph Zerilli. Illegal activities, listed by the McClellan committee, include gambling, bootlegging, burglary, robbery, larceny, and tax evasion. Rise to power in Detroit had beginning in the 1930's, when the Italian mobsters took over from the non-Mafia members of the famous Purple Gang. Son, Anthony, is married to Carmela, daughter of the late Joseph Profaci of Brooklyn.

Santo Trafficante, Jr.: FBI #482531B. Maintains residence in Tampa and Miami, where he operates lucrative rackets operation. Lived at one time in Havana, Cuba, operating gaming casinos under the Batista regime. With advent of Castro, returned to the U.S., where he inherited rackets controlled by his father, Santo Trafficante, Sr., who died in 1954. According to government files, attended Apalachin meeting and is an associate of such criminals as Meyer Lansky, Joseph Bonanno, Sam Giancana, Sam Mannarino, and Joseph Riccobono. Was among guests at the marriage of Carmela Profaci to Anthony Tocco in June, 1955. Later appeared at a reception in the Hotel Commodore with others, including 13 men who attended the Apalachin gathering. Early in 1968 visited, for reasons unknown, Singapore, Hong Kong, and South Vietnam. Is an intimate of Louisiana Mafia chieftain Carlos Marcello.

Joseph Valachi: FBI #554, also known as "Joe Cago," "Joe Cargo," "Joe Kato," "Joseph Siano." Born Sept. 22, 1903, in New York City. Criminal associates included, before his arrest and appearance before the McClellan committee, Joe Adonis, Anthony Strollo, John Stopelli, etc. Criminal record includes arrests for burglary, robbery, and carrying concealed weapons. In 1960 pleaded guilty to federal narcotics-law violations and was thereafter instrumental in exposing the inner workings of the Mafia. Bailiwick was the upper East Side of New York City, where was, among other things, a wholesaler of heroin.

Joseph Zerilli: FBI #795171C. Born in Terrasina, Sicily. One of the five ruling dons of the Detroit Mafia family. Supposed to have exercised the greatest continuing influence through the years on the Detroit syndicate structure, though some police officials claim that Pete Licavoli, whose brother Dominic is married to Zerilli's daughter Rosalie, really is the Detroit boss. Listed by McClellan committee as having been involved in almost every form of illegal activity: extortion, mayhem, and murder; burglary, robbery, and larceny; bootlegging and illegal possession of weapons. En route to the Apalachin meeting but turned back when he found out there was trouble, according to Detroit police.

APPENDIX II

Las Vegas Casino Licensees

The following is a listing of licensees in some of the larger downtown and Strip casinos in Las Vegas. Gambling licenses are issued by the Nevada State Gaming Control Board, and those listed here were in effect as of May 1, 1968.

(*C.O. stands for Corporate Officer.*)

Desert Palace, Inc., dba CAESAR'S PALACE
Las Vegas, Nevada

	Shares
ADLER, Abraham: 6304 Fairlane Dr., Baltimore, Md.	100
AGRETTO, Ralph: 3322 Berwyck, Las Vegas, Nev.	50
ALPERSTEIN, Jerome: 1701 Woodholme Ave., Pikesville, Md.	50
AXELROD, Max: 15610 Van Aken Blvd., Cleveland, O.	150
BEALLO, Herman: 3570 Las Vegas Blvd., Las Vegas, Nev.	110
COHEN, John (deceased): 115 Peterborough St., Boston, Mass.	100
DEVERELL, George: 1639 Parkchester Dr., Las Vegas, Nev.	100
FACCINTO, Albert: 1337 St. Jude Circle, Las Vegas, Nev.	100
FRANK, Walter B.: 7107 Grand Ave., Cleveland, O.	110
GLICKMAN, Howard: 1422 N. Sweetzer, Dept. 300, Los Angeles, Calif.	100
GOLDBERG, Nathaniel: 1444 E. Baltimore St., Baltimore, Md.	400
GRASMICK, Louis J.: 303 Valdene Ct., Tinonium, Md.	50

GROBER, Bert M.: 356 Desert Inn Rd., Las Vegas, Nev. 200

GUNION, Fred A., M.D.: 1148 N.E. 99th St., Miami, Fla. 50

JACOBS, Nathaniel: 7505 Long Meadow Rd., Baltimore, Md. 366

JACOBSON, Edward: 1 Charles Center, Baltimore, Md. 110

JACOBSON, Morris: 4201 Cathedral Ave., N.W., Apt. 810, West Washington, D.C. 100

JACOBSON, Nathan S.: 1 Charles Center, Baltimore, Md. 650

JANIEN, Cedric: 416 E. 50th St., New York, N.Y. 400

KADAN, Leonard: 13937 Cedar Rd., Cleveland, O. 75

KLIM, William: 3051 Kishner Dr., Apt. 201, Las Vegas, Nev. 100

KLINE, Sam: 8201 16th St., #18, Silver Springs, Md. 100

KOREN, Eugene B.: 445 Desert Inn Rd., Las Vegas, Nev. 100

KOVENS, Irvin S.: 6203 Verdene, Baltimore, Md. 100

KRAUSE, Marvin: 350 Desert Inn Rd., Las Vegas, Nev. 100

KURLAND, Sanford: 13937 Cedar Rd., Cleveland, O. 75

LEVIN, Leonard: 3512 Autumn Dr., Baltimore, Md. 100

MALLIN, Stanley: 2367 Mohigan, Las Vegas, Nev. 555

McINTOSH, Jud: 7 Lake Shore Dr., Avondale Estates, Ga. 325

NEWMAN, Jake: 2220 Juana Vista, Las Vegas, Nev. 100

PERENCHIO, Robin: 13240 Stone Ridge Pl., Sherman Oaks, Calif. 100

RACKIN, Martin L.: 628 N. Foot Hill Rd., Beverly Hills, Calif. 110

RAINESS, Julius: 3407 Midfield Rd., Baltimore, Md. 110

ROGERS, Ben J.: 2030 Thomas Rd., Beaumont, Tex. 150

ROGERS, Nathan: 2190 Thomas Rd., Beaumont, Tex. 150

ROGERS, Sol J.: 2195 Thomas Rd., Beaumont, Tex. 150

ROGERS, Victor J.: 2025 Thomas Rd., Beaumont, Tex. 150

ROSENBERG, Harry: 8211 Anita Rd., Baltimore, Md. 50

SARNO, Jay: 3541 Maricapa Way, Las Vegas, Nev. 1400

SCHUMAN, Ruth: 1701 Woodholme, Pikesville, Md.	50
STEIN, Daniel: 4849 Koval Lane, Las Vegas, Nev.	200
WALD, Harry: 4793 Koval Lane, Las Vegas, Nev.	100
WATNER, Lloyd: 1112 Race St., Baltimore, Md.	55
WEINBERGER, William S.: 4777 Koval Lane, #3, Las Vegas, Nev.	200
SHENDAL, Dean: 548 Ellen Way, Las Vegas, Nev.	200
CLAIBORNE, Robert C.	50
HORTON, Starr W.	100
JOHNS, Charles B.	100
KAMINSKY, Moe	50
PEARLMAN, Samuel	100
PLATT, Leonard	40

Casino Operations, Inc., dba LAS VEGAS HACIENDA
Las Vegas, Nevada

Casino Operations, Inc. Proprietary Interests	*Percentage*
WARREN BAYLEY INVESTMENT COMPANY	81.88
BAYLEY, Warren (Estate) (Judith Bayley, Executrix): c/o Hacienda Hotel, Las Vegas Blvd., Las Vegas, Nev.	100.00
MAGLEBY, C.: 109 S. 3rd St., Las Vegas, Nev.	C.O.
INMAN, B.: 93 E. Reno Ave., Las Vegas, Nev.	C.O.
CURFEW, L. S.	10.62
SEIDEMAN, Ben: 1532 S. 7th St., Las Vegas, Nev.	3.75
SEIDEMAN, R.: 117 N. Hamilton Dr., Beverly Hills, Calif.	3.75
Casino Operations, Inc., Beneficial Interests	
SOUTHERN NEVADA INVESTORS LTD.	60 N.P.

JARRATT, Charlotte: 9069 Chaney Ave., Downey, Calif. 6.63

BAYLEY, Warren (Estate) (Judith Bayley, Executrix): c/o Hacienda Hotel, Las Vegas Blvd., Las Vegas, Nev. 31.38

MATTHEWS, V.: Litchfield Rd., Norfolk, Conn. 4.42

OVERHOLSER, J. H.: 4961 Palomar, Tarzana, Calif. 5.44

SEIDEMAN, Ben: 1532 S. 7th St., Las Vegas, Nev. 3.32

SEIDEMAN, R. M.: 117 N. Hamilton Dr., Beverly Hills, Calif. 3.32

SEXTON, Sophia: 10017 Wiley Burke, Downey, Calif. 2.20

MULCONNERY, Florence: Belair Apts. Apt. 118, 2001 Beverly Plaza, Long Beach, Calif. 2.20

MULCONNERY, William J. (Estate) (Florence Mulconnery, Executrix): Belair Apts, Apt. 118, 2001 Beverly Plaza, Long Beach, Calif. 6.18

TERRAZZI, E.:1218 S. St. Andrews, Santa Ana, Calif. 2.20

CURFEW, Harold: 7913 Melva St., Downey, Calif. 5.52

HOFUES, F. (Estate): 6803 Lakewood Blvd., Dallas, Tex. 2.20

DESSEL, Louis: 4502 Highland Pl., Riverside, Calif. 4.42

CRAFT, Shields B.: 2451 Brickell Ave., Apt. PH-T, Miami, Fla. 5.52

MARTELL, LeRoy and Emma: 114 S. Locust, Visalia, Calif. 3.72

BORIS, James E.: 6333 S. 3rd, Los Angeles, Calif. 2.20

RANKAITIS, John: 7401 Naylor, Los Angeles, Calif. 1.33

MILLER, Hubert: 7953 Mt. Vernon, Lemon Grove, Calif. 1.13

HESSE, R. E.: 933 E. Gross, Tulare, Calif. 3.05

JAME, Mabel E.: 1130 Fiske St., Pacific Palisades, Calif. 2.20

BAYLEY, Patrick K.: 179 'S' St., Salt Lake City, Utah 1.33

Consolidated Casino Corporation, MINT HOTEL Division
Las Vegas, Nevada

	Percentage
HUGHES, John P.: 750 Rancho Circle, Las Vegas, Nev.	30
JAMES, Howard P.: Las Vegas, Nev.	70
THOMPSON, Earle: 3501 Maryland Pkwy., Villa 74, Las Vegas, Nev.	C.O.
FITZGERALD, Maurice E.: 1701 Ivanhoe Way, Las Vegas, Nev.	Casino Mgr.
HINKLE, Jess W.: 1808 Ivanhoe Way, Las Vegas, Nev.	C.O.
BENNETT, William G.: 4113 Fortune Ave., Las Vegas, Nev.	Adm. Ofc.

Consolidated Casino Corporation, SAHARA HOTEL Division
Las Vegas, Nevada

	Percentage
HUGHES, John P.: 750 Rancho Circle, Las Vegas, Nev.	30
JAMES, Howard P.: 2020 Bannies, Las Vegas, Nev.	70
HINKLE, Jess W.: 1808 Ivanhoe Way, Las Vegas, Nev.	C.O.
THOMPSON, Earle F.: 3501 Maryland Pkwy., Villa 74, Las Vegas, Nev.	C.O.

Consolidated Casino Corporation, THUNDERBIRD HOTEL Division
Las Vegas, Nevada

	Percentage
HUGHES, John P.: 750 Rancho Circle, Las Vegas, Nev.	30
JAMES, Howard P.: Skyland, Zephyr Cove, Nev.	70

THOMPSON, Earle F.	C.O.
HINKLE, Jess W.	C.O.
BENNETT, William G.	C.O.

Flamingo Resort, Inc., dba FLAMINGO HOTEL
Las Vegas, Nevada

Owner	*Percentage*
TRACY INVESTMENT COMPANY	100
KERKORIAN, Kirk: 37 Country Club Lane, Las Vegas, Nev.	Pres.
BENNINGER, Fred	V.P.
ALJIAN, James D.	Sec./Treas.
PECHULS, Rose	Dir.
Licensees, Operating Company	
KERKORIAN, Kirk	Chmn.
BENNINGER, Fred	Pres./Dir.
ALJIAN, James D.	Sec./Treas.
PECHULS, Rose	V.P./Dir.
GOODWIN, Ernest	V.P./C.O.
NEWMAN, James W.	V.P./C.O.
SCHOOFEY, Alex J.	C.O.

Four Queens, Inc., dba FOUR QUEENS CASINO-HOTEL
Las Vegas, Nevada

	Percentage
ABRAMSON, Einar: 1816 S. 17th St., Las Vegas, Nev.	1.5
ADELSON, Mervyn: La Costa Country Club, Costa Del Mar Rd., Rancho La Costa, Calif. 92008	2.0

BARNES, F. E., Jr.: 2917 Mason Ave., Las Vegas, Nev.	1.5
BELLANGER, H. L.: 2913 Colanthe Ave., Las Vegas, Nev.	4.0
CALLAHAN, T. J.: 367 Desert Inn Rd., Las Vegas, Nev.	7.5
COULTHARD, G. W.: 601 Rancho Circle, Las Vegas, Nev.	1.0
GABRIELE, Julius: 1201 Buehler Dr., Las Vegas, Nev.	1.0
GAMBARANA, Edgar: 501 Park Way E., Las Vegas, Nev.	2.0
GARTH, Max: 3115 Dona Marta Dr., Studio City, Calif.	1.0
GINSBURG, M. E.: 1100 N. Alta Loma Rd., Los Angeles, Calif.	2.0
GOFFSTEIN, Ben, Estate: 353 Desert Inn Rd., Las Vegas, Nev.	15.0
GOLDMAN, H. A.: 1001 N. Crescent Dr., Beverly Hills, Calif.	4.0
GOLDMAN, Norris J.: 1634 Tower Grove Dr., Beverly Hills, Calif.	1.0
HAM, A. W., Jr.: 1337 Cashman Dr., Las Vegas, Nev.	4.0
HAM, A. W., Jr. (Trustee for Pattea Reid Tueller): 1337 Cashman Dr., Las Vegas, Nev.	1.0
HAZAN, M. A.: 1822 Doheny Dr., Los Angeles, Calif.	2.5
KRAFT, B. F.: 531 Park Way E., Las Vegas, Nev.	2.0
LAXER, G. B.: 7813 Chesterfield, Knoxville, Tenn.	1.0
MACK, J. D.: 1501 S. 6th St., Las Vegas, Nev.	6.0
MACK, J. D. (Trustee and Melvin MOSS, Trustor, for Ellen Joy Moss and Rosemary Beth Moss): 1501 S. 6th St., Las Vegas, Nev.	4.0
MACK, J, D. (Trustee for the Center Trust): 1501 S. 6th St., Las Vegas, Nev.	2.0
MACK, J. D. (Trustee for the Peter Trust): 1501 S. 6th St., Las Vegas, Nev.	2.0
MOLASKY, Irwin A.: 43 Country Club Lane, Las Vegas, Nev.	2.0
MORSE, H. S.: 712 N. Sierra Dr., Beverly Hills, Calif.	3.0
NABAT, A. S.: Fremont Hotel, Las Vegas, Nev.	1.0
PAPAGNA, William T.: 1932 E. Oakey Blvd., Las Vegas, Nev.	1.0

PARVIN, Albert B.: 2220 Avenue of the Stars, Los Angeles, Calif.	3.0
ROTHBERG, G. Harry: 321 S. Beverly Dr., Beverly Hills, Calif.	4.0
WELLS, H. A.: 750 Brown St., Reno, Nev.	4.0
WELLS, Joe (Estate): 725 Rancho Circle, Las Vegas, Nev.	4.0
WELLS, Robert: 1580 Circle Dr., Reno, Nev.	2.0
WHITE, N. L.: 55 Country Club Lane, Las Vegas, Nev.	1.0
LANDWIRTH, Michael	3.0
MISSLER, Earl B.	1.0
STEWART, John D.	2.0

FREMONT CASINO CORPORATION
Las Vegas, Nevada

	Percentage
PARVIN, Albert B.: 2220 Avenue of the Stars, Los Angeles, Calif.	45
GOLDMAN, Harry A.: 9105 Carmelita, Beverly Hills, Calif.	45
GOLDMAN, Norris: 1634 Tower Grove Dr., Beverly Hills, Calif.	10
FALBA, Frank: 4777 Koval Lane, Apt. 4, Las Vegas, Nev.	C.O.
HILL, James: 27 Country Club Lane, Las Vegas, Nev.	C.O.
NABAT, Abe: c/o Fremont Hotel, Las Vegas, Nev.	C.O.

GOLDEN NUGGET
Las Vegas, Nevada

	Shares
BLAINE, G. C.: 1623 Hastings Ave., Las Vegas, Nev.	8,827
KING, C. C.: 880 Rancho Circle, Las Vegas, Nev.	4,100
GREENE, W. E.: 1224 Park Circle Dr., Las Vegas, Nev.	12,000
HIRSCH, C. J.: 2104 Santa Rita Dr., Las Vegas, Nev.	C.O.

BRICK, Arthur: P.O. Box 610, Las Vegas, Nev.	68,856
CAFFERTY, Jack D.: 2411 Mason, Las Vegas, Nev.	100
GRIFFITH, R. B.: 400 Rancho Circle, Las Vegas, Nev.	% Rentals
MARTIN, W. M.: 2824 Ashby, Las Vegas, Nev.	% Rentals
MARK, M. H.: 611 First Federal Bldg., Indianapolis, Ind.	% Rentals
DAHLIN, Ray: 298 S. Anza, El Cajon, Calif.	% Rentals
BOYD, William: 1110 Douglas Rd., Las Vegas, Nev.	% Card Room
PIEPER, Jack K.: 3609 Fortune, Las Vegas, Nev.	% Casino
ROSE, Gordon: 2339 Sandy Lane, Las Vegas, Nev.	% Casino
WILLIAMS, John: 2209 Mesquite Ave., Las Vegas, Nev.	% Casino
WORTHEN, Robert: 1315 Norman, Las Vegas, Nev.	% Casino
ABRAMS, Lucille: 1599 Williams St., Denver, Colo.	20,000
BERNSTEIN, Dr. Peter M.: 2531 W. McNichols Rd., Detroit, Mich.	26,000
CAHLAN, A. E.: 3211 Ashby, Las Vegas, Nev.	41,600
CASTELLUCCI, Bernard and Jennie: 919 W. 84th St., Los Angeles, Calif.	22,000
COOPER, Chester C.: 3000 Ashby Ave., Las Vegas, Nev.	30,490
HAUGEN, Marian Virginia: 5229 Morgan Ave. S., Minneapolis, Minn.	40,200
HOUSSELS, Mrs. J. Kell: 1012 S. 6th St., Las Vegas, Nev.	20,000
IDE, Mrs. Rozan: c/o Crown Jewelry Store, Great Falls, Mont.	20,000
KELLER, Mitzi H. (Executrix for Norman Keller): 905 Ironwood Dr., Las Vegas, Nev.	32,000
KROLOFF, Robert: 2650 California St., Apt. 1, Mountain View, Calif.	26,000
McAFEE, Guy (Estate): Box 610, Las Vegas, Nev.	45,200

McMICHAEL, J. W.: 1615 Maryland Pkwy., Las Vegas, Nev.	26,000
MASEK, Irma D.: 13421 Fairfield Lane, Apt. 55–1, Seal Beach, Calif.	20,000
PURCELL, Kermit	20,000
RYAN, Martin S.: 1231 Bartlett Bldg., Los Angeles, Calif.	24,000
STEIN, Freida: Box 610, Las Vegas, Nev.	20,000
WITTUS, Max and Lucille (Trust): 2121 Santa Ynez Dr., Las Vegas, Nev.	10,000
LAZARD-VANIER, Marie Louise	25,800

Hotel Conquistador, Inc., dba HOTEL TROPICANA Las Vegas, Nevada

	Shares
DENVER, Edward J.: 860 DeWitt Pl., Apt 1407, Chicago, Ill.	200.0
FEINBERG, Preston: 401 Parkway W., Las Vegas, Nev.	2,284.3
FIELDS, Jackie: 1313 S. 16th St., Las Vegas, Nev.	516.0
HOUSSELS, J. K., Jr.: 380 Rancho Circle, Las Vegas, Nev.	3,066.6
HOUSSELS, J. K., Sr.: 1012 S. 6th St., Las Vegas, Nev.	3,066.6
KALLIS, Jack A.: 1130 S. Canal, Chicago, Ill.	918.8
KALLIS, Morton: 1130 S. Canal, Chicago, Ill.	281.6
MIRSKY, Solomon B.: 3180 Lake Shore Dr., Chicago Ill.	2,189.3
SALTZ, Sidney: 412 S. Wells St., Chicago, Ill.	1,976.0
URBAN, Louis: Route 1, Dundee, Ill.	525.0
VALENTINE, Grace A.: 1040 Bayview Dr., Suite 520, Fort Lauderdale, Fla.	400.0

Hughes Tool Company, dba THE CASTAWAYS CASINO
Las Vegas, Nevada

	Percentage
HUGHES, Howard R.: 3145 Las Vegas Blvd. S., Las Vegas, Nev.	100
HOLLIDAY, Raymond M.	Pres.
GAY, Frank W.	Sr. V.P.
MONTROSE, Maynard E.	Sr. V.P.
COLLIER, Calvin H., Jr.	V.P./Treas.
CONNER, Earl M.	V.P.
KISTLER, William A., Jr.	V.P.
LESCH, James R.	V.P.
MARTIN, Daniel J.	V.P.
MYERS, Park L.	V.P.
PAYNE, Lyle L.	V.P.

Hughes Tool Company, dba DESERT INN
Las Vegas, Nevada

	Percentage
HUGHES, Howard R.: 3145 Las Vegas Blvd. S., Las Vegas, Nev.	100
BRADY, Rodney H.	C.O.
COLLIER, Calvin H., Jr.	C.O.
CONNER, Earl M.	C.O.
GAY, Frank W.	C.O.
HARNED, Malcom S.	C.O.
HOLLIDAY, Raymond M.	C.O.
HOOPER, Rea E.	C.O.

KISTLER, William A., Jr.	C.O.
LESCH, James R.	C.O.
MONTROSE, Maynard E.	C.O.
MYERS, Park L.	C.O.
PAYNE, Lyle L.	C.O.
PEDERSON, Don E.	C.O.
RANKIN, William E.	C.O.
SCHAAF, Charles E.	C.O.
STINSON, Leon B.	C.O.

Hughes Tool Company, dba FRONTIER HOTEL
Las Vegas, Nevada

	Percentage
HUGHES, Howard R.: 3145 Las Vegas Blvd. S., Las Vegas, Nev.	100
HOLLIDAY, Raymond M.	Pres.
GAY, Frank W.	Sr. V.P.
MONTROSE, Maynard E.	Sr. V.P.
COLLIER, Calvin H., Jr.	V.P./Treas.
CONNER, Earl M.	V.P.
KISTLER, William A., Jr.	V.P.
LESCH, James R.	V.P.
MARTIN, Daniel J.	V.P.
MYERS, Park L.	V.P.
PAYNE, Lyle L.	V.P.

Hughes Tool Company, dba SANDS HOTEL
Las Vegas, Nevada

	Percentage
HUGHES, Howard R.: 3145 Las Vegas Blvd. S., Las Vegas, Nev.	100
HOLLIDAY, Raymond M.	Pres.
GAY, Frank W.	Sr. V.P.
MONTROSE, Maynard E.	Sr. V.P.
COLLIER, Calvin H., Jr.	V.P./Treas.
CONNER, Earl M.	V.P.
KISTLER, William A., Jr.	V.P.
LESCH, James R.	V.P.
MARTIN, Daniel J.	V.P.
MYERS, Park L.	V.P.
PAYNE, Lyle L.	V.P.

Hughes Tool Company, dba SILVER SLIPPER
Las Vegas, Nevada

	Percentage
HUGHES, Howard R.	100
HOLLIDAY, Raymond M.	Pres.
GAY, Frank W.	Sr. V.P.
MONTROSE, Maynard E.	Sr. V.P.
COLLIER, Calvin H., Jr.	V.P./Treas.
CONNER, Earl M.	V.P.
KISTLER, William A., Jr.	V.P.
LESCH, James R.	V.P.

MARTIN, Daniel J.	V.P.
MYERS, Park L.	V.P.
PAYNE, Lyle L.	V.P.

M. & R. Investment Company, dba DUNES HOTEL
Las Vegas, Nevada

	Percentage
RIDDLE, M. A.: 2808 Brown Circle, Las Vegas, Nev.	35.28
RICH, Charles: 2622 W. Charleston Blvd., Las Vegas, Nev.	12.00
WYMAN, Sidney: c/o Dunes Hotel, 3650 Las Vegas Blvd. S., Las Vegas, Nev.	21.00
RICE, Robert: 1311 S. 5th Pl., Las Vegas, Nev.	7.72
DUCKWORTH, George: 1400 Westwood, Las Vegas, Nev.	6.00
ENGEL, Howard I.: 1621 Westwood, Las Vegas, Nev.	5.00
BASSINGER, Wilbert: Route 1, Industry, Pa.	1.00
GENGERELLA, Louis: 1109 Beaver, Midland, Pa.	1.00
HERSCH, Joseph: 1805 N. Whitley, Hollywood, Calif.	1.00
STEINBAUM, Jerome: 1109 Tower Rd., Beverly Hills, Calif.	2.00
GOLDSTEIN, David: 3478 Paradise Rd., Las Vegas, Nev.	2.00
SCHAFER, Leonard: 1716 Chapman Dr., Las Vegas, Nev.	1.00
APCAR, Frederick: 1499 Cayuga Pk., Las Vegas, Nev.	5.00
RIDDLE, Norma: 2808 Brown Circle, Las Vegas, Nev.	C.O.
CAMPBELL, Leonard J.: 400 Parkway, East Las Vegas, Nev.	C.O.

N.L.V. Casino Corporation, dba SILVER NUGGET
North Las Vegas, Nevada

	Percentage
RIDDLE, Major A.: 2122 Edgewood, Las Vegas, Nev.	51

RIDDLE, Norma F.: 2122 Edgewood, Las Vegas, Nev.	C.O.
WIENER, Louis, Jr.: 1700 Chapman Dr., Las Vegas, Nev.	C.O.
THOM, Arthur	C.O.
ROVINSKY, Meyer	5
KAUFMAN, David M.	5
RUBIN, Gabriel	5
COHEN, Herbert S.	5
APCAR, Frederic	10

Prell Hotel Corporation, dba ALADDIN HOTEL
Las Vegas, Nevada

	Shares
ATOL, Elias J.: 908 Benedict Canyon, Beverly Hills, Calif.	12
AGRON, Oscar: 1812 E. St. Louis, Las Vegas, Nev.	8
BERMAN, Adolph (deceased: Estate of): 907 S. Gramercy Pl., Los Angeles, Calif.	4
BRILL, John H.: 2100 Jefferson St., San Francisco, Calif.	2
CLARK, Paula C.: 3784 Central Park Dr., Las Vegas, Nev.	2
COBLENTZ, Alexander: 1609 S. 6th St., Las Vegas, Nev.	4
FEINBERG, Harry: 3187 Silver Saddle St., Las Vegas, Nev.	4
GARBIAN, Albert: 449 Desert Inn Rd., Apt. 47, Las Vegas, Nev.	8
GARFIELD, Pearl: 1001 N. Odgen Dr., Los Angeles, Calif.	2
GILBERT, Gil: 1700 Rexford Dr., Las Vegas, Nev.	20
GILBERT, Sanford L.: 3177 Brazos St., Las Vegas, Nev.	2
GOLDMAN, Harry A.: 9105 Carmelita, Beverly Hills, Calif.	20
HASTIE, Carl J., Jr.: 241 Sands Ave., Apt. 105D, Las Vegas, Nev.	4

HILTON, Harriet Z.: 6904 Munsee Lane, Indianapolis, Ind.	8
HOFFMAN, Jack: 3944 Lemon Ave., Long Beach, Calif.	4
KEAYS, John E.: 809 Chabot Dr., Las Vegas, Nev.	2
KONYS, James J.: 561 Bonita Ave., Las Vegas, Nev.	10
KRANTZ, James J.: 2224 Juana Vista, Las Vegas, Nev.	2
KRYSTAL, Sydney D.: 9255 Doheny Rd., Los Angeles, Calif.	14
McLEOD, Norval B.: 804A S. 3rd St., Las Vegas, Nev.	2
MELVIN, Jack: 1924 S. 6th St., Las Vegas, Nev.	4
MESSER, Saul: 6332 Shawnee, Las Vegas, Nev.	10
MORSE, Harvey S.: 110 E. 9th St., Los Angeles, Calif.	8
PARVIN, Albert B.: 2220 Avenue of the Stars, Los Angeles, Calif.	8
PORTNOY, Sylvia: 1010 Pamela Dr., Beverly Hills, Calif.	12
POSNER, Stanley M.: 252 N. Kenter Ave., Los Angeles, Calif.	2
PRELL, Melvin S.: 2280 Mahigan Way, Las Vegas, Nev.	8
PRELL, Milton: 3667 Las Vegas Blvd., S., Las Vegas, Nev.	80
PRELL, Sheila L.: 3667 Las Vegas Blvd., S., Las Vegas, Nev.	20
RIVERA, James: 908 Hassett St., Las Vegas, Nev.	4
ROTHBERG, G. Harry: 400 N. Oakhurst Dr., Beverly Hills, Calif.	20
ROWAN, Hyman L.: 107 W. Broadway, Long Beach, Calif.	4
ROWAN, Sam: 3649 Country Club Dr., Lakewood, Calif.	4
SCHAYER, Charles M.: 100 Locust St., Denver, Colo.	3
SIMS, Ernest A.: 4673 Happy Valley Ave., Las Vegas, Nev.	4
SPECKS, Granville I.: 1421 Dobson St., Evanston, Ill.	10
STERN, Martin, Jr.: 8221 Sunset Blvd., Los Angeles, Calif.	4
STERN, Stuart: 8506 Spring View Dr., Indianapolis, Ind.	10
TOPPER, Ronald: 2630 Sherwood, Apt. 6, Las Vegas, Nev.	4
ZICKLER, Joyce F.: 7150 N. Pennsylvania St., Indianapolis, Ind.	12
MAJOR, Bernard A.	10

HOTEL RIVIERA, Inc.
Las Vegas, Nevada

	Shares
GOLDMAN, Harry A.: 120 N. Robertson Blvd., Los Angeles, Calif.	1,600
SILBERT, Harvey L.: 9601 Wilshire Blvd., Beverly Hills, Calif.	4,000
MAGNA CORPORATION: 246 W. 44th St., New York, N.Y.	4,000
HARRISON, Charles J.	1,600
ABRAMS, Samuel	800
ATOL, Frank	1,200
MARTIN, Tony	1,600
KREMS, Nathan S.	1,600
CARTER, Charles T.	800
MILLER, Herschel M.	1,600
MILLER, Louis	1,600
MILLER, Ross	3,200
ROSENBERG, Joe	800
STOKES, E. Yale	800
GOODMAN, J. Dee	800

New Hotel Showboat, Inc., dba SHOWBOAT CASINO
Las Vegas, Nevada

	Percentage
CONWAY, Nelson: 319 S. 3rd St., Las Vegas, Nev.	9.0
HOUSSELS, J. K., Jr.: 380 Rancho Circle, Las Vegas, Nev.	18.0
HOUSSELS, J. K., Sr.: 1012 S. 6th St., Las Vegas, Nev.	31.5

KELLEY, Joseph: 830 Kenny Way, Las Vegas, Nev.	8.0
MOORE, R. Julian: 273 Sands Ave., Apt. 3, Las Vegas, Nev.	5.0
MORLEDGE, Fred: 2040 Edgewood Dr., Las Vegas, Nev.	5.0
PARKER, Judd: 605 Lacy Lane, Las Vegas, Nev.	4.0
ZETTLER, George: 2043 Canosa, Las Vegas, Nev.	2.5
VALENTINE, Harold L.: 1040 Bayview Dr., Fort Lauderdale, Fla.	10.0
SHUGART, James W. (Executor of the Estate of James C. Shugart): 1656 Christy Lane, Las Vegas, Nev.	7.0

STARDUST HOTEL
Las Vegas, Nevada

DALITZ, Moe B.: Stardust Hotel, Las Vegas, Nev.

JONES, C. J.: Desert Inn Hotel, Las Vegas, Nev.

DREW, John F.: 333 Desert Inn Rd., Las Vegas, Nev.

JAFFE, Milton: Stardust Hotel, Las Vegas, Nev.

DONNELLEY, John A.: Stardust Hotel, Las Vegas, Nev.

BENEDICT, Alvin: Stardust Hotel, Las Vegas, Nev.

STILLINGS, George L.: 5101 Evergreen Ave., Las Vegas, Nev.

APPENDIX III

Charts

The following fourteen charts are provided in the hope that they will help the reader define his ideas concerning the nature and scope of organized crime in the country.

Charts 1–11 are adapted from the charts published in the printed "Hearings (Organized Crime and Illicit Traffic in Narcotics) before the Permanent Subcommittee on Investigations of the Committee on Government Operations, United States Senate, Eighty-Eighth Congress, September 1963–August 1964."

Chart 12 is taken from the "Task Force Report: Organized Crime, 1967" (prepared for the President's Commission on Law Enforcement and Administration of Justice).

Chart 13 is adapted from a document drawn up by the Los Angeles police department.

Chart 1

THE VITO GENOVESE FAMILY

Vito Genovese *Boss*

Thomas Eboli *Acting Boss* Gerardo Catena *Underboss* Michael Genovese *Messenger* Michele Miranda *Consigliere*

Capiregime

Vincent Alo
James Angelina
Michael Coppola
Pasquale Eboli
Thomas Greco
Richard Boiardi

Vincent Alo Regime	James Angelina Regime	Michael Coppola Regime	Pasquale Eboli Regime		Richard Boiardi Regime	Michele Miranda Regime
Soldiers—Buttons	*Soldiers—Buttons*	*Soldiers—Buttons*	*Soldiers—Buttons*	*Soldiers—Buttons*	*Soldiers—Buttons*	*Soldiers—Buttons*
Nicholas Belangi	Louis Barbella	Charles Albero	Dominic Alongi	Joseph Agone	Settimo Accardi	John Gregory Ardito
Lawrence Centore	Joseph Barra	Alfred Cupola	Edward Capobianco	Philip Albanese	Albert Barrasso	Lorenzo Brescia
Francesco Cucola	Morris Barra	Anthony DeMartino	Joseph DeNegris	Ottilio Caruso	Anthony Boiardi	Anthony Carillo
Aniello Ercole	Earl Coralluzzo	Benjamin DeMartino	Cosmo DiPietro	Mike Clemente	Paul Bonadio	Frank Celano
Frank Galluccio	Tobias DeMiccio	Theodore DeMartino	Alfred Faicco	George Filippone	Thomas Campisi	Salvatore Celembrino
August Laietta	Mattew Fortunato	Pasquale Erra	Anthony Florio	Joseph Lapi	Antonio Caponigro	Alfred Criscuolo
Gaetano Martino	Paul Marchione	Anthony Ferro	Mario Gigante	George Nobile	Charles Tourine, Sr.	Pete DeFeo
Aldo Mazzarati	John Savino	Joseph Lanza	Vincent Gigante	Michael Spinella	Peter LaPlaca	Joseph Lanza
Sabato Milo		Frank Livorsi	Michael Maione		Ernest Lazzara	Alfonso Marzano
Rocco Perrotta		Philip Lombardo	Vincent Mauro		Andrew Lombardino	Barney Miranda
James Picarelli		Felix Monaco	Gerardo Mosciello		Paul Lombardino	Carmine Persico, Jr.
Louis Prado		Louis Pacella	Sebastian Ofrica		Anthony Marchitto	David Petillo
Rudolph Prisco		Joseph Paterra	Joseph Pagano		Anthony Peter Riela	Mathew Principe
Nicholas Ratenni		Al Rosato	Pasquale Pagano		Salvatore Chiri	Frank Tieri
Batisto Salvo		Anthony Salerno	Armando Perillo			Eli Zaccardi
George Smurra		Anthony Salerno	Girolamo Santuccio			
Gaetano Somma		Ferdinand Salerno	Fiore Siano			
		Angelo Salerno	John Stopelli			
		Dan Scarglatta	Joseph Valachi			
		Giovanni Schillaci				
		Frank Serpico				
		Joseph Stracci				
		Joseph Tortorici				

Chart 2

THE CARLO GAMBINO FAMILY

CARLO GAMBINO *Boss*

JOSEPH BIONDO *Underboss* JOSEPH RICCOBONO *Consigliere*

Capiregime

Paul Castellano
Paolo Gambino
Arthur Leo
Rocco Mazzie
Anthony Sedotto
Anthony Zangarra
Joseph Colazzo
Aniello Dellacroce
Charles Dongarro
Peter Ferrara
Carmine Lombardozzi
Ettore Zappi

Soldiers—Buttons

Andrew Alberti
Germaio Anaclerio
Joseph Armone
Eduardo Aronica
Peter Baratta
Charles Barcellona
Frank Barranca
Ernesto Barese
Sebastiano Bellanca
Salvatore Bonfrisco
Michael Bove
Anthony Carminati
James Casablanca
Matthew Cuomo
Alex D'Allesio
John D'Allesio
Mike D'Allesio
Charles DeLutro
Nicholas DiBene
Alex DeBrizzi
Charles Gagliodotto
Frank Gagliardi
Michael Galgano
Pasquale Genese
Anthony Granza
Frank Guglieimini
Sally Guglieimini
Joseph Indelicato
Giuseppe LoPiccolo
Frank Luciano
Aniello Mancuso
Genaro Mancuso
Joseph Manfredi
James Massi
Frank Moccardi
Sabato Muro
Frank Pasqua
Michael Pecoraro
Dominick Petito
Larry Pistone
Anthony Plate
Hugo Rossi
Giacomo Scalici
Joseph Scalici
Salvatore Scalici
Giacomo Scarpulla
Mike Scandifia
Al Seru
James Stassi
Joseph Stassi
Felice Teti
Arthur Tortorella
Peter Tortorella
Paul Zaccaria

Chart 3

THE GAETANO LUCCHESE FAMILY

GAETANO LUCCHESE *Boss*

STEFANO LASALLE *Underboss*

VINCENT JOHN RAO *Consiglieri*

Capiregime

Ettore Coco
Anthony Corallo
Joseph Laratro
Joseph Lucchese
John Ormento
James Plumeri
Joseph Rosato
Salvatore Santoro
Carmine Tramunti
Natale Evola

Soldiers—Buttons

Frank Arra
Nicholas Bonina
Frank Campanello
Paul John Carbo
Sam Cavalieri
Donato Laietta
Edward D'Argenio
John Di Carlo
Thomas Dioguardi
John Dioguardi
Charles DiPalermo
Vincent Corrao
Joseph DiPalermo
Salvatore Granello
Anthony Lisi
Salvatore LoProto
Salvatore Maneri
Neil Migliore
Vic Panica
Andinno Pappadia
Anthony LoPinto
Vincent Potenza
Calogero Rao
Charles Scoperto
Salvatore Shillitani
Joseph Silesi
Nicholas Tolentino
Angelo Tuminaro
Joseph Vento
Anthony Vadala
Sam Valente
Tom Valente
James Vintaloro

Chart 4

THE GIUSEPPE MAGLIOCCO FAMILY

GIUSEPPE MAGLIOCCO *Boss*

SALVATORE MUSSACHIO *Underboss*

Capiregime

Sebastiano Aloi
Simone Andolino
Salvatore Badalamenti
Leo Carlino
Joseph Colombo

Harry Fontana
John Franzese
Ambrose Magliocco
Nicholas Forlano
John Oddo

Soldiers—Buttons

Anthony Abbattemarco
Cassandros Bonasera
Alphonse D'Ambrosio
Salvatore D'Ambrosio
Bartolo Ferrigno
Cosmo Frasca

Albert Gallo, Jr.
Joseph Gallo
Lawrence Gallo
Philip Gambino
Gaetano Marino
Sebastiano Nani

Frank Profaci
James Sabella
Modesto Santora
Joseph Schipani
Giuseppe Tipa
Joseph Yacovelli

Chart 5

THE JOSEPH BONANNO FAMILY

JOSEPH BONANNO *Boss*
CARMINE GALANTE *Underboss*
FRANK GARAFOLO *Consigliere*
JOSEPH NOTARO *Caporegime*

Soldiers—Buttons

James Colletti
Michael Consolo
Rosario Dionosio
Nicholas Marangello
Frank Mari
John Petrone
Angelo Presinzano
Frank Presinzano
Philip Rastelli
George Rizzo
Michael Sabella
Joseph Spadaro
Costenze Valente
Frank Valente
Nicholas Zapprana

other capiregime unidentified

Chart 6

BUFFALO, NEW YORK, ORGANIZATION

STEFANO MAGADDINO *Boss*
FREDRICO RANDACCIO *Underboss*

Lieutenants

John Cammillieri
Pascal Natarelli
Roy Carlisi
Steven Cannarozzo

Section Leaders

Salvatore Brocato
Joseph Fino
Salvatore Bonito
Daniel Sansanese
Paul Briandi
Anthony Perna
Salvatore Rizzo
Pascal Politano
Sam Lagattuta
Salvatore Miano
Michael Tascarella

Relatives of Boss

Antonio Magaddino
James LaDuca

Chart 7

RHODE ISLAND AND BOSTON, MASSACHUSETTS, ORGANIZATION

PHILLIP BRUCCOLA *Former Boss* RAYMOND PATRIARCA *Boss* GENARO J. ANGIULO

RHODE ISLAND	BOSTON, MASS.
Henry Tamello	Frank Cucchiara
Antonio Lopreato	Anthony Sandrelli
Americo Bucci	Larry A. Zannino
Louis J. Taglinetti	Joseph Lombardi
Frank Morrelli	Francesco P. Intiso
John Candelmo	Leo Santaniello
Dominic J. Biafore	Peter J. Limone
Francis Joseph Patriarca	Michael Rocke
Alphonse Capalbo	Joseph Anselmo
Albert Le Pore	Santo Rizzo
Santino Ruggerio	John Gugliemo
Giuseppe Simonelli	Ralph Lamattina
Frank Forti	Theodore Fuccillo
Richard Ruggerio	Henry Selvitelli
Frank Ferrara	Nicholas A. Giso
Albert Joseph Vitali	Samuel Granito
Alfredo Rossi	

Chart 8

THE MAFIA ORGANIZATION IN THE TAMPA, FLORIDA, AREA

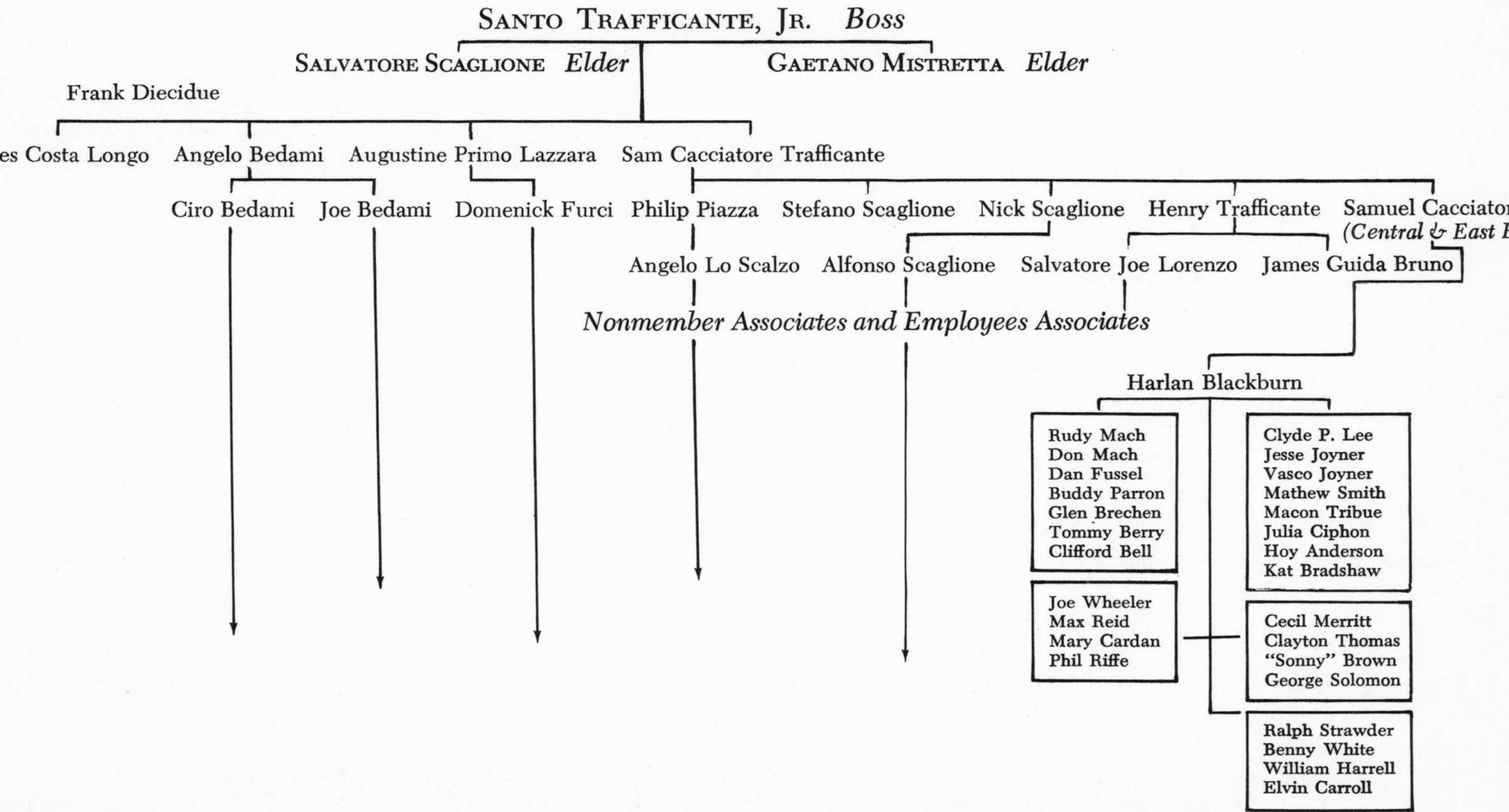

Chart 9

THE MAFIA ORGANIZATION IN THE DETROIT AREA

Ruling Council

JOSEPH ZERILLI
JOHN PRIZIOLA
ANGELO MELI
WILLIAM TOCCO
PETER LICAVOLI

Administrators and Heirs Apparent

Michael Rubino
Salvatore Lucido
Joseph Massei
Dominic P. Corrado
Joseph Bommarito
Santo Perrone
Raffaele Quasarano
Michael Polizzi
Anthony Giacalone
Vincent A. Meli

Chiefs

Dominic Corrado
Joseph Triglia
Tony Teramine
Anthony Cimini
Vito Giacalone
Peter Vitale
Paul Vitale
Joseph Barbara, Jr.
Joseph Bommarito
Joseph Moceri

Lieutenants

Frank Meli
Benedict Bommarito
Sam Finazzo
Dominic Cavataio
Eddie Guarella
Julian Cavataio
Peter Cavataio
Salvatore Serra
Sam Caruso

Section Leaders

Peter Maniaci
Dominic Bommarito
Joe Coppola
Pete Lombardo
Angelo Lombardi
Anthony Imburnone
Danny Bruno
Pete Trupiano
Nick Ditta
Vincent Finazzo
Michael Bartalotta
Sam Lobaido
James Macagnone
James Galici
Joseph Lobaido
Leonardo Monteleone
Mario Agosta
Sam Giordano
Arthur Gallo
Frank Mudaro
Frank Randazzo
Joe Brooklier
Ricco Priziola
Tony Randazzo
Dominic Allevato
Paul Cimino

Windsor, Canada, Segment

Onofrio Minaudo (*Lieutenant*)
Joe Catalanotte (*Lieutenant*)
Nicolas Cicchini (*Section Leader*)

Chart 10

CHICAGO-ITALIAN ORGANIZATION

Overall Chicago Area, Bosses and Lieutenants

Salvatore Giancana	Dominic Brancato	John Cerone
Sam Battaglia	Felix Anthony Alderisio	Giuseppe Glielmi
Anthony Accardo	Rocco Fischetti	Rocco DeStefano
Paul Ricca	Ross Prio	Frank Caruso
Dominic Nuccio	Frank Ferrera	Fiore Buccieri
Dominic DiBella	Marshall Caifano	William Aloisio
	Francesco Cironato	

West Side

William Daddano	Leonard Gianola	Mario A. DeStefano	Ned Bakes	Joseph A. Ferriola	Rocco Potenza	Frank Fratto
Charles English	James Mirro	Sam DeStefano	Dominic Blasi	Ernest Infelice	Louis Rosanova	Frank Eulo
Frank Buccieri	Charles Nicoletti	Vito DeStefano	Samuel Cesario	Vincent J. Inserro	Rocco Salvatore	James Torello
Joseph Aiuppa	Anthony Pitello	John DeBiase	Eco James Coli	John Lardino	Joseph Siciliano	Phillip Mesi
Albert Capone	Louis Briatta	Rocco DeGrazia	Dominic Cortina	John L. Manzella	Tarquin Simonelli	Frank Manno
John Capone	Albert Frabotta	Charles Tourino, Jr.	Joseph Colucci	Sam Mesi	Frank Teutonico	Nick Manno, Jr.
Matthew Capone	Joseph Gagliano	Dominic Volpe	Americo DePietto	William Messino	Nick Visco	Sam Manno
Ralph Capone	Joseph Fusco	Sam Ariola	Anthony Eldorado	Rocco Paternoster	Joseph A. Accardo	Thomas Manno

North Side

Placideo Divarco	Frank Orlando	James Policheri	Anthony DeMonte	Michael Glitta	L. Buonaguidi	Joseph LaBarbara
	Joseph Liscandrella	Samuel Liscandrella	Frank Lisciandrella	Cosmo Orlando	Ben J. Policheri	

South Side

George Tuffanelli	James Roti	James Catura	James R. Cordovano	Anthony DeLordo	Charles B. DiCaro	Joseph N. DiCaro
	Anthony Panzica	Louis Tornabene	Frank C. Tornabene	Joseph Caruso	Anthony DeRosa	

Chart 11

NONMEMBER ASSOCIATES OF CHICAGO-ITALIAN ORGANIZATION

Overall Chicago Area

MURRAY HUMPHREYS
RALPH PIERCE
GUS ALEX
LESTER KRUSE
FRED THOMAS SMITH
LEONARD PATRICK
DAVID YARAS

West Side

Joseph Corngold
Elias Argyropoulos
August Dierolf Liebe
Edward Vogel
Leo Rugendorf
John Wolek
William Block
Nick Bravos
George J. Bravos
Maish Baer
Frank Zimmerman
Gus Spiro Zapas
Jack Patrick

North Side

William Goldstein
Joseph Arnold
Robert Furey
Phillip Katz
Irving Dworetzky

South Side

Bernard Posner
Arthur Markovitz
Michael Markovitz
Hyman Gottfried

Chart 12

AN ORGANIZED CRIME FAMILY

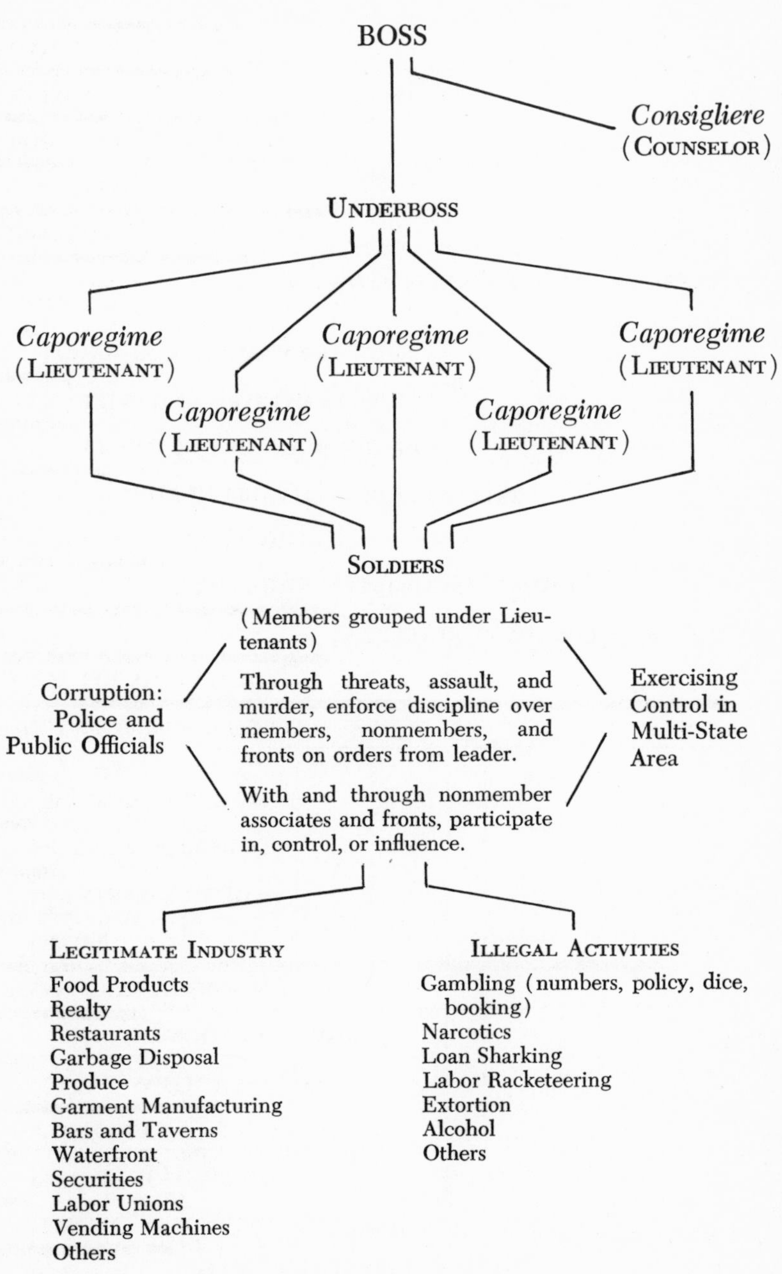

Chart 13

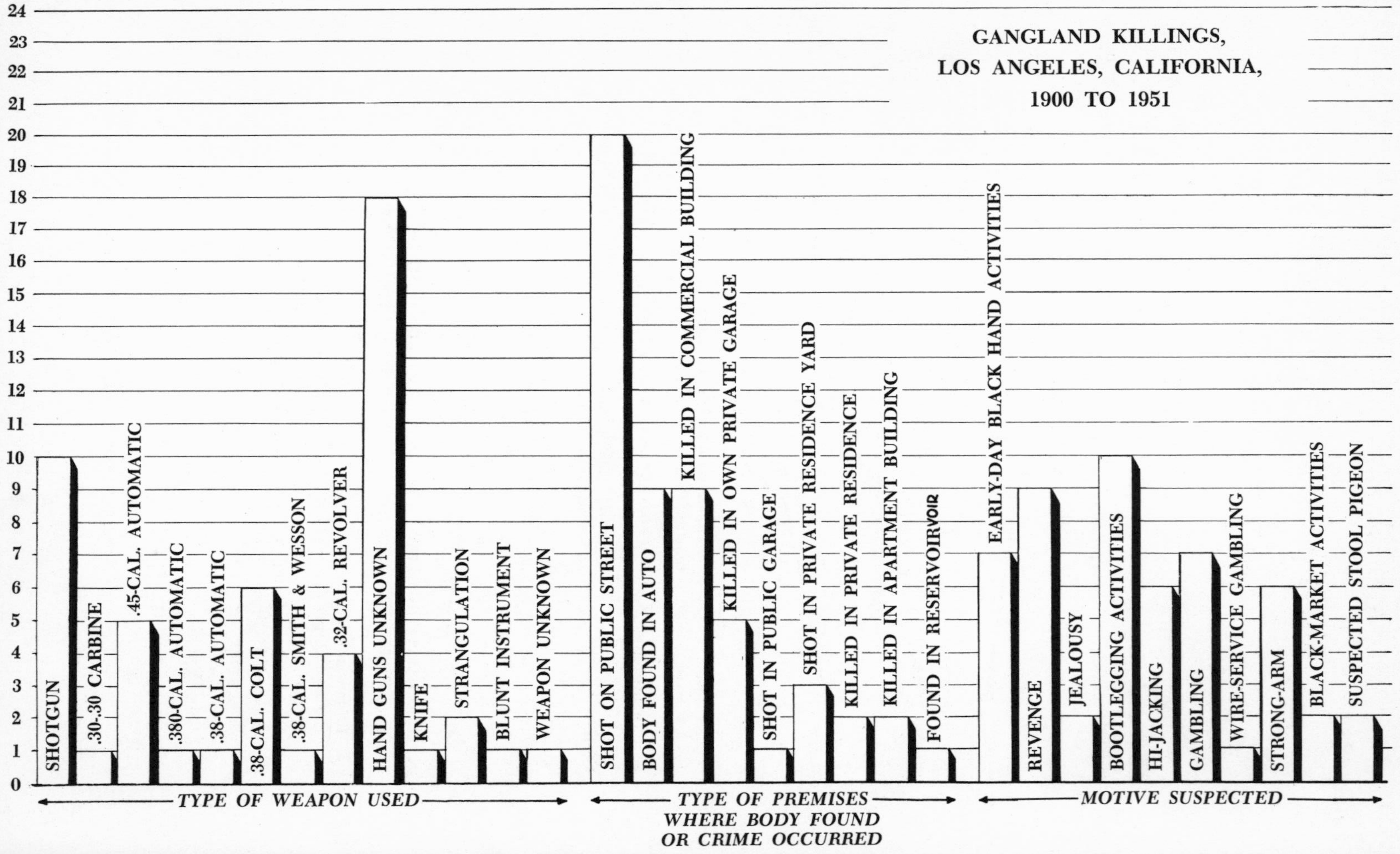

GANGLAND KILLINGS, LOS ANGELES, CALIFORNIA, 1900 TO 1951

24
23
22
21
20
19
18
17
16
15
14
13
12
11
10
9
8
7
6
5
4
3
2
1
0

TYPE OF WEAPON USED

SHOTGUN
.30-.30 CARBINE
.45-CAL. AUTOMATIC
.380-CAL. AUTOMATIC
.38-CAL. AUTOMATIC
.38-CAL. COLT
.38-CAL. SMITH & WESSON
.32-CAL. REVOLVER
HAND GUNS UNKNOWN
KNIFE
STRANGULATION
BLUNT INSTRUMENT
WEAPON UNKNOWN

TYPE OF PREMISES WHERE BODY FOUND OR CRIME OCCURRED

SHOT ON PUBLIC STREET
BODY FOUND IN AUTO
KILLED IN COMMERCIAL BUILDING
KILLED IN OWN PRIVATE GARAGE
SHOT IN PUBLIC GARAGE
SHOT IN PRIVATE RESIDENCE YARD
KILLED IN PRIVATE RESIDENCE
KILLED IN APARTMENT BUILDING
FOUND IN RESERVOIRVOIR

MOTIVE SUSPECTED

EARLY-DAY BLACK HAND ACTIVITIES
REVENGE
JEALOUSY
BOOTLEGGING ACTIVITIES
HI-JACKING
GAMBLING
WIRE-SERVICE GAMBLING
STRONG-ARM
BLACK-MARKET ACTIVITIES
SUSPECTED STOOL PIGEON

Chart 14

LA STELLA RESTAURANT

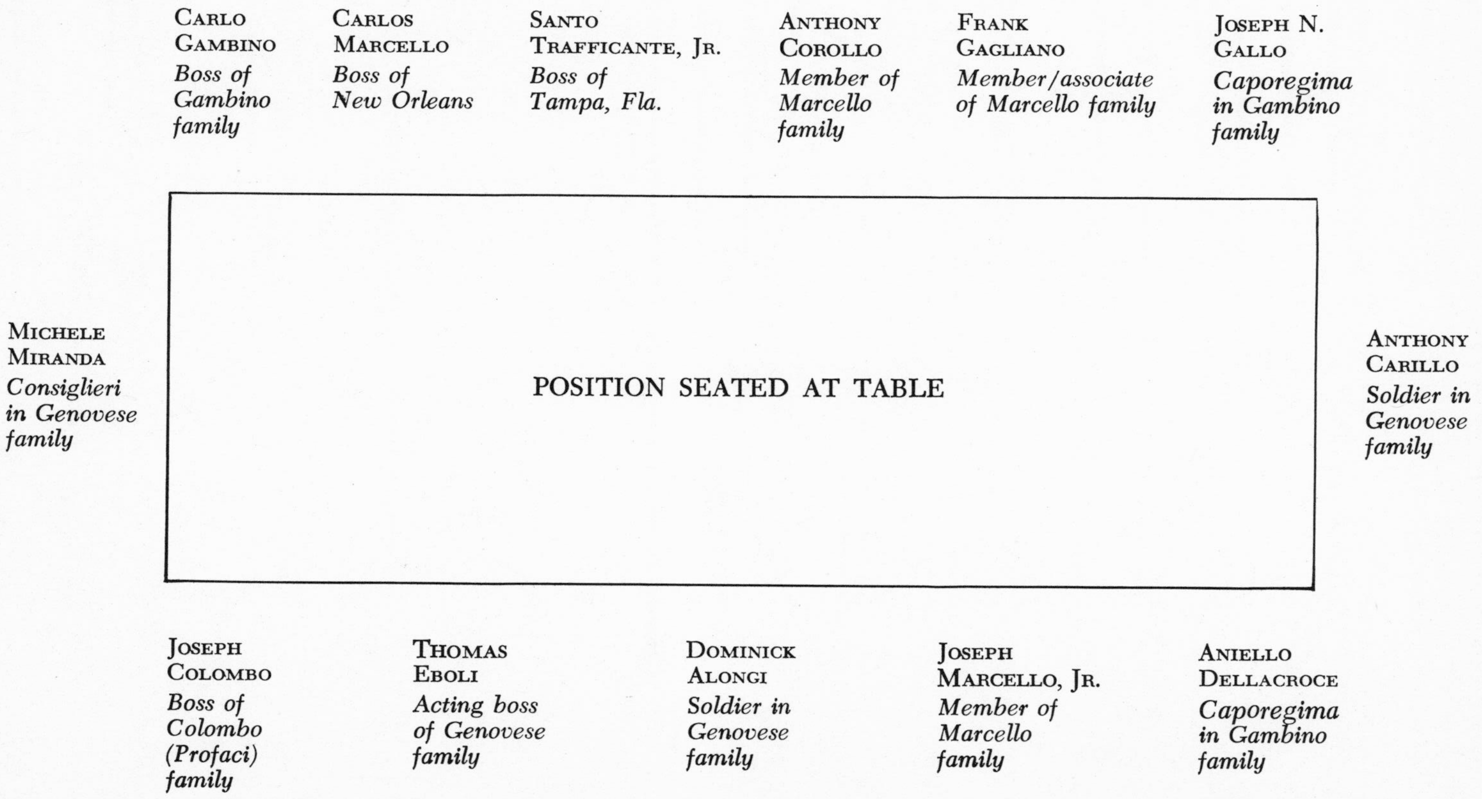

Carlo Gambino
Boss of Gambino family

Carlos Marcello
Boss of New Orleans

Santo Trafficante, Jr.
Boss of Tampa, Fla.

Anthony Corollo
Member of Marcello family

Frank Gagliano
Member/associate of Marcello family

Joseph N. Gallo
Caporegima in Gambino family

Michele Miranda
Consiglieri in Genovese family

POSITION SEATED AT TABLE

Anthony Carillo
Soldier in Genovese family

Joseph Colombo
Boss of Colombo (Profaci) family

Thomas Eboli
Acting boss of Genovese family

Dominick Alongi
Soldier in Genovese family

Joseph Marcello, Jr.
Member of Marcello family

Aniello Dellacroce
Caporegima in Gambino family

INDEX

C

D

E

M

S

T

U

V

W

Y

Z